MILL'S PROGR
PRINCIPL

MILL'S PROGRESSIVE PRINCIPLES

DAVID O. BRINK

CLARENDON PRESS · OXFORD

UNIVERSITY PRESS

Great Clarendon Street, Oxford, OX2 6DP,
United Kingdom

Oxford University Press is a department of the University of Oxford.
It furthers the University's objective of excellence in research, scholarship,
and education by publishing worldwide. Oxford is a registered trade mark of
Oxford University Press in the UK and in certain other countries

© David O. Brink 2013

The moral rights of the author have been asserted

First published 2013
First published in paperback 2015

All rights reserved. No part of this publication may be reproduced, stored in
a retrieval system, or transmitted, in any form or by any means, without the
prior permission in writing of Oxford University Press, or as expressly permitted
by law, by licence or under terms agreed with the appropriate reprographics
rights organization. Enquiries concerning reproduction outside the scope of the
above should be sent to the Rights Department, Oxford University Press, at the
address above

You must not circulate this work in any other form
and you must impose this same condition on any acquirer

Published in the United States of America by Oxford University Press
198 Madison Avenue, New York, NY 10016, United States of America

British Library Cataloguing in Publication Data
Data available

Library of Congress Cataloging in Publication Data
Data available

ISBN 978–0–19–967214–1 (Hbk.)
ISBN 978–0–19–874439–9 (Pbk.)

Links to third party websites are provided by Oxford in good faith and
for information only. Oxford disclaims any responsibility for the materials
contained in any third party website referenced in this work.

Contents

Preface	viii
A note on Mill's texts	xviii

1. Mill's radical background — 1
1. Psychological egoism — 3
2. Utilitarianism — 8
3. Evaluative hedonism — 10
4. Duty and interest — 15
5. Why utilitarianism? — 21

2. Varieties of motivation — 26
6. Mill's apparent egoism — 26
7. Mill's rejection of psychological egoism — 30
8. Reservations about the Radical legacy — 33
9. The sanctions of utilitarianism — 34
10. The demands of utilitarianism — 38

3. Perfectionism about happiness and higher pleasures — 46
11. The higher pleasures doctrine — 46
12. Subjective and objective pleasures — 51
13. Problems for hedonism about higher pleasures — 52
14. Attitudinal and hybrid hedonism — 58
15. Perfectionism — 60
16. Reconciling the elements of happiness — 63
17. Perfectionism about happiness — 67
18. Perfectionism and pluralism about happiness — 72
19. Unanswered questions about perfection and happiness — 73

4. Ambivalence about duty — 79
20. Varieties of utilitarianism — 80
21. Utilitarianism as a standard of conduct — 82
22. The case for act utilitarianism — 84
23. Felicific tendencies — 85
24. Principles and rules — 89
25. Sanction utilitarianism — 98
26. An apparent virtue of sanction utilitarianism — 103

27. The vices of sanction utilitarianism	106
28. The Art of Life	108
29. Considered, but not consistent, act utilitarianism	110

5. The justification of utilitarianism — 113
30. Methodological naturalism	113
31. A traditional reading of the proof	118
32. Spot the howler	119
33. An alternative reading of the proof	121
34. Bottom-up justification	125
35. Utilitarianism's prospects	132

6. Liberal preliminaries — 135
36. One very simple principle and the categorical approach	135
37. The self/other asymmetry	139
38. The scope of liberty	141
39. The harm principle and liberal rights	142
40. Categories, rights, and utility	146

7. Freedom of expression in a liberal context — 149
41. The blanket prohibition on paternalism	150
42. Against censorship	152
43. The truth-tracking rationale	152
44. The deliberative rationale	154
45. From expressive liberties to liberal principles	156
46. Limits on liberty	158
47. Limits on freedom of expression	161
48. Deliberative values and First Amendment categories	162
49. From liberal principles to expressive liberties	165
50. Free speech and other liberal principles	171

8. Liberal principles refined — 173
51. The harm principle	173
52. Is harm sufficient?	176
53. Is harm necessary?	180
54. Moralizing harm?	187
55. Paternalism	190
56. Offense	196
57. A balancing test	198
58. Legal moralism	203
59. The Devlin debate	206
60. Beyond the Devlin debate	208
61. The categorical approach revisited	212

9. Liberalism, utilitarianism, and rights — 214
62. The apparent tension between utility and rights	215

63.	The sanction theory of rights	217
64.	Rights as secondary principles	223
65.	Rights as pre-eminent goods	226
66.	Reconciling utility and rights	232

10. Liberal democracy 234
67.	The case for representative democracy	234
68.	The scope of the franchise, weighted voting, and expertocracy	238
69.	The trouble with weighted voting	244
70.	Liberal democracy and the common good	249
71.	Old and new liberalisms	253
72.	Perfectionist liberalism	255

11. Sexual equality 260
73.	The case for sexual equality	260
74.	Rebutting the case for inequality	265
75.	The vices of charity and self-abnegation	268
76.	Is the sexual division of labor natural?	269
77.	Transitional justice?	271
78.	Millian feminism	276

Epilogue 277
79.	Making utilitarianism more progressive	278
80.	From progressive utilitarianism to liberalism	280
81.	Equality as a progressive principle	282
82.	Mill's legacy	287

Bibliography   290
Index   297

Preface

> It is proper to state that I forego any advantage which could be derived to my argument from the idea of abstract right as a thing independent of utility. I regard utility as the ultimate appeal on all ethical questions; but it must be utility in the largest sense, grounded on the permanent interests of man as a progressive being [*On Liberty*, Chapter I, paragraph 11].

John Stuart Mill (1806–73) was the most famous and influential British moral philosopher of the nineteenth century. He was one of the last systematic philosophers, making significant contributions in logic, metaphysics, epistemology, ethics, political philosophy, and social theory.[1] He was also an important public figure, articulating the liberal platform, pressing for various liberal reforms, and serving in Parliament. Nowadays, it is fair to say, Mill's greatest philosophical influence lies in moral and political philosophy, especially his articulation and defense of utilitarian moral theory and liberal political philosophy.[2] Utilitarianism is the doctrine that people, actions, and institutions should be assessed by the extent to which they promote happiness. The liberal tradition claims that individuals have rights, in particular, rights to certain important interests and liberties, which determine what other individuals and the state owe them and may do to them. This book is a study of key concepts and principles in Mill's moral and political philosophy that aims to reconstruct and assess the central elements of his contributions to the utilitarian and liberal traditions. To understand Mill's defense of

---

1. The best comprehensive discussion of Mill's philosophical commitments is John Skorupski, *John Stuart Mill* (London: Routledge, 1989).
2. Though it is fair to say that Mill's greatest philosophical influence nowadays lies in his moral and political philosophy, especially his defense of utilitarianism and liberalism in *Utilitarianism* and *On Liberty*, this has not always been true. As Nicholson documents, during and shortly after his own lifetime, Mill was better known and more widely admired for his work in theoretical philosophy and political economy. See Peter Nicholson, "The Reception and Early Reputation of Mill's Political Thought," in *The Cambridge Companion to Mill*, ed. J. Skorupski (Cambridge: Cambridge University Press, 1998), pp. 464–67.

utilitarian and liberal principles, I will focus on his two most popular and best-known works—*Utilitarianism* (1861) and *On Liberty* (1859)—but I will also draw on other texts, including *A System of Logic* (1843), the *Autobiography* (1873), and various essays, when this sheds light on our interpretation of his utilitarian and liberal principles. To see how he understands these principles, it will also be instructive to see how he applies them to issues of political and sexual equality in *Considerations on Representative Government* (1859), *Principles of Political Economy* (1848), and *The Subjection of Women* (1869).

Historically, both utilitarianism and liberalism have been progressive doctrines. Mill was raised in the tradition of *Philosophical Radicalism*, made famous by Jeremy Bentham (1748–1832) and his followers, including Mill's father, James Mill (1773–1836), which applied utilitarian principles in a self-conscious and systematic way to issues of institutional design and social reform. Utilitarianism assesses actions and institutions in terms of their effects on happiness and enjoins us to perform actions and design institutions so that they promote—in one formulation, maximize—happiness. Utilitarianism was a progressive doctrine historically, principally because of its *universal scope*—its insistence that everyone's happiness matters—and its *egalitarian conception of impartiality*—its insistence that everyone's happiness matters equally. Because of these general characteristics of utilitarianism, the Radicals' application of utilitarian principles to social institutions tended to challenge traditional institutions of class and privilege. For instance, these commitments led the Radicals to advocate the extension of the franchise to previously disenfranchised classes. This progressive character is also characteristic of Mill's utilitarian commitments.

Mill's defense of liberal principles, in particular, his recognition of individual rights that protect basic interests and liberties of individuals from private or state interference, was also a progressive influence. Mill distinguishes old and new threats to liberty. The old threat to liberty is found in traditional societies in which there is rule by one (a monarchy) or a few (an aristocracy). Though one could be worried about restrictions on liberty by benevolent monarchs or aristocrats, the traditional worry is that when rulers are politically unaccountable to the governed they will rule in their own interests, rather than the interests of the governed. In particular, they will restrict the liberties of their subjects in ways that benefit the rulers, rather than the ruled. It was these traditional threats to liberty that the democratic reforms of the Philosophical Radicals were meant to address. But Mill thinks that these traditional threats to liberty are not the only ones to worry about. He makes clear that democracies contain their own threats to liberty—this is the tyranny, not of the one or the few, but of the majority. Mill sets out to articulate the principles that should regulate how governments and societies, whether democratic or not, can restrict individual liberties.

Mill's contributions to the utilitarian and liberal traditions are of more than historical interest. While utilitarianism is a controversial moral and political doctrine, it remains an influential theory or family of theories in both public debate and academic discussions. Though liberalism is not without its critics, it is fair to say that some form of liberalism is now the dominant political philosophy in the Western tradition. As a founding contributor to both traditions, Mill has much to tell us about how to understand some of our most important moral and political commitments. But, as I hope to show, Mill's discussion also draws our attention to important issues and options about how best to understand these two traditions, and so a study of Mill's principles can itself be an important contribution to the systematic, and not merely historical, task of identifying the best conceptions of utilitarianism and liberalism.

Mill's commitments to utilitarianism and liberalism are thought by some to be problematic, because they see a tension between the pursuit of the general welfare and individual rights that seem to constrain the pursuit of collective goods. By contrast, as the epigraph at the head of this Preface demonstrates, Mill thinks we can and should give individual rights a utilitarian foundation. Because Mill challenges this perceived tension between utility and rights, understanding and assessing his position promises to shed light on both utilitarian and liberal commitments.

This is one prominent example of apparent intellectual tensions that Mill tries to resolve. Some of Mill's philosophical significance lies in his attempt to synthesize the insights of different traditions—such as Enlightenment and Romantic traditions, Liberal and Conservative traditions, naturalist and intuitionist traditions, and utilitarian and natural rights traditions. But synthesis sometimes brings the risk of introducing inconsistency. Mill's syncretic aims raise questions about his overall consistency, such as whether utilitarianism can succeed in mixing accommodation of common moral precepts with calls for moral and political reform, whether the perfectionist elements in his moral and political theory can be reconciled with his commitment to hedonism, whether duty should be understood in terms of optimal actions, optimal rules, or optimal sanctioning responses, whether he really does think that harm prevention is the essence of liberalism, and whether his apparently categorical liberal principles are compatible with utilitarianism. Whether or not we agree that Mill can reconcile these disparate traditions and beliefs, his synthetic ambitions are instructive. He shows us what is attractive about each tradition, and he attempts to show how the truths in one can be squared with those in another. Even if his reconciliations are unsuccessful, we learn something interesting about the resources and limitations of each tradition. If his reconciliations are successful, we learn that some standard antinomies are unnecessary and that it is possible to incorporate the insights of rival traditions into an attractive comprehensive view.

I have been reading, teaching, and writing about Mill's moral and political philosophy for twenty-five years now, trying to understand and assess his contributions to the utilitarian and liberal traditions and trying to gauge when his ambitions for synthesis have been successful and when they have produced genuine inconsistency. This book represents a progress report on these efforts. My interpretation of Mill is still evolving, but its main features are reasonably settled and sufficiently different from other interpretations, I think, to be worth sharing with others.

Nonetheless, my treatment of Mill's moral and political philosophy is selective and incomplete in several respects. It is selective in its attention to texts and issues in Mill's moral and political philosophy. My emphasis is on Mill's understanding of his first principles. Though I do look at what his application of his principles to issues of democracy, political economy, and sexual equality tells us about how he understands those principles, I have not attempted to provide a thorough account of his views on these practical issues. Even on issues concerning utilitarianism or liberalism that I do discuss in some depth, my analysis is sometimes incomplete in the sense that I don't always reach definite conclusions about which view makes most interpretive or systematic sense. For instance, I see ambivalence in Mill between rival direct and indirect utilitarian conceptions of duty and rights and between moralized and non-moralized conceptions of the harm principle. But where my interpretive or systematic verdicts are not decisive, I try to assess the intellectual costs and benefits of alternative views and give reasons for these mixed verdicts. I also try in places to explore and assess in a very limited way the implications of Millian principles for moral or political issues that Mill did not address directly, such as the demandingness of utilitarianism, limitations on freedom of expression, the extent of principled exceptions to the usual prohibition on paternalism, the permissibility of nuisance regulation, and the prospects for legal moralism. These discussions are meant to illustrate places and ways that we might want to test and assess Millian principles. They are not intended to serve as an exhaustive examination of Millian principles or as self-standing discussions of those complex practical issues.

Despite these limitations in my study, I hope that it will be of interest to students and scholars of Mill's moral and political philosophy. It has certainly been worthwhile for me to try to bring together and extend my previous efforts on disparate topics in Mill's moral and political philosophy into a continuous study of his utilitarian and liberal commitments. But I hope my interpretation will be of some interest to others, as well. My account of key concepts in Mill's moral and political philosophy—his theory of motivation, his conception of happiness, his theories of duty and rights, his justification of utilitarianism, his understanding of the harm principle, his defense of expressive liberties and anti-paternalism, and his conceptions of and rationale for democratic and sexual equality—differs in significant ways from extant accounts of these matters in the secondary literature. I hope my interpretive and systematic claims about these elements in Mill's theory help stir the intellectual pot of Mill scholarship in constructive ways. But the most distinctive contribution of this study is to make the case for a perfectionist reading of Mill's conception of happiness and explore the significance of this kind of perfectionism for other aspects of his moral and political philosophy. Here, I have in mind his allusion to the importance of "utility in the largest sense, grounded on the permanent interests of man as a progressive being," quoted in the epigraph to this Preface from *On Liberty*. This is a conception of persons as autonomous agents, for whom the principal ingredient of happiness consists in the exercise of capacities for practical deliberation and decision—capacities that make us responsible agents and, hence, progressive beings. Millian perfectionism, on my interpretation, is not just a claim about what things *cause* happiness but also a claim about what happiness *consists in*. This perfectionist conception of happiness is also reflected, I believe, in his doctrine of higher pleasures in *Utilitarianism*. I would not claim that Mill's perfectionism permeates every theoretical commitment he makes in his moral or political philosophy, but I do think that the influence of his perfectionism is quite pervasive and significant. Once we become aware of this perfectionist theme, we can see Mill drawing on it at various points in his discussion of liberalism, rights, democratic government, and sexual equality. Even when Mill does not explicitly invoke this perfectionist theme, we can often see it as a further resource for defending his principles or for applying them in particular ways. Something like Mill's perfectionism strikes me as a plausible conception of happiness or welfare and, to my mind, marks much of what is distinctive and attractive in his contributions to utilitarian and liberal traditions.

Hence, on my reading, Mill's principles are progressive in two senses. His utilitarian and liberal commitments have exerted a progressive influence historically, combating institutions and policies of class and privilege and defending the rights of individuals against majoritarian coalitions, prejudice, and pressures for conformity. Some of these progressive aims and influences are attributable to structural features of utilitarianism and liberalism, independently of any particular assumptions about human nature or happiness. They could perhaps be supported by a consistent application and extension of the hedonistic assumptions of the Philosophical Radicals. But Mill's best case for these progressive aspirations, and much of his philosophical legacy, rests on his distinctive progressive assumptions about human nature and happiness that set him apart from the Radicals. That, at least, is a central contention of this book.

Studies in the history of philosophy are sometimes characterized as *analytical* or as *contextualist*, depending on whether the study emphasizes the adequacy of the philosophical ideas and arguments under discussion or their intellectual and historical context. Of course, analytical and contextual perspectives are not mutually exclusive, and good historical work partakes of both. Nonetheless, it is possible to mix these dimensions in different ratios responsibly, and it's only fair for me to confess that my study emphasizes analytical concerns. While I try to be aware of historical and intellectual context, I am especially interested in identifying what is distinctive and constructive in Mill's contributions to the utilitarian and liberal traditions, in part because I think that these are interesting and attractive traditions with enduring significance. I feel constrained by Mill's philosophical milieu and especially by his texts, and I don't assume that Mill's concerns are always the same as those of contemporary utilitarians or liberals. But I do see him as an important influence on these traditions, and I think that comparing his formulations of issues with contemporary ones can often provide mutual illumination. Mill's explicit remarks are not always fully transparent or obviously consistent, which is part of what makes interpreting his ideas interesting and rewarding. Contemporary distinctions, options, and conceptions may allow us to formulate rival readings of Mill's claims more clearly or identify interpretive possibilities worth exploring. The other side of this comparison is that we may come away from our study of Mill with interesting lessons about the utilitarian and liberal traditions—either new information about the origins of familiar utilitarian and liberal commitments or perhaps ideas from the past about promising options that have been unduly neglected in more recent discussions of these traditions. So my project mixes interpretation, rational reconstruction, and assessment at different points in different ways. Sometimes the result is a claim about what Mill asserted and what he meant. Sometimes the result is a claim about indeterminacy or tension within Mill's explicit remarks and a claim about how to understand Mill's considered view, or what is most plausible in his commitments. Sometimes the result is a claim about what Mill should or should not have said, given his most central and most attractive commitments. As I say, there are many responsible ways to mix contextual and analytical concerns, and this is one that has some genuine virtues, not least of which is that it allows us to see how interpretive and systematic perspectives can be mutually illuminating.

In writing this book, I am conscious of several intellectual debts. My biggest debts are to Fred Berger, David Lyons, Dick Arneson, and Terry Irwin. Though I never met Fred Berger, I have learned much from his wonderful study, *Happiness, Justice, and Freedom: The Moral and Political Philosophy of John Stuart Mill*, which sympathetically examines many of Mill's utilitarian and liberal commitments.[3] Berger's discussion has influenced me at many points, and on other issues I have tried to determine how my interpretive claims would fit with or modify his analysis. David Lyons's landmark essays on Mill's theories of duty, justice, and rights—many of which are collected in his book *Rights, Welfare, and Mill's Moral Theory*—have also shaped my discussion in important ways.[4] Interestingly, I did not study Mill with David while I was a graduate student at Cornell. He had completed most of his Mill essays a few years before my arrival at Cornell (in 1980) and was mostly working on issues in analytical jurisprudence in the early 1980s. Though we did discuss general issues about the prospects for utilitarianism, it was only after leaving Cornell and beginning to work on Mill's ethics that

---

3. Fred Berger, *Happiness, Justice, and Freedom: The Moral and Political Philosophy of John Stuart Mill* (Berkeley: University of California Press, 1984).
4. David Lyons, *Rights, Welfare, and Mill's Moral Theory* (New York: Oxford University Press, 1994).

I discovered these landmark essays and their importance. I discuss here many aspects of Mill's moral and political philosophy that David does not address, but on the topics we do both discuss my debt to his work is significant. Though my colleague Dick Arneson has published important essays on Mill's claims about paternalism, democracy, and political economy, from which I have learned a great deal,[5] my debt to him is only in small part to his writings on Mill. I have learned even more from countless discussions over the years about the resources of utilitarianism and consequentialism and from a graduate seminar we co-taught in 2009 on Mill's moral and political philosophy. I know Dick will disagree with me at many points, but I hope he will appreciate how much my interpretation and assessment of Mill owe to his philosophical friendship. I owe a different kind of debt to Terry Irwin. Though Terry and I have not discussed Mill in much depth, Terry introduced me to the pleasures of the history of ethics, both ancient and modern, and, to my mind, his work sets the standard for how to combine interpretive and systematic concerns in the history of philosophy in rich and constructive ways. I hope he sees the mark of his scholarly and pedagogical influence, however faint, in these pages.

There is a vast and growing secondary literature on Mill's moral and political philosophy that sets a very high standard of scholarship from which I have tried to profit. Some of it is by scholars from earlier eras, some of whom are themselves significant figures in the history of ethics. Much of it is by recent or contemporary scholars. I am indebted to this secondary literature at many points and in many ways and have done my best to record these debts along the way. However, I am sure that I cannot remember all my debts, my knowledge of this extensive literature is limited, and I have undoubtedly failed in places to benefit where I should have. One could measure my debt by how much more there is to learn from others. Equally important, I think, is how much I have already learned.

Several people have read and commented on earlier versions of the book manuscript. Among them are Roger Crisp, Sam Rickless, Don Rutherford, and three readers for Oxford University Press—Ben Saunders, C.L. Ten, and David Weinstein. I would like to thank them for flagging errors, identifying issues requiring fuller treatment, and offering constructive suggestions. The

---

5. See especially, Richard Arneson, "Mill Versus Paternalism," *Ethics* 90 (1980): 470–89, and "Paternalism, Utility, and Fairness," reprinted in *Mill's On Liberty: Critical Essays*, ed. G. Dworkin (New York: Rowman & Littlefield, 1997).

input of Ben Saunders was really supererogatory. He provided copious and judicious comments and suggestions that saved me from several errors and led to several significant changes and improvements. In addition, I am extremely grateful to a reading group of faculty and graduate students at the University of California, San Diego that met over several weeks early in 2012 to discuss the penultimate version of the manuscript. These sessions were humbling but also incredibly fruitful. I would like to thank Saba Bazargan, Eric Watkins, Matt Braich, Nanhee Byrnes, Adam Streed, Michael Tiboris, and Danny Weltman. Special thanks go to Dick Arneson, Craig Agule, Amy Berg, and Theron Pummer for their careful and constructive engagement with the book. These discussions really helped me put the central arguments in perspective and better assess the intellectual costs and benefits of various interpretive and systematic possibilities. Significant changes in the final revision owe much to their thoughtful input.

I would also like to thank several groups of students at UCSD for serving as willing and responsive guinea pigs as I tried out the ideas here. In particular, undergraduates in two courses (2009 and 2012) and graduate students in two seminars (2005 and 2009) provided useful feedback on many issues here. In this connection, I would especially like to thank Zachary Bachman, Christopher Dohna, Dale Dorsey, Charlie Kurth, Justin Lim, Violet McKeon, Omari Mikaberidze, Theron Pummer, Luke Robinson, Mellania Safarian, Sharon Skare, Adam Streed, and Dong Tran for their own ideas about Mill and their discussion of mine.

Parts of this study were presented to various audiences over many years, including a Boston University School of Law conference in honor of David Lyons, a Georgetown University law and philosophy seminar, the International Society for Utilitarian Studies held at Dartmouth University, and philosophy colloquia at the University of California, Santa Barbara, Middlebury College, the University of Pennsylvania, the University of Texas, Cornell University, the University of Kansas, the University of Connecticut, and Dartmouth College. I would like to thank audiences on those occasions for constructive feedback.

Various people provided useful commentary and feedback on proper parts of the present study, for which I am grateful. They include Michael Bratman, Joshua Cohen, David Copp, Garrett Cullity, Steve Darwall, Wendy Donner, James Fleming, Robert Fogelin, Samuel Freeman, Alan Fuchs, Paul Guyer, Michael Hardimon, Diane Jeske, Monte Johnson, Philip Kitcher, David Lyons, James Messina, Susan Sauvé Meyer, John Mikhail, Richard Miller,

Mark Murphy, Peter Nicholson, Alastair Norcross, Derek Parfit, Gerald Postema, Henry Richardson, Jonathan Riley, Kory Schaff, Fred Schauer, Ed Sherline, Ken Simons, David Sosa, Bob Stalnaker, Kyle Stanford, Jason Stanley, Nick Sturgeon, C.L. Ten, Aaron Zimmerman, and Matt Zwolinksi.

Earlier versions of some of the ideas presented here were published previously: "Mill's Deliberative Utilitarianism," in *Philosophy & Public Affairs* 21 (1992): 67–103; "Millian Principles, Freedom of Expression, and Hate Speech," in *Legal Theory* 7 (2001): 119–57; "Mill's Moral and Political Philosophy," in *The Stanford Encyclopedia of Philosophy*, ed. E. Zalta <http://plato.stanford.edu/archives/fall2007/entries/mill-moral-political>; "Mill's Liberal Principles and Freedom of Expression," in *Mill's On Liberty: A Critical Guide*, ed. C.L. Ten (New York: Cambridge University Press, 2008); "Mill's Ambivalence about Rights," in the *Boston University Law Review* 90 (2010): 1669–1704; and "Mill's Ambivalence about Duty," in *Mill on Justice*, ed. L. Kahn (London: Palgrave, 2012). I thank the publishers of those articles for permission to re-use some of that material here.

Peter Momtchiloff, my editor at Oxford University Press, provided just the right blend of encouragement and patience on this project. I am grateful to the staff at the Press, especially Sarah Parker, Carla Hodge, Melleoni Sapphire Lagrama, Eleanor Collins, and Rosemary Campbell for their sensible and efficient guidance during the publication process. Craig Agule provided invaluable help in various stages of preparing and proofing the manuscript.

Finally, I would like to thank my wife, Bonny Sweeney, for her love, support, and example over these years. She has taught me all I know about the content and importance of Mill's ideal of friendships among equals.

A note on Mill's texts

There are many editions of Mill's more popular and influential works, including many of his writings in moral and political philosophy. The definitive edition of Mill's writings is *The Collected Works of John Stuart Mill* [*CW*], 33 volumes, ed. J. Robson (Toronto: University of Toronto Press, 1965–91), which is available online and free of charge through the Online Library of the Liberty Fund <http://oll.libertyfund.org>. In order to facilitate common reference among readers using different editions of *Utilitarianism*, *On Liberty*, *A System of Logic*, and *Principles of Political Economy*, I will refer to those works using natural divisions in his texts, such as chapter, section, and/or paragraph. Otherwise, I will refer to Mill's works using pagination in his *Collected Works*. I refer to the following works, employing the associated abbreviations and conventions.

- "Remarks on Bentham's Philosophy" ["Remarks on Bentham"] (1833) [*CW* X]. *CW* pagination.
- "Civilization" (1836) [*CW* XVIII]. *CW* pagination.
- "On Bentham" ["Bentham"] (1838) [*CW* X]. *CW* pagination.
- *A System of Logic* [*SL*] (1843) [*CW* VII–VIII]. References by book, chapter, and section number.
- *Principles of Political Economy* [*PPE*] (1848) [*CW* II–III]. References by book, chapter, and section number.
- "Chapters on Socialism" (1850) [*CW* V]. *CW* pagination.
- "Whewell on Moral Philosophy" (1852) [*CW* X]. *CW* pagination.
- "Thoughts on Parliamentary Reform" (1859) [*CW* XIX]. *CW* pagination.
- *On Liberty* [*OL*] (1859) [*CW* XVIII]. References by chapter and paragraph number.

- *Utilitarianism* [*U*] (1861) [*CW* X]. References by chapter and paragraph number.
- *Considerations on Representative Government* [*CRG*] (1861) [*CW* XIX]. References by chapter and *CW* pagination.
- "August Comte and Positivism" (1865) [*CW* X]. *CW* pagination.
- *The Subjection of Women* [*SW*] (1869) [*CW* XXI]. *CW* pagination.
- *Autobiography* (1873) [*CW* I]. *CW* pagination.
- Notes to James Mill, *Analysis of the Phenomena of the Human Mind* [Notes], 2 vols, 2d ed., J.S. Mill, London: Longmans, 1869.

So, for instance, *OL* I 11 refers to paragraph 11 of chapter I in *On Liberty* and *SL* VI.xii.6 refers to book VI, chapter xii, section 6, of *A System of Logic*. I will cite *CW* by volume number. To make a pinpoint reference, I will use volume and page number. So, for instance, "Bentham" *CW* X 110 refers to page 110 in Mill's essay "On Bentham" in volume X of Mill's *Collected Works*.

1
Mill's radical background

One cannot properly appreciate the development of Mill's moral and political philosophy without some understanding of his intellectual background. He was raised in the tradition of *Philosophical Radicalism*. The Radicals were British intellectuals and political figures in the first half of the nineteenth century who advocated for social and political reform. They included figures such as David Ricardo (1772–1823), John Austin (1790–1859), George Grote (1794–1871), and William Molesworth (1810–55). The intellectual leadership of the Radicals came primarily from Bentham and, to a lesser extent, from James Mill. John Stuart Mill is himself usually regarded as a Radical, perhaps the most important one. But our interest here is in Mill's Radical inheritance. The Radicals applied utilitarian principles in a self-conscious and systematic way to issues of institutional design and social reform. Utilitarianism assesses actions and institutions in terms of their effects on happiness and enjoins us to perform actions and design institutions so that they promote—in one formulation, maximize—happiness. As I've noted already, utilitarianism was a progressive doctrine historically, principally because of its universal scope—its insistence that everyone's happiness matters—and its egalitarian conception of impartiality—its insistence that everyone's happiness matters equally. Because of utilitarianism's universal scope and impartiality, the Radicals' application of utilitarian principles to social institutions tended to challenge traditional institutions and policies of class and privilege. Bentham, of course, was famous for his numerous and quite detailed plans for legislative and penal reform. Prominent among the reforms proposed by Bentham and other Radicals were democratic reforms, such as the 1832 Reform Bill, that aimed to extend the franchise to the working classes, which would give them a say indirectly in legislation and make members of Parliament more widely accountable.

As recounted in his *Autobiography* (1873), Mill was groomed from birth by his father to become the ultimate Victorian intellectual and utilitarian reformer. As part of this apprenticeship, Mill was exposed to an extremely demanding education, shaped by utilitarian principles. He began Greek at the age of three. He had read considerable Greek and Latin history, poetry, and philosophy by the age of eight. At the age of eleven he helped edit his father's *History of India*. At the age of thirteen he began a systematic study of political economy. While Mill followed the strict intellectual regimen laid down by his father for many years, the intellectual and emotional stress that he was asked to shoulder eventually proved too much. He suffered a profound intellectual and emotional crisis in the period 1826–30. Mill discusses this emotional crisis in his *Autobiography*. In contrast with contemporary memoirs, Mill does not rush to blame his father for all of his troubles, though blame would have been well deserved. He appreciated the attention his father gave to his education, but he regarded that education as one-sided. He thought that his training was too strictly intellectual and ignored his emotional needs and development. Mill's recovery was assisted by friendships he formed with Thomas Carlyle and Samuel Coleridge, who introduced him to ideas and texts from the Romantic and Conservative traditions. As Mill emerged from his depression, he became more concerned with the development of well-rounded individuals and with the role of feeling, culture, and creativity in the happiness of individuals.[1] Though Mill never renounced the liberal and utilitarian tradition and mission that he inherited from his father, his mental crisis and recovery greatly influenced his interpretation of this tradition. He became critical of the moral psychology of Bentham and his father and of some of the social theory underlying their plans for reform. It is arguable that Mill tends to downplay the significance of his innovations and to underestimate the intellectual discontinuities between himself and his father. One measure of the extent of Mill's departure from the views of Bentham and James Mill is that Mill's contributions to the utilitarian tradition apparently led his father to view him as a defector from the utilitarian cause (*Autobiography*, *CW* I 189). We need to try to understand the extent of the transformation Mill brings to the utilitarian and liberal principles of the Radicals.

Mill embraced the utilitarianism of the Philosophical Radicals. Utilitarianism, in its most general form, claims that the moral value of persons, actions, and

---

1. For useful accounts of Mill's life and intellectual development, see Michael St. John Packe, *The Life of John Stuart Mill* (New York: Macmillan, 1954), and Nicholas Capaldi, *John Stuart Mill: A Biography* (New York: Cambridge University Press, 2004).

institutions depends on how well they promote human (or perhaps sentient) happiness. This claim Mill shares with his forebears. But he modified their assumptions about human motivation, the nature of happiness, the relationship between happiness and duty, and the justification of utilitarianism. Some of Mill's most significant innovations to the utilitarian tradition concern his claims about the nature of happiness and the role of happiness in human motivation. Bentham and James Mill understand happiness hedonistically, as consisting in pleasure, and they believe that the ultimate aim of each person is predominantly, if not exclusively, the promotion of the agent's own happiness (pleasure). Mill rejects their psychological egoism (hedonism) and significantly modifies their assumptions about happiness when he introduces his doctrine of higher pleasures. To appreciate Mill's innovations here, we need to understand some aspects of the Radical legacy he inherited.

1. Psychological egoism

The Radicals embraced both psychological and evaluative hedonism. Bentham begins his *Introduction to the Principles of Morals and Legislation* (1789) with this hedonistic assumption about human motivation.[2]

> Nature has placed mankind under the governance of two sovereign masters, *pain* and *pleasure* [Ch. I §1].

Bentham allows that we may be moved by the pleasures and pains of others. But he appears to think that these other-regarding pleasures can move us only or primarily insofar as we take pleasure in the pleasure of others (V 32). This suggests that Bentham endorses a version of psychological egoism, which, on one common formulation, claims that the agent's own happiness is and can be the only ultimate object of his desires. If one's own happiness is one's only ultimate object of desire, this implies an explanatory structure to one's desires and behavior. If one's own happiness is one's only ultimate desire, then one's other desires are always subordinated to this desire, and the ultimate object of one's intentional actions is the promotion of one's own

---

2. Jeremy Bentham, *An Introduction to the Principles of Morals and Legislation* [1789], ed. J. Burns and H. Hart (London: Athlone Press, 1970). I refer to passages in the *Principles* by chapter and paragraph number in this edition.

happiness. In his unfinished *Constitutional Code* (1822–32), Bentham seems to endorse these commitments.[3]

> On the occasion of every act he exercises, every human being is led to pursue that line of conduct which, according to his view of the case, taken by him at the moment, will be in the highest degree contributory to his own greatest happiness [*Works* IX: Introduction, §2].

Bentham is a hedonist about utility or happiness, treating happiness as consisting in pleasure.

> By utility is meant that property of any object, whereby it tends to produce benefit, advantage, pleasure, good, or happiness, (all of this in the present case comes to the same thing) or (what comes again to the same thing) to prevent the happening of mischief, pain, evil, or unhappiness to the party whose interest is considered: if the party be the community in general, then the happiness of the community: if a particular individual, then the happiness of that individual [*Principles* I 3].

Someone skeptical of hedonism might well wonder if these different predicates all designate the same property. Perhaps happiness or advantage does not consist in pleasure. But Bentham affirms that they do express the same property and so embraces hedonism. So the version of psychological egoism to which Bentham is attracted is psychological hedonism.

James Mill also endorses psychological hedonism in his *Essay on Government* (1824).[4] For instance, he claims

> The desire, therefore, of that power which is necessary to render the persons and properties of human beings subservient to our pleasures, is the grand governing law of human nature [*Essay* IV].

Later, he describes this assumption in somewhat greater detail.

> The positions...with regard to human nature, and which we assume as foundations, are these: That the actions of men are governed by their wills, and their wills by their desires: That their desires are directed to pleasure and the relief from pain as *ends*, and to wealth and power as the principal means: That to the desire of these means there is no limit; and that the

---

3. Unless specified otherwise, references to Bentham's works are to natural divisions in the text of *The Works of Jeremy Bentham* [1838–43], ed. J. Bowring (New York: Russell & Russell, 1962). So, "*Constitutional Code* (*Works* IX: Introduction, §2)" refers to section 2 of the Introduction to the *Constitutional Code* in volume IX of Bowring's edition of Bentham's *Collected Works*.
4. James Mill, *An Essay on Government* [1824] reprinted in *Utilitarian Logic and Politics*, ed. J. Lively and J. Rees (Oxford: Clarendon Press, 1978).

actions that flow from the unlimited desire are the constituents whereof bad Government is made. Reasoning correctly from these laws of nature, we shall presently discover what opinion, with respect to the mixture of the different species of Government, it will be incumbent upon us to adopt [*Essay* V].

In these passages, Bentham and James Mill appear to say that all behavior is self-interested. Neither says much about his reasons for making this assumption. In fact, both treat the assumption as "axiomatic," implying that is not supported by other claims. But there is also evidence that Bentham saw his legislative science built on an empirical foundation, and so he may have seen his egoistic axiom as a generalization from his observations of human behavior.

In these and other pronouncements about human motivation, the Radicals are psychological egoists and hedonists. However, sometimes Bentham appears to allow for a more diverse set of ultimate motives or interests, including other-regarding motives, as in this passage from his *A Table of the Springs of Action*.

> 1. In regard to *interest*, in the most extended—which is the original and only strictly proper sense—of the word *disinterested*, no human act ever has been, or ever can be, *disinterested*. For there exists not ever any voluntary action, which is not the result of the operation of some *motive* or *motives*: nor any motive, which has not for its accompaniment a corresponding *interest*, real or imagined.
> 2. In the only sense in which *disinterestedness* can with truth be predicated of human action,... it must be understood to denote, being—not the absence of *all* interest—a state of things which, consistently with voluntary action, is not possible—but only the absence of all interest of the *self-regarding* class...
> 3. If what is above be correct, the most *disinterested* of men is not less under the dominion of *interest* than the most *interested* [*Works* I: II (Observations) §2].[5]

Here, Bentham recognizes interests on which agents act that are not self-regarding. However, he still claims that all behavior is a reflection of the agent's interests, while allowing that some of these interests might be non-derivative

---

5. This fact is noticed by Sir Leslie Stephen, *The English Utilitarians* (originally published 1900) (New York: Augustus Kelley, 1968), vol. 1, p. 311.

other-regarding interests. In several places, Bentham indicates that among these other-regarding interests are sympathetic interests (*Principles* V 10, 32; X 25; XI 31; *Table of the Springs of Action* in Works I: Table X). This seems like a potentially very important qualification to his otherwise egoistic assumptions about motivation. Indeed, it seems inconsistent with his egoistic assumptions—it can't be true both that everyone's ultimate motivation is self-interest and that some people have ultimate desires that are other-regarding. How could he not notice this inconsistency?

Bentham's use of the term "interest" is potentially misleading. When we talk about an agent's interests, we might be talking about what is in her self-interest or we might be talking about what interests her or what she cares about. In the former case, we are talking about her own happiness or well-being, but, in the latter case, her interests might be other-regarding. Unless psychological egoism is true, we can't assume that what an agent cares about is always her own happiness or welfare. The danger here is of confusing these two ways of talking about an agent's interests. If we believe that agents always act to satisfy their desires and identify an agent's interests with what she cares about, then we might well assume that an agent always acts to promote her interests.

1. An agent always acts to promote her own interests (what interests her).
2. Hence, an agent always acts self-interestedly (so as to promote her own happiness).

By distinguishing these two senses of an agent's interests, we can see that this inference to psychological egoism is fallacious, resting on a tacit equivocation. The mistake involves inferring something about the *content* of an agent's desires from a fact of *ownership*, whose desires they are.

Another way to try to square other-regarding motives with psychological hedonism is to insist that agents expect to experience pleasure at satisfying their desires, including their other-regarding desires. If so, then agents can expect to experience self-interested rewards for altruistic motivation. But this point does not show that apparently altruistic motivation is at bottom self-interested. Bishop Butler famously argued that we could not infer psychological hedonism from the expectation of pleasure at satisfying our desires.

> That all particular appetites and passions are towards *external things themselves*, distinct from the *pleasure arising from them*, is manifested from hence; that there

could not be this pleasure, were it not for that prior suitableness between the object and the passion: there could be no enjoyment or delight from one thing more than another, from eating food more than swallowing a stone, if there were not an affection or appetite to one thing more than another.[6]

Butler's point is that it is a fallacy to suppose that we aim at the pleasure we expect to accompany the satisfaction of our desires. The pleasure in getting x (P1) is predicated or consequential on the prior desire for x (D1); the desire is not predicated on that pleasure. So even if the anticipation of P1 gives rise to a new desire for x (D2), that gives no reason to think that the original desire for x (D1) is predicated on the expectation of pleasure.

Neither of these considerations shows that psychological egoism or hedonism—conceived as a substantive theory about the nature of human motivation—is incoherent or false. Rather, they show that some common ways of defending psychological egoism and reconciling it with sympathetic and altruistic motivation are misguided. As a result, I think it's hard to avoid the conclusion that Bentham cannot square his defense of psychological hedonism with his own more plausible pluralist assumptions about human motivation. Should we just conclude that Bentham is inconsistent?

It's worth noting that Bentham's concessions to psychological pluralism are exceptional. Even in contexts where he recognizes motivation that is not ultimately self-interested, he appears to treat it as weaker and less dependable than self-interested motivation. For instance, in his *Constitutional Code* Bentham acknowledges that the ratio of sympathy and self-regard are different in different individuals. But he notes that it is natural for self-regard to predominate and advises the legislator to assume this in crafting policy.

> But, in regard to sympathy, the less the proportion of it is, the natural and actual existence of which he assumes as and for the basis of his arrangements, the greater will be the success of whatever endeavours he uses to give increase to it [*Works* I: Bk. II, Ch. vi, §31/p. 192].

In these claims, Bentham makes a psychological claim that is weaker than psychological egoism, which we might call *predominant egoism*.[7] Predominant

---

6. Bishop Joseph Butler, *Fifteen Sermons Preached at the Rolls Chapel Sermons* (originally published 1726) (London: Bell & Sons, 1953), Sermon XI, para. 6.
7. Kavka introduces the concept of predominant egoism in his discussion of Hobbes, claiming that Hobbesian political theory requires no more than predominant egoism. See Gregory Kavka, *Hobbesian Moral and Political Theory* (Princeton: Princeton University Press, 1986), pp. 64–80. A predominant egoist reading of Bentham is suggested by Stephen, *The English Utilitarians*, vol. I, p. 313.

egoism claims that while there might be a plurality of ultimate aims that people have, self-interested motivation predominates for most people most of the time. Other ultimate motives are not always present, and, even when they are present, they tend to be weaker than, and are often overridden by, self-interested concerns. Predominant egoism is weaker and, hence, more plausible than egoism.

Predominant egoism does not acquit Bentham of inconsistency, because it is not strictly compatible with psychological egoism, to which he sometimes commits himself. Nonetheless, predominant egoism might be the best way to make sense of his twin commitments to psychological egoism and pluralism about ultimate motives. We might say that while Bentham does commit himself to psychological egoism in various places, when he is being careful he commits himself to no more than predominant egoism. As we will see, many of the reforms that Bentham and James Mill endorse make good sense whether egoism or predominant egoism is true. And predominant egoism is not as implausible psychologically as egoism is.

2. Utilitarianism

Bentham claims that utility not only describes human motivation but also sets the standard of right and wrong (*Principles* I 1).

> By the principle of utility is meant that principle which approves or disapproves of every action whatsoever, according to the tendency which it appears to have to augment or diminish the happiness of the party whose interest is in question: or, what is the same thing in other words, to promote or oppose that happiness. I say of every action whatsoever; and therefore not only of every action of a private individual, but of every measure of government [I 2].

It remains to be determined whose happiness matters. One might imagine that it is the utility of the agent. This would be the ethical counterpart to psychological egoism. However, Bentham's answer, and the answer characteristic of utilitarianism, is the happiness of the community or the happiness of all (I 4–10). In fact, Bentham believed that the scope of the utilitarian concern with happiness should be wide indeed, insofar as it should include sentient happiness, as well as human happiness (XVII 4). Though Bentham thinks that the scope of utilitarian concern should include sentient happiness, it will be convenient to focus, as Bentham himself normally does, on the utilitarian concern with human happiness. Bentham says that our account of right action, obligation, and duty ought to be governed by the principle of utility (I 9–10). This seems to imply that an action is right or obligatory only insofar as it promotes utility. But then the right or obligatory act would seem to be the one that promotes utility the most or *maximizes* utility. This is how Bentham describes the principle of utility in *A Fragment on Government* (1776). He identifies it as the greatest happiness or greatest felicity principle:

> that principle which states that the greatest happiness of all those whose interest is in question, as being the right and proper, and only right and proper and universally desirable, *end* of human action in every situation; and, in particular, in that of a functionary, or set of functionaries, exercising the powers of Government [*Works* I: Ch. I §48].

A common way to formulate this claim is in terms of *act utilitarianism*.

> An agent should perform that action, among those available to her, whose consequences for happiness are at least as good as any other available to her.

Bentham clearly thinks that a proper science of legislation should endorse institutions and policies that will promote or maximize happiness. No doubt, he thinks that legislators should often calculate expected utility, and many of his own recommendations for reform reflect his own calculations of expected utility. But he is sensitive to the idea that the consequences of calculating utility might not always be best.

> 'The principle of utility, (I have heard it said) is a dangerous principle: it is dangerous on certain occasions to consult it.' This is as much to say, what? that it is *not* consulting it, to consult it [*Principles* I 13].

Bentham is not clear what these occasions are or in what sense consulting the principle in such cases is not consulting it. Though we might expect a utilitarian to calculate expected utility in all her decisions, it is a practical question how to deliberate, and utilitarianism implies that this practical question, like all practical questions, is correctly answered by what would in fact maximize utility. Utilitarian calculation is time-consuming and often unreliable or subject to bias and distortion. For such reasons, we may in such cases better approximate the utilitarian standard if we don't always try to approximate it. Bentham does not elaborate how we should identify these cases or how we should reason about them. But he is consistent in recognizing the utilitarian limits of utilitarian reasoning.

3. Evaluative hedonism

Hedonistic utilitarianism contains two normative elements: one is the claim that the good is happiness, specifically, pleasure, and the other is that we should promote—in one formulation, maximize—the good, so understood. We've seen that Bentham endorses the utilitarian moral claim. Let's look more closely at his evaluative hedonism.

Bentham is content to identify the good to be promoted as utility or advantage or happiness or pleasure, treating these as interchangeable concepts (*Principles* I 3). But this is a substantive and potentially controversial claim. Utility might be viewed as a term of art, naming whatever it is that is good for a person or that one should care about insofar as one cares about that person for his own sake. But it is a substantive claim that utility, in this sense, should be identified with either happiness or pleasure. One might think that utility is not a matter, or not only a matter, of happiness. Even if one does identify utility and happiness, it is a further substantive and potentially controversial claim to understand happiness in terms of pleasure, as hedonism claims. There are various alternative non-hedonic conceptions of utility and happiness. As we will see, one could in principle identify utility or happiness with satisfying one's desires, with self-realization, or with acquiring various objective goods, such as knowledge, friendship, and personal achievement.

It is common to understand utilitarianism as the doctrine that one has a duty to promote human happiness or welfare. While many of Bentham's formulations of utilitarianism are agnostic about how happiness or welfare is to be conceived, he does accept a hedonistic conception of happiness or welfare. But his account of hedonism is very incomplete. Nowadays, it is common to understand hedonism as the claim that pleasure is the one and only intrinsic good and that pain is the one and only intrinsic bad. On this conception, other things can have only extrinsic value; they are extrinsically valuable (or disvaluable) insofar as they are responsible for bringing about pleasure (or pain).

Perhaps surprisingly, the Radicals do not have much to say about precisely what sort of mental state or sensation pleasure is. On one view, pleasure is a mental state or sensation with a particular kind of feel or qualia. Bentham is sometimes interpreted as this sort of hedonist, though the grounds for this interpretation are unclear. This conception of pleasure is problematic insofar as it can be difficult to believe that there is a single qualia or feel common to all the diverse sorts of pleasures that people experience—for instance, the pleasures of sex and drugs, gustatory pleasures, the pleasures of hard work, the pleasure in parental pride, and the pleasures of discovery. Those who despair of finding a common feel among disparate pleasures sometimes conceive of pleasures as mental states or sensations that are preferred. At one point in his *Analysis of the Phenomena of the Human Mind*, James Mill suggests a conception along these lines.

> Some sensations...are what we call indifferent. They are not considered as either painful, or pleasurable. There are sensations, however,...some of which are painful, some pleasurable. The difference is that which is felt. A man knows it by feeling it; and this is the whole account of the phenomenon. I have one sensation, and then another, and then another. The first is of such a kind, that I care not whether it is long or short; the second is of such a kind that I would put an end to it instantly if I could; the third is of such a kind, that I like it prolonged. To distinguish these feelings, I give them names. I call the first Indifferent; the second, Painful; the third, Pleasurable.[8]

We can develop this appeal to preferences among our sensations in functional terms. On this conception, pleasures are mental states or sensations that the subject prefers and, other things being equal, would take steps to prolong. In a parallel fashion, pains, on this functional conception, are mental states or sensations that the subject dislikes and, other things being equal, would take steps to discontinue. Of course, other things may not be equal. There may be reasons not to prolong a particular pleasure, and there may be reasons why a particular pain should be prolonged. But this is compatible with the functional view of pleasures as sensations one is disposed to prolong and of pains as sensations one is disposed to cut short. Whereas Bentham is largely silent on the nature of pleasure, James Mill suggests such a preference or functional conception.

Nonetheless, in *Principles* Chapter IV Bentham does have several things to say about the *value* of pleasures. First, he sets out four aspects of pleasures that, considered in themselves, affect their value (IV 2–3):

1. Intensity
2. Duration

---

8. James Mill, *An Analysis of the Phenomena of the Human Mind*, vols I–II (originally published 1829), 2d. ed. A. Bain, A. Findlander, G. Grote, and J.S. Mill (London: Longmans, 1878), vol. II, p. 184.

3. Certainty or uncertainty
4. Propinquity or remoteness in time.

In understanding these four dimensions of pleasure, it may help to think of what hedonism apparently implies. It says that pleasure is the one and only intrinsic good and that pain is the one and only intrinsic evil. All other things have only extrinsic or instrumental value depending on whether they produce pleasure or pain and, if so, how much. To make comparative assessments, therefore, we need to be able to determine the *amount* or *magnitude* of pleasure. These four dimensions are supposed to affect the magnitude of the pleasure and, hence, its value.

The first two dimensions are straightforward. It is easy to see how a pleasure's intensity or duration might bear on its magnitude. All else being equal, a more intense pleasure is more pleasurable than a less intense pleasure. And, all else being equal, a longer lasting pleasure is more pleasurable than a more short-lived pleasure. If hedonism is true, a pleasure's value should be directly proportional to its intensity and duration.

The second two dimensions of pleasurableness are more problematic. Certainty is a problematic dimension, because it seems to be a feature not of the pleasure itself, but of our cognitive relation to the pleasure. Whereas intensity and duration affect a pleasure's *value*, certainty seems to affect its *expected value*. If so, certainty might be relevant to someone's attempt to maximize expected value, but it seems irrelevant to what in fact maximizes value. That's a matter of which pleasures do or will occur, not how certain we are that they will occur.

Propinquity—temporal proximity—is also a puzzling dimension of pleasurableness. Bentham implies that, all else being equal, a more remote pleasure is less valuable than a more proximate one. Though it is perhaps descriptively true that humans often engage in temporal discounting, that sort of temporal bias is hard to defend. A future pleasure is no less a pleasure than a present pleasure. Why should it be any less valuable for the hedonist? Indeed, temporal bias is typically viewed as a paradigmatic form of irrationality. We condemn as irrational the person who knowingly prefers the smaller short-term good to the greater, later good. The one way in which the proximity of a pleasure may have rational significance is its bearing on the pleasure's certainty. For the more temporally remote a potential pleasure, the more uncertain may be its occurrence. Just as my own future existence is less certain the further into the future we project, so too the occurrence of a given pleasure or pain is less certain the further in the future it lies. In the *Methods of Ethics* Henry Sidgwick (1838–1900) criticizes Bentham on precisely this score.[9]

> [P]roximity is a property [of pleasures and pains] which it is reasonable to disregard except in so far as it diminishes uncertainty. For my feelings a year hence should be just as important to me as my feelings next minute, if only I could make an equally sure forecast of them. Indeed this equal and impartial concern for all parts of one's conscious life is perhaps the most prominent element in the common notion of the *rational*—as opposed to the merely *impulsive*—pursuit of pleasure [*Methods of Ethics* 124n; cf. 111].

Later, Sidgwick rejects any pure time preference.

> Hereafter *as such* is to be regarded neither less nor more than Now. It is not, of course, meant, that the good of the present may not reasonably be preferred to that of the future on account of its greater certainty: or again, that a week ten years hence may not be more important to us than a week now, through an increase in our means or capacities of happiness. All that the principle affirms is that the mere difference of priority and posteriority in time is not a reasonable ground for having more regard to the consciousness of one moment than to that of another. The form in which it practically presents itself to most men is 'that a smaller present good is not to be preferred to a greater future good' (allowing for differences of certainty). . . . [*Methods* 381]

If Sidgwick is right, then Bentham is wrong to say that propinquity is a distinct dimension of a pleasure's value. It should have no intrinsic relevance. It is relevant only insofar as it affects a pleasure's certainty, and certainty affects not a pleasure's value, but its expected value.[10]

These four dimensions are supposed to bear on the value of a pleasure itself. Bentham mentions three other considerations affecting the value of pleasures, not of pleasures considered individually and intrinsically, but of some pleasures considered in relations to other pleasures (IV 3–4):

1. Fecundity, which is the tendency of a pleasure (pain) to be accompanied by more pleasures (pains).

---

9. Henry Sidgwick, *The Methods of Ethics*, 7th ed. (London: Macmillan, 1907).
10. Bentham's mistaken claim that certainty and propinquity affect the value of a pleasure may reflect his tendency to elide the distinction between hedonistic and utilitarian standards, on the one hand, and the perspective of someone, such as a legislator, trying to apply these standards and attempting to maximize expected value or utility, on the other hand. This sort of elision is easy enough to do, but it is illicit. What is part of a standard and what is part of its application are different things.

2. Purity, which is the tendency of a pleasure (pain) not to be followed by a pain (pleasure).[11]
3. Extent, which is the number of times a given kind of pleasure (pain) is had, whether by a single person or others.

These three dimensions and their evaluative significance are reasonably straightforward. All else being equal, we should prefer pleasures that are more fecund, more pure, and greater in extent. Of course, all else is not always equal. For instance, we may produce more pleasure overall with mixed or impure pleasures than with pure pleasures if the pleasures associated with the mixed pleasure are sufficiently greater in extent, duration, or intensity than those associated with the pure pleasure.

But one might well find Bentham's whole taxonomy unnecessarily complex. To promote happiness, conceived of as pleasure, whether within a single life or across lives, one must be able to make sense of quantities or magnitudes of pleasure associated with different options, and be able, at least in principle, to compare the total pleasure associated with different options. Intensity, duration, and extent would appear to be the only genuinely relevant variables. Each option is associated with various pleasures and pains both within a single life and across lives. For any given option we must find out how many pleasures and pains it produces, and whether those occur in a single life or in different lives. For every distinct pleasure and pain, we must calculate its intensity and its duration to determine its magnitude. The total amount of net pleasure (or pain) associated with each option represents the difference between the magnitude of the pleasures and the magnitude of the pains. The best option is the one with the greatest total of net pleasure. If there are two (or more) options with the greatest total, we are free to select any of these.[12] We can, of course, still talk about the fecundity or purity of pleasures and say that, all else being equal, we should prefer more fecund or purer pleasures. But those properties of pleasures have no independent significance.

11. Bentham conceives of purity as a diachronic property of pleasures (pains), but we could also think of it as a synchronic property of pleasures (pains). So conceived, pleasures (pains) would be pure insofar as they were unmixed at a time or over time.
12. For a clear statement of the essentials of classical hedonism, see Fred Feldman, *Pleasure and the Good Life* (Oxford: Clarendon Press, 2004), ch. 2, esp. p. 27. Feldman is describing what he calls Default Hedonism. Default Hedonism recognizes only sensory pleasures and pains. For this reason, I doubt any of the classical utilitarians accepts Default Hedonism. But if we abstract from this restriction, Default Hedonism provides a clear conception of the basics of hedonism and hedonistic arithmetic.

4. Duty and interest

It is reasonably clear how the Radicals intended to articulate a science of legislation that incorporated both utilitarian and egoist elements. Utilitarianism gives us our normative end or duty—what we should be aiming at in all action, including legislation. But what in concrete circumstances will promote happiness, and how best to achieve that, are matters that are constrained by facts of human psychology. According to the Radicals, human psychology is egoistic, or at least predominantly so. So we must find ways to harness people's self-interested motives to achieve outcomes that are beneficial for all. We need to pursue institutions and policies that make utilitarian duty and individual interest coincide.

But there is a problem with this attempt to marry duty and interest. It is problematic to combine the ethical claim that each of us ought to aim at the general happiness (or pleasure) with the psychological claim that each of us can only aim (ultimately) at his own happiness (or pleasure). It's true that utilitarianism is a normative claim and egoism is a descriptive claim, but they give agents conflicting ends. The worry is not unique to combining egoism with utilitarianism. Here we seem to have a special case of the conflict between psychological egoism and morality's other-regarding or altruistic demands.

Though the problem may not be unique to a utilitarian conception of duty, a utilitarian conception of duty may make the problem worse. For there is a clear sense in which the problem is worse the greater the conflict between duty and self-interest. Any moral theory that recognizes even modest duties of altruism in which one might be required to forego a small benefit or risk a small loss for the sake of producing a much greater good for others will recognize some moral duties that conflict with self-interest. But because of its wide scope—its insistence that everyone's happiness matters—and its impartiality—its insistence that everyone's happiness matters equally—utilitarianism appears to be potentially very demanding. As long as I can do more good for others with my time and energy than I could do for myself, utilitarianism would seem to require that I benefit others at my own expense (for more discussion, see §10). If so, the conflict between egoism and utilitarianism seems potentially great.

The problem with this conflict is that in a significant range of cases utilitarianism is telling agents that they ought to behave in ways that are contrary to natural motivational patterns. This might make utilitarianism look unattractive, utopian, or even irrelevant. But matters might be worse still. For egoism is usually understood not just as a claim about how people happen to be motivated, viz. that everyone just happens to have his own happiness as his only ultimate aim, but rather as a modal claim about how human nature constrains what is motivationally possible for us. On this view, we can't help but act self-interestedly. But if this is how egoism is understood, then we can see a further problem squaring utilitarianism, or any moderately altruistic moral theory, with the *voluntarist principle* that ought implies can.

1. What maximizes total happiness (or pleasure) often is not what maximizes the agent's own happiness (or pleasure).
2. Necessarily, an agent acts so as to maximize his own happiness (or pleasure).
3. Ought implies can; you can only be obligated to do what it is possible for you to do.
4. Hence, it cannot be one's duty to maximize happiness (or pleasure).

It's bad enough if utilitarianism proved to be unattractive, utopian, or irrelevant. But if we accept egoism and voluntarism, that shows that utilitarianism must be false as well.

However, the utilitarian can take comfort in knowing that this is not a very discriminating argument, inasmuch as egoism and voluntarism cannot be squared with any moderately altruistic moral conception either. If this argument against utilitarianism proves too much, that strongly suggests that there is something wrong with it. Because the argument is valid, that means that we should rethink the truth of the premises. There are, in effect, three premises—egoism, voluntarism, and the extensional inequivalence of duty and interest. Though voluntarism is occasionally questioned, it makes a remarkably plausible claim about the limits of moral demands. It seems harsh and unfair to hold people to duties that they could not perform. This is especially plausible if wrongdoing licenses blame. Fairness seems to require that we only be blamed for things that that were up to us. If wrongdoing licenses blame, then fairness requires the opportunity to avoid wrongdoing. That leaves egoism and the inequivalence of duty and interest to question. As we will see, Bentham does want to challenge the extent of the inequivalence of duty and interest. But it's hard to believe in the perfect coincidence of duty, especially utilitarian duty, and self-interest. As long as this coincidence is imperfect, that leaves the argument intact.[13]

This leaves egoism as the most likely culprit, which is hardly surprising, inasmuch as it is, as we have already observed, a very implausible claim about the content and structure of human motivation. Utilitarians, and anyone attracted to a moderately altruistic moral theory, should respond to this worry by denying psychological egoism. There is good independent reason to do so, and doing so blocks this argument.

Even if rejecting egoism is a sensible response, it seems like a major concession for the Radicals. Is there any way to soften this blow? Recall that I said that Bentham sometimes allowed for ultimate aims that are other-regarding and I suggested that his considered view might be best interpreted as predominant egoism. I also said that the reforms defended by Bentham and James Mill seemed to presuppose no more than predominant egoism (more on this below). So perhaps the Radicals could avoid this objection to utilitarianism without renouncing egoism altogether, provided they switch from egoism to predominant egoism. Making this work would place some constraints on the formulation of predominant egoism. To avoid ascribing impossible duties, predominant egoism not only must avoid the claims that self-interest is our only motive and that everyone always acts self-interestedly but also must claim that even in cases when we do act self-interestedly we have the *capacity* to act otherwise. A natural formulation would make several claims.

1. The vast majority of us have both self-interested and other-regarding ultimate aims.
2. The self-interested impulses tend to be stronger, so that most, but not all, of us tend to act self-interestedly most of the time.
3. Most of us do not act self-interestedly all the time.
4. Some of us are quite unselfish.

---

13. A different attempt to avoid the anti-utilitarian conclusion might insist on construing utilitarianism as the demand to perform the best option *available to the agent*. It might then be claimed that psychological egoism greatly constrains the actions available to the agent. Indeed, according to egoism, the only actions available to the agent are those that maximize her utility. This move would undermine the inequivalence thesis. But this is not a good way of defending utilitarianism, for it collapses the distinction between utilitarianism and ethical egoism and turns utilitarianism into an unattractive parochial doctrine. This just shifts the lump under the philosophical carpet; it does not remove it.

5. The vast majority of us have the capacity to refrain from acting on self-interested motivation, even when we do, in fact, act self-interestedly.

While not uncontroversial as a claim about human motivation, predominant egoism, so understood, has some plausibility and is vastly more plausible than psychological egoism.[14] Understood this way, predominant egoism avoids the voluntarist argument against utilitarianism. In particular, claim (5) ensures that utilitarian demands are not impossible to meet, which allows us to reconcile utilitarianism and voluntarism.

So if the Radicals switch from egoism to predominant egoism they can avoid the voluntarist objection to utilitarianism. This is surely a step in the right direction, but it does not get the Radicals out of the woods entirely. For even if predominant egoism allows that agents are always able to refrain from self-interested behavior, it does say that self-interested behavior is the norm and that this is no accident. Even if human nature includes sympathetic or altruistic impulses, predominant egoism implies that these are weaker and regularly overridden. But then even if it is possible to act on utilitarian demands, it will often be motivationally hard and often won't happen. While utilitarianism won't be inconsistent with voluntarism, it may nonetheless make demands that seem unattractive or utopian. If predominant egoism is true, this problem will afflict any moderately altruistic moral theory, and not just utilitarianism. But in light of utilitarian demands, it may be a bigger problem for utilitarianism than for other moral theories.

What do the Radicals say about the tension between duty and interest? Bentham and James Mill are not unaware of this tension. Bentham addresses part of the problem in the political context in other writings, notably his *Plan for Parliamentary Reform* (1817) (*Works* III). There the problem is how we can get self-interested rulers to rule in the interest of the governed, as utilitarianism implies that they should. Bentham's answer invokes his

---

14. To appreciate the difference between egoism and predominant egoism, consider Hume. Hume is a clear critic of psychological egoism, recognizing sympathy and other ultimate passions, in addition to self-love. See David Hume, *Enquiry Concerning the Principles of Morals* (originally published 1777), ed. P.H. Nidditch (Oxford: Clarendon Press, 1975) §V, part ii and appendix II. But on several occasions, he allows that sympathy is fainter than self-love and that self-love tends to be the strongest single passion. See *A Treatise of Human Nature* (originally published 1739), ed. P.H. Nidditch (Oxford: Clarendon Press, 1978) III.ii.2 and III.iii.1 and *Enquiry* V.ii. It seems clear that Hume sees local sympathy (for relations and intimates) and extended sympathy (for those with whom one has no special relationship) as more powerful passions than Bentham does. But if one is a predominant egoist insofar as one recognizes the comparative strength of self-love, then Hume and Bentham are both predominant egoists, even if Bentham's egoism predominates more than Hume's.

commitment to representative democracy. We can reconcile self-interested motivation and promotion of the common good if we make rulers democratically accountable to (all) those whom they govern, for this tends to make the interest of the governed and the interest of the governors coincide.[15] Bentham's argument, elaborated influentially by James Mill in his *Essay on Government*, is something like this.

1. Each person acts only (or predominantly) to promote his own interests.
2. The proper object of government is the interest of the governed.
3. Hence, rulers will pursue the proper object of government if and only if their interests coincide with those of the governed.
4. A ruler's interest will coincide with those of the governed if and only if he is politically accountable to the governed.
5. Hence, rulers must be democratically accountable.

It was this reasoning that led Bentham and Mill to advocate democratic reforms that included extending the franchise to workers. This is a classic illustration of Radical attempts to pursue utilitarian goals in psychologically realistic ways and to harness self-interest for the promotion of the common good. This model for reconciling duty and interest is ingenious and has been an incredibly influential idea in theories of institutional design.

Whether it is an adequate response to the tension between utilitarianism and psychological egoism is another matter. Even in the political context this strategy only reduces the conflict between egoistic motivation and impartial utilitarian demands. Though the democratic reforms of the Radicals extended the franchise, they did not call for universal suffrage. Without wide scope accountability, the reconciliation of duty and interest must be incomplete. Also notice that the coincidence Bentham and James Mill seek between the interest of the governed and the interest of the governors is artificial. Political accountability will not effectively curb political egoism if rulers are sufficiently good at deceiving the public through outright deception or propaganda. So political accountability, even wide scope accountability, is not itself sufficient to reconcile self-interest and the interest of the governed.

Finally, notice that the Radical solution to the tension is framed exclusively in political terms. Though it may be true that Bentham and James

---

15. Also see Stephen, *The English Utilitarians*, vol. I, pp. 284–85.

Mill were especially interested in the public or political application of utilitarian principles, Bentham is very clear that utilitarianism is a comprehensive doctrine, meant to apply to personal, as well as political, ethics. Their strategy for the political reconciliation of duty and interest has no obvious counterpart in the case of personal conduct. What would be needed is a mechanism for ensuring that it is in the individual interests of each to conform her conduct to the common good, as interpreted in utilitarian terms. Of course, there are strategic reasons for individuals to comply with familiar other-regarding moral norms of cooperation, forbearance, and aid, even when doing so involves opportunity costs. Each individual has an interest in the fruits of interaction conducted according to these norms. Though it might be desirable to reap the benefits of other people's compliance with such norms without incurring the burdens of one's own, the opportunities to do this are infrequent. Noncompliance is generally detectable, and others won't be compliant toward those who are known to be non-compliant. For this reason, compliance is typically necessary to enjoy the benefits of others' continued compliance. While communities can improve this reconciliation by trying to monitor compliance, and encouraging compliance and discouraging non-compliance, there is no single institutional mechanism, such as the franchise, for securing these conditions. Moreover, this informal coincidence of duty and self-interest is limited in scope and fragile. We can have duties of beneficence and aid, which utilitarianism will recognize, to those with whom we do not regularly interact or have any prospect of interacting, where there will be no strategic reason to be concerned about them. Duties to the infirm and to future generations are prominent examples. Moreover, even if this informal coincidence of duty and interest were extensionally adequate, it would be unstable. As Plato's Ring of Gyges makes clear, if one had some way of ensuring that one's own non-compliance would go undetected, one could enjoy the benefits of non-compliance with impunity (*Republic* book II). Presumably, the Ring of Gyges is an allegory, meant to draw our attention to the fact that even in the real world people can often act unjustly with impunity.

These considerations suggest that the Radicals do not have a general and satisfactory answer to the tension created by their embrace of a utilitarian conception of duty and psychological egoism. Though the tension is less stark if they retreat from egoism to predominant egoism, the tension remains unresolved.

5. Why utilitarianism?

Bentham and James Mill are more interested in the thorough application of utilitarian principles to legislation and reform than they are in the justification of those principles. For the most part, the Radicals treat utilitarianism as an axiom, unnecessary to defend. It may have just seemed obvious to them that in moral matters everyone's happiness matters and matters equally. Though Bentham is often treated as the founder of utilitarianism, utilitarian ideas had already been championed by other figures, including Claude Adrien Helvetius (1715–71), Cesare Beccaria (1738–94), Joseph Priestley (1733–1804), and William Paley (1743–1805).[16] But even if utilitarian ideas were familiar when the Radicals wrote, the doctrine was controversial then, as it is now. In particular, it was opposed by rational intuitionists, such as Richard Price (1723–91), Thomas Reid (1710–96), Dugald Stewart (1753–1828), and William Whewell (1794–1866), who recognized a plurality of fundamental moral precepts, including juridical or deontic principles about the right or duty alleged to hold independently of teleological principles concerning self-love and benevolence.[17]

Critics of utilitarianism typically worry that the doctrine has counter-intuitive moral implications. It will be useful to keep three such worries in mind.

1. *Categorical Rules*: There are categorical moral rules that must be followed, independently of their consequences.
2. *Demandingness*: In making it an agent's duty to do things that promote the happiness of everyone, counting his own interest as only one among many interests, utilitarianism demands too much of agents.
3. *Justice*: A just outcome depends on the distribution, and not just the sum, of happiness within a group.

These are reasons one might be skeptical about utilitarianism. The uncommitted need a reason to accept utilitarianism, and even the committed might like some assurance that their commitment is not arbitrary and should be maintained.

---

16. For some discussion, see Stephen, *The English Utilitarians*, vol. I, ch. V, and Ross Harrison, *Bentham* (London: Routledge, 1983), ch. 7.
17. For some discussion of the relation between rational intuitionism and utilitarianism, see Henry Sidgwick, *Outlines of the History of Ethics* (London: Macmillan, 1886), ch. IV, and Terence Irwin, *The Development of Ethics*, 3 vols. (Oxford: Clarendon Press, 2007–09), ch. 79.

Toward the end of Chapter I of the *Principles* Bentham does address the justification of utilitarianism and offers a flurry of disparate considerations in favor of it. Unfortunately, these rationales are breathtakingly compressed and of very uneven value. I will consider them, not in sequence, but in what I take to be a progression from least to most promising.

First, Bentham says that the words "ought" and "right" mean the same as "promotes utility."

> When thus interpreted, the words *ought*, and *right* and *wrong*... have meaning: when otherwise, they have none [I 10].

This claim about meaning looks like semantic legislation, which should change no one's mind. Ordinary speakers can doubt that it is always one's duty to promote utility, for instance, because that might violate categorical rules, be too demanding, or sacrifice justice. These doubts may be misplaced or answerable, but the person who expresses them is not confused about the meanings of words or an incompetent speaker. One cannot defend a substantive moral commitment by linguistic fiat.

Second, Bentham also claims that those who attempt to refute the principle of utility necessarily presuppose it (I 13). This would be an impressive transcendental defense of utilitarianism. This is where Bentham (in a footnote) considers the objection that it might be inexpedient sometimes to calculate expected utility, presumably because time is short, one's calculations are subject to bias or distortion, or there are significant opportunity costs to calculation. Bentham is right that *this* sort of objection seems to presuppose that utilitarianism is the correct moral standard. But not all critics of utilitarianism complain that it is inexpedient. It is not at all clear that the proponent of categorical rules, moderate demands, or distributive justice need be appealing to utility, explicitly or tacitly.

Third, Bentham suggests that the alternative to embracing utilitarianism is to appeal to one's personal sentiments and that this will lead to anarchy (I 14). Here, he writes as if utilitarianism is the only principled form that moral reasoning might take, the only alternative being case-by-case assessment on impressionistic grounds. But the opponent of utilitarianism need not appeal to mere intuition (in this sense). Instead, she can seek to replace the principle of utility with a rival principle or set of principles about one's duties and rights. Of course, there can be disagreement about the content of these principles, and, sometimes, moral disagreement can become inconvenient or even dangerous. But disagreement is hard to avoid. Not only can there be disagreement among the critics of utilitarianism and disagreement between utilitarians and their critics, but also there can be disagreement among utilitarians about how best to conceive utility or how best to apply utilitarian principles. We seem to struggle on in the face of this kind of disagreement, often trying to find common ground among rival moral principles. And if, contrary to fact, agreement was some kind of superlative value that trumped all others, this would hardly explain why we should all coalesce around utilitarianism, rather than some rival principle or set of principles.

Fourth, Bentham claims that utilitarianism, as a first principle, is incapable of proof.

> Is it susceptible of any direct proof? it should seem not: for that which is used to prove everything else, cannot itself be proved: a chain of proofs must have their commencement somewhere. To give such a proof is as impossible as it is needless [I 11].

Here, Bentham invokes a common idea in the history of modern ethics, one which will find echoes, among other places, in John Stuart Mill and Sidgwick, viz. that ultimate or first principles cannot be derived from other claims or principles, because, if they could, they would not be ultimate principles after all. The Radicals like to refer to the principle of utility as an axiom, and it's true that other things admit of proof by derivation from axioms but that axioms themselves do not admit of proof within the axiomatic system.

But what does this show? In particular, does this show that first principles, like utilitarianism, cannot be justified? Even if the fact that first principles can't be proven within an axiomatic system showed that first principles cannot be justified, this would be cold comfort for utilitarians. For even if there is an axiomatic system in which utility figures as an axiom, there are presumably rival axiomatic systems in which other principles, perhaps the Ten Commandments, figure as axioms. Rival first principles could each claim to be incapable of proof because of their roles as axioms within their own systems. Knowing that utilitarianism is a first principle in one system, when other systems have other first principles, gives us no reason to prefer the utilitarian axiom to its rivals. They are equally incapable of proof.

Fortunately, proof, in this sense, is not essential for justification. We can ask why we should accept some axioms as true and why we should prefer one axiomatic system to another. The answer depends on what things we can prove within the system and how that compares with what we believe, independently, to be true. Does the axiomatic system allow us to prove all the things that we believe to be true? Does it entail claims that we don't believe to be true? Sometimes axiomatic systems have surprising implications. Here, we need to decide if we should accept these implications after all, partly on the strength of all the welcome implications of the system, or whether it is a defect in the system that it has such consequences. Typically, we are trying to decide if we should accept a given axiom or axiomatic system, rather than another. To do so, we want to make comparative assessments of the implications of the alternative axioms or systems.

The situation is similar with ethical principles. We might identify *structure* within an ethical system. The truth of moral claims about particular actions (action tokens) depends on the truth of certain moral rules that articulate morally relevant factors, which make moral claims about classes or types of actions. Correct moral rules subsume and explain particular moral truths. If these rules are not ultimate, then they, in turn, can be subsumed under some more general or abstract moral principle or principles. But eventually we must reach moral factors that are genuinely ultimate, which explain why other moral claims are true, but which cannot be subsumed under any more ultimate principle. Utilitarians claim that utilitarianism is such a first principle. In this way, more particular moral truths are dependent on first principles, but not vice versa. This is a kind of *asymmetrical metaphysical dependence*.

Bentham and others seem to assume that this asymmetrical metaphysical dependence implies an asymmetric epistemic dependence. We can justify more particular moral claims by tracing them to the first principle(s) on which they depend, but we cannot justify first principles in terms of anything else—otherwise, they wouldn't be ultimate moral principles.

But *epistemic dependence need not be asymmetric*. We can't ask in virtue of what other morally relevant factor a first principle obtains. But we can ask whether a putative first principle is true, or why we should accept one putative first principle, rather than another. A plausible answer is that we should accept those putative first principles as true that subsume and explain more particular judgments that, on reflection, we think are true. It might be that no principle subsumes and explains all and only the things we take to be true antecedently, in part because our antecedent beliefs are likely to be incomplete in some respects and inconsistent in others. But we can reasonably prefer to accept a principle or set of principles that subsumes and explains more that we are prepared on suitable reflection to accept, over principles that subsume and explain less of what we believe to be true or more of what we believe to be false. Metaphysical dependence may be top-down, but epistemic dependence can be bottom-up. (Also see §34.)

Finally, Bentham suggests that utilitarianism is what in fact guides most people's moral motivations and behavior, whether consciously or not, most of the time (*Principles* I 12). He does not develop this claim in any detail, but he may have in mind the sort of claim Sidgwick later makes when he says commonsense morality is "unconsciously" and "inchoately and imperfectly" utilitarian (*Methods* 424–27).

> It may be shown, I think, that the Utilitarian estimate of the consequences not only supports broadly the current moral rules, but also sustains their generally received limitations and qualifications: that, again, it explains the anomalies in the Morality of Common Sense, which from any other point of view must seem unsatisfactory to the reflective intellect; and moreover, where the current formula is not sufficiently precise for the guidance of conduct, while at the same time difficulties and perplexities arise in the attempt to give it additional precision, the Utilitarian method solves these difficulties and perplexities in general accordance with the vague instincts of Common Sense, and is naturally appealed to for such solution in ordinary moral discussions. It may be shown further, that it not only supports the generally received view of the relative importance of different duties, but is also naturally called in as arbiter, where rules commonly regarded as co-ordinate come into conflict... [*Methods* 425–26].

We will see that John Stuart Mill can and should be read as sympathetic with Sidgwick's thesis (§34). If Sidgwick's thesis about the imperfectly and inchoately utilitarian character of commonsense morality were true, that would provide just the sort of bottom-up proof or justification of which first principles admit. Of course, it is controversial whether Sidgwick's thesis is true, and Bentham does not defend this thesis, as Mill and Sidgwick do. But his brief comments here might be read as an inchoate and imperfect recognition of the probative value of this approach to justifying utilitarianism.

2

Varieties of motivation

We have now seen some elements of Benthamite utilitarianism. What exactly is Mill's attitude toward this Radical legacy? Though he never renounced the utilitarian tradition and Radical mission that he inherited from his father, Mill's mental crisis and recovery greatly influenced his interpretation of this tradition. One measure of the extent of Mill's departure from his Radical legacy is that Mill's contributions to the utilitarian tradition apparently led his father to view him as a defector from that legacy (*Autobiography* CW I 189). Part of Mill's disagreement with the Radicals concerns their assumptions about human motivation.

6. Mill's apparent egoism

Some commentators see little difference between Mill and his forebears on matters of motivation. Sidgwick, for one, reads Mill as a psychological egoist (*Methods* 42–44). This is not just guilt by association. Sidgwick appeals to claims Mill makes in Chapter IV of *Utilitarianism*, discussing the proof of the principle of utility. Later, we will discuss the proper reading of the proof and its epistemological significance. Here, we are interested in psychological claims Mill makes there. In particular, Sidgwick draws our attention to a passage at the end of that discussion in which Mill appears to identify desiring something and finding it pleasurable.

> I believe that these sources of evidence [practiced self-consciousness and self-observation, assisted by the observation of others], impartially consulted, will declare that desiring a thing and finding it pleasant, aversion to it and thinking of it as painful, are phenomena entirely inseparable, or rather two parts of the same phenomenon; in strictness of language, two different modes of naming the same psychological fact: that to think of an object as desirable (unless for

the sake of its consequences), and to think of it as pleasant, are one and the same thing; and that to desire anything, except in proportion as the idea is pleasant, is a physical and metaphysical impossibility [*U* IV 10].

Here Mill seems to say that my ultimate desires are desires for things insofar as they are pleasant, and this seems to endorse the egoist claim that my ultimate desires are always for my own happiness and, in particular, pleasure. At least, this is how Sidgwick reads the passage. Moreover, this egoist assumption may seem to be at work in the proof itself. Mill aims to show that happiness is the one and only thing desirable in itself (IV 2). To do this, he argues that happiness is desirable in itself (IV 3), and a central premise in this argument is that everyone desires his own happiness (IV 3). Mill later argues that only happiness is desirable in itself (IV 4).

However, there are good philosophical and interpretive reasons to avoid reading Mill as a psychological egoist and hedonist in these passages. Consider, first, his equation of desiring with finding pleasant and thinking desirable with thinking pleasant. On the face of it, it seems quite implausible that I desire things just insofar as I expect them to be pleasant for myself. I desire many things, including a job well done, personal integrity, and the happiness of my loved ones, out of proportion to the pleasure it produces for me. Indeed, often I act on desires associated with these personal commitments when I know that doing so requires foregoing more pleasure for myself. Perhaps Mill's claim is that in desiring these things for their own sakes I take pleasure in satisfying these desires, so that when I act for the sake of these desires I can expect to promote my own pleasure. So far, this is unobjectionable, but it falls short of Mill's equating desiring and thinking pleasurable, and would, in any case, provide no support to psychological hedonism. This is because of Butler's point (§1). As Butler argues, the pleasure expected from the satisfaction of desire is *consequential* on the pre-existing desire and its perceived (or anticipated) satisfaction. This shows two things. First, it shows that the desire cannot be identified with the pleasure expected from its satisfaction. Second, it shows that if the action is explained by the agent's desires, then the expected pleasure does not explain the agent's behavior and is instead a by-product of what does.

This common but problematic reasoning does not explain why Mill would identify desiring and finding pleasant or finding desirable and finding pleasant, as he does in the passage quoted above. The psychological egoist reading of Mill's identification assumes that he is saying that in desiring x or believing x desirable one perceives x as pleasurable for oneself. This, we have seen, is psychologically very implausible. Mill's real point might be different. In the proof Mill says that desire is evidence of desirability (IV 3). As we will see later (§33), one way to understand this claim is as the claim that desire is defeasible evidence of desirability or value. In identifying thinking desirable and finding pleasant, he might be claiming instead that in taking something to be valuable we delight or take pleasure in it. But even if there is this sort of *valuational pleasure* that is consequential on the perception of value, not all pleasure is valuational pleasure, and valuational pleasure provides no support for egoism. For there is nothing in the idea that one takes a kind of pleasure in what one finds desirable for its own sake to suggest that what one finds desirable for its own sake is some state or condition of oneself. On this reading, the pleasure Mill is talking about is consequential on a perception of value and should not be identified with that perception. But if valuational pleasure is consequential on a perception or belief that the object of the pleasure is valuable, then it places no constraints on the nature of those objects and their value, and so gives no support to psychological egoism.

What about aspects of the proof that suggested egoism? The apparent egoism of the proof evaporates on closer inspection. First, notice that in the proof Mill is explicitly concerned with happiness, not pleasure, as an object of desire (IV 2–6). Hedonism is just one conception of happiness. That doesn't require him to distinguish the two, but it does mean that any support for psychological egoism in the proof would not *ipso facto* be support for psychological hedonism.

More importantly, Mill does not endorse psychological egoism. To see this, consider the structure of his proof. Mill claims that the utilitarian must claim that happiness is the one and only thing desirable in itself (IV 2). He claims that the only proof of desirability is desire (IV 3) and proceeds to argue that happiness is the one and only thing desired. He argues that a person does desire his own happiness for its own sake and that, therefore, happiness, as such, is desired by and desirable for its own sake for humanity as a whole (IV 3). He then turns to defend the claim that happiness is the only thing desirable in itself, by arguing that apparent counterexamples (e.g. desires for virtue for its own sake) are not inconsistent with his claim (IV 4–6).

Later, we will look at the proof in more detail and discuss various worries about its cogency (Chapter 5). The important point, for present purposes, is that Mill does not endorse psychological egoism here. He does say that each person has an ultimate desire for her own happiness, but he does not say that this is each person's only ultimate desire. Indeed, in the second half of the proof he allows that some agents have a disinterested concern for virtue and that they care about virtue for its own sake (IV 4–5). And what is true of virtue is no less true of less grand objects of desire, such as money, power, and fame (IV 6). These too it is possible to desire for their own sakes.

In fact, Mill offers an associationist story about the evolution of such intrinsic or ultimate desires. Like everyone else, the miser initially desires money only instrumentally, for the sake of the things that it allows him to buy. But, over time, the miser's desire transfers from the ends to the means such that he develops a concern for money for its own sake, independently of its instrumental value. Whether all of our desires originated in self-interested or specifically hedonistic desire Mill does not say. But he is clear that our own happiness and certainly our own pleasure are not the only intrinsic aims we have. If psychological egoism claims that one's own happiness is the only thing that is desired for its own sake, then this shows that Mill is not a psychological egoist.

Of course, he does say that these things are desired as parts of happiness, and this might seem to be compatible with a sophisticated version of psychological egoism, according to which one's own happiness is a complex whole that can have non-self-regarding parts. Egoism of this stripe would be a far cry from the psychological egoism and hedonism of the Radicals. But there is room for doubt that Mill is endorsing even a sophisticated psychological egoism. First, he does say that people can develop a purely "disinterested" desire for virtue itself, "without looking to any end beyond it" (IV 5). So it's not clear that he thinks one need desire virtue as a part of happiness. Moreover, if the concern with virtue is disinterested, it's hard to see how this involves pursuing one's own interest. Indeed, it's not clear that Mill is here talking about desiring virtue for its constitutive contribution to (a) the agent's own happiness or (b) the general happiness. Only (a) could possibly provide some comfort to psychological egoism. But presumably Mill's proof requires (b); it requires that it be the general happiness that is the one and only thing desirable for its own sake. But if Mill has (b) in mind, then he's given up on psychological egoism.

Difficulties with the proof itself make it hard to know just what Mill is assuming about human motivation. Some passages seem to contradict psychological egoism, but others are less clear. Perhaps all we can say for sure is that the proof does not provide unequivocal reason to read Mill as a psychological egoist.

7. Mill's rejection of psychological egoism

If we look outside of *Utilitarianism* we can find clearer evidence of Mill's doubts about psychological egoism and hedonism. In a note to his edition of his father's *Analysis of the Phenomena of the Human Mind* Mill diagnoses a possible equivocation in his father's doctrine.

> That the pleasures or pains of another person can only be pleasurable or painful to us through the association of our own pleasures and pains with them, is true in one sense, which is probably that intended by the author, but not true in another, against which he has not sufficiently guarded his mode of expression. It is evident, that the only pleasures or pains of which we have direct experience...[are] those felt by ourselves...[and] that the pleasure or pain with which we contemplate the pleasure or pain felt by someone else, is itself a pleasure or pain of our own. But if it be meant that in such cases the pleasure or pain is consciously referred to self, I take this to be a mistake [II 217–18].

In his "Remarks on Bentham's Philosophy" (1833) Mill urges a similar caution in understanding Bentham.

> In laying down as a philosophical axiom that men's actions are always obedient to their interests, Mr. Bentham did no more than dress up the very trivial proposition that all people do what they feel themselves most disposed to do... He by no means intended by this assertion to impute universal selfishness to mankind, for he reckoned the motive of sympathy as an interest [*CW* X 13–14].

Indeed, here Mill echoes a caution Bentham himself urges. In a footnote to a discussion of the efficacy of legal sanctions in *Of Laws in General* (1782), Bentham claims that the observation that no man acts without a motive

> is of a piece with another observation equally trite concerning man in general, that he is never governed by anything other than his own interest. This observation in a large and extensive sense of the word interest (as comprehending all sorts of motives) is indubitably true; but as indubitably false in any of the confined senses in which upon such an occasion the word *interest* is wont to be made use of.[1]

These passages suggest what is now a familiar diagnosis of the troubles with psychological egoism. Mill thinks that psychological egoism is ambiguous

---

1. Jeremy Bentham, *Of Laws in General* (originally 1782), ed. H.L.A. Hart (London: Athlone Press, 1970), Ch. VI, para. 19.

between a true but trivial thesis about the *ownership* of desire—an agent necessarily acts on his own desires—and a substantive but very implausible thesis about the *content* of desires—an agent's ultimate desire is always and necessarily to promote his own interests or pleasure. If so, there is no thesis that is both substantive and plausible. The substantive thesis may seem speciously attractive if we tacitly confuse it with the trivially true thesis.

The passage from Bentham shows that he (Bentham) was at least sometimes alive to the difference between the claims about the ownership and content of desires. However, we have seen that this didn't keep Bentham and James Mill from asserting the substantive thesis about the content of desire. Moreover, it is clear from the Radicals' worries about the conflict between rulers' interests and the interest of the ruled that they construe egoism as a substantive psychological thesis. But if they do so because they conflate it with the trivial but true thesis, then they commit the fallacy of equivocation.

In *A System of Logic* Mill again provides a critique of psychological hedonism that relies on an associationist account of the development of plural ends that are psychologically autonomous.

> When the will is said to be determined by motives, a motive does not mean always, or solely, the anticipation of a pleasure or of a pain. I shall not here inquire whether it be true that, in the commencement, all our voluntary actions are mere means consciously employed to obtain some pleasure, or to avoid some pain. It is at least certain that we gradually, through the influence of association, come to desire the means without thinking of the end: the action itself becomes an object of desire, and is performed without reference to any motive beyond itself. Thus far, it may be objected, that, the action having through association become pleasurable, we are, as much as before, moved to act by the anticipation of a pleasure, namely, the pleasure of the action itself. But granting this, the matter does not end here. As we proceed in the formation of habits, and become accustomed to will a particular act or a particular course of conduct because it is pleasurable, we at last continue to will it without any reference to its being pleasurable. Although, from some change in us or in our circumstances, we have ceased to find any pleasure in the action, or perhaps to anticipate any pleasure as the consequence of it, we will still continue to desire the action and consequently to do it. In this manner it is that habits of hurtful excess continue to be practised although they have ceased to be pleasurable; and in this manner also it is that the habit of willing to persevere in the course which he has chosen, does not desert the moral hero, even when the reward, however real, which he doubtless receives from the consciousness of well-doing, is anything but an equivalent for the sufferings he undergoes, or the wishes which he may have to renounce [VI.ii.4].

Something one desires originally only as an instrumental means to pleasure comes, by a process of association, to be desired for itself. In the process, Mill claims, the desire acquires psychological autonomy such that it can conflict with the prudential or hedonist concerns from which it originated. For instance, this is true of the miser. He starts off, like others, desiring money only as a means, for the pleasures that it can buy him. But he comes, over time, by a process of association or habituation, to care about money itself. In this way, the miser's concern for money can acquire psychological autonomy. Freed of its instrumental origin, the miser's desire for money can conflict with and override the prudential concern from which it originated. Here Mill denies the psychological hedonist view that pleasure is the sole ultimate object of our desires. Likewise, he denies the more general psychological egoist thesis that one's own happiness is the sole ultimate object of desire.

Psychological egoism (and its special case, psychological hedonism), as traditionally formulated, makes a claim about the *structure* of one's desires—everything one desires one desires for the sake of the happiness (pleasure) it brings or is expected to bring—and a claim about the *content* of one's desires—the only thing one desires for its own sake is one's own happiness (pleasure). Mill denies these claims here, as we have seen. However, he alludes to a different thesis about the *origin* of desire—that all desires have their origins in desires for the agent's own happiness (pleasure). Mill allows that his associationist account of the origin of non-self-interested desires is compatible with the *genetic* claim that all our desires for things other than our own happiness originated in desires for things as instruments to our happiness (pleasure). This genetic version of egoism is not undermined by the falsity of traditional egoist claims about the structure and content of desires.[2]

Whether it is a plausible claim is another matter. As a developmental hypothesis, it's hard to believe that all the desires of an infant or child are mediated by a conception of her own self-interest. Indeed, it's unlikely that the concept of self-interest is original equipment in infants and children. In any case, it seems quite likely that they are hard-wired to desire food and to respond to maternal care independently of any conception that these things promote their self-interest. Of course, it may well be that individuals are

---

2. Michael Slote discusses the possibility of a genetic version of psychological egoism in "An Empirical Basis for Psychological Egoism," *Journal of Philosophy* 61 (1964): 530–37.

better off for having these desires, but that doesn't mean that their content is self-interested. Moreover, in his discussion of the sanctions of utilitarianism (§9), Mill claims that Conscience is an important source of human motivation and that even though Conscience itself may not be innate it is built out of social sentiments, such as sympathy and empathy, that are innate (*U* III 8–11).

So Mill is committed to rejecting psychological egoism (hedonism), both as a claim about the structure and content of our desires and as a claim about the origins of our desires. Though his attitude toward predominant egoism is less clear, presumably he would reject it as well. In discussing moral motivation in Chapter III of *Utilitarianism*, Mill appeals to our social sentiments, not to our self-interest. He appeals to sympathy, empathy, and a sense of community.

> In an improving state of the human mind, the influences are constantly on the increase which tend to generate in each individual a feeling of unity with all the rest; which, if perfect, would make him never think of, or desire, any beneficial condition for himself in the benefits of which they are not included [III 10].

I suspect that Mill thinks that Conscience is already distributed widely enough and is already strong enough in those in whom it is present so as to render predominant egoism false. But predominant egoism, like psychological egoism, is a modal claim about human nature and its limits. In this passage, Mill makes very clear that he thinks that human nature and motivation are malleable and that in a progressive state of society Conscience would completely supersede self-interested motivation. Whether this sort of optimism about Conscience is justified or realistic is a large and difficult issue that we cannot resolve here. We will return to the significance of some of these claims about Conscience shortly (§9). The important point, for present purposes, is that Mill's claims about Conscience show that he is not a predominant egoist.

8. Reservations about the Radical legacy

So it seems clear that Mill rejects the traditional substantive doctrines of psychological egoism and hedonism that Bentham and James Mill sometimes defended or suggested. This is really part of a larger criticism of the conception of psychology and human nature underlying Benthamite utilitarianism, which Mill elaborates in his essays "Remarks on Bentham's Philosophy" (1833) and "On Bentham" (1838). Psychological egoism is an overly narrow doctrine in not recognizing the existence and importance of motives other than self-interest. But Mill thinks that Bentham's psychology was narrow in other ways too, ignoring people's spiritual aspirations, the importance of the emotions, such as sympathy and empathy, and the value of tradition, culture, and the arts. Mill links Bentham's faults to the narrowness of his philosophy and personality.

> Bentham's contempt, then, for all other schools of thinkers; his determination to create a philosophy wholly out of the materials furnished by his own mind, and by minds like his own; was his first disqualification as a philosopher. His second, was the incompleteness of his own mind as a representative of universal human nature. In many of the most natural and strongest feelings of human nature he had no sympathy; from many of its graver experiences he was altogether cut off; and the faculty by which one mind understands a mind different from itself, and throws itself into the feelings of that other mind, was denied him by his deficiency of Imagination ["Bentham" *CW* X 91].

This narrowness of vision accounted for both the strengths and weaknesses of Bentham's philosophical system.

> This, then, is our idea of Bentham. He was a man both of remarkable endowments for philosophy, and of remarkable deficiencies for it: fitted, beyond almost any man, for drawing from his premises, conclusions not only correct, but sufficiently precise and specific to be practical: but whose general conception of human nature and life, furnished him with an unusually slender stock of premises ["Bentham" *CW* X 93].

The extent of Mill's departure from Benthamite assumptions about human nature and psychology is also reflected in Mill's conception of happiness and his doctrine of higher pleasure (which will be discussed in the next chapter).

9. The sanctions of utilitarianism

Mill's theory of motivation includes his discussion of the sanctions of utility. Though we have not yet looked at the details of Mill's utilitarianism—especially, his conceptions of duty and happiness—his discussion of the sanctions of utilitarianism appeals to quite general features of that doctrine.

In what is probably the most understudied chapter of *Utilitarianism*, Mill addresses the question of the ultimate sanction of the principle of utility. He understands this alternately as a question about "the motives to obey it" and the "source of its obligation... [or] binding force" (III 1). Nor does Mill think that this issue about the sanction of the principle of utility is an idle one. There is a potential worry about the sanctions of utilitarianism that apparently has its source in prudence or self-interest.

> [A] person... says to himself, I feel that I am bound not to rob or murder, betray or deceive; but why am I bound to promote the general happiness? If my own happiness lies in something else, why may I not give that the preference [III 1]?

But we can imagine this person unmoved by the moral demands in question and not just by a utilitarian reconstruction of these demands. Why should I not murder, rob, or deceive if this would promote my own happiness? And Mill is very clear that he thinks this issue about the sanction of utilitarianism arises for any moral theory and so poses no special problem for utilitarianism (III 1, 2, 3, 6).

Mill is not entirely clear how he understands the sanctions worry. Is it a problem about *motivation*—the extent to which people are motivated to comply with utilitarianism or other moral conceptions and the extent to which, and manner in which, they might be brought to comply more fully or more easily? Or is it more a problem of *authority*—the extent to which people have reason to comply with utilitarianism or other moral conceptions? The sort of self-interested challenge that Mill identifies at the beginning (III 1) is often part of an amoralist challenge to the authority of other-regarding morality. That challenge asks "Why should I be moral?" and seeks an account of the rational authority of other-regarding moral demands. But much of Mill's actual discussion seems more addressed to the motivational issue.

Either way, we can ask what role the appeal to self-interest or prudence plays in framing the concern about the sanctions of utilitarianism. If the challenge is motivational, it seems to appeal to the importance of self-love. This appeal could flow from a commitment to psychological egoism, which we should expect Mill to reject. Alternatively, the appeal to self-interest could presuppose only predominant egoism. If so, we might expect Mill to defend utilitarianism's motivational commitments either by accepting, but perhaps softening, predominant egoism, or by rejecting it. Alternatively, if the challenge is to the authority of utilitarianism, it seems to appeal to the special authority of prudence. If so, Mill might either try to reconcile duty and interest or challenge the special authority of prudence.

Mill thinks that an account of the sanctions of utilitarianism or any other moral conception should distinguish between *external* and *internal* sanctions. The external sanctions are those penalties that can be visited on those who flout duty (noncompliers) by another, whether the others are mortals, individually or collectively, or God (III 3). Penalties might include official acts of the state (legal punishment) or community (official ostracism or public censure) or God (punishment meted out on Judgment Day). They might also include more informal and diffuse sanctions, such as those incurred when my bad acts have bad reputational effects that harm my social or economic prospects and opportunities. Of course, mortals are neither omniscient nor omnipotent. So there's no guarantee that non-compliers will be visited with external sanctions, at least in this world. If noncompliers can conceal their noncompliance, concealing either the fact of noncompliance or their responsibility for the noncompliance, they will suffer no external sanctions. And existing external sanctions may be insufficient to deter noncompliance even if the noncompliance cannot be concealed. For instance, I may not be deterred from violating our agreement for mutually beneficial exchange of services by the bad reputational effects of noncompliance if you have already performed your part of the contract and the benefits of "taking the money and running" for me in this one case dwarf the costs of being excluded from future cooperation with you and other members of my community. Of course, we can collectively try to ratchet up the costs for detected noncompliance by criminalizing noncompliance, adopting draconian punishments for noncompliance, and pursuing extradition treaties with other communities. In this sense, the provision of adequate external sanctions is not entirely outside our control and could be treated as a political or social goal and achievement.

Mill spends somewhat more time discussing internal sanctions for noncompliance (III 4–11). The primary internal sanction for noncompliance is Conscience (III 4). The issue that interests Mill most about Conscience seems to be whether it is innate (III 6–11). He represents the intuitionists (transcendentalists) as claiming that it is innate (II 6). He seems to equate Conscience being innate with its not being analyzable into other desires, passions, or emotions. Conscience might involve a desire to please God (III 4); it might involve the desire to be liked by others (III 4); it might involve the desire to form a union with others (III 10); or it might involve sympathy and empathy (III 7). Mill endorses the claim that Conscience is not innate (III 8–11). He thinks that Conscience involves these other emotions, passions, and desires and is built up out of them.

As we have seen, Mill's claims about Conscience represent a real break with Radical psychology. He appeals to our social sentiments, especially sympathy, empathy, and a sense of community, not to our self-interest. Moreover, as we saw, he thinks that society can and should encourage individuals to identify with the interests of others to an extent that they will not seek goods at the expense of others (III 10). Mill makes clear that this aspect of Conscience—the identification with the interests of others—is a tender plant in need of nourishment. But he also has a progressive view of Conscience according to which features of modern life contribute to the growth of Conscience. In his essay "Civilization" (1836) Mill insists that "wherever...we find human beings acting together for common purposes in large bodies, and enjoying the pleasures of social intercourse, we term them civilized" (*CW* XVIII 120–24). And in *The Principles of Political Economy* he frequently remarks that economic development goes hand-in-hand with greater economic cooperation and interdependence and that these aspects of modern economic life create a school of social sentiments in which workers develop common interests (II.i.3, IV.vii.1, IV.vii.6). So Conscience draws on capacities for sympathy and empathy that are themselves innate, but their proper development and exercise is a historical accomplishment that is not yet complete and that is fragile. So it is within our power individually—but, more importantly, collectively—to change social conditions so as to make Conscience and the internal sanctions of duty more robust. In making these claims, Mill makes his rejection not only of psychological egoism, but also of predominant egoism, very clear.

In these claims Mill seems clearly to be focused on the motivational dimension of the internal sanctions of duty. But we might wonder what he has to say about the authority of these sanctions. The capacities underlying Conscience may not be distributed equally, and these capacities can wither or flower. *Why* should we care about Conscience? Is there anything wrong with me—in particular, any failure of practical reason—if I do not have a Conscience or it is weak? Is there any good reason I should cultivate a Conscience if I don't have one (assuming that's possible) or that I should invest resources in maintaining my Conscience if I do have one? Unfortunately, Mill seems not to address these questions directly. However, he may address them insofar as he addresses the question whether utilitarianism is too demanding.

10. The demands of utilitarianism

Is Mill right to claim that the worry about sanctions is really a general worry about the sanctions for noncompliance with other-regarding morality of any sort and so poses no special problem for utilitarianism? One might wonder whether utilitarianism makes greater demands on agents than other moral theories.

To appreciate this point, we should distinguish between two different tendencies within the utilitarian tradition—*accommodation* and *reform*. Sometimes, utilitarians stress ways in which the correct application of their theory can accommodate commonsense moral distinctions and claims. Sidgwick's claim that commonsense morality is inchoately and imperfectly utilitarian includes important accommodationist claims. However, at other times, utilitarians stress the revisionary implications of their theory. Because of its conception of impartiality—that everyone's happiness matters and that everyone's happiness matters equally—utilitarianism can challenge moral complacency and parochialism. The most interesting versions of utilitarianism contain elements of both accommodation and reform, though they may mix these elements in different ratios. Perfect accommodation is probably impossible if only because there is no reason to assume that our current moral convictions are complete, consistent, and coherent. So any principled accommodation of our moral beliefs is likely to extend and revise our current moral outlook in some ways. But if a moral principle implied complete and total revision of our current moral views, we'd want to know why we should go in for that. That would likely look more like a change of subject matter than an attractive moral theory. So most reform has to be partial. We might agree that a principled account of all of our moral beliefs is impossible and agree to revise some of our moral beliefs to make them cohere with a principle that subsumes and explains other parts of our current moral outlook. If so, reform is like the hole in a doughnut, made possible by the surrounding substance of accommodation. However, to say that reform must be partial is not to say that it cannot be significant. How revisionary a principled moral theory might be is not something we can decide in advance of looking at the principle, its degree of accommodation, and the nature of its reforms. (For further discussion of these issues, see §§34–35.)

Some contemporary writers stress the revisionary character of utilitarianism. In particular, they argue that utilitarianism seems to be potentially very demanding, much more so than commonsense morality. For instance, in "Famine, Affluence, and Morality" Peter Singer argues that utilitarianism implies that even moderately affluent agents must make significant personal sacrifices for the benefit of the world's needy.[3] If, as utilitarianism seems to claim, we have a duty to assist others provided we don't sacrifice anything of comparable value, then each of us has a duty to benefit others up to the point where the cost of our sacrifices exceeds the benefits those sacrifices confer. This reformist utilitarian argument entails extensive duties of mutual aid that would call for enormous changes in the lifestyles of all those who are even moderately well-off.[4]

Moreover, some critics of utilitarianism treat the demandingness of utilitarianism as one of its principal flaws. In *A Theory of Justice* John Rawls argues that the sort of interpersonal sacrifice that utilitarianism requires violates the strains of commitment in a well-ordered society.[5] And in his influential "Critique of Utilitarianism" Bernard Williams argues that the demandingness of utilitarianism threatens the sort of personal projects and partial relationships that help give our lives meaning.[6] The common complaint among the critics of utilitarianism is that its demands threaten to offend against a requirement of *psychological realism*, according to which the demands of an acceptable moral theory must be ones that can be incorporated into a reasonable and satisfying life plan.[7]

This worry about the demands of utilitarianism is not easy to assess. One might wonder how to interpret and whether to accept the psychological realism constraint. If the constraint is relative to people's actual psychologies and patterns of concern, then it represents a potentially conservative constraint on

---

3. Peter Singer, "Famine, Affluence, and Morality," *Philosophy & Public Affairs* 1 (1972): 229–43.
4. Singer is a utilitarian. Though his reformist conclusions can be derived from utilitarian premises, Singer himself appeals to what he regards as a more ecumenical premise that it is a duty to prevent significant harm if this can be done without the agent sacrificing anything of comparable moral importance. However, this premise is less ecumenical than it seems inasmuch as Singer measures comparable moral importance in purely welfarist terms.
5. John Rawls, *A Theory of Justice* (Cambridge, MA: Harvard University Press, 1971), pp. 176–77.
6. Bernard Williams, "A Critique of Utilitarianism," in J.J.C. Smart and Bernard Williams, *Utilitarianism: For and Against* (Cambridge: Cambridge University Press, 1973).
7. Also see Samuel Scheffler, *Human Morality* (Oxford: Clarendon Press, 1994).

moral theorizing that one might well reject. After all, utilitarianism is a *normative* claim, telling us how we *should* behave. We would be denying the normativity of ethics if we assumed that how we should behave is constrained by our actual motivations. By contrast, the voluntarist constraint assumes only that how we should behave is constrained by what we can do and how we can be motivated (§4). But if the psychological realism constraint is relative to possible or ideal psychology, then it is not clear that even a highly revisionary moral theory need flout the constraint.[8] Certainly, we can't tell whether a revisionary moral theory makes impossible or unattractive motivational demands from the fact that it flouts actual motivational patterns in contingent social and ideological circumstances.

Then there is a question about how demanding or revisionary utilitarianism actually is. Though Mill agreed with the Radicals that utilitarianism is a reformist doctrine in many respects, he also thought an intelligent application of the utilitarian first principle would sustain many of our common moral precepts, and he spends a considerable portion of *Utilitarianism* trying to show that utilitarianism is not as much at variance with commonsense moral thinking as some critics think. In particular, Mill thinks that utilitarianism does not demand pure disinterested benevolence and unrelenting self-sacrifice.

> The objectors to utilitarianism cannot always be charged with representing it in a discreditable light. On the contrary, those among them who entertain anything like a just idea of its disinterested character, sometimes find fault with its standard as being too high for humanity. They say that it is exacting too much to require that people shall always act from the inducement of promoting the general interests of society. But this is to mistake the very meaning of a standard of morals, and to confound the rule of action with the motive of it. It is the business of ethics to tell us what are our duties, or by what test we may know them; but no system of ethics requires that the sole motive of all we do shall be a feeling of duty; on the contrary, ninety-nine hundreths of all our actions are done from other motives, and rightly so done, if the rule of duty does not condemn them.... [I]t is a misapprehension of the utilitarian mode of thought, to conceive it as implying that people should fix their minds upon so wide a generality as the world, or society at large. The great majority of good actions are intended, not for the benefit of the world, but for that of individuals, of which the good of the world is made up; and the thoughts of the most

---

8. For a discussion of some related issues about the plausibility of a psychological realism constraint on political theorizing, see David Estlund's critique of utopophobia in *Democratic Authority* (Princeton: Princeton University Press, 2008), ch. 14.

virtuous man need not on these occasions travel beyond the particular persons concerned, except so far as is necessary to assure himself that in benefiting them he is not violating the rights—that is, the legitimate and authorized expectations—of any one else. The multiplication of happiness is, according to the utilitarian ethics, the object of virtue: the occasions on which any person (except one in a thousand) has it in his power to do this on an extended scale, in other words, to be a public benefactor, are but exceptional; and on these occasions alone is he called on to consider public utility; in every other case, private utility, the interest or happiness of some few persons, is all he has to attend to [U II 19].[9]

Mill is not very clear about *why* utilitarianism does not demand a greater concern with public, and not merely private, utility.

One thing Mill does say here is that utilitarianism is a standard of morality and a rule of action, but not a claim about motives. As we will see later (§§21, 24), part of what he means is that utilitarianism is a claim about what makes an action our duty, not itself a claim about how we should reason or be motivated. If we ignore this distinction, we might expect a utilitarian to be motivated by pure disinterested benevolence and to deliberate by calculating expected utility on each and every occasion for action. But it is a practical question how to reason or be motivated, and utilitarianism implies that this practical question, like all practical questions, is correctly answered by what would in fact best promote utility. Utilitarian calculation is time-consuming and often unreliable or subject to bias and distortion. For such reasons, we may better approximate the utilitarian standard if we don't always try to approximate it. Bentham recognized this (§2), and so does Mill. This is what he means when he warns us not to confound moral standards and motives.

But how exactly does making this distinction between standards and motives insulate an agent from what would otherwise be the reformist demands of utilitarianism? First, there is the question what duties the utilitarian standard recognizes. If, as Singer argues, modest sacrifices by the comparatively affluent can produce significantly more good for the distant needy, then it would seem that a standard that enjoins conduct that promotes the good should demand these sacrifices. That's a reformist claim about our duties. Moreover, we can agree that a theory of what determines duty need not itself determine the content of an agent's motives. What motives we

---

9. This passage in *Utilitarianism* might be compared with a similar passage in a letter Mill wrote to George Grote (*CW* XV 762–63).

should operate with is itself a practical question to be answered by appeal to what in fact promotes utility. But if the standard itself is utilitarian, then why shouldn't the comparatively affluent be substantially more benevolent and beneficent than they are, and why shouldn't they be substantially more committed to improving the lives of others than they are?

Perhaps Mill has in mind the sort of reasons that will later lead Sidgwick to claim that special obligations and concern for the near and dear can be accommodated by utilitarianism. Sidgwick claims that our knowledge of what others want and need and our causal powers to do good are greater in cases involving those near and dear to us and other associates with whom we have regular contact, with the result that—as individuals—we do better overall by focusing our energies and actions on associates of one kind or another, rather than the world at large (*Methods* 361–69). This is one traditional way utilitarians try to accommodate partiality, at least in private life, which could then be used to respond to the worry that utilitarianism is too demanding. If Sidgwick is right, this would explain why Mill is right to think that we are justified in focusing on private, rather than public, utility.

But it is arguable that even if this sort of utilitarian accommodation was tenable in nineteenth-century Britain, technological development and globalization have rendered utilitarian demands more revisionary. Our information about others and our causal reach are not limited as they once were. Given the high benefit-to-cost ratio of many modern relief agencies, it seems hard to resist something like Singer's conclusions about the reformist demands of utilitarianism. So even if Mill was right to think that the motivational demands of utilitarianism were not so different from those of other moral theories at the time he wrote, that claim would need to be reassessed today.

Perhaps Mill would pursue other avenues of accommodation. He might claim that associational relationships—ties to family, friends, and neighbors—are essential to the happiness of each, so that partiality is important, even from the impartial point of view. Later, we will see various ways in which Mill thinks that associations—especially, associations of equals—contribute to the happiness and welfare of their members. But it is not clear that this point alone blunts the demandingness worry. Think of association as a big utility boost for associates. Even if I have associates who make a special contribution to my utility (and to whose utility I make a special contribution), the distant needy also have their own associates. But then it's not clear why the benefits of association aren't better promoted by my making personal sacrifices to benefit the distant needy; there is a cost to me and my associates, but one that should be compensated for by the greater benefits to the distant needy and their associates.

Perhaps, instead, or, in addition, Mill might try to accommodate partiality by insisting on the psychological limits of pure beneficence. Given the importance to each of us of intimate and non-intimate associations, we are unable to be happy, for various reasons, if our own associations are repressed. But if we aren't happy, it will be difficult, if not impossible, for us to be successful benefactors to others. We are unlikely to be successful enough to be benefactors in the first place, and, without the sustenance we get from our own associates, we won't be able to sustain a significant level of beneficence. Like the phenomenon of compassion fatigue, the importance of associational ties to the psychic health of would-be benefactors may place an internal limit on the demands of beneficence. This seems like a legitimate limit on utilitarian beneficence, but it is unclear just how significant a limit it is, because it is unclear just how much private utility would-be benefactors need to be successful public benefactors.[10]

Mill might try to render utilitarian demands less revisionary in another way. We should distinguish assessing actions and assessing responses to those actions. If the utilitarian assesses actions directly by the value of their consequences, then she should assess separately an agent's actions (or omissions) and our responses, such as praise or blame, for those actions (or omissions). According to this sort of direct utilitarianism, it is possible for actions to be wrong, because suboptimal, but not blameworthy if it is not optimal to blame them. While we may think that it is not too burdensome for the affluent to give more than they typically do, we may think that demanding that they give to the point of diminishing marginal utility is quite burdensome. If so, we might conclude that while utilitarianism was quite demanding, it was not blameworthy to fail to meet its more burdensome demands. This would be one way for the direct utilitarian to cushion the blow of utilitarian demands. Alternatively, the utilitarian might assess actions (or omissions) indirectly by the value of praising or blaming them. According to this sort of indirect utilitarianism, actions are not automatically wrong if they are suboptimal; they are wrong if

---

10. Some of these issues appear structurally similar to issues at stake in the debate about what inegalitarian incentives for the better-off, if any, are necessary to raise the prospects of the worse-off. See, for example, the provocative discussion in G.A. Cohen, *Rescuing Justice & Equality* (Cambridge, MA: Harvard University Press, 2008), ch. 1, for concerns about this rationale for inequality and incentives.

and only if they are optimal to blame. But if it were not optimal to blame agents for failing to comply with especially burdensome demands, then such failures would not be wrong, even if they were suboptimal. This would be another way to moderate utilitarian demands. Both direct and indirect utilitarianism appeal to utilitarian assessments of blame, but they draw different conclusions about our duties. Whereas the indirect utilitarian limits moral demands themselves to those that it is optimal to blame, the direct utilitarian limits blame for failing to meet some demands to do the optimal thing. As we will see (Chapter 4), Mill is ambivalent between direct and indirect utilitarian claims about duty. However that ambivalence gets resolved, he can appeal to the consequences of blame to address some concerns about utilitarian demands.

So Mill can recognize some limits on the demands of beneficence and some justification of partiality, though it is not yet clear if he can rationalize the strong form of partiality expressed in the passage quoted above. But he need not insulate us from the demands of beneficence completely. For he does think that Conscience is motivated by both sympathy for and empathy with the plight of others (*U* III 8–11). Conscience allows us to identify with the interests of others and to take an interest in institutions, policies, and actions that benefit others, especially others less well-off than ourselves. And, as we have seen, Mill thinks that progressive societies cultivate this kind of Conscience. So utilitarian moral demands involve some mix of beneficence and partiality, and human motives involve some mix of self-love, sympathy, and empathy, among other motives. What's not clear is whether Millian morality and psychology mix these elements in the same ratios. Of course, they need not be mixed in exactly the same ratios. Even predominant egoism allows that agents can act on impartial demands, and Mill rejects predominant egoism as too narrowly focused on self-love. As long as utilitarian demands make some provision for self-love and partiality, even if they also include significant demands or beneficence, Mill may have the psychological resources in Conscience to claim that utilitarianism is psychologically realistic. Psychological realism should not require a perfect match between existing motivational patterns and moral demands; otherwise, it becomes a parochial and conservative ethical constraint. It looks like Mill can claim a substantial match between moral demands and natural motivational patterns. And because he thinks that Conscience becomes stronger in progressive societies, he thinks that the match can in principle be improved over time.

Rawls and Williams might suspect that the degree of psychological identification with others required to provide this sort of rough match between utilitarian demands and natural human motivation is too great or otherwise unattractive. But we have raised some questions about how demanding Mill thinks utilitarian morality is. Also, as we will see (§34), Mill, like Sidgwick, thinks that commonsense morality is inchoately and imperfectly utilitarian. In particular, he thinks that utilitarianism is revisionary, but he thinks that these revisions are forced on us by a principle that otherwise accommodates our reflective moral convictions quite well. If so, local revisions are required by considerations of global or systematic accommodation, and this realization can affect our motivations. Someone who was otherwise comfortable with the ethos of his slave-holding society might become uncomfortable if convinced that the very same principles about equal opportunity that subsume and explain psychologically resonant claims about the rights that slave-holders possess demand similar rights for slaves and so call for abolition. This conviction could change his motivations and lower psychological barriers to demands that were initially perceived as burdensome and alien. In a similar way, Mill may think that he can bridge any remaining gap between utilitarianism's revisionary demands and limited sympathy and empathy. If and when we see that more revisionary demands come from the very same principle that best subsumes and explains those convictions that are motivationally resonant for us, we are likely to revise our motivations in ways that make the new demands seem less burdensome and alien. In the end, this may be Mill's best answer to the question about the authority of utilitarian demands that he does not face squarely in Chapter III of *Utilitarianism*.[11]

---

11. A more thorough discussion of utilitarian demands would explore more fully both how demanding utilitarianism is and how demanding it is reasonable to suppose morality is or can be. These issues are discussed in more detail by others, including Liam Murphy, *Moral Demands in Nonideal Theory* (Oxford: Clarendon Press, 2000); Tim Mulgan, *The Demands of Consequentialism* (Oxford: Clarendon Press, 2001); and Garrett Cullity, *The Moral Demands of Affluence* (Oxford: Clarendon Press, 2004).

3
Perfectionism about happiness and higher pleasures

Whatever his differences with the Radicals, Mill never abandons their commitment to utilitarianism. But he does reinterpret this commitment. We've seen how he criticizes their motivational assumptions, rejecting their egoism. Equally important, Mill modifies their assumptions about happiness or utility. This modification is clearest in his higher pleasures doctrine, introduced in Chapter II of *Utilitarianism*, though his own conception of happiness is reflected in *On Liberty* and other writings as well.

11. The higher pleasures doctrine

Chapter II of *Utilitarianism* is where Mill purports to say what the doctrine of utilitarianism is and isn't. Early in the chapter, he explains the doctrine this way.

> The creed which accepts as the foundations of morals "utility" or the "greatest happiness principle" holds that actions are right in proportion as they tend to promote happiness; wrong as they tend to produce the reverse of happiness. By happiness is intended pleasure and the absence of pain; by unhappiness, pain and the privation of pleasure [II 2].

This famous passage is sometimes called the Proportionality Doctrine. It sounds very much like Bentham. The first sentence appears to endorse utilitarianism, while the second sentence appears to endorse a hedonistic conception of utilitarianism.

Mill immediately goes on to introduce his doctrine of higher pleasures, which he contrasts with Benthamite utilitarianism. Mill worries that some will reject hedonism as a theory of value or happiness fit only for swine (II 3). In particular, he worries that opponents will assume that utilitarianism favors sensual or voluptuary pursuits over higher or nobler pursuits. The canonical expression of this contrast is between the lower pleasure of pushpin (a Victorian parlor game for children) and the higher pleasure of poetry (the intended contrast could be with writing poetry, reading poetry, or both). Mill attempts to reassure readers that the utilitarian can and will defend the superiority of higher pleasures, such as poetry.

He begins by noting, with fairly obvious reference to Bentham, that the hedonist can defend higher pursuits as extrinsically and instrumentally superior on the ground that they produce more intense, durable, and fecund pleasures (II 4). To see his point, we should remind ourselves of hedonistic essentials. Classical hedonism says that the mental state of pleasure is the only thing having *intrinsic* value and that the mental state of pain is the only intrinsic evil or bad. As claims about intrinsic value, they are claims about what is valuable (or disvaluable) in itself. All other things have only, or at most, *extrinsic* value; they have value in relation to or for the sake of something else that has intrinsic value. One thing x can be extrinsically good because it brings about another extrinsic good y, but for either to be extrinsic goods, they must eventually lead to something else z that is intrinsically good. In this way, all extrinsic value must be grounded ultimately in intrinsic value. For the classical hedonist all extrinsic value would appear to be *instrumental* value, that is, good (or bad) not in itself but as a causal means to what is intrinsically valuable (or intrinsically disvaluable).[1] Things that are not themselves pleasures or pains—including actions, character traits, policies, and institutions—have value only insofar as they causally produce pleasure or pain, and it would seem that their value should

---

1. Extrinsic goods, as such, need not have only instrumental value. X might be good in relation to y without being good only as a causal means to y, for instance, if x is good for its constitutive contribution to y. For instance, for Aristotle, virtue is a complete good, but not an unconditionally complete good, because it is chosen for the sake of its constitutive contribution to eudaimonia (*Nicomachean Ethics* 1097a26–1097b6). So, for Aristotle, virtue is an extrinsic good, but not thereby an instrumental good; in fact, it is good in itself by virtue of its contribution to eudaimonia. Cf. Christine Korsgaard, "Two Distinctions in Goodness," *Philosophical Review* 92 (1983): 169–95. However, even if extrinsic goods, as such, need not be instrumental goods, the classical hedonist does conceive of all extrinsic value as instrumental, because extrinsic goods are valuable only as causal means to pleasure.

depend entirely upon the *quantity* or *magnitude* of pleasure that they produce, where quantity is a function of the number of pleasures, their intensity, and their duration. This would mean that one kind of activity or pursuit is intrinsically no better than another. If we correctly value one more than another, it must be because the first produces more numerous, intense, or durable pleasures than the other. So presumably, Mill is claiming that the Benthamite can think that neither poetry nor push-pin is intrinsically good. *A fortiori* neither is intrinsically superior to the other. We can only compare their extrinsic value based on the quantity of pleasure they produce, and this must be an empirical issue. As Mill remarks in the essay "On Bentham,"

> He [Bentham] says somewhere in his works, that, "quantity of pleasure being equal, push-pin is as good as poetry" [*CW* X 113].

So the Benthamite can defend the extrinsic superiority of higher pleasures, as Mill allows, but this must be an empirical claim.

Interestingly, Bentham appears to have thought not simply that push-pin could be as valuable as poetry in some possible circumstances but that in fact it was *more* extrinsically valuable. In *The Rationale of Reward* Bentham writes:

> The utility of all these arts and sciences...is exactly in proportion to the pleasure they yield. Every other species of preeminence which may be attempted to be established among them is altogether fanciful. Prejudice apart, the game of push-pin is of equal value with the arts and sciences of music and poetry. If the game of push-pin furnish more pleasure, it is more valuable than either. Everybody can play at push-pin; poetry and music are relished only by a few. The game of push-pin is always innocent: it were well could the same always be asserted of poetry. Indeed, between poetry and truth there is a natural opposition: false morals and fictitious nature.... If poetry and music deserve to be preferred before a game of push-pin, it must be because they are calculated to gratify those individuals who are most difficult to be pleased [*Works* II: Bk. III, Ch. 1].

Actually, the difficulty of pleasing high-brows must be a count against music and poetry, for it raises their opportunity costs. Moreover, the education that it takes to appreciate music and poetry is also more costly than that required to appreciate push-pin. So Bentham seems to be making out a case for the fecundity, purity, and extent of the pleasures of push-pin. He should have concluded that if poetry is better than push-pin it must because the few high-brows who enjoy it get much more pleasure out of it than the masses do from push-pin, something about which he appears to be skeptical.[2]

Presumably, Mill's claim is that Bentham's actual view of the comparative value of push-pin and poetry might be rejected. Indeed, this is one place where Mill thinks that Bentham wrongly projects from his own narrow experience and interests, specifically from his failure to understand and appreciate the value of the arts. Mill apparently thinks that the arts broaden one's sensibilities and imagination, so that even if the pleasures associated with the arts are sometimes impure or costly they nonetheless produce intense and durable pleasures directly and produce much more pleasure indirectly by cultivating our emotional sensibilities and imagination in valuable ways.

So Mill thinks that the Benthamite hedonist can defend the extrinsic superiority of higher pleasure. Nonetheless, he is not content with this defense of the superiority of higher pleasures. While agreeing with the strict hedonist that the higher pleasures produce a larger quantity of pleasure and so are extrinsically more valuable, he also insists that the greater value of intellectual pleasures can and should be put on a more secure footing, revealing them to be intrinsically superior (U II 4).

Mill famously explains these higher pleasures and links them with the preferences of a competent judge, in the following manner.

> If I am asked what I mean by difference of quality in pleasures, or what makes one pleasure more valuable than another, merely as a pleasure, except its being greater in amount, there is but one possible answer. If one of the two is, by those who are competently acquainted with both, placed so far above the other that they prefer it, even though knowing it to be attended with a greater amount of discontent, and would not resign it for any quantity of the other pleasure which their nature is capable of, we are justified in ascribing to the preferred enjoyment a superiority in quality so far outweighing quantity as to render it, in comparison, of small account [II 5].

2. It's possible that Bentham's claim here represents an unusual interpretation of utilitarianism. Utilitarianism is usually understood as the demand that we promote or maximize total happiness. Requiring the most total happiness does not require a distributed concern for the happiness of any one person or group of persons. For instance, it does not require a distributed concern for those who are especially hard to please. The opportunity costs of pleasing them imply that we promote total happiness better by concentrating our resources on those who are less hard to please. Bentham famously formulates utilitarianism as a principle about "the greatest happiness of the greatest number." It's possible that he thinks that utilitarianism involves a commitment to make each happy as well as a commitment to promote total happiness. If so, then he may think that there is a utilitarian duty to promote the happiness of those who are hard to please, despite the high opportunity costs of doing so.

Mill goes on to affirm the antecedent of the conditional with which this passage ends—competent judges do have a categorical preference for higher pleasures (II 6). Indeed, he seems to claim here not just that higher pleasures are intrinsically more valuable than lower ones but also that they are discontinuously better.[3]

In stating the case for higher pleasures, Mill claims that a competent judge, who is capable of higher pleasures, would not renounce these pleasures "for the most complete satisfaction" of the lower pleasures (II 6). Is he claiming that no amount of lower pleasures could ever exceed in value the least amount of higher pleasures? If so, he must think that higher pleasures are infinitely or lexically better than lower pleasures. This would seem to imply that one should never indulge lower pleasures at the cost of even the smallest increase in higher pleasures. On this reading, we should be tireless and pure in our pursuit of higher pleasures, never admitting any lower ones, no matter how pleasurable, so long as there is an opportunity cost to them, however modest, in terms of higher pleasures.[4]

This seems to be an extreme and unattractive claim about happiness.[5] Fortunately, Mill does not commit himself to it. Notice two things. First, Mill says only that *if* competent judges categorically prefer one pleasure to another, then the first is discontinuously better than the second. So categorical preference is a sufficient, rather than a necessary, condition of higher pleasures. That opens up the possibility that qualitative differences need not always be discontinuous.[6] One kind of pleasure might be preferred to another by a competent judge in the sense that he would prefer one unit of the first pleasure to several units of the second without its being true that there is no amount of the lower pleasure that would outweigh the higher pleasure. Second, when Mill introduces the idea of a competent judge, in

---

3. Mill's own doctrine of higher pleasures is strikingly similar to that of Francis Hutcheson, *A System of Moral Philosophy* (1755), Book I, 476–77, excerpted in *British Moralists*, 2 vols., ed. L.A. Selby-Bigge (Oxford: Clarendon Press, 1897). Hutcheson says that true happiness needs to reckon different kinds of pleasures, as well as their intensity and duration, that even small amounts of higher pleasures are "incomparably more excellent and beatifick" than the largest amount of lower pleasures, and that it is our sense of dignity that explains our categorical preference for higher pleasures.
4. For a defense of this interpretation of Mill, see Jonathan Riley, "On Quantities and Qualities of Pleasure," *Utilitas* 5 (1993): 291–300, and "Is Qualitative Hedonism Incoherent?," *Utilitas* 11 (1999): 347–58.
5. This verdict is shared by Roger Crisp, *Mill on Utilitarianism* (London: Routledge, 1997), p. 41, and Dale Miller, *J.S. Mill: Moral, Social, and Political Thought* (Cambridge: Polity, 2010), pp. 58–59.
6. See Christoph Schmidt-Petri, "Mill on Quality and Quantity," *The Philosophical Quarterly* 53 (2003): 102–04.

the passage quoted above, he does imagine that a competent judge might compare pleasures or pursuits individually. But when he goes on in the next paragraph to consider the superiority of higher pleasures, what Mill imagines the competent judge comparing are not individual activities but total lives.[7] Moreover, his comparison of lives is quite limited. He compares a life including substantial self-examination and directive control, such as the life of Socrates, with a life containing few or no higher pleasures, such as the life of a satisfied pig or fool. It is in this comparison, Mill claims, that competent judges express a categorical preference for the life containing higher pleasures.

> Now it is an unquestionable fact that those who are equally acquainted with, and equally capable of appreciating and enjoying, both, do give a most marked preference to the manner of existence which employs their higher faculties. Few human creatures would consent to be changed into any of the lower animals, for a promise of the fullest allowance of a beast's pleasures.... It is better to be a human being dissatisfied than a pig satisfied; better to be Socrates dissatisfied than a fool satisfied [II 6].

Here, Mill is comparing the life of Socrates with a life containing only lower pleasures. He does not claim that competent judges have a categorical preference for the pure Socratic life over a predominantly Socratic life, judiciously seasoned with olives, wine, and push-pin. So Mill's defense of the superiority of higher pleasures does not commit him to their pure and tireless pursuit.

12. Subjective and objective pleasures

The higher pleasures doctrine certainly goes beyond Bentham's quantitative hedonism. But to see what conception of happiness it commits Mill to we need to look more closely at the nature and value of higher pleasures. What exactly are higher pleasures, and what does their superior value consist in? Mill's position is hard to pin down, in part because he uses the term "pleasure" sometimes to refer to a certain kind of mental state or sensation and at other times to refer to non-mental items, such as actions, activities, and

---

7. Henry West offers a similar defense of Mill's discontinuity thesis against worries that it is extreme in *An Introduction to Mill's Utilitarian Ethics* (New York: Cambridge University Press, 2004), pp. 64–65.

pursuits that can and often do cause pleasurable mental states. It will be useful to refer to these as *subjective pleasures* and *objective pleasures*, respectively. Especially in the context of a discussion of hedonism, it would be natural to assume that pleasures are subjective pleasures. But we do sometimes recognize objective pleasures, as when someone refers to sexual activity as a bodily pleasure or says that his greatest pleasure is playing hockey, and, as we will see, there are many places where Mill also recognizes objective pleasures. One question then is whether higher pleasures are subjective or objective pleasures, that is, whether they are mental states or sensations caused by activities that exercise our higher faculties or those activities themselves.

Even if we recognize this question as legitimate, it might seem clear that we should interpret higher pleasures as subjective pleasures. After all, Mill has just told us that he is a hedonist about happiness. The Radicals may not have always been clear about the kind of mental state or sensation they take pleasure to be, but it seems clear that they conceive of it as some kind of mental state or sensation. This is certainly the way the hedonist tradition is usually understood. Some, like Bentham, appear to conceive of pleasure as a sensation with a distinctive kind of qualitative feel. Others, perhaps despairing of finding qualia common to all disparate kinds of pleasures, tend to understand pleasures functionally, as mental states or sensations that the subject, whose states these are, wants to continue and is disposed, *ceteris paribus*, to prolong. Pleasures, understood functionally, could have very different qualitative feels and yet still be pleasures. Insofar as Mill does discuss subjective pleasures, he is not clear which, if either, of these conceptions of pleasure he favors. Nonetheless, it may seem natural to assume that as a hedonist he conceives of pleasures as subjective pleasures. According to this interpretation, Mill is focusing on pleasurable sensations and then distinguishing higher and lower pleasures by reference to their causes. Higher pleasures are pleasures caused by the exercise of our higher faculties, whereas lower pleasures are pleasures caused by the exercise of our lower faculties.

13. Problems for hedonism about higher pleasures

This interpretation of the higher pleasures doctrine raises various issues. One is how to square this reading with hedonism. Hedonism presumably says that pleasure is the one and only intrinsic good and that other things are good insofar as they are pleasurable. One thing is better than another, for the hedonist, insofar as it is more pleasurable. But this makes superiority sound like a quantitative relation. So, as Sidgwick notes, a puzzle arises when Mill says that quality, independently of quantity, makes one pleasure better than another. If higher pleasures are better, but not because they are more pleasurable, then how can the higher pleasures doctrine be reconciled with hedonism?[8]

One possible answer is that Mill thinks that there are two factors affecting the magnitude of a pleasure: its quantity, as determined by its intensity and duration, and its quality or kind. On this proposal, one pleasure can be greater than another independently of its quantity by virtue of its quality.[9]

But the hedonistic credentials of this reading are still in doubt. We can distinguish among pleasures between those that are caused by the exercise of our higher faculties and those that are caused by the exercise of our lower faculties. But why should this difference itself affect the pleasurableness of the state in question? Of course, Mill thinks that competent judges have a categorical preference for the higher pleasures. Mill, we said, is largely silent about the nature of (subjective) pleasures. Were he to hold the sort of preference or functional conception of pleasure apparently held by his father, he could claim that preferred pleasures are more pleasurable pleasures. However, he says that competent judges have this preference for the higher pleasure, "even though knowing it to be attended with a greater amount of discontent" (II 5). This suggests that higher pleasures may not be more pleasurable even for competent judges, and in any case it's not clear we could infer what was more pleasurable for someone who was not a competent judge from what was more pleasurable for someone who was. So, even if we can distinguish higher and lower pleasures, according to their causes, it remains unclear how the hedonist is to explain how higher pleasures are inherently more pleasurable.

A related concern is how this interpretation of the higher pleasures doctrine makes sense of Mill's contrast between happiness and contentment or satisfaction. After explaining higher pleasures in terms of the categorical preferences of competent judges and insisting that competent judges would not trade any amount of lower pleasures for higher pleasures, he claims that this preference sacrifices contentment or satisfaction, but not happiness.

---

8. See Henry Sidgwick, *Outlines of the History of Ethics* (originally published 1886) (London: Macmillan, 1967), p. 247.
9. Nicholas Sturgeon develops an interesting version of this interpretation in "Mill's Hedonism," *Boston University Law Review* 90 (2010): 1705–29.

> Whoever supposes that this preference takes place at a sacrifice of happiness—that the superior being, in anything like equal circumstances, is not happier than the inferior—confounds two very different ideas, of happiness, and content.... It is better to be a human being dissatisfied than a pig satisfied; better to be Socrates dissatisfied than a fool satisfied [II 6].

Presumably, subjective pleasure is a matter of contentment or satisfaction, even if there are different kinds of contentment. But Mill does not here say that the preference of competent judges is for one kind of contentment over another or that Socrates has more contentment than the pig or fool by virtue of enjoying a different kind of contentment. Instead, he contrasts happiness and contentment and implies that Socrates is happier than the fool, even if less contented. It's hard to see how Mill can square these claims with hedonism, even one that treats quality and quantity as independent variables affecting the magnitude of a pleasure. Instead, these claims read like a rejection of hedonism in favor of a conception of happiness that prizes the exercise of a person's higher faculties.

Another problem for understanding higher pleasures as subjective pleasures is that various features of Mill's discussion suggest that he understands higher pleasures as objective pleasures.[10] First, we have independent evidence that Mill sometimes uses the word "pleasure" to refer to objective pleasures. For instance, in the second part of the proof of the principle of utility in Chapter IV Mill counts music, virtue, and health as pleasures (IV 5). These are pursuits or conditions that can and often do cause subjective pleasures. As such, they are objective pleasures, not subjective ones. Elsewhere in his discussion of higher pleasures, in Chapter II, Mill equates a person's pleasures with his "indulgences" (II 7) and with his "mode of existence" (II 8). Here too he seems to be discussing lifestyles and pursuits, which would be objective pleasures. When Mill introduces higher pleasures (II 4) he is clearly discussing, among other things, intellectual pursuits and activities. He claims to be arguing that what the quantitative hedonist finds extrinsically more valuable is also intrinsically more valuable (II 4, 7). But what the quantitative hedonist defends as extrinsically more valuable are

---

10. Related claims are made in Ben Saunders, "J.S. Mill's Conception of Utility," *Utilitas* 22 (2010): 52–69. Like me, he interprets Mill's higher pleasures to be (what I call) objective pleasures. It's less clear whether he thinks that higher pleasures essentially involve a subjective, as well as an objective, element. I think that they do not, which renders the higher pleasures doctrine inconsistent with hedonism, as ordinarily understood. If he thinks that higher pleasures do essentially involve both subjective and objective elements, then his interpretation might be closer to attitudinal or hybrid hedonism (see §14).

complex activities and pursuits, such as writing or reading poetry, not mental states. For the quantitative hedonist, the mental states themselves have intrinsic value. Because Mill claims that these very same things are intrinsically, and not just extrinsically, more valuable, his higher pleasures would appear to be intellectual activities and pursuits, rather than mental states. Finally, in paragraphs 4–8 Mill links the preferences of competent judges and the greater value of the objects of their preferences. But among the things Mill thinks competent judges would prefer are activities and pursuits. And, in particular, in commenting on the passage quoted above (II 5), Mill writes:

> Now it is an unquestionable fact that those who are equally acquainted with and equally capable of appreciating and enjoying both do give a most marked preference to the *manner of existence which employs their higher faculties* [II 6, emphasis added].

Here Mill is identifying the higher pleasures with activities and pursuits that exercise our higher capacities. He also claims that happiness includes "many and various pleasures, with a decided predominance of the active over the passive…" (II 12). Whereas activities and pursuits can be passive or active, it is not clear if pleasures themselves could be passive or active.

Insofar as Mill's higher pleasures doctrine concerns objective pleasures, it appears anti-hedonistic for several reasons. First, if the higher pleasures are objective pleasures, then Mill does not accept the idea that higher pursuits are valuable only insofar as they cause pleasure or enjoyment.[11] Second, he claims that the intellectual pursuits have value out of proportion to the amount of contentment or pleasure (the mental state) that they produce. This would contradict the traditional hedonist claim that the extrinsic value of an activity is proportional to the amount of pleasure associated with it. Third, Mill claims that these activities are intrinsically more valuable than the lower pursuits (II 7). But the traditional hedonist claims that the mental state of pleasure is the one and only intrinsic good; activities can have only extrinsic value, and no activity can be intrinsically more valuable than another.

Whichever way we read Mill's higher pleasures doctrine, it is hard to square that doctrine with hedonism, as traditionally formulated. This apparent inconsistency has been noted by many of Mill's subsequent critics,

---

11. Contrast Crisp, *Mill on Utilitarianism*, p. 35.

including Sidgwick, F.H. Bradley, T.H. Green, and G.E. Moore.[12] Green's discussion in his *Prolegomena to Ethics* is especially instructive. After raising some of these questions about the compatibility of the higher pleasures doctrine with hedonism, Green focuses on Mill's explanation of the preferences of competent judges for modes of existence that employ their higher faculties. Higher pleasures are those things (e.g. activities) that a competent judge would prefer, even if they produced less pleasure *in her* than the lower "pleasures" would (II 5). But *why* should competent judges prefer activities that *they* often find less pleasurable unless they believe that these activities are more valuable? Mill explains the fact that competent judges prefer activities that exercise their rational capacities by appeal to their sense of *dignity*.

> We may give what explanation we please of this unwillingness [on the part of a competent judge ever to sink into what he feels to be a lower grade of existence]...but its most appropriate appellation is a sense of dignity, which all human beings possess in one form or other, and in some, though by no means in exact, proportion to their higher faculties...[II 6].

Green thinks that the dignity passage undermines hedonism (*Prolegomena* §§164–66, 171). In claiming that it is the dignity of a life in which the higher capacities are exercised and the competent judge's sense of her own dignity that explains her preference for those activities, Mill implies that her preferences reflect judgments about the value that these activities have independently of their being the object of desire or the source of pleasure. We take pleasure in these activities because we recognize their value; they are not valuable because they are pleasurable. This means that the preferences of competent judges should be understood as *evidence* of the greater value of the object of their preferences, rather than as constituting the object of their preferences as more valuable.[13]

To see Green's point, think of competent judges as demi-gods. In the dignity passage, Mill is making the same sort of point that Socrates does in discussing Euthyphro's definition of piety as what all the gods love (*Euthyphro*

---

12. Sidgwick, *Methods*, pp. 93n, 94, 121; F.H. Bradley, *Ethical Studies* (originally published 1876), 2d ed. (Oxford: Clarendon Press, 1927), pp. 116–20; T.H. Green, *Prolegomena to Ethics* (originally published 1883), ed. D. Brink (Oxford: Clarendon Press, 2003), §§162–63; and G.E. Moore, *Principia Ethica* (Cambridge: Cambridge University Press, 1903), pp. 71–72, 77–81.
13. For this reason, I think that the dignity passage is evidence against those commentators who would treat the preferences of competent judges as constitutive of the superiority of the objects of their preferences. See, for example, Elijah Millgram, "Mill's Proof of the Principle of Utility," *Ethics* 110 (2000), pp. 296–97.

9c–11b). Socrates thought the gods' attitudes would be principled, not arbitrary. But this means that their love presupposes, rather than explains, piety and justice. Similarly, Mill thinks that the preferences of competent judges are not arbitrary, but principled, reflecting a sense of the value of the higher capacities. But this would make his doctrine of higher pleasures fundamentally anti-hedonistic, insofar as it explains the superiority of higher activities, not in terms of the pleasure they produce, but rather in terms of the dignity or value of the kind of life characterized by the exercise of higher capacities. It is sensitivity to the dignity of such a life that explains the categorical preference that competent judges supposedly have for higher activities.

On this reading, the preference of competent judges for higher activities is evidential, rather than constitutive, of the superior value of those activities. Some additional support for this evidential reading comes from a passage in which Mill says that the appeal to competent judges must be final on matters of quality as well as quantity.

> From this verdict of the only competent judges, I apprehend there can be no appeal. On a question which is the best worth having of two pleasures, or which of two modes of existence is the most grateful to the feelings, apart from its moral attributes and from its consequences, the judgment of those who are qualified by knowledge of both, or, if they differ, that of the majority among them, must be admitted as final. And there needs be the less hesitation to accept this judgment respecting the quality of pleasures, since there is no other tribunal to be referred to even on the question of quantity [II 8].

The finality of the preference of competent judges might be thought to be support for the constitutive reading.[14] However, this is not so. First, finality is not the same as infallibility. Since Mill appeals to competent judges, a judicial analogy might be useful. Judges in superior courts might be final arbiters about how to interpret the legal rules in a given system, but it does not follow from the finality of their verdicts that they cannot be mistaken about what the law, properly interpreted, requires. The constitutive reading requires that the verdicts of competent judges be infallible.[15] The finality of their verdicts does not establish this. Moreover, Mill says that competent judges are equally authoritative about matters of quality and quantity. But the quantity of pleasure produced by an activity (or mode of existence) is

---

14. See Millgram, "Mill's Proof of the Principle of Utility," p. 297.
15. See H.L.A. Hart, *The Concept of Law*, 2d ed. (Oxford: Clarendon Press, 1994), pp. 141–47.

plainly an objective matter that depends on the extent, duration, and intensity of the subjective pleasures. The preferences of a competent judge could be at most evidence about the quantity of pleasure associated with a given pursuit. So if the preference of competent judges is final in matters involving quality in the same way it is in matters involving quantity, then it seems that their preference for higher pleasures is evidence of their greater value.[16]

14. Attitudinal and hybrid hedonism

I have argued against a consistent hedonist reading of the higher pleasures doctrine that treats higher pleasures as subjective pleasures. But Mill certainly seems to endorse hedonism in the Proportionality Doctrine, and he focuses, especially in Chapter II, on the value of pleasures. So it might be worth exploring further whether there is a way of squaring these claims about the intrinsic superiority of higher pursuits with some form of hedonism.

One suggestion worth considering is Fred Feldman's proposal that Mill's higher pleasures doctrine introduces and defends a form of *attitudinal hedonism*.[17] Feldman contrasts sensory pleasures, which are pleasurable feelings or sensations, with attitudinal pleasures, which are pleasures taken in certain objects, perhaps in the contemplation or appreciation of those objects. Feldman's idea is that higher pleasures are attitudinal pleasures that take higher pursuits as their objects. They are pleasures *in* certain kinds of activities.[18] Feldman takes the concept of attitudinal pleasure to be primitive.[19] But this is not necessary. We could apply our preferred analysis of pleasure, whatever that is, to the mental state that is directed at higher pursuits. So, for instance, we could understand higher pleasures in preference or functional terms as mental states, the having of which the subject wants to persist and will, other things being equal, take steps to prolong. These would be attitudinal pleasures taken in the higher pursuits or their contemplation. This does not yet explain the intrinsic superiority of higher pleasures in relation to other sorts of attitudinal pleasure. Feldman's proposal is that we can distinguish the value of different attitudinal pleasures

---

16. Crisp, *Mill on Utilitarianism*, p. 36, makes a similar point.
17. Fred Feldman, *Pleasure and the Good Life* (Oxford: Clarendon Press, 2004), ch. 4, esp. pp. 71–78.
18. For a similar idea, see Dale Dorsey, "The Authority of Competence and Quality as Extrinsic," *British Journal of the History of Philosophy* (forthcoming).
19. This assumption is implicit in Feldman's discussion of Mill and attitudinal pleasure in *Pleasure and the Good life*. It is explicit in Fred Feldman, *What is this Thing Called Happiness?* (Oxford: Clarendon Press, 2010), pp. 110–11.

in terms of the pleasure-worthiness of their objects. In particular, he suggests that we understand the higher pleasures doctrine to distinguish among attitudinal pleasures by the "altitude" of the objects of those pleasures. Higher pleasures are "altitude-adjusted" attitudinal pleasures. Though Feldman's proposal is in some ways quite elegant, there are two problems with this as an attractive hedonistic reading of Mill's doctrine of higher pleasures—one philosophical, and one interpretive.

The interpretive problem is that to read Mill as an attitudinal hedonist we have to see higher pleasures as attitudinal pleasures, and this requires treating higher pleasures as higher pursuits *just insofar* as subjects take altitude-adjusted pleasure in them. But, as we have seen, in Mill's discussion of higher pleasures, the pleasures he refers to are, at least typically, activities or pursuits themselves. In these cases, higher pleasures are objective pleasures, not subjective attitudinal pleasures.

The philosophical problem is that in explaining how attitudinal pleasures with higher objects are intrinsically better than attitudinal pleasures with lower objects Feldman appeals to the higher objects being more pleasure-worthy than the lower objects.[20] But this appeals to a kind of value that these objects have prior to and independently of their being the object or source of pleasure. Indeed, this is another way of putting Mill's crucial claim in the dignity passage. Taking pleasure in these pleasure-worthy objects may itself be good or valuable, but this value is in addition to the value of the pleasure-worthy objects themselves. There is nothing wrong with recognizing both kinds of value. Their subjective appreciation may add value, but the activities and pursuits have value independently of their appreciation. In fact, it is the value of the activities and pursuits that *merits* their appreciation. But the value of the higher altitude objects, independently of their causing or being the object of pleasure, is inconsistent with the hedonist claim that pleasure is the *only* good.

Similar remarks apply to the related suggestion that Mill's higher pleasures doctrine is a *hybrid* of valuable activity and subjective pleasure taken in that activity or its contemplation.[21] The hybrid view recognizes that subjective pleasure is consequential on activities and pursuits that express

---

20. A similar issue arises when assessing Feldman's defense of attitudinal hedonism in terms of "merit-adjusted" and "desert-adjusted" attitudinal pleasure. See *Pleasure and the Good Life*, chs. 7 and 9.
21. Both Steve Darwall and Dick Arneson suggested the possible appeal of this sort of hybrid interpretation to me. Wayne Sumner ascribes this sort of view to Mill in *Welfare, Happiness, and Ethics* (New York: Oxford University Press, 1996), pp. 110, 112, 163–64.

our dignity. But then it looks like the value of the activities is prior to and independent of their subjective appreciation. Their subjective appreciation may add value, but the activities and pursuits have value independently of their appreciation. We might think that a good poet's life is better still when she subjectively enjoys her work. But the appreciation of her work is parasitic on her work's having value independently of its appreciation. This is why it merits appreciation. But then value attaches to the poetry itself, independently of its appreciation. So her life has substantial value even if or when she does not appreciate her work properly. But then happiness cannot consist in pleasure alone, as hedonism claims.

Indeed, precisely because the value of the subjective appreciation is consequential on the value of that which is appreciated, it seems clear that the value of the activities and pursuits must be greater than the value of their appreciation. A meal with a dessert may be better than a meal without one, but dessert is an embellishment of the main course and should not be mistaken for a meal. A complete conception of happiness may have to include some hedonistic elements, but that does not establish the hedonist claim that happiness consists in pleasure alone. Indeed, it seems that if we compare the contributions of the activities themselves and their subjective appreciation, attitudinal pleasure must be the junior partner in happiness.

The hybrid conception faces the same interpretive worry as the other hedonistic interpretations. They foundered on the fact that Mill uses the term "pleasure" in the higher pleasures doctrine to refer to objective pleasures, that is, activities, pursuits, and modes of life—just the things that the quantitative hedonist claims have only extrinsic value. If in these passages Mill is talking about higher activities and pursuits, then not only is he not talking about subjective pleasures but also he is not talking about higher activities and pursuits only when they are conjoined with subjective pleasure.

15. Perfectionism

If we read Mill's higher pleasures doctrine as Green suggests, and note these problems for a hedonistic reading of that doctrine, then we can begin to see the possibility and some of the appeal of reading Mill as a kind of perfectionist about happiness who claims that human happiness consists in a kind of self-realization involving the proper exercise of those capacities essential to our nature. Such a reading fits with various claims Mill makes. For instance, early in *On Liberty* he describes the utilitarian foundation of his defense of individual liberties but insists that "it must be utility in the largest sense, grounded on the permanent interests of man as a progressive being" (I 11). Mill apparently believes that the sense of dignity of a (properly self-conscious) progressive being would give rise to a categorical preference for activities that exercise his or her higher capacities. In claiming that "it is better to be a human being dissatisfied than a pig satisfied; better to be Socrates dissatisfied than a fool satisfied" (*U* II 6), Mill recognizes capacities for self-examination and practical deliberation as among our higher capacities. This concern with self-examination and practical deliberation is, of course, a central theme in *On Liberty*. There he articulates the interest that progressive beings have in reflective decision-making.

> He who lets the world, or his own portion of it, choose his plan of life for him has no need of any other faculty than the ape-like one of imitation. He who chooses his plan for himself employs all his faculties. He must use observation to see, reasoning and judgment to foresee, activity to gather materials for decision, discrimination to decide, and when he has decided, firmness and self-control to hold his deliberate decision. And these qualities he requires and exercises exactly in proportion as the part of his conduct which he determines according to his own judgment and feelings is a large one. It is possible that he might be guided in some good path, and kept out of harm's way, without any of these things. But what will be his comparative worth as a human being [III 4]?

Here Mill contrasts human and merely animal (ape-like) nature and identifies capacities for practical deliberation with human nature. Mill need not suppose that practical reason is unique to our species or that the difference between humanity and other species is not a matter of degree. Nor does he think that all humans possess these capacities. Early in *On Liberty* he places limits on the scope of his liberal principles, telling us that they do not apply to individuals that do not possess a suitably developed normative competence.

> It is, perhaps, hardly necessary to say that this doctrine is meant to apply only to human beings in the maturity of their faculties. We are not speaking of children or of young persons below the age which the law may fix as that of manhood or womanhood. Those who are still in a state to require being taken care of by others must be protected against their own actions as well as against external injury. For the same reason we may leave out of consideration those backward states of society in which the race itself may be considered as in its nonage.... Liberty, as a principle, has no application to any state of things

anterior to the time when mankind have become capable of being improved by free and equal discussion.... [A]s soon as mankind have attained the capacity of being guided to their own improvement by conviction or persuasion (a period long since reached in all nations with whom we need here concern ourselves), compulsion, either in the direct form or in that of pains and penalties for noncompliance, is no longer admissible as a means to their own good, and justifiable only for the security of others [I 10; cf. *PPE* V.xi.9].

This passage raises interesting questions about the scope of his liberal principles.[22] The important point, for present purposes, is that here Mill recognizes that children have immature deliberative faculties and that some adults have very limited normative competence, whether due to congenital defects or social circumstance.

So the normative competence Mill values is imperfectly correlated with humanity, understood as a biological category. Instead, I think we should understand him to be invoking humanity as a *normative category*, one that can be linked to the normative concept of a *person*. This is what underlies his talk about humanity as a "progressive" force and the "comparative worth of a human being." Persons are moral agents, who can be responsible and accountable for their actions. Mill discusses responsibility in *A System of Logic* in the section entitled "Of Liberty and Necessity" (VI.ii.3). There he claims that capacities for practical deliberation are necessary for responsibility. In particular, he claims that moral responsibility involves a kind of self-mastery or self-governance in which one can distinguish between the *strength* of one's desires and impulses and their *suitability* or *authority*, and in which one's actions can reflect one's deliberations about what is suitable or right to do. Non-responsible agents, such as brutes or small children, appear to act on their strongest desires or, if they deliberate, to deliberate only about the instrumental means to the satisfaction of their strongest desires. By contrast, responsible agents must be able to deliberate about the appropriateness of their desires and regulate their actions according to these deliberations. This kind of normative competence is essential to our humanity, conceived of as a normative category.

---

22. An obvious question concerns the threshold of normative competence below which a society is sufficiently "backward" that Mill's anti-paternalistic principles do not apply. Here, one might suspect Mill has in mind a defense of British colonialism. However, he does say that the threshold has been long since reached in the nations with whom we need concern ourselves. This could just be evidence of Mill's parochial concerns. But Mill was obviously very concerned about India and other colonies, so a case could be made that he thinks the normative competence threshold is very widely met.

If this is right, then Mill can claim that possession and use of our deliberative capacities mark us as progressive beings, because they are what mark us as moral agents who are responsible. If our happiness should reflect the sort of beings we are, then Mill is in a position to argue that higher activities that exercise these deliberative capacities form the principal or most important ingredient in human happiness. This is a perfectionist claim about happiness.

16. Reconciling the elements of happiness

Where exactly does this recognition of Mill's perfectionism leave our interpretation of his conception of happiness? Is Mill a consistent perfectionist? It is worth noting that any interpretation of Mill's conception of happiness faces significant worries about his consistency. Part of the problem is that Mill appears to endorse three distinct conceptions of the good and happiness.

1. *Hedonism*: Pleasure is the one and only intrinsic good, things are good insofar as they are pleasant, and happiness consists in pleasure.
2. *Desire-satisfaction*: The one and only intrinsic good is the satisfaction of desire (actual or idealized), things are good insofar as they satisfy desire, and happiness consists in the satisfaction of desire.
3. *Perfectionism*: The exercise of one's higher capacities is the one and only intrinsic good, things are good insofar as they exercise higher capacities, and happiness consists in the exercise of higher capacities.

Hedonism is apparently introduced in the Proportionality Doctrine, when Mill identifies happiness and pleasure (*U* II 2). In introducing the doctrine of higher pleasures, Mill appears to want to make some refinement within hedonism (II 3–5). But the higher pleasures doctrine appeals to the informed or idealized preferences of a competent judge and identifies higher pleasures with the object of their preferences (II 5). Moreover, he treats this appeal to the preferences of competent judges as final (II 8). But competent judges prefer higher activities, and not just subjective pleasures caused by those activities, and their preference for higher pursuits is based on their sense of the dignity inherent in a life lived that way (II 6). Moreover, in *On Liberty* and elsewhere he embraces a "progressive" conception of happiness in terms of reflective self-examination and directive self-control. Since these are three distinct and rival claims about Mill's conception of the final good, any reading must explain away inconsistency as best it can and say something about how these three elements are to be reconciled with one another. Perhaps no reading can avoid attributing some inconsistency to Mill, but it would be nice to find a plausible reading of the texts that minimized his inconsistency. Perhaps there is more than one way to try to reconcile these three elements. But I will concentrate on the perfectionist reconciliation, because I take its systematic and interpretive credentials to be strongest.

If there were no other problems with a hedonist reading of the higher pleasures doctrine, it would be an interesting question whether to read Mill as a hedonist or preference-satisfaction theorist. For then he would think that pleasure is the one and only intrinsic good but that what makes higher pleasures especially valuable is the fact that competent judges prefer all and only those kinds of pleasures. Perhaps the best solution would be to distinguish between evaluative *substance* and *metaethics*. Perhaps one should say that Mill is a substantive hedonist and a metaethical desire-satisfaction theorist, claiming that happiness consists in (altitude-adjusted) pleasure, because that is what competent judges would prefer. But the situation is not so simple. Mill's other claims about higher pleasures and his introduction of perfectionist elements make this simple solution untenable.

There are several problems for the hedonist reading. It's hard to see why the cause of a given (subjective) pleasure should affect its magnitude. But then it's hard to see how we could square the higher pleasures doctrine, conceived as a doctrine about subjective pleasures, with hedonism. Moreover, higher pleasures cannot be understood as subjective pleasures during much of Mill's discussion. For what competent judges allegedly prefer and what Mill defends as intrinsically superior are higher pursuits and modes of existence consisting of such pursuits (*U* II 4–8). A hedonist should deny that such objective pleasures have intrinsic value and should insist that their extrinsic value is proportional to the (subjective) pleasure they produce. But Mill denies both claims. Instead, he distinguishes between happiness and contentment (II 6). These problems are not avoided by attitudinal or hybrid readings. These readings do not explain Mill's focus on objective pleasures, and they appeal to the value of higher pursuits, independently of their being the object of pleasure, which is inconsistent with the hedonist claim that pleasure alone is intrinsically good.

These problems for the hedonist reading do not, as such, affect the merits of the desire-satisfaction reading. Indeed, one could try to reconcile the desire-satisfaction and perfectionist elements in a fashion parallel to the potential reconciliation of desire-satisfaction and hedonism. One could claim that Mill is a substantive perfectionist with a desire-satisfaction meta-ethic, claiming that happiness consists in the development and exercise of one's capacities for practical deliberation, because this is what competent judges would prefer. But just as that reconciliation of hedonism and desire-satisfaction is untenable, so too is this proposed reconciliation of perfectionism and desire-satisfaction. The problem for the desire-satisfaction reading is Mill's claim in the dignity passage that it is a competent judge's sense of his own dignity that explains his preference for a life of higher pursuits. The dignity passage requires us to read the preferences of competent judges as evidential, rather than constitutive, of the higher value of the object of their preferences. Though this requires us to deny a desire-satisfaction conception of happiness, it does allow us to make sense of Mill's appeal to the preferences of competent judges.

How, if at all, are we to reconcile perfectionist and hedonist elements? The perfectionist reading must deny hedonism as a conception of happiness. But can it make any sense of Mill's apparent endorsement of hedonism and focus, much of the time, on pleasure? After all, it is awkward for a perfectionist reading of the higher pleasures doctrine that Mill equates happiness and pleasure in the Proportionality Doctrine (II 2). It seems one couldn't ask for a clearer statement of hedonism. Must the perfectionist reading just say that Mill is inconsistent when he goes on to introduce the higher pleasures doctrine that is best read in perfectionist terms? If so, then we should conclude that Mill is inconsistent, but has a considered view. The interpretive and systematic credentials of the perfectionist reading make this Mill's considered view. But we can do better, I think. There is a good case to be made for a consistent perfectionist reading of Mill's conception of happiness.

For one thing, the apparently hedonistic formulation at the beginning of Chapter II, Mill insists, is only a first approximation that needs further articulation.

> To give a clear view of the moral standard set up by the theory, much more requires to be said; in particular, what things it includes in the ideas of pain and pleasure, and to what extent this is left an open question [II 2].

This should be a puzzling claim if we assume, as Bentham seems to have, that the term "pleasure" refers to a simple, qualitative mental state or sensation, for then, it is not clear what further analysis of pleasure should be necessary or even possible. There is no puzzle if Mill is speaking here, as he does elsewhere, of objective pleasures. If he uses the word "pleasure" here to refer, not to any mental state, but to the activities that typically produce pleasurable mental states, then he can consistently say that happiness consists in pleasure—objective pleasure—and offer an objective or even perfectionist conception of happiness whose dominant component is the exercise of deliberative capacities. And this is just what he seems to do. His defense of higher pleasures in the paragraphs immediately following this initial statement of utilitarianism should be read as an important articulation of this initial statement that, I have argued, yields an anti-hedonistic perfectionist conception of happiness.

There is an additional source of support for this reading of the apparent hedonism in terms of objective pleasure. Recall the passage Sidgwick cites from Chapter IV of *Utilitarianism* in support of reading Mill as a psychological hedonist.

> I believe that these sources of evidence [practiced self-consciousness and self-observation, assisted by the observation of others], impartially consulted, will declare that desiring a thing and finding it pleasant, aversion to it and thinking of it as painful, are phenomena entirely inseparable, or rather two parts of the same phenomenon; in strictness of language, two different modes of naming the same psychological fact: that to think of an object as desirable (unless for the sake of its consequences), and to think of it as pleasant, are one and the same thing; and that to desire anything, except in proportion as the idea is pleasant, is a physical and metaphysical impossibility [U IV 10].

As we saw before (§6), Sidgwick reads Mill as making the psychological hedonist claim that all desire is directed toward the agent's own pleasure. But we rejected that claim as implausible and inconsistent with criticisms Mill makes of psychological hedonism. We suggested instead that Mill should be read as claiming that we delight or take pleasure in that which we regard as valuable. On this reading, Mill is introducing an extended or technical sense of pleasure in which we take pleasure in whatever we regard as valuable. But this kind of pleasure is consequential on a perception of value and imposes no substantive constraint on what is valuable. *A fortiori*, appeal to pleasure in this sense does not involve a commitment to hedonism. So if Mill is using the word "pleasure" in the Proportionality Doctrine as he does in his discussion of the proof, then the Proportionality Doctrine appeals to an extended or technical sense of pleasure and not hedonism. When he goes on in the text immediately following the Proportionality Doctrine to defend a perfectionist conception of higher pleasures, he introduces no inconsistency, because he never committed himself to hedonism.

There is no doubt that Mill could have been clearer and invites charges of inconsistency. His initial formulation of his conception of happiness in terms of pleasure easily leads us to expect a defense of hedonism and greater continuity between his own brand of utilitarianism and Benthamite utilitarianism than we actually find. Mill's break with the hedonistic utilitarianism of Bentham and his father would have been clearer if he had avoided defining utilitarianism in terms of pleasure and pain and eschewed talk of "higher pleasures," simply arguing for a conception of happiness that recognizes the intrinsic superiority of the higher pursuits. However, this seems to be how we should understand the doctrine of higher pleasures. The fact that he uses the word "pleasure" to refer to objective pleasures or whatever we take to be intrinsically valuable allows us to recover a consistent and coherent perfectionist doctrine from his somewhat disparate claims.

This gives us a largely consistent perfectionist reading of Mill's conception of happiness and his doctrine of higher pleasures. But just how plausible are these claims? There are several dimensions of the perfectionist reading worth discussing.

17. Perfectionism about happiness

No doubt, one can be a perfectionist about the good, claiming that the value we should try to promote is self-realization or perfection. That is, whatever its ultimate merits, perfectionism is a coherent conception of the good. But can one be a perfectionist about happiness?[23] Isn't happiness an essentially subjective condition? Isn't happiness a matter of contentment or getting what one wants, and doesn't the perfectionist insist that what is good is an objective matter, independent of one's experiences and desires?

---

23. In the course of defending perfectionism, Thomas Hurka, *Perfectionism* (Oxford: Clarendon Press, 1993), pp. 17–18, asserts, without justifying, the related idea that perfectionism should not be understood as a conception of well-being.

Though modern conceptions of happiness do tend to be subjective, we can see the possibility and appeal of objective conceptions of happiness.[24] To see this, we need to make explicit two common assumptions about happiness.

1. *Happiness is subjective*: It consists in or depends upon a person's variable psychological states.
2. *Happiness is what matters*: When we care about someone for her own sake, we care about her happiness.[25]

Some reflection and some attention to Mill's claims show that these two assumptions are in tension and that it is difficult to maintain both. If we insist that happiness is subjective, then we may experience pressure to deny that happiness is what matters. Alternatively, we might retain the assumption that happiness is what matters and reject the assumption that happiness needs to be subjective. This is what perfectionists about happiness should claim.

Consider subjective conceptions of happiness. It is worth distinguishing two varieties: *extreme subjectivists* say that happiness consists in psychological states alone, whereas *moderate subjectivists* say that happiness depends on such states but does not consist in such states. The most familiar form of extreme subjectivism is classical hedonism, which claims that happiness just consists in pleasurable mental states or sensations. The most familiar form of moderate subjectivism is a desire-satisfaction or preference-satisfaction view, which says that happiness depends on a person's desires but consists in the satisfaction of those desires.

---

24. My discussion of the possibility and appeal of objective conceptions of happiness has been influenced by Richard Kraut's wonderful article "Two Conceptions of Happiness," *Philosophical Review* 88 (1979): 167–97. He contrasts ancient conceptions of happiness, which tend to be objective, and modern conceptions, which tend to be subjective, and argues, among other things, that they are rival conceptions of a common concept.
25. We might identify the good life as the life that is good in itself for the one who lives it. The assumption that happiness is what matters is the assumption that the good life is the happy life. A good test for the good life is Feldman's "crib test," which asks what sort of life I would want for my newborn insofar as I cared about her for her own sake. See Fred Feldman, "On the Advantages of Cooperativeness," *Midwest Studies in Philosophy* 13 (1988): 308–23. Cf. Stephen Darwall, *Welfare and Rational Care* (Princeton: Princeton University Press, 2002). Feldman now has qualms about the crib test, because he worries that one's preferences for another's life might be moralistic. For instance, I might want my loved one to lead a life of virtue or to be a martyr for a moral cause. See Feldman, *Pleasure and the Good Life*, p. 10, and *What is this Thing Called Happiness?*, p. 164. But either such moralistic preferences do not reflect what one wants for another *for her own sake*, in which case they don't pass the crib test, or they do, in which case they reflect a partly moralistic conception of the other's good. So, I think that the crib test is a defensible test for conceptions of the good life. I am claiming, in effect, that both happiness and perfectionism pass the crib test.

It is possible to confuse the two views, because both can be formulated in terms of satisfaction. But whereas the hedonist identifies happiness with a feeling of satisfaction, the desire-satisfaction view identifies happiness with the satisfaction of desire. As long as one desires things other than one's own pleasure, the two views will diverge. Indeed, as long as one desires things other than subjective states of oneself, the desire-satisfaction view implies that one's happiness will consist in more than psychological states alone.

Both forms of subjectivism are problematic, as long as one accepts that happiness is what matters. Extreme subjectivism is problematic, because we can imagine someone with the specified experiences and mental states who is nonetheless not connecting with what's valuable in the right way. In *Anarchy, State, and Utopia*, Robert Nozick famously describes an experience machine that allows one to have any experience one chooses.

> Suppose there were an experience machine that would give you any experience you desired. Superduper neuropsychologists could stimulate your brain so that you could think and feel you were writing a great novel, or making a friend, or reading an interesting book. All the time you would be floating in a tank, with electrodes attached to your brain. Should you plug into this machine for life, preprogramming your life's experiences?[26]

Nozick expresses reservations about the prospect of hooking oneself up to such a machine for life on the ground that we want to do certain things and be related to others and the world in certain ways and not just have experiences as if we were engaged in such activities and relationships. Indeed, as long as we prefer a set of experiences grounded in real activities, relationships, and accomplishments to the same set of experiences ungrounded, this shows that it is not experiences alone that matter.

Or consider the case of the deluded schoolboy.[27] His greatest desire is to be the most popular boy in school. His classmates, who despise him, construct an elaborate hoax in which they stage a mock election in which he is chosen the most popular boy in school. As long as the deception is successful, he is euphoric. But his euphoria is based on a false belief. We pity his bliss, and should he later discover the deception, we can imagine him ruing those days as contemptible.

With both the experience machine and the deluded schoolboy we have reservations about the value of these experiences; our reservations reveal

---

26. Robert Nozick, *Anarchy, State, and Utopia* (New York: Basic Books, 1974), p. 42.
27. Kraut discusses this case in "Two Conceptions of Happiness."

that experiences are not all that we wish for ourselves or our loved ones when we wish someone well for his own sake. Mill presumably shares these concerns insofar as he denies that a satisfied fool is happy and claims that competent judges prefer the exercise of their higher capacities and not just the pleasure that might arise from that exercise.

The moderate subjectivist about happiness can concede these doubts about extreme subjectivism. Nozick's claim shows that we have desires that the experience machine does not satisfy, and the deluded schoolboy may be satisfied but does not have his desires satisfied, because he is not the most popular boy in school.

But there are other problems with moderate subjectivism. One problem is that such conceptions attach significance to satisfying desire without in any way constraining the content of desire. But most of us think that people can be satisfying their deepest desires and yet lead impoverished lives if their desires are for unimportant or inappropriate things. For instance, we are unlikely to view the life of someone devoted to collecting lint as a richly valuable life, no matter how successful a lint collector he is.[28] This is not the sort of life I would want for someone whom I care about, at least not if that person has a normal set of capacities and talents.

Another worry about moderate subjectivism is that in its focus on the satisfaction of desire it seems to counsel adaptation of our desires to fit our circumstances, for by adapting our desires, we increase the probability of satisfying them. Such adaptive views of happiness are familiar from Plato's *Gorgias* and from Epicurean ethics. No doubt there is some truth in this adaptive maxim, at least insofar as it is often advisable to maintain some degree of realism in one's aspirations and ambitions. But, as a general strategy, unrestricted adaptation is unattractive, for it counsels us always to change our desires, rather than changing the world. That strategy is effectively criticized in Aldous Huxley's dystopia *Brave New World* in which Deltas and Epsilons form the working classes who are genetically engineered and psychologically programmed to acquiesce in and indeed embrace intellectually and emotionally limited lives that are liberally seasoned with mood-altering drugs.[29] Deltas and Epsilons lead contented lives precisely because their

---

28. In *A Theory of Justice*, p. 432, Rawls discusses a person whose chief desire is to spend his life counting the blades of grass in the fields around him.
29. Aldous Huxley, *Brave New World*, 2d ed. (New York: Harper and Row, 1946). I take Huxley's Brave New World to be not merely a dystopia but also an allegory for certain aspects of modern life. Interestingly, Huxley suggests that the proper lesson to be drawn from such a dystopia is recognition of a higher (perfectionist) form of utilitarianism (viii–ix).

desires are satisfied. They've got what they want. It's their desires that are frightening. We do not (in general) improve the quality of lives by lowering our sights, even if by doing so we increase the frequency of our successes.

Mill agrees with these sorts of doubts about moderate subjectivism when he claims that the contented fool is not happy and that happiness requires the exercise of one's higher capacities.

We could accept these reservations about extreme and moderate subjectivism and conclude so much the worse for happiness. This reaction holds subjectivism about happiness fixed and concludes that happiness is not what matters. Especially if we distinguish between happiness, on the one hand, and a person's welfare, well-being, or interest, on the other hand, this reaction might be understandable. For then, utilitarianism could and should be reformulated not in terms of the promotion of happiness but rather in terms of the promotion of welfare or well-being, for on this view, it is welfare or well-being, rather than happiness, that is what matters.

But there is an alternative possibility. If one holds fixed the assumption that happiness is what matters, then one can accept these reservations about extreme and moderate subjectivism and conclude that we should reject subjective conceptions of happiness in favor of more objective ones. False happiness may be essentially subjective, but true or genuine happiness is an objective matter. It is this sense of happiness that we have in mind when we wish for our children to lead happy lives. We wish them a complete life that contains the objective goods that matter, not just a life of satisfaction or one that meets whatever goals they happen to have. On this reading, perfectionist views emerge as potentially viable conceptions of happiness. Mill's doubts in *On Liberty* about "the comparative worth" of the life of a human being not involving reflective self-examination and decision-making show that he does believe that happiness is what matters (III 4). Insofar as he distinguishes between happiness and contentment and offers a conception of happiness in terms of the exercise of our rational or deliberative capacities, he can be read as holding a perfectionist conception of happiness.

Mill's perfectionism about happiness has an advantage in explaining why happiness matters. For any conception of happiness, we can ask the normative question about why we should care about happiness, so understood. That question is not easy to answer and raises a legitimate question about the significance of some conceptions of happiness. For instance, it is unclear why we should care about promoting happiness if hedonism is true. Perhaps there is a good answer to that question, but it is not obvious. By contrast,

Mill's perfectionist conception of happiness has a promising answer to the question about why happiness matters. He grounds his conception of happiness in those capacities for practical deliberation that mark us as moral persons, subject to reasons for action, and responsible for our actions. This promises to explain why a rational agent should be especially concerned about his happiness, conceived in terms of the exercise of such capacities.

18. Perfectionism and pluralism about happiness

One source of the appeal of subjectivism about happiness is its recognition that happiness can come in many forms. Because people's preferences and plans vary, they can take pleasure in different activities, and different activities will satisfy their desires. So happiness, according to subjective conceptions, is pluralistic. By contrast, more objective conceptions of happiness, such as perfectionism, may seem to deny this kind of pluralism, precisely because they say that there is one particular conception of a good or happy life, the value of which is independent of what people want or find pleasing. Can only the subjectivist embrace pluralism about happiness? If so, this might be a legitimate worry about perfectionism.

However, an objective conception of happiness can be pluralist. The details depend on the form the objective conception takes. Some objective conceptions conceive of happiness in terms of a list of disparate intrinsic goods, such as knowledge, achievement, and friendship. Activities and lives could combine these goods in different ratios, yielding the result that lives structured in different ways could contain equivalent or comparable value. For a perfectionist, such as Mill, who understands the primary ingredient in a happy life to be the cultivation and exercise of capacities for practical deliberation, happiness can be as multifarious as practical reason can be. Shallow and undemanding lives will not be especially happy lives. But many different lifestyles will exemplify practical reason. For instance, the artisan who makes important decisions about the organization of her craft and the production and distribution of her product exercises a form of deliberative control within her life comparable to that exercised by the intellectual or artist. Recognition of this diversity is part of what explains Mill's insistence in *On Liberty* on the value of experiments in living. Such experiments are an important part of Mill's conception of liberalism. But also they show Mill's recognition of pluralism. So there is reason to doubt that Mill thinks that pluralism is the exclusive province of subjective conceptions of happiness. Perfectionists must be discriminating but need not be elitists.

Moreover, it matters how one justifies pluralism. There is an important sense in which subjective conceptions of happiness are not just pluralist but relativist. The classical hedonist thinks that pleasure is good independently of whether anyone recognizes this fact or not. In this sense, hedonism is an objective conception of happiness. But the hedonist also thinks that what makes something good for someone depends entirely on her contingent and variable psychology. In this sense, the classical hedonist recognizes no restrictions on what might be good for someone. Similarly, desire-satisfaction theories of happiness make happiness depend on a person's contingent and variable desires. So both forms of subjectivism are in a certain sense *content-neutral*, placing no substantive constraints on what might contribute to a person's happiness. But we saw that this kind of content-neutrality is problematic. Most of us are not prepared to judge that there are no substantive constraints on happiness. If we assume that happiness is what matters, then we have doubts about whether shallow and undemanding lives could be happy ones for people with a normal range of talents and capacities. So it is a vice of subjective conceptions insofar as they derive their commitment to pluralism from the more extreme and unsustainable commitment to content-neutrality. It is a virtue of objective conceptions, such as perfectionism, that they can defend pluralism without the unsustainable commitment to content-neutrality.

19. Unanswered questions about perfection and happiness

So far, a perfectionist reading of Mill's conception of happiness looks promising on both interpretive and systematic grounds. But the perfectionist conception of happiness that we have found in Mill is incomplete in several respects. This conception will become somewhat more complete as we see how Mill applies his perfectionist assumptions in moral and political argument. But there are several issues about his perfectionist commitments that he never faces squarely. These are worth raising and discussing, if only briefly, both to see how Mill's conception of happiness is incomplete and to see the issues that any more complete conception would have to address.

One aspect of happiness about which Mill says very little is pain. Though Mill mentions pain as the counterpart to pleasure in the Proportionality Doctrine (*U* II 2), he never elaborates about pain or its role in his conception of happiness. The Proportionality Doctrine appears to suggest that pain is intrinsically bad. However, if, as I have argued, the pleasures referred to in the Proportionality Doctrine are objective pleasures, this raises the question whether pains are objective too. On this interpretation, pains are activities that tend to cause subjective pain. We do sometimes speak this way, as when we describe an unpleasant person or task as a pain. If Mill understood pains objectively, then he need not think that subjective pain is inherently bad. Subjective pain could still be instrumentally bad insofar as it impeded the exercise of valuable activities. Pain is distracting and, in extreme cases, disabling. This might lead one to suppose that pain was bad insofar as it disabled or distracted one from the pursuit of pleasures, especially higher pleasures.

But some might think that subjective pain is intrinsically, and not just relationally, bad. It is bad in itself, independently of what it might impede. We saw that Mill does seem to recognize the intrinsic value of subjective pleasure, even if its value is inferior to higher objective pleasures. To make his position symmetrical, he could recognize the intrinsic disvalue of subjective pain, even if he also recognizes the intrinsic disvalue of objective pains. Even if Mill does recognize the inherent disvalue of subjective pain, this still poses at least two further questions.

One question is whether there are higher and lower pains. One might deny this, claiming that pain is just the counterpart to lower sensory pleasure. But we might instead interpret pains symmetrically with Mill's commitments about pleasure. On the perfectionist reading that I have defended, there are four kinds of pleasures. There are two kinds of objective pleasures, higher and lower; these are activities and pursuits that exercise our higher capacities and lower capacities, respectively. There are also two kinds of subjective pleasures, higher and lower; higher subjective pleasures are altitude-adjusted attitudinal pleasures, and lower subjective pleasures are sensory pleasures. If Mill were to treat pain symmetrically, he would recognize four kinds of pain, two kinds of objective pain and two kinds of subjective pain. As we have seen, one can recognize objective pains as things and activities that tend to cause subjective pain. One could presumably distinguish among objective pains between higher and lower. Higher objective pains would be events or activities that thwart the exercise of higher capacities, such as squandering one's talents and rational capacities or the loss of a valued friend. By contrast, lower objective pains would be events or activities that thwart the exercise of our lower capacities, such as activities that dull one's sensory capacities or induce painful sensation. Moreover, one could distinguish higher and lower subjective pains. Lower subjective pains would be sensory pains, such as the sort of sensations caused by physical trauma or present in toothaches. Higher subjective pains would be attitudinal pain taken in the sacrifice or loss of higher pursuits, such as the anguish caused by the recognition of squandered potential or by the loss of loved ones.

What would such an approach to pain imply about the comparative value of pleasure and pain? Again, in the absence of explicit suggestions from Mill, one might treat pain and pleasure symmetrically. On our perfectionist understanding of pleasure, objective pleasures are pre-eminently valuable. They are superior to lower pleasures, whether these be subjective or objective, and they are also superior to altitude-adjusted attitudinal pleasure taken in the higher pursuits. Symmetry would require making higher objective pains as bad as higher objective pleasures are good. These higher pains would be worse than lower objective pains and subjective pains, whether sensory pains or altitude-adjusted attitudinal pain.

These remarks about the nature of pains and their value are extremely sketchy, and it's hard to tell if they have the same degree of plausibility as Mill's perfectionist treatment of pleasure has. Perhaps there is reason for Mill to treat pleasure and pain differently. But, in the absence of explicit guidance from Mill himself about the nature and value of pain, symmetry is one way to start the conversation.

A different question about Mill's conception of happiness concerns the purity of his perfectionism and the role, if any, of subjective pleasure in his perfectionism. Mill distinguishes higher and lower pleasures, and we have seen reason to interpret higher pleasures as objective pleasures that support a perfectionist conception of happiness. Should we interpret lower pleasures as subjective pleasures? If so, then Mill accepts a mixed conception of happiness, containing both perfectionist and hedonistic elements, in which the perfectionist elements dominate the hedonistic ones. We could call this *predominant perfectionism*.

But it's not clear that Mill is this sort of predominant perfectionist. This case for predominant perfectionism requires interpreting higher and lower pleasures asymmetrically—higher pleasures being objective pleasures and lower pleasures being subjective pleasures. Since Mill does use the word "pleasure" objectively in this context, that gives us some reason to interpret higher and lower pleasures symmetrically, so that both are objective pleasures. On this reading, just as higher pleasures refer to higher activities or pursuits, so too lower pleasures refer to lower activities or pursuits. On this reading, subjective pleasures aren't in play at all.

But perhaps we should not interpret lower pleasures objectively, or at least not always. After all, lower pleasures are associated with contentedness and satisfaction (II 5, 6). So perhaps lower pleasures are, or at least can be, subjective pleasures. Moreover, though we rejected attitudinal and hybrid conceptions of higher pleasures, we allowed that it was plausible to claim that taking attitudinal pleasure in higher pursuits added value to those pursuits. Though higher pleasures themselves are objective pleasures, it is also valuable to take subjective pleasure in these objective pleasures. Here, we said, the attitudinal pleasure is parasitic on the non-hedonic value of the higher pursuits. If attitudinal pleasure adds value to the higher pursuits themselves, the hedonistic value added must be less than the perfectionist value on which it is parasitic (§14).

Do these hedonistic claims support a mixed conception of happiness? Consider first these last claims about altitude-adjusted attitudinal pleasure. Though they imply that a kind of subjective pleasure is valuable, this need not require any departure from perfectionism. This is because we might accept a purely *cognitive* conception of altitude-adjusted attitudinal pleasure. On this view, the attitudinal pleasure associated with higher activities should be understood as an appreciation and delight in their non-hedonic value. Indeed, this is how I suggested we should understand Mill's claim that finding pleasurable and finding desirable or valuable are one and the same (IV 10). Because appreciation of value is a fitting response to value, we can understand the appreciation of perfectionist value as itself a perfectionist value. This kind of hedonic value can be part of perfectionism. What about the hedonic value at least sometimes involved in lower pleasures? If these are also to be understood cognitively as appreciations of the non-hedonic value of lower pleasures, then their recognition involves no departure from perfectionism. Mill is forced to a mixed conception of happiness only if the subjective pleasures associated with lower pleasures cannot be understood cognitively. For then their value would consist solely in their being pleasant and not in their perception of non-hedonic value. I don't think that Mill clearly faced this question. Though a purely cognitive conception of (subjective) pleasure is not obviously wrong, neither is it obviously right. If one does not accept a purely cognitive conception of the hedonic value of lower pleasures, then one must embrace a mixed conception of happiness, combining independent perfectionist and hedonist elements. But even if the Millian were to opt for a mixed view, it's clear that the resulting view would be a form of predominant perfectionism in which perfectionist elements dominate hedonistic elements.

A different question about the purity of Mill's perfectionist conception of happiness concerns whether perfection itself requires appeal to intrinsic goods independent of perfection. Perfectionism would be pure in this sense just in case the ideal of perfection provided adequate normative guidance by itself without being supplemented by distinct values. In Mill's case the issue is whether his ideal of self-realization understood in terms of the exercise of rational or deliberative capacities provides the right sort of guidance, at least in principle, about the content of happiness and well-being, without being supplemented by other goods. It may be easier to understand and assess this issue about purity by considering its denial. Here, we need to distinguish more and less radical denials of purity. A less radical denial of purity would allow that a deliberative ideal gives content to happiness and well-being but insist that this guidance must remain incomplete until supplemented by other values. A more radical denial of purity would insist that by itself the deliberative ideal is empty and provides no guidance whatsoever.[30]

We can start with the more radical critique of perfectionism. If Mill's perfectionist ideal consists in the exercise of rational or deliberative capacities, we may conclude that the ideal could offer no guidance by itself without some list of independent values. For deliberation is among alternatives and aims at reaching conclusions about which course of action or option is best. But then the process of deliberation seems to require some prior and independent conception of the merits of options, which deliberation recognizes and compares. On this view, a deliberative ideal is itself empty until supplemented with a list of good-making factors.

We've already seen reason to reject this more radical critique of Mill's perfectionism. Mill's perfectionist emphasis on the importance of exercising deliberative capacities has consequences. It discriminates between higher and lower pleasures, between a life of self-examination and a life of sensory contentment, between a life of an artisan who has control over the nature

30. It might be helpful to compare this critique of perfectionist purity with apparently similar worries about the adequacy of appeals to rational nature in Kant and other rationalists. See, e.g., Donald Regan, "The Value of Rational Nature," *Ethics* 112 (2002): 267–91. I take Regan to endorse the less radical concern that the appeal to rational nature is in principle incomplete.

of her work and the distribution of her products and the life of a successful lint collector. Later, we will see, for example, that Mill's perfectionist ideal provides a defense of freedom of expression and a critique of contracts in perpetuity. It will also provide a defense of the value of friendship among equals and a defense of sexual equality. Something's content is a function of what it excludes. An ideal of a life that exercises one's higher capacities and exhibits deliberative control excludes many possibilities. As we noted earlier (§18), though it is pluralistic, Mill's perfectionism is not content-neutral.

The less radical critique of incompleteness is harder to assess. This critique concedes that Mill's deliberative ideal has content capable of providing guidance about the requirements of happiness and well-being. But it insists that proper deliberation requires more guidance than provided by the concepts of self-realization and deliberation themselves. In addition to the value of rational nature, we need to appeal to substantive values, such as achievement, knowledge, friendship, and (subjective) pleasure. Such a charge of incompleteness can, I think, only be decided on a case-by-case basis by assessing claims that it has left out something important that should help determine our prudential judgments. A thorough assessment of this kind is not possible here. But one can see how the discussion might proceed. We have already seen how one might try to reconcile some pleasures with perfectionism by adopting a cognitive conception of pleasure as an appreciation of perfectionist value. Later, we will see the beginnings of an account of how friendship engages deliberative values and so might be brought under the perfectionist umbrella. Though the details would have to be worked out, it's not too hard to see how one might begin to try to understand achievement and knowledge as perfectionist values. Whether the perfectionist justification of these goods is plausible and whether there are other goods that defy perfectionist analysis are open questions that require more extended examination.

If there is a legitimate worry about the viability of pure perfectionism, it is the worry about incompleteness, not the worry that perfectionism is empty. Even this less radical critique is far from conclusive. There are perfectionist justifications of several plausible intrinsic goods that are worth exploring. Even if we did decide that the good of perfection needs to be supplemented with other goods, there would still be a strong case to be made for predominant perfectionism and an even stronger case to be made for the weaker but significant perfectionist claim that our understanding of happiness would be seriously incomplete without recognizing the importance of perfectionist goods.

4
Ambivalence about duty

In the last chapter, we focused on Mill's conception of happiness, defending a perfectionist reading of Mill's conception of happiness on both interpretive and systematic grounds. If utilitarianism is a form of consequentialism that understands the good to be promoted in terms of well-being or happiness, perfectionism is a viable conception of happiness, and Mill is a perfectionist about happiness, then Mill is best understood as a perfectionist utilitarian.[1] But this conclusion does not yet tell us exactly how duty is related to happiness. It is to these issues that we should turn now. As Mill's Proportionality Doctrine makes clear, he endorses the utilitarian idea that duty or right action involves the promotion of happiness. But exactly how Mill thinks duty is related to happiness is not yet clear. Mill's conception of duty is also bound up with his conception of justice and rights, because he thinks of these as involving special kinds of duties.

On these issues Mill is especially interesting, because his claims about duty and justice have been subject to widely different interpretations. There is a tradition of reading Mill as an act utilitarian, who thinks that it is our duty to perform the action with the best consequences for the general happiness. We will see good evidence for this tradition. However, J.O. Urmson famously argued against this act utilitarian reading of Mill and defended a rule utilitarian reading, according to which an act is obligatory, not because of its consequences, but because it conforms to a rule with optimal accept-

---

1. So I disagree with commentators who equate utilitarianism with hedonistic utilitarianism and conclude that Mill is not a (consistent) utilitarian from the premise that he is not a (consistent) hedonist. For example, Irwin correctly sees that Mill's conception of happiness has important perfectionist or eudaimonist elements, which are anti-hedonistic. But he does not conclude that Mill is a perfectionist utilitarian; instead, he treats this as evidence that Mill is not a (consistent) utilitarian. See Irwin, *The Development of Ethics*, §1141. There is no need to draw this radical conclusion as long as utilitarianism is a form of consequentialism that identifies the good as happiness or well-being and Mill defends a perfectionist conception of happiness.

ance value for the general happiness.[2] More recently, David Lyons has defended a different reading of Mill's theory of duty, according to which right and wrong are determined by the utility of sanctioning conduct.[3]

These three utilitarian conceptions of duty are, I shall argue, mutually inconsistent. Mill cannot consistently embrace more than one of them. Against Urmson, I argue that most of Mill's claims about duty are best interpreted in act utilitarian, rather than rule utilitarian, terms. However, I agree with Lyons that in Chapter V of *Utilitarianism* Mill introduces a different form of utilitarianism that is inconsistent with act utilitarianism. Because I think that Mill's other claims are best interpreted in act utilitarian terms, I believe that Chapter V introduces inconsistency into Mill's conception of duty. I conclude by exploring the comparative advantages of the two forms of utilitarianism to which Mill is attracted and suggest that there is reason to prefer the act utilitarian conception.

20. Varieties of utilitarianism

In order to understand what is at stake among some different interpretations of Mill's theory of duty, it may help to make some now generally familiar distinctions within consequentialist and utilitarian ethics. Though these are contemporary distinctions, they may help us locate Mill's conception of duty in a familiar space of possibilities or, when we compare Mill's claims with this space, we may decide to expand our conception of this space.

Consequentialists generally agree that deontic notions such as obligation, permission, and prohibition should be understood in terms of evaluative notions about the good. For instance, duty or obligation should be understood as serving or promoting the good in some way. In a familiar slogan, consequentialists believe that *the good is prior to the right*.[4] Utilitarians are consequentialists who conceive of the good in terms of happiness or well-being. Within the constraints set by consequentialist and utilitarian essentials, there are several important intrafamily disputes. Among these disputes is how best to understand the exact relation between the good and the right.

---

2. J.O. Urmson, "An Interpretation of the Philosophy of J.S. Mill," reprinted in *Mill's Utilitarianism: Critical Essays*, ed. D. Lyons.
3. See David Lyons, "Mill's Theory of Morality" and "Mill's Theory of Justice" both reprinted in his *Rights, Welfare, and Mill's Moral Theory*.
4. See Rawls, *A Theory of Justice*, §§5–6.

One important question is whether the utilitarian assessment of persons, actions, institutions, and policies should be direct or indirect.

- *Direct Utilitarianism*: Any object of moral assessment (e.g. action, motive, policy, or institution) should be assessed by and in proportion to the value of its consequences for the general happiness.
- *Indirect Utilitarianism*: Any object of moral assessment (e.g. an action) should be assessed, not by the value of its consequences for the general happiness, but by its conformity to something else (e.g. rules, norms, or motives) that has (have) good or optimal acceptance value for the general happiness.

So formulated, direct and indirect utilitarianism are general theories that apply, at least in principle, to any object of moral assessment. But our immediate focus is on right action or duty. Act utilitarianism is the most familiar form of direct utilitarianism applied to action, whereas the most common indirect utilitarian theory of duty is rule utilitarianism.[5]

- *Act Utilitarianism*: An act is right insofar as its consequences for the general happiness are at least as good as any alternative available to the agent.
- *Rule Utilitarianism*: An act is right insofar as it conforms to a rule whose acceptance value for the general happiness is at least as good as any alternative rule available to the agent.

This conception of act utilitarianism is both *maximizing*, because it identifies the right action with the best available action, and *scalar*, because it recognizes that rightness can come in degrees, depending on the action's proximity to the best.[6] The right act is the optimal act, but some suboptimal

---

5. Notice that indirect utilitarianism is really a *hybrid* of indirect and direct elements. It offers an indirect utilitarian assessment of one thing in terms of another and a direct utilitarian assessment of the second thing. So, for example, rule utilitarianism offers an indirect utilitarian assessment of actions in terms of rules, which are then assessed in direct utilitarian terms. This allows us to say that rule utilitarianism is a form of indirect utilitarianism but only in its treatment of right action. I'm not sure that there are any purely indirect forms of utilitarianism. The hybrid character of indirect utilitarianism is a potential source of theoretical difficulty, which I explore later (§27).
6. This conception of act utilitarianism might be contrasted with *satisficing* act utilitarianism, which says that an act is right just in case its consequences for the general happiness are *good enough*. Though satisficing act utilitarianism is also a form of direct utilitarianism, Mill shows no signs of being attracted to it, and I will not discuss it further here. Similar remarks apply *mutatis mutandis* to the possible and relevant forms of rule utilitarianism. Alastair Norcross, "A Scalar Approach to Utilitarianism," in *The Blackwell Guide to Mill's Utilitarianism*, ed. H. West (Oxford: Blackwell, 2008), recognizes the scalar character of consequentialist reasons and concludes that utilitarians should eschew deontic notions. He is right to recognize scalar consequentialism but wrong to think that this requires rejecting deontic notions of duty and obligation. In fact, Mill's Proportionality Doctrine combines the two.

acts can be more right and less wrong than others. Similarly, this conception of rule utilitarianism assesses rules in both maximizing and scalar fashion.

Act utilitarianism appears to say that we should adhere to familiar moral precepts about honesty, fidelity, and nonmaleficence only when doing so has the best consequences. It is a counter-intuitive doctrine to the extent that we regard some of these precepts as categorical moral rules or principles. Honesty and fidelity may be the best policies, but some think that we have duties of honesty and fidelity even in situations in which their consequences are suboptimal. Rule utilitarianism may seem less counter-intuitive, because it can explain why one ought to adhere to certain rules or precepts, even when doing so does not have the best consequences, provided doing so is generally optimal. Act utilitarianism must condemn following rules when doing so is suboptimal; rule utilitarianism need not. But not everyone agrees that this makes rule utilitarianism superior to act utilitarianism. Some think that we are wrong to embrace categorical moral rules and principles. Though these rules and principles might be good rules of thumb, they are not exceptionless generalizations. Moreover, rule utilitarianism may seem ad hoc. If utility is the appropriate test for rules, then why shouldn't we assess actions by the same criterion? Isn't rule utilitarianism a form of irrational rule worship? I raise these issues here, not to take a stand on them, but to indicate what might be at stake in the debate between direct and indirect utilitarianism.

21. Utilitarianism as a standard of conduct

Recall that in Chapter II of *Utilitarianism* Mill explains utilitarianism by introducing the Proportionality Doctrine.

> The creed which accepts as the foundations of morals "utility" or the "greatest happiness principle" holds that actions are right in proportion as they tend to promote happiness; wrong as they tend to produce the reverse of happiness. By happiness is intended pleasure and the absence of pain; by unhappiness, pain and the privation of pleasure [II 2].

As we will see, the Proportionality Doctrine has been interpreted in both act utilitarian and rule utilitarian ways. But before we get to these issues, we should attend to a different question about the sort of principle that utilitarianism is. We might expect a utilitarian (act or rule) to apply the utilitarian principle in her deliberations. Consider act utilitarianism for a moment. We might expect such a utilitarian to be motivated by pure disinterested benevolence and to deliberate by calculating expected utility on each and every occasion for action. But it is a practical question how to reason or be motivated, and direct utilitarianism implies that this practical question, like all practical questions, is correctly answered by what would in fact maximize utility. Utilitarian calculation is time-consuming and often unreliable or subject to bias and distortion. Because utilitarian calculation is often complex and time-consuming, it can involve significant opportunity costs, especially if one misses the opportunity to do good as the result of performing complex calculations. Moreover, agents often engage in temporal discounting of future benefits and harms, thereby underestimating temporally distant benefits and harms. Similarly, agents often engage in interpersonal discounting of benefits and harms to others, thereby underestimating benefits and harms to others to whom they stand in no special relationship. For such reasons, we may better approximate the utilitarian standard if we don't always try to approximate it. As we saw earlier (§2), Bentham recognized this, and so does Mill. Mill, we saw (§10), says that to suppose that one must always consciously employ the utilitarian principle in making decisions

> ...is to mistake the very meaning of a standard of morals and confound the rule of action with the motive of it. It is the business of ethics to tell us what are our duties, or by what test we may know them; but no system of ethics requires that the sole motive of all we do shall be a feeling of duty; on the contrary, ninety-nine hundredths of all our actions are done from other motives, and rightly so done if the rule of duty does not condemn them [II 18].

Later utilitarians, such as Sidgwick, have emphasized this point, insisting that utilitarianism provides a standard of right action.

> Finally, the doctrine that Universal Happiness is the ultimate *standard* must not be understood to imply that Universal Benevolence is the only right or always the best *motive* of action. For, as we have observed, it is not necessary that the end which gives the criterion of rightness should always be the end at which we consciously aim: and if experience shows that the general happiness will be more satisfactorily obtained if men frequently act from other motives than pure universal philanthropy, it is obvious that these other motives are reasonably to be preferred on Utilitarian principles [*Methods* 413].

Both Mill and Sidgwick distinguish between a moral standard and a set of motives. Another way to make their point would be to distinguish between a moral principle or theory supplying a *standard* of right conduct and supplying a *guide* to action or a *decision procedure*. They understand first principles, such as utilitarianism, as providing a standard, rather than a guide.

If utilitarianism is itself the standard of right conduct, not a guide, then what sort of decision procedure should the utilitarian endorse, and what role should the principle of utility play in moral reasoning? Utilitarianism, if true, is the *first principle* of morality. As we will see (§24), Mill thinks that much moral reasoning should be governed by *secondary principles* about such things as fidelity, fair play, and honesty that make no direct reference to utility but whose general observance does promote utility. These secondary principles should be set aside in favor of direct appeals to the utilitarian first principle in cases in which adherence to the secondary precept would have obviously inferior consequences or in which such secondary principles conflict (*U* II 19, 24–25).

We can now specify more precisely that the question that concerns us here is what kind of utilitarian standard Mill endorses.

22. The case for act utilitarianism

Mill is often read as an act utilitarian, and with good reason.[7] Several of his characterizations of utilitarianism imply or naturally suggest a form of direct utilitarianism, specifically act utilitarianism. Chapter II, we saw, is where Mill purports to say what the doctrine of utilitarianism does and does not say. In the opening paragraph, he tells us that utilitarians are "those who stand up for utility as the test of right and wrong" (II 1). According to the Proportionality Doctrine, introduced in the next paragraph, utilitarianism holds "that actions are right in proportion as they tend to promote happiness; wrong as they tend to produce the reverse of happiness" (II 2). Later in that chapter, he says that it requires that "utility or happiness [be] considered as the directive rule of human conduct" (II 9). Still later in Chapter II, he describes utilitarianism as a "standard of what is right in conduct" (II 17). Even Chapter V, which will eventually introduce some indirect elements, begins with Mill asserting that utilitarianism is "the doctrine that utility or happiness is the criterion of right and wrong" (V 1).

---

7. Berger, *Happiness, Justice, and Freedom*, ch. 3, is perhaps the best statement of the act utilitarian reading to date. Also see D.G. Brown, "Mill's Act-Utilitarianism" reprinted in *Mill's Utilitarianism: Critical Essays*, ed. D. Lyons.

These passages all say that actions are right or wrong depending on their utility, which is a direct utilitarian claim. The Proportionality Doctrine says that actions are right insofar as they promote utility or happiness. According to this criterion, an act is more right the more it promotes (net) utility or happiness, and presumably the most right action is the one that most promotes or maximizes (net) utility or happiness. So the canonical passages all seem to endorse a form of direct utilitarianism, specifically act utilitarianism.

23. Felicific tendencies

But not everyone agrees. In his influential paper, "An Interpretation of the Philosophy of J.S. Mill," J.O. Urmson famously defended a rule utilitarian reading of Mill. One of Urmson's reasons for this rule utilitarian reading appeals to Mill's reliance on various rules and secondary principles in moral reasoning. We will examine that rationale shortly. But, perhaps surprisingly, Urmson also appeals to the Proportionality Doctrine as requiring a rule utilitarian interpretation of Mill.

Recall that the Proportionality Doctrine says, in part, that utilitarianism "holds that actions are right in proportion as they tend to promote happiness; wrong as they tend to produce the reverse of happiness [II 2]." Urmson claims that we can make sense of an action's tendency to produce good or bad consequences only as a claim about what is true of a *type* of action or *class* of actions. Token actions produce specifiable consequences; only types of actions have tendencies. On Urmson's interpretation, Mill is really saying that an action is right if it is a token of a type of act that tends to have good or optimal consequences. But then the Proportionality Doctrine would espouse a form of rule utilitarianism. This is a natural interpretive claim. But several considerations count against Urmson's interpretation of the Proportionality Doctrine.

First, it was common among the Philosophical Radicals to formulate utilitarianism, as the Proportionality Doctrine does, in terms of the felicific tendencies of individual actions. For instance, Bentham does this early in his *Principles*.

> By the principle of utility is meant that principle which approves or disapproves of every action whatsoever, according to the tendency which it appears to have to augment or diminish the happiness of the party whose interest is in question: or, what is the same thing in other words, to promote or oppose that

happiness. I say of every action whatsoever; and therefore not only every action of a private individual, but of every measure of government [I 2; cf. I 3, 6].

Here Bentham clearly ascribes the felicific tendency to action tokens, and he equates an action's felicific tendency with the extent to which it promotes utility. Later, Bentham repeats this understanding of tendencies.

> The general tendency of an act is more or less pernicious, according to the sum total of its consequences: that is, according to the differences between the sum of such as are good, and the sum of such as are evil [VII 2; cf. IV 5].

John Austin, who was a rule, rather than an act, utilitarian, nonetheless shared Bentham's understanding of the felicific tendencies of particular acts, as he makes clear in *The Province of Jurisprudence Determined* (1832).[8]

> Now the *tendency* of a human action (as its tendency is thus understood) is the whole of its tendency: the sum of its probable consequences, in so far as they are important or material: the sum of its remote and collateral, as well as of its direct consequences, in so far as any of its consequences may influence the general happiness [Lecture II/38].

In the first passage from Bentham and in this passage from Austin, there is a concern with expected, rather than actual, utility, presumably because they are concerned in these passages with the calculation of expected utility required when one is trying to apply the utilitarian standard. But presumably neither wants to formulate the utilitarian standard itself in terms of expected, rather than actual, utility.[9] If we abstract from this apparent concern with expected utility, Austin and Bentham are claiming that action tokens have felicific tendencies and that an action's felicific tendency consists in the value of its actual consequences. We might call this the *extensional* reading of the felicific tendencies of action tokens.[10] But if we

---

8. John Austin, *The Province of Jurisprudence Determined*, ed. H.L.A. Hart (New York: Noonday Press, 1954).
9. In Bentham's case, this is reasonably clear from his doubts about the actual utility of trying to calculate expected utility in some circumstances (*Principles* IV 6). However, the matter is complicated by the fact that Bentham treats both certainty and propinquity (temporal proximity) as intrinsic dimensions of pleasures that affect their intrinsic value (IV 2–3). But here, I think, Bentham is confusing the standard and its application. Certainty and propinquity are not features of pleasures themselves, but of their relation to planners, and they affect not actual utility, but expected utility.
10. I call it an extensional reading of the felicific tendency of an act, even though it can apply to possible or hypothetical acts, because the felicific tendency of a hypothetical act consists in what would be the actual, not the probable, consequences of such an act, were it performed.

interpret Mill's Proportionality Doctrine against the background of these extensional claims held by his utilitarian forebears, then we have strong evidence against Urmson's reading and in favor of an act utilitarian reading of the Proportionality Doctrine.[11]

Second, we might note another, related extensional reading of felicific tendencies within the Proportionality Doctrine. Particular actions have many consequences that are distributed both across persons and across times. The felicific or hedonic valence of these various consequences can be *mixed*. A given act may have consequences that are good for A and B but bad for C or bad for A and B in the short-run but better for them in the long-run. We could speak of an action's tendency to promote happiness either as a way of picking out its beneficial consequences or perhaps as a way of signaling that its beneficial consequences outweigh or predominate over its harmful consequences. Sometimes, Bentham does just this.

> Sum up all the values of all the *pleasures* on the one side, and those of all the *pains* on the other. The balance, if it be on the side of pleasure, will give the *good* tendency of the act upon the whole, with respect to the interests of that *individual* person; if on the side of pain, the *bad* tendency of it upon the whole [*Principles* IV 5].

But then the Proportionality Doctrine would be asserting that an action is right insofar as it has beneficial consequences or insofar as its beneficial consequences predominate. But these are also direct act utilitarian claims.

Third, in some non-ethical contexts Mill understands tendencies as *powers* or *dispositions* of things to produce a certain sort of effect that will produce that effect unless some countervailing force interferes. For instance, in his understanding of the laws of mechanics in *A System of Logic*, Mill denies that an object subjected to a force always moves in the direction of the force.

> To accommodate the expression of the law to the real phenomena, we must say, not that the object moves, but that it *tends* to move, in the direction and with the velocity specified. We might, indeed, guard our expression in a different mode, by saying that the body moves in that manner unless prevented, or except insofar as prevented, by some counteracting cause [III.x.5].

Tendencies in this sense are possessed not only by types of things but also by tokens. Moreover, tokens have the tendency even when they don't manifest

---

11. My claims here are indebted to Berger, *Happiness, Justice, and Freedom*, pp. 73–78.

it (produce the associated effect) due to interference. If Mill understands talk of tendencies in the Proportionality Doctrine in this way, then there's no need to read him, as Urmson does, as talking about types of actions, rather than action tokens. He would be ascribing to token actions powers to produce pleasure or pain—powers which, though present, may be masked by interfering factors.

But if we read Mill's tendency talk in the Proportionality Doctrine in this dispositional way, then he is endorsing something other than act utilitarianism, as traditionally conceived. Act utilitarianism is a form of direct utilitarianism, and it identifies the rightness of an act with the value of its consequences. These are actual consequences. But the dispositional version of the Proportionality Doctrine denies this. For on this view, rightness tracks not actual value but dispositional value—not actual consequences but the consequences an action would produce were it not interfered with. This view might be equivalent to rule utilitarianism if an action's dispositional value was always the same as the normal or average value of the consequences of that type of action. If so, then there would be merit to Urmson's rule utilitarian reading of the Proportionality Doctrine even though he would be wrong to defend it by appeal to the claim that only action types have tendencies. However, it is not reasonable to assume that dispositional value is the same as usual or average value. For a genuine disposition may be regularly or systematically masked if interference is regular. Water may boil at 100°C (at sea level), but few samples of water may boil at that exact temperature due to interfering conditions, such as impurities in the water or atmospheric pressure that is lower or higher than at sea level.

So a dispositional reading of proportionality would not result in rule utilitarianism. But it would result in an odd form of utilitarianism—one that implied that an action might be right even though it doesn't have good consequences, even though it does not belong to a class of actions that generally has good consequences, and even though that same action might not have good consequences in relevantly similar possible situations. This leads me to think that, even though Mill clearly understands tendencies as dispositions or powers that might not be manifest in some non-ethical contexts, this is not how he understands talk of tendencies in the Proportionality Doctrine. There it seems more plausible to read him as assuming a purely extensional reading of tendencies of the sort employed by Bentham and Austin in their own canonical statements of utilitarianism.

24. Principles and rules

But Urmson does not appeal only to the Proportionality Doctrine to support his rule utilitarian interpretation. He also defends this interpretation as a reading of Mill's claims about the importance of secondary principles and rules in our moral reasoning. He recognizes that an act utilitarian might appeal to rules or principles as rules of thumb in doing utilitarian calculations, but he insists that Mill's secondary principles are not mere rules of thumb.

We can see the need for rules and principles that do not refer to utility by remembering Mill's distinction between a moral standard and a decision procedure (*U* II 19). In his *Autobiography* Mill notes the case for pursuing our own happiness indirectly.

> I never, indeed, wavered in the conviction that happiness is the test of all rules of conduct, and the end of life. But I now thought that this end was only to be attained by not making it the direct end. Those only are happy (I thought) who have their minds fixed on some object other than their own happiness; on the happiness of others, on the improvement of mankind, even on some art or pursuit, followed not as a means, but as itself an ideal end. Aiming thus, at something else, they find happiness by the way [*CW* I 145].

Here, Mill describes the importance of *indirection* in pursuing one's own happiness. The need for indirection in the pursuit of one's own happiness is sometimes called the paradox of egoism or prudence. It requires that one pursue things other than one's own happiness for their own sakes in order to be happy. Mill treats these plural ends as secondary principles. It is reasonable to treat them as secondary principles, subordinate to prudence, if their pursuit is suitably regulated by their prudential value. On this picture, these plural ends are not consciously pursued as a means to happiness, but they are pursued as ends because this contributes to happiness. If their pursuit did not promote the agent's happiness, they would lose their status as ends.

Mill holds similar views about the need for secondary principles in the promotion of universal happiness. For instance, in *Utilitarianism* he defends the utilitarian's appeal to various moral precepts as secondary principles, such as veracity, fidelity, and fair play (II 24–25). But it is not entirely clear how these secondary principles are related to the utilitarian first principle. Mill's discussion of the indirect pursuit of one's own happiness suggests one possible relationship.

- Secondary principles are false targets for the successful pursuit of one's primary objective, as when one shouldn't think too hard about making a free throw if one wants to sink the basket or when one shouldn't think too much about impressing one's interviewer if one wants to perform well in the interview.

However, the immediate context of discussion in Chapter II of *Utilitarianism* suggests that Mill is there focusing on a somewhat different relationship.

- Secondary principles are generally but imperfectly reliable guides to doing what will maximize happiness in the sense that trying to follow secondary principles generally, but not always, produces optimal results.

Secondary principles, so understood, might sound like mere rules of thumb. But Mill does not regard them as mere heuristics in a utility calculation. They don't themselves make reference to utility, and he thinks they should be adhered to uncritically in ordinary circumstances. He goes so far as to describe the rule against lying as "sacred" (II 23). He seems to believe that secondary principles, such as the principle of veracity, often satisfy two conditions.

1. Employing the principle generally but imperfectly leads to optimal results.
2. One cannot in general reliably discriminate whether or, if so, when adherence to the principle would produce suboptimal results.

When these two conditions are met, Mill believes, agents should follow these principles automatically and uncritically most of the time. In these cases, agents consult only secondary principles; they do not use them as heuristics in a utility calculation. They have genuine deliberative autonomy. But to say this is not to say that agents should never consult the utilitarian first principle or assess the acceptance value of secondary principles. They should periodically step back and review, as best they can, whether the principle continues to satisfy conditions (1) and (2). Also, they should set aside these secondary principles and make direct appeal to the principle of utility in unusual cases in which it is especially clear that the effects of adhering to the principle would be significantly, and not merely marginally, suboptimal, and in cases in which secondary principles, each of which has a utilitarian justification, conflict (II 19, 24–25). But, otherwise, they should regulate their conduct according to these secondary principles without recourse to the utilitarian first principle.[12]

Should everyone operate by the same secondary principles, or might the optimal ones vary among agents? Mill does not address this issue directly, but we can see what his conception of secondary principles might imply. In theory, the secondary principles that might be optimal for agents to employ might vary among different agents. Broadly speaking, secondary principles are justified by our cognitive limitations, including limitations in our abilities to make optimal exceptions to coarse-grained rules. But these limitations might vary, which might in principle justify agents in adopting different secondary principles. This seems not to be just a theoretical possibility. It is a familiar fact that we employ more coarse-grained moral rules when dealing with young children than when dealing with adolescents or adults. For instance, it may be better for young children to internalize a coarse-grained rule against lying, even if we expect adults to adopt more fine-grained rules that make exceptions for white lies designed to spare others unnecessary offense. The more coarse-grained rules appropriate for children gradually give way to more fine-grained rules appropriate for adults. But just as there are cognitive differences between adults and children that make different rules appropriate for them, so too there may be cognitive differences among adults that justify different secondary principles.

This possibility can't be denied. But two considerations place significant limits on individual variability in optimal secondary rules. First, the precedential value of more fine-grained rules limits the conditions under which they are optimal. If more discriminating agents act according to more fine-grained rules, this is likely to set a precedent that the less discriminating will feel entitled to follow. But, by hypothesis, it will be suboptimal for the less discriminating to employ more fine-grained rules. So even if it would otherwise be more optimal for the more discriminating to employ more fine-grained rules, the spillover effects on the less discriminating constrain the more discriminating from operating by different rules. Second, rule-governed behavior in many contexts carries advantages of securing expectations and coordinating behavior. But to achieve these benefits, people must operate with the same rules. These

---

12. Scheffler provides a very useful discussion of related ideas about the possible roles of first principles in ordinary moral reasoning in *Human Morality*, ch. 3.

benefits of predictability and coordination operate to limit the variability in optimal secondary principles.

Regulating one's behavior in this way by secondary principles is what will best promote happiness. Mill summarizes this picture in *A System of Logic*.

> I do not mean to assert that the promotion of happiness should be itself the end of all actions, or even all rules of action. It is the justification, and ought to be the controller, of all ends, but it is not itself the sole end. There are many virtuous actions, and even virtuous modes of action (though the cases are, I think, less frequent than is often supposed) by which happiness in the particular instance is sacrificed, more pain being produced than pleasure. But conduct of which this can be truly asserted, admits of justification only because it can be shown that on the whole more happiness will exist in the world, if feelings are cultivated which will make people, in certain cases, regardless of happiness [VI.xii.7].

Mill makes similar claims in his essay "On Bentham."

> We think utility, or happiness, much too complex and indefinite an end to be sought except through the medium of various secondary ends, concerning which there may be, and often is, agreement in persons who differ in their ultimate standard; and about which there does exist a much greater unanimity among thinking persons, than might be supposed from their diametrical divergence on the great questions of moral metaphysics.... Those who adopt utility as a standard can seldom apply it truly except through the secondary principles; those who reject it, generally do no more than erect those secondary principles into first principles. It is when two or more of the secondary principles conflict, that a direct appeal to some first principle becomes necessary; and then commences the practical importance of the utilitarian controversy...[*CW* X 110–11].

Mill's claims about the nature and importance of secondary principles and precepts that are and ought to be regulated by utilitarian first principles form an important part of his views about moral reasoning.

His utilitarian justification of discrete secondary principles is intended as a contrast with the intuitionism of William Whewell and others. As he makes clear in his essay "Whewell on Moral Philosophy" (1852), Mill thinks that the intuitionist wrongly treats familiar moral precepts as ultimate moral factors whose justification is supposed to be self-evident to reason (*CW* X). By contrast, Mill's account of secondary principles recognizes their importance in moral reasoning but insists that they are neither innate nor infallible. They are precepts that have been adopted and internalized because of their acceptance value, and their continued use should be suitably regulated by their ongoing comparative acceptance value. Far from undermining utilitarian first principles, Mill thinks, appeal to the importance of such moral principles actually provides support for utilitarianism. He makes this argument in considerable detail in the case of precepts of justice in Chapter V of *Utilitarianism*, where he argues that justice is not, as intuitionists allege, a principle independent of utility, but rather a principle and associated set of emotions protecting security and other essentials of happiness and, hence, justified by their good consequences (see especially V 1–3, 32–38).

It seems clear that Mill is assigning to secondary principles or rules a role that goes beyond rules of thumb in a utilitarian calculation. In the passage from *A System of Logic* above he claims that utility justifies which principles or rules we follow. Does this commit Mill to rule utilitarianism? Urmson thinks it does.

John Rawls may too. In "Two Concepts of Rules" Rawls motivates a rule utilitarian justification of punishment by appeal to a difference between *legislative* and *judicial* attitudes toward rules.[13] Rawls asks us to distinguish the legislative issues of whether to punish conduct, which conduct to punish and how to punish such conduct from the judicial issue about the conditions under which particular individuals ought to be punished. This is, Rawls thinks, a special case of the more general distinction between reasons for having a practice and the rules or reasons that regulate its proper operation. Forward-looking utilitarian reasons are relevant to these legislative issues, but only backward-looking retributive reasons are relevant to addressing the judicial issue.

> The decision whether or not to use the law rather than some other mechanism of social control, and the decision as to what laws to have and what penalties to assign, may be settled by utilitarian arguments; but if one decides to have laws then one has decided on something whose working in particular cases is retributive in form.[14]

This is a rule utilitarian approach to punishment. Interestingly, as Rawls himself notes, Mill begins his own account of the relationship between first principles and secondary principles in *A System of Logic* by making the same

---

13. John Rawls, "Two Concepts of Rules" reprinted in John Rawls, *Collected Papers*, ed. S. Freeman (Cambridge, MA: Harvard University Press, 1999).
14. Ibid., p. 23.

distinction between legislative and judicial perspectives on punishment (VI.xii.2). So perhaps he too is drawing rule utilitarian conclusions.[15]

But Mill's claims about secondary principles are not inconsistent with direct utilitarianism or act utilitarianism.[16] Some writers understand indirect utilitarianism as including any utilitarian theory that permits psychological indirection, in the form of false targets or secondary principles, as a way of satisfying the utilitarian standard.[17] It should be uncontroversial that Mill is an indirect utilitarian in *this* sense, because he recognizes secondary principles that are not mere rules of thumb in an expected utility calculation. But this is not something that the act utilitarian need deny. These forms of indirection do not require that the standard *itself* be formulated in indirect terms. The issue of interest is whether Mill's standard itself is direct or indirect.

So far, Mill's claims about secondary principles do not imply that his standard of duty is not direct. For one thing, though Mill does not treat secondary principles as mere rules of thumb in utilitarian calculation, he does not think that they should be followed uncritically or independently of their consequences. He thinks that they should be set aside in favor of direct appeal to the principle of utility when following them would be clearly suboptimal or when there is a conflict among secondary principles.

Moreover, act utilitarianism permits one to act on discrete moral precepts or principles that make no direct reference to utility if this results in one performing the optimal action. Indeed, the act utilitarian can allow the agent to follow principles or rules even when this sometimes results in suboptimal acts being performed. Recall that act utilitarianism is a species of direct utilitarianism, which assesses things by their (actual) consequences. But the direct utilitarian assesses things other than actions, including motives, principles, and rules. Now it might be true that for a particular agent the

---

15. For another rule utilitarian reading of Mill, see Dale Miller, *J.S. Mill,* ch. 6. Also see Rex Martin, "Mill's Rule Utilitarianism in Context," David Weinstein, "Interpreting Mill," Ben Eggleston, "Rules and their Reasons: Mill on Morality and Instrumental Rationality," and Dale Miller, "Mill, Rule Utilitarianism, and the Incoherence Objection," all in *John Stuart Mill and the Art of Life,* ed. B. Eggleston, D. Miller, and D. Weinstein (Oxford: Clarendon Press, 2011).
16. Rolf Sartorius, *Individual Conduct and Social Norms* (Encino: Dickenson, 1975), esp. ch. 4, reaches a similar conclusion that the act utilitarian can defend the use of secondary principles or norms that are not mere rules of thumb.
17. For instance, I think that it is something like this ecumenical sense of indirect utilitarianism that is employed in R.M. Hare, *Moral Thinking: Its Levels, Methods, and Point* (Oxford: Clarendon Press, 1981), and Lyons, *Rights, Welfare, and Mill's Moral Theory.*

rules with the optimal acceptance value direct him to perform actions some of which are suboptimal. If he cannot reliably identify in advance those cases where adherence to the rule would be suboptimal or if he is not sufficiently fine-grained psychologically to deviate from the rule here where doing so is optimal without deviating from the rule in other cases where it is not, then he will do more good by following the rules uncritically even though he knows that by doing so he will perform some suboptimal actions. In such a situation, a direct utilitarian should want the agent to follow the optimal rules, rather than perform the optimal action. This would be rule utilitarianism (not direct utilitarianism) only if we made the further claim that the right action is to follow the optimal rules. But the direct utilitarian will refuse this further move. She will say that an action's deontic status depends on the value of its consequences and that the right action is the optimal action, but that for some agents it can in principle be best to act from optimal motives, rather than perform the right action. The suboptimal actions the agent thus performs will be wrong, but because they are part of the best pattern of behavior, they can be treated as cases of *blameless wrongdoing*, perhaps even *praiseworthy wrongdoing*.

So whether Mill's claims about the importance of secondary principles imply rule utilitarianism depends, in part, on whether he wants to define right action in terms of the best set of secondary principles or whether they are just a reliable way of doing what is in fact best. If he defines right action in terms of conformity with principles with optimal acceptance value, then he is a rule utilitarian. But if the right action is the best action, and secondary principles are just a reliable (though imperfect) way of identifying what is best, then Mill is an act utilitarian. It's not clear that Mill ever commits himself to the rule utilitarian reading of secondary principles, and the act utilitarian reading could be reconciled with his other commitments to act utilitarianism, such as the Proportionality Doctrine.

It might be thought that the optimal action and the action based on optimal motives could not come apart in this way, because the negative effects of departing from optimal rules must always count against the optimality of departing from them. If this assumption were true, then there would be no conflict between act and rule utilitarianism and indeed rule utilitarianism would collapse into act utilitarianism. But Mill believes there can be such a conflict and so, at least implicitly, rejects this assumption. This is a complicated issue, but I think Mill's assumptions are defensible. Our actions do affect our motives and dispositions. But while an individual action has some small effect on forming or sustaining motives or dispositions, one act does not a motive or disposition make or sustain. If the single action cannot be ascribed all the negative effects of producing a suboptimal motive, then we cannot argue that following the best motives could not produce some suboptimal outcomes. From this it follows, I believe, that we cannot assume that the best action is always the same as the action required by the best motives or rules.[18]

For the most part, Mill gives no indication that he does not accept this direct utilitarian justification of acting from optimal rules or motives, even when this might result in suboptimal acts. However, there is one passage that suggests an indirect utilitarian account. As we have seen (§10), in the middle of Chapter II of *Utilitarianism* Mill argues that utilitarianism permits most people most of the time to concentrate on promoting the well-being of a comparatively small circle of people and that only a few are required to concern themselves with promoting the human good impartially on a regular basis. He goes on to suggest that moral compunction might be obligatory even in cases in which it would be beneficial to violate the rule.

> In the case of abstinences indeed—of things which people forbear to do, from moral considerations, though the consequences in the particular case might be beneficial—it would be unworthy of an intelligent agent not to be consciously aware that the action is of a class which, if practiced generally, would be generally injurious, and that this is the ground of the obligation to refrain from it [II 19].

Here, Mill commits himself to an indirect utilitarian conception of duty if he says that an act is right or required by duty, though suboptimal, because it is an instance of a rule with optimal acceptance value. That is certainly a possible reading of this passage. But it introduces inconsistency with the direct utilitarian claims Mill makes elsewhere.

Indeed, Mill elsewhere insists on the direct, act utilitarian claim that an action's deontic status depends on the value of its consequences, claiming that the value of generally acting like that has only evidential significance about the consequences in the particular case. In an 1872 letter to John Venn, Mill writes:

> I agree with you that the right way of testing actions by their consequences, is to test them by the natural consequences of the particular action, and not

---

18. Here, I agree with West, *An Introduction to Mill's Utilitarianism*, p. 93.

by those which follow if every one did the same. But, for the most part, the considerations of what would happen if every one did the same, is the only means we have of discovering the tendency of the act in the particular case [CW XVII 1881].[19]

One might try to read the abstinence passage in a way that squares with this direct utilitarian claim. For instance, one could claim that his talk of "obligation" in the abstinence passage is loose and not to be taken literally. An act utilitarian who believes that there are cases of blameless or even praiseworthy wrongdoing could claim that Mill is saying only that the agent has a good reason or justification to follow the optimal rule even in particular cases in which doing so is suboptimal and, hence, by act utilitarian lights, wrong. So when Mill says that the ground of the obligation is the acceptance value of the practice, he really only means that this is the agent's reason for following the optimal practice, not a ground of obligation or duty to forbear in the particular case. This reading has the advantage of making this passage consistent with Mill's other commitments to act utilitarianism, but it has the disadvantage of requiring a non-literal reading of the passage.

Instead of endorsing a loose reading of the passage, the act utilitarian might advocate greater attention to Mill's actual language. There are two different things Mill says in this passage that make the rule utilitarian reading of the passage problematic or at least non-mandatory.

First, notice that Mill discusses cases in which it is good to follow a practice of forbearance even though this means foregoing beneficial consequences in particular cases. He says we have reason to regard it as our duty to abstain from certain actions even when these would have beneficial consequences. He says that the prohibited actions would be beneficial, not that they would be optimal. But then he does not actually assert that we have a duty to perform suboptimal acts.

There is a second, independent way to resist the rule utilitarian reading. Suppose, for the sake of argument, that Mill is thinking about cases in which abstinence is suboptimal. He does not say that it is our duty to abstain even when doing so is suboptimal. Instead, he says "it would be unworthy of an intelligent agent not to be consciously aware that the action is of a class which, if practiced generally, would be generally injurious, and that this is the ground of the obligation to refrain from it." But then he is saying that a good

---

19. This passage was brought to my attention by Brown, "Mill's Act-Utilitarianism," reprinted in *Mill's Utilitarianism: Critical Essays*, ed. D Lyons (New York: Rowman and Littlefield, 1997).

agent will regard duty as consisting in conformity to rules with optimal acceptance value—not that duty will so consist. The direct utilitarian agrees that agents with limited powers of discrimination might do best by following optimal rules even though this may produce some individual actions that are suboptimal and, hence, by her lights, wrong. So the direct utilitarian might think that it was best for an agent to regard her duty as consisting in conformity with the best rules, even if her duty actually consisted in what was optimal. Once we see that "the ground of the obligation" falls within the scope of what it would be "worthy of an intelligent agent" to consider, we can see how the passage admits of a direct, act utilitarian reading after all.

To say that we can reconcile the abstinence passage with direct utilitarianism is not to say that this is the most natural reading of the passage or that there is nothing to be said for a rule utilitarian reading of it. But if we continue to abstract, for the moment, from complexities to be introduced in Chapter V of *Utilitarianism* (discussed later in this chapter), then, given Mill's commitments to direct utilitarianism elsewhere, a direct utilitarian reading of the abstinence passage appears to be the only way for him to maintain a consistent position. The fact that we can read the abstinence passage in a way that is consistent with direct utilitarianism is, therefore, reason to do so. This allows us to read Mill's claims about secondary principles in a way that is consistent with his commitment to direct utilitarianism, though not without some interpretive strain. Whatever Mill may have said, it should be clear that his principal claims about the importance of secondary principles do not, as such, force a choice between direct, act utilitarianism and indirect, rule utilitarianism. *A fortiori*, they do not provide reason to reject the act utilitarian strand in Mill's formulation of the utilitarian doctrine.

25. Sanction utilitarianism

So far, the picture we get is that Mill pretty consistently endorses act utilitarianism as a standard of right conduct or duty, even if he does not require it to be a guide or a decision procedure. Though he believes in the importance of secondary rules that can and should regulate much moral reasoning, this does not require any departure from direct utilitarianism. However, Chapter V of *Utilitarianism* introduces claims about duty, justice, and rights that are hard to square with direct or act utilitarianism. The central passage here is one in which Mill links duty with sanctions.

> For the truth is, that the idea of penal sanction, which is the essence of law, enters not only into the conception of injustice, but into that of any kind of wrong. We do not call anything wrong unless we mean to imply that a person ought to be punished in some way or other for doing it—if not by law, by the opinion of his fellow creatures; if not by opinion, by the reproaches of his own conscience. This seems the real turning point of the distinction between morality and simple expediency [V 14].

Here Mill defines wrongness and, by implication, duty, not directly in terms of the nature of the action or its consequences, but indirectly in terms of appropriate responses to it. He appears to believe that one is under an obligation or duty to do something just in case failure to do it is wrong and that an action is wrong just in case some kind of external or internal sanction—legal punishment, social censure, or self-reproach—ought to be applied to its performance.

In this context, sanction seems to be understood quite broadly, so that it includes any kind of censure or blame, whether or not that censure is accompanied by sanctions in the narrower sense of punishment. Legal punishment involves both censure and sanctions in this narrower sense of fines or imprisonment. Social censure may or may not involve further informal forms of punishment, such as shunning or ostracism. Presumably, self-reproach typically involves only censure or blame, not self-inflicted punishment, though the force of Conscience can nonetheless be quite severe. Here, as in Chapter III of *Utilitarianism*, Mill appeals to this broader sense of sanction as involving censure and blame.

Sanctions determine when conduct is wrong, which allows Mill to say that an act is one's duty just in case its omission would be appropriate to sanction. In this way, the sanction test distinguishes duty from expediency (V 14, 15). Not all suboptimal or inexpedient acts are wrong, only those in which one ought to apply some sort of sanction (at least, self-reproach) to them.

Justice is a proper part of duty. Justice involves duties that are perfect duties—that is, duties that are correlated with rights (V 15).

> Justice implies something which it is not only right to do, and wrong not to do, but which some individual person can claim from us as a matter of right [V 15].

An act is unjust just in case it is wrong and violates someone's rights (V 23). Someone has a right just in case she has a claim that society ought to protect by force of law or public opinion.

> When we call anything a person's right, we mean that he has a valid claim on society to protect him in the possession of it, either by the force of law, or by that of education and opinion. If he has what we consider a sufficient claim, on whatever account, to have something guaranteed to him by society, we say that he has a right to it. If we desire to prove that anything does not belong to him by right, we think this is done as soon as it is admitted that society ought not to take measures for securing it to him, but should leave it to chance, or to his own exertions [V 24].

Mill makes or implies several claims here.

1. An act is wrong just in case some sort of sanction ought to be applied to its performance.
2. An act is obligatory or one's duty just in case failure to do it is wrong.
3. Hence, an act is obligatory or one's duty just in case some sort of sanction ought to be applied to the failure to do it.
4. An act is permissible just in case it is not wrong to perform it.
5. Hence, an act is permissible just in case it is not the case that some sort of sanction ought to be applied to its performance.
6. Not all inexpedient or suboptimal acts are wrong.
7. Hence, it is not always one's obligation or duty to perform the optimal act.
8. Hence, some suboptimal acts are permissible.
9. There can be supererogatory acts—acts that are praiseworthy, though their omission is not wrong.
10. Justice is a species of duty in which the failure to act justly is not only wrong but also violates rights.
11. Someone has a right to x just in case society ought to protect her claim to x by force of law or public opinion.
12. Hence, unjust acts are wrongs that society ought to prohibit by force of law or opinion.
13. Hence, just acts are duties that society ought to require by force of law or opinion.

Notice that these relationships among duty, justice, and rights and other deontic notions do not yet introduce any utilitarian elements. But Mill does think that whether sanctions ought to be applied to an action—and hence whether it is wrong—and whether society ought to enforce an individual's claim—and hence whether she has a right—both depend upon the utility or expediency of doing so (V 25).

Mill does not say precisely what standard of expediency he has in mind. In particular, he does not say whether something counts as wrong just in case it is optimal to sanction that conduct or just in case it would be beneficial on-balance to sanction it, etc. The class of wrong acts is narrower if we require that sanctions be optimal than if we require that they be merely beneficial. Unless otherwise noted, I will ignore this interesting question about the proper utilitarian standard for applying sanctions, because its resolution won't affect our main conclusions.

Because this account of duty defines the rightness and wrongness of an act, not in terms of its utility, as act utilitarianism does, but in terms of the utility of applying sanctions to the conduct, it is an indirect form of utilitarianism. Because justice is a species of duty, it inherits the indirect character of sanction utilitarianism. In "Mill's Theory of Morality" and other essays, David Lyons has drawn attention to this indirect aspect of Mill's utilitarianism. Lyons does not have a name for this form of indirect utilitarianism. Because it makes the rightness and wrongness of conduct depend upon the utility of sanctioning that conduct in some way, we might call it *sanction utilitarianism*. Because sanction utilitarianism is a species of indirect utilitarianism, it is inconsistent with act utilitarianism.

While I am indebted to Lyons' analysis of Mill's theory of duty in Chapter V of *Utilitarianism*, I disagree with his interpretation on one point and dispute the significance he attaches to sanction utilitarianism.

It is worth noticing that Lyons' interpretation of Mill's theory of duty is *doubly* indirect. It is indirect, as we have seen, because it makes an action's rightness or wrongness a function not of its utility but rather of the utility of others responding to it in certain ways. But on Lyons' reading Mill's theory is indirect in another way as well.

> To call an act wrong is to imply that guilt feelings, and perhaps other sanctions, would be warranted against it. But sanctions assume coercive rules. *To show an act wrong, therefore, is to show that a coercive rule against it would be justified.*[20]

Lyons believes that for Mill an action's deontic status turns, not on its utility, but on the utility of sanctioning responses, not to it, but to actions of

---

20. Lyons, "Mill's Theory of Morality," p. 55.

that type or class. This second layer of indirection is the appeal to rules, shared with rule utilitarianism. However, I see no justification for this second layer of indirection. In particular, I see no evidence that Mill wants to introduce rules or principles into his formulation of the utilitarian standard. Of course, as we have seen, he is a firm believer in the need for secondary principles in ordinary moral deliberations. But this is a claim about how we are likely to best satisfy the utilitarian standard, not a claim about the formulation of the standard itself. When Mill defines wrong action in terms of sanctions, he says that an act is wrong if *it* ought to be sanctioned in some way, not if it's enjoined by a principle, violations of which ought to be sanctioned. If so, sanction utilitarianism is only singly indirect, which means that it is even further removed from the sort of indirection embodied in rule utilitarianism. Sanction utilitarianism is really a distinct form of indirect utilitarianism.

Lyons concludes from the fact that Mill's indirect account of duty is not act-utilitarian that Mill is not an act utilitarian. But whereas I agree with the premise, the conclusion does not follow. The fact that Mill sometimes makes claims that do not fit with act utilitarianism does not mean that he does not elsewhere make commitments to act utilitarianism. Lyons reminds us that Mill sometimes identifies utilitarianism as a theory of ends.[21]

> Questions about ends are, in other words, questions about what things are desirable. The utilitarian doctrine is, that happiness is desirable, and the only thing desirable as an end; all other things being desirable only as a means to that end [*U* IV 2].

It is true that utilitarianism is in part a theory of ends or the good; it insists that the good is happiness or well-being. But it is also a theory of the right, as both direct and indirect forms of utilitarianism recognize. The problem is simply that Mill is attracted to different utilitarian conceptions of right action. While the account of duty in Chapter V represents an indirect form of utilitarianism, Mill elsewhere—and on several occasions—assigns utility a direct role in the determination of right and wrong action. We examined these above (§22). The natural conclusion is that Mill does not have a consistent theory of duty. The introduction of indirect utilitarian ideas in Chapter V of *Utilitarianism* into an account

---

21. *Rights, Welfare, and Mill's Moral Theory*, pp. 50, 59–60.

of utilitarianism that is otherwise act utilitarian reveals a fundamental tension in Mill's conception of duty.[22]

26. An apparent virtue of sanction utilitarianism

Given Mill's ambivalence between direct and indirect utilitarianism, it is natural to inquire whether one view is more plausible than the other. Some of Mill's claims in Chapter V suggest a possible advantage that sanction utilitarianism might have. In articulating sanction utilitarianism, Mill claims that it allows him to distinguish duty and expediency and claim that not all inexpedient acts are wrong. Inexpedient acts are only wrong, according to sanction utilitarianism, when it is good or optimal to sanction them. This suggests that sanction utilitarianism may be preferable to act utilitarianism, because it has a more plausible account of the relation among different deontic categories.

Consider some of the implications of act utilitarianism. Act utilitarianism implies that I do wrong every time I fail to do the very best action, even when the suboptimal act that I perform is very good indeed. That may seem harsh and overly demanding. To see why, consider a familiar fourfold deontic distinction among acts:

(a) wrong or impermissible,
(b) permissible,
(c) obligatory, and
(d) supererogatory.

---

22. Daniel Jacobson, "J.S. Mill and the Diversity of Utilitarianism," *Philosophers' Imprint* 3 (2003): 1–35, defends an *ecumenical* reading according to which Mill is not endorsing any one utilitarian conception of duty but is instead putting forward and popularizing the essentials of utilitarianism, common to diverse conceptions. On Jacobson's view, utilitarian essentials consist in a naturalistic approach to moral theory that is teleological in the broad sense that it makes moral assessment turn in some way on the value of the objects of assessment. Mill's main aspiration, on this reading, is to describe and defend a family of moral theories that can usefully be contrasted with the rational intuitionism of Whewell and others. Jacobson's evidence for this deflationary reading of Mill's ambitions strikes me as not decisive. Moreover, there is a serious worry about this ecumenical interpretation. Mill spends much of *Utilitarianism* responding to various objections to utilitarianism by appealing to resources available to various sectarian conceptions. Even if each objection admits of a sectarian response, it is not clear that these various responses are consistent and that there is some single theory or family of theories that has an adequate response to all critics.

According to commonsense thinking, the obligatory is just a proper part of the permissible. All permissible acts are not wrong, but many permissible acts are not obligatory either. Common sense also recognizes a class of supererogatory acts that are above and beyond the call of duty, which would presumably include many good but suboptimal acts. After all, Mother Teresa's succor for the poor of Calcutta may not have always been optimal, but her actions were very good indeed and supererogatory.

By contrast, act utilitarianism seems unable to account for this fourfold distinction. Because it makes the optimal obligatory and the suboptimal wrong, it appears to expand the domain of the impermissible. The act utilitarian must treat all suboptimal acts, even very good ones, as wrong. Act utilitarianism also collapses the distinction between the permissible and the obligatory, treating all non-obligatory acts as impermissible. Moreover, act utilitarianism recognizes no supererogatory acts. If the optimal is already one's duty, there appears to be no room for the supererogatory. When Mother Teresa's aid was optimal, it was just her duty; when it was slightly suboptimal, it was wrong. These seem like problematic implications of act utilitarianism.

By contrast, sanction utilitarianism does not appear to have these problems. It offers a distinct account of each category.[23]

(a) Wrong or impermissible acts are those whose performance it is optimal to blame.

(b) Permissible acts are those whose performance it is not optimal to blame.

(c) Obligatory acts are those whose omission it is optimal to blame.

(d) Supererogatory acts are permissible acts that are especially expedient.

In this way, sanction utilitarianism appears to respect this common fourfold distinction and, in particular, to make room for the supererogatory.

In "Auguste Comte and Positivism" (1865) Mill discusses the need to recognize categories of the permissible but not obligatory and the supererogatory—"There is a standard of altruism to which all should be required to come up, and a degree beyond which it is not obligatory, but meritori-

---

23. Recall that Mill's sanction utilitarianism is agnostic about whether the utilitarian standard for applying sanctions should be optimality or something less, such as net benefit. For ease of comparison with act utilitarianism, I focus on the optimality criterion. But similar claims would apply, *mutatis mutandis*, for the comparison with the net benefit criterion.

ous" (*CW* X 337). He does not say or imply that this is a problem for act utilitarianism or an argument for linking duty with sanctions. Nonetheless, it might seem that only sanction utilitarianism can accept these claims.

Is this a genuine advantage of sanction utilitarianism? I think not. The direct utilitarian can and should distinguish between the moral assessment of an act and the moral assessment of the act of praising or blaming that act. Each should be assessed, the direct utilitarian claims, by the utility of doing so. But then it is possible for there to be wrongdoing (a suboptimal act) that is blameless or even praiseworthy. But then the direct utilitarian can appeal to the same distinctions among praiseworthiness and blameworthiness that the sanction utilitarian appeals to, while allowing that these distinctions line up differently with her own deontic distinctions.

(a) *Acts whose performance it is optimal to blame.* This class would typically include only those suboptimal (wrong) acts that rise to the level of meriting blame.

(b) *Acts whose performance it is not optimal to blame.* This class will include optimal (obligatory) acts and some, but not all, suboptimal (wrong) acts that do not merit any kind of blame.

(c) *Acts whose omission it is optimal to blame.* This class would typically include only those acts whose nonperformance was so suboptimal (wrong) as to merit blame.

(d) *Acts whose performance it is not optimal to blame and whose performance is optimal to praise.* This class will include especially expedient acts, including the optimal (obligatory) act and several somewhat suboptimal (wrong) acts.

Because this fourfold distinction is made, not directly in terms of deontic status, but in terms of patterns of praise and blame, it represents a kind of *pragmatic* reconstruction of the commonsense classification.

Notice also that in distinguishing between the moral assessment of the act and the moral assessment of praise and blame, and in providing a pragmatic account of the supererogatory, the direct utilitarian introduces a resource to address worries about the demandingness of utilitarianism. As we noted earlier (§§6, 10), because the act utilitarian identifies one's duty with doing what's optimal, it can seem very demanding. In particular, it appears to demand that everyone divert their resources to the needy until the point at which the costs of beneficence to them equal the magnitude of the benefits that they confer on others (call this the point of marginal disutility). For even moderately affluent people, this would seem to require very significant changes in lifestyle and patterns of concern for oneself and one's close associates. While it may not seem too much to ask for greater levels of aid and better (more widespread) compliance with these demands, the requirement to give until the point of marginal disutility might seem unusually burdensome. We noted that by distinguishing between the assessment of an agent's actions and the assessment of our responses to her actions, the direct utilitarian could make room for the possibility of actions that were suboptimal and, hence, wrong, but nonetheless not optimal to blame. We are now in a better position to appreciate the significance of this strategy. The act utilitarian should recognize the category of *blameless wrongdoing*. Indeed, some forms of wrongdoing will be not only blameless but even *praiseworthy*. One reaction to heavy moral demands is to reject them outright. A different reaction is to be prepared to excuse failures to meet these demands, especially the most burdensome. Whereas commonsense morality and sanction utilitarianism pursue the first strategy, direct utilitarianism and, hence, act utilitarianism pursue the second. It's not immediately obvious that the first strategy is superior to the second.

While there is no a priori guarantee that the direct utilitarian fourfold classification in terms of praise and blame will track perfectly the commonsense classification of deontic status, there is some reason to think that it will sort options in roughly the same ways and to wonder whether the direct utilitarian's classification might not provide reflectively acceptable guidance and correction where the commonsense classification provides uncertain or questionable guidance. In any case, it is hard to see how sanction utilitarianism could be preferable to act utilitarianism here, because they offer the same classification in terms of praise and blame. The only difference is that whereas sanction utilitarianism ties rightness and wrongness to praise and blame, act utilitarianism does not. But this looks more like a difference in moral book-keeping systems than a substantive moral difference.

27. The vices of sanction utilitarianism

However, sanction utilitarianism appears to have disadvantages that act utilitarianism does not. One such cost is that sanction utilitarianism appears to provide the *wrong sort of reason* for thinking an action wrong. Sanction utilitarianism involves a response-dependent conception of duty, claiming that wrong actions are those that merit a certain response, in particular, blame or sanction of some kind. It makes the wrongness of an act depend upon the appropriateness of sanctioning it. But this inverts what many would regard as the usual dependency between wrongness and sanction.[24] Many think that sanctions are appropriate for wrong acts because they are wrong. This requires grounding their wrongness in some independent account; it is not the suitability for sanction that makes an act wrong. Perhaps one ought to sanction wrong acts, but it doesn't seem that they are wrong because one ought to sanction them.

Retributivism is the view that sanction and punishment should be consequential on, and proportional to, the wrongness of the conduct in question. But then the retributivist owes us some independent account of what makes actions wrong. Usually, this debt is paid in deontological currency. So the retributivist can explain how wrongness is prior to sanction and punishment. By contrast, direct utilitarianism must deny that an act's wrongness is either a necessary or a sufficient condition for sanction or punishment, because whether an act should be sanctioned depends on the consequences, not of the original action, but of the act of sanctioning it. Though they disagree about whether sanction and punishment are always and only consequential on wrongness, the direct utilitarian and the retributivist agree on the need for an account of an action's wrongness that is independent of its suitability for sanction. It is only sanction utilitarianism that denies the independence of these two concepts.

Another disadvantage of sanction utilitarianism is its *hybrid* structure. Sanction utilitarianism is impurely indirect. For while it provides an indirect utilitarian theory of duty, the account it provides of when sanctions should be applied to conduct is direct—it depends upon the consequences of applying sanctions. This isn't just the worry that sanction utilitarianism is a *mixed* theory—combining direct and indirect elements in an unmotivated or ad hoc way—though that would be cause for concern too. There is a deeper worry afoot. Sanction utilitarianism provides an indirect utilitarian account of the conditions under which an action—any action—is right or wrong. This general indirect criterion is that any action is wrong to which

---

24. For a similar diagnosis, see David Lyons, "Human Rights and the General Welfare," reprinted in *Rights*, ed. D. Lyons (Belmont, CA: Wadsworth, 1979), p. 181. This is, I think, a special case of a general concern about response-dependent analyses in many domains that invert the explanatory priority between property and response.

one ought to attach sanctions. But imposing sanctions is itself a kind of action, and we can ask whether the imposition of a particular sanction would be right or wrong. The general criterion implies that we should answer this question about the rightness of applying sanctions in sanction-utilitarian terms too, namely, by asking whether it would be right to sanction the failure to apply sanctions. This introduces a second-order sanction, about whose rightness we can now ask. We seem to be off on an infinite regress of sanctions. This is a cause for concern, inasmuch as this infinite regress looks vicious, because there appears to be no determinate fact to ground an answer to the original question about whether it is right to apply the first-order sanction. But matters are worse for sanction utilitarianism inasmuch as it avoids the regress by giving a direct utilitarian answer to the question of whether it is right to apply sanctions that is inconsistent with the general criterion. In effect, sanction utilitarianism combines indirect and direct elements.

1. Any act is right if and only if and because it is optimal to apply sanctions to its omission (the indirect claim).
2. Applying sanctions is right if and only if and because doing so is optimal (the direct claim).

But these two claims are inconsistent, which renders sanction utilitarianism internally inconsistent.[25]

28. The Art of Life

These are serious worries about sanction utilitarianism, which would appear to make act utilitarianism more attractive. Before reaching this conclusion, it is worth looking at Mill's remarks on the Art of Life, which some commentators take to support sanction utilitarianism, rather than act utilitarianism. In his discussion of the Art of Life in *A System of Logic*, Mill divides practical reason into three spheres—morality, prudence, and aesthetics—

---

25. As I indicated above, Lyons does not treat Mill's account of when to apply sanctions as a direct utilitarian account; it is indirect inasmuch as it adverts to optimal rules. But Mill's form of sanction utilitarianism faces a parallel structural dilemma even on Lyons' view—Mill can avoid the vicious regress only by introducing a direct account of the duty to apply sanctions that is inconsistent with the doubly indirect general account of duty that is provided by sanction utilitarianism.

each of which is to be governed by teleological principles of expediency (VI.xii.6).[26] What distinguishes these spheres then must be something about their domains. In "Utilitarianism without Consequentialism: The Case of John Stuart Mill," Daniel Jacobson has argued for a particular interpretation of the domain of morality that he claims is inconsistent with act utilitarianism and fits with sanction utilitarianism.[27] Jacobson appeals to a passage in *On Liberty* in which Mill claims that actions that cease to be self-regarding and harm the interests of others become "amenable to moral disapprobation in the proper sense of the term" (IV 10). Jacobson concludes that Mill here demarcates the domains of the moral and the prudential: the domain of the moral is limited to actions that affect—in particular, harm—others, whereas the domain of prudence concerns self-regarding actions. This claim about the restricted domain of the moral is incompatible with the act utilitarian claim that any action is morally assessable by the value of its consequences, precisely because the latter claim contains no restriction on the domain of morality. Act utilitarianism applies to any action whatsoever, including purely self-regarding acts.[28]

Mill's claims about the Art of Life raise interesting questions, which I cannot address adequately here. But even if we were to accept Jacobson's interpretation of the Art of Life, this would not support the sanction utilitarianism of Chapter V or show that Mill is not elsewhere committed to act utilitarianism.

First, notice that the Art of Life seems to counsel maximization within the spheres of morality and prudence, whereas sanction utilitarianism does not. So even if the Art of Life were inconsistent with act utilitarianism, it would not be consistent with sanction utilitarianism. The Art of Life, on this reading, would be yet a third distinct commitment.

Second, sanction utilitarianism is also inconsistent with the claims about morality's limited domain within the Art of Life. For sanction utilitarianism also has universal scope, implying that any action is morally wrong just in case some kind of sanction, whether external or internal, is appropriate on utilitarian grounds. But there is every reason to believe that it will often be

---

26. For further discussion of the significance of Mill's claims about the Art of Life, see Alan Ryan, "John Stuart Mill's Art of Living," *The Listener* 21 (1965): 620–22, and *John Stuart Mill and the Art of Life*, ed. Eggleston, Miller, and Weinstein.
27. Daniel Jacobson, "Utilitarianism without Consequentialism: The Case of John Stuart Mill," *Philosophical Review* 117 (2008): 159–91.
28. Cf. D.G. Brown, "Mill on Liberty and Morality," *Philosophical Review* 81 (1972): 133–58.

useful or even optimal to sanction imprudence. Remember that an act is wrong provided any kind of sanction, whether external or internal, is appropriate. So actions are wrong even if the only sanctions that would be appropriate are those of self-reproach. But it is very plausible that it would often, perhaps typically, be beneficial or optimal for an agent to experience self-reproach in connection with gross imprudence. In such cases, gross imprudence would be morally wrong by sanction utilitarian lights. But then sanction utilitarians should deny that matters of prudence (and imprudence) lie outside of morality.

Third, this interpretation about the Art of Life makes claims about the restricted domain of morality that are contradicted by those passages in *Utilitarianism*, which we have already examined, that endorse act utilitarianism and its implications about the unrestricted domain of morality, notably the Proportionality Doctrine's claim "that actions are right in proportion as they tend to promote happiness; wrong as they tend to produce the reverse of happiness" (II 2). Here, the utilitarian theory of duty applies to any action and so makes no restrictions on the domain of morality.

So Mill's claims in the Art of Life, interpreted as Jacobson recommends, are consistent with neither act nor sanction utilitarianism and introduce further inconsistency into Mill's theory of duty. My own suspicion is that this is reason to look for another interpretation of the Art of Life. Perhaps Mill's compartmentalization of practical reason into three separate spheres is not meant to signal deep and principled divisions within practical reason that Mill endorses, but only something about the ways the three domains are conventionally distinguished. Mill says that discussing the foundations of morality "would be out of place" in *A System of Logic* (VI.xii.7). When he does present his theory in *Utilitarianism* he presents a theory (actually, theories) that has (have) universal scope. Whether or not we can find a better interpretation of Mill's Art of Life, I think that doctrine should not fundamentally alter our previous assessment of the comparative advantages of act and sanction utilitarianism.

29. Considered, but not consistent, act utilitarianism

So our worries about sanction utilitarianism make act utilitarianism more attractive. They make the introduction of sanction utilitarianism in Chapter

V of *Utilitarianism* an unwelcome development, both because this introduces inconsistency into Mill's conception of duty but also because sanction utilitarianism is, despite its apparent appeal, problematic. In the face of these worries about sanction utilitarianism, it may be tempting to try to reconcile Mill's apparent commitment to sanction utilitarianism with his otherwise largely consistent commitment to act utilitarianism. One such interpretive strategy involves noticing that in the crucial passage introducing sanction utilitarianism Mill says that "we do not *call anything wrong* unless we mean to imply that a person ought to be punished in some way or other for doing it—if not by law, by the opinion of his fellow creatures; if not by opinion, by the reproaches of his own conscience" (V 14, emphasis added). One might argue that Mill is giving an account of when we *call* something wrong, not when it *is* wrong. Whereas being wrong is, as the act utilitarian claims, a matter of being suboptimal, we only bother to call something wrong if it rises to the level that it would be good or optimal to sanction. This is a kind of *pragmatic* or *deflationary* reading of sanction utilitarianism. Considered in itself, this act utilitarian reading of the significance of sanction utilitarianism is reasonably plausible. The problem is that the surrounding text makes it difficult to sustain this reading as an interpretive claim without strain. For in the previous sentence Mill says that "the idea of penal sanction...enters...into any kind of wrong," and in the sentence immediately following the statement of sanction utilitarianism he says "that this seems to be the real turning point of the distinction between morality and simple expediency." Here, Mill seems to be speaking in his own voice, not merely analyzing what people say is wrong, and insisting on distinguishing one's duty from what is or would be optimal.[29]

Convenient as it might be, we cannot plausibly read Mill's sanction utilitarian claims in Chapter V in act utilitarian terms. Because Mill is otherwise attracted to act utilitarianism, we cannot, I think, avoid seeing Mill's theory of duty as an inconsistent mix of direct and indirect utilitarian claims. But to say that Mill is not consistent is not to say that he does not have a considered

---

29. Some confirmation for this can be found in an 1859 letter to William George Ward in which Mill expresses related ideas. He writes, in part:

> I...pass to the case of those who have a true moral feeling, that is, a feeling of pain in the fact of violating a certain rule, quite independently of any expected consequences to themselves. It appears to me that to them the word *ought* means, that if they act otherwise, they shall be punished by this internal & perfectly disinterested feeling [*CW* XV 649].

I am indebted to Miller, *J.S. Mill*, p. 87, for drawing this letter to my attention.

view. As we have seen, Mill's commitment to direct utilitarian claims is much more consistent than his commitment to indirect claims of the sort contained in sanction utilitarianism. Mill makes regular commitments to direct utilitarianism throughout Chapter II and even in Chapter V, which later introduces indirect elements. Indeed, sanction utilitarianism is itself an inconsistent hybrid of direct and indirect utilitarian claims. Direct utilitarianism is also at work in *A System of Logic*, and his essays and correspondence (as we have seen). In these ways, direct utilitarianism arguably has deeper textual roots than indirect utilitarianism. Moreover, we saw that sanction utilitarianism's apparent advantages over act utilitarianism are spurious and that it has significant theoretical problems that act utilitarianism does not. Whatever the ultimate merits of act utilitarianism, it seems a more coherent and plausible form of utilitarianism than sanction utilitarianism. These textual and systematic considerations are reasons to read Mill's considered conception of duty as an act utilitarian one.

5

The justification of utilitarianism

We have now examined Mill's account of the content of utilitarianism in some detail, reconstructing his conceptions of happiness and duty. We have also explored his understanding of the demands of utilitarianism and the issues they raise about the psychological resonance and authority of those demands. Clarifying these matters is important, but it does not tell us why we should believe utilitarianism. What is the justification of utilitarianism? Mill insists that we cannot profitably investigate the justification of utilitarianism until we understand the content of that doctrine (*U* I 6). Presumably, his idea is that you cannot sensibly ask why you should assent to a proposition before you know what that proposition is, which is why his discussion of the proof of utilitarianism does not come until Chapter IV. But now that we have examined the content of utilitarianism in some depth, we can turn to its justification. Mill discusses this topic explicitly in two main places within *Utilitarianism*. Chapter I discusses some significant methodological preliminaries, and Chapter IV discusses the proof. After examining Mill's claims in these two chapters, we will explore a different justificatory strategy that underlies Mill's claims about the relation between the utilitarian first principle and the precepts of commonsense morality.

30. Methodological naturalism

In Chapter I, Mill makes several methodological remarks about the proof or justification of which utilitarianism admits. He begins by lamenting what he sees as the limited progress in moral theory concerning first principles

(I 1). This leads him to suggest an apparent methodological symmetry between science and ethics.

> The truths which are ultimately accepted as the first principles of a science, are really the last results of metaphysical analysis, practised on the elementary notions with which the science is conversant; and their relation to the science is not that of foundations to an edifice, but of roots to a tree, which may perform their office equally well though they be never dug down to and exposed to light. But though in science the particular truths precede the general theory, the contrary might be expected to be the case with a practical art, such as morals or legislation. All action is for the sake of some end, and rules of action, it seems natural to suppose, must take their whole character and colour from the end to which they are subservient. When we engage in a pursuit, a clear and precise conception of what we are pursuing would seem to be the first thing we need, instead of the last we are to look forward to. A test of right and wrong must be the means, one would think, of ascertaining what is right or wrong, and not a consequence of having already ascertained it [I 2].

In science, Mill says, particular truths come before theory. It is not entirely clear if this is just a claim about the normal *chronological order of discovery* or whether it is supposed to reflect a fact about the *structure of justification* being bottom-up. By contrast, Mill suggests, it might seem as if the correct method in ethics would put theory before particular judgments or truths. As a claim about the order of discovery in ethics, this claim seems especially implausible. Ordinary people do not begin with first principles and proceed to formulate judgments about particular cases. Rather, moral reflection begins with particulars. We begin with a conviction about what ought to be done in a particular case or perhaps with moral perplexity about what to do in a particular case. Reflecting on perplexities about particular cases or perhaps trying to reconcile apparently different judgments about apparently similar cases or perhaps responding to someone's challenge to our apparently settled convictions about a case can lead to theorizing, as we attempt to subsume and explain disparate particular claims under more general morally relevant factors. It is not clear if Mill endorses this methodological contrast. His language in the passage only insists on an expected or apparent contrast. But if he does endorse the contrast, then he must understand the direction of ethical method as a claim about the structure of justification, rather than the order of discovery. Perhaps he is saying that justification in ethics must be top-down.

But this might be surprising given Mill's own "inductive" or naturalistic approach to matters of justification (I 3). The term "naturalism" can mean different things in different philosophical contexts. In this context, Mill evidently understands naturalism as a methodological and epistemological doctrine or perspective. Naturalism involves a bottom-up approach in which theoretical claims are justified by appeal to particulars, in particular, by appeal to "observation and experience" (I 3). The naturalist, Mill thinks, eschews purely top-down reasoning. In science, laws and principles are justified by appeal to their ability to subsume and explain our observations and perceptions. Another aspect of Mill's naturalism is fallibilism. Any given belief about the world might be mistaken, and correction must come from observation and experience (*A System of Logic* III.xxi.2). In ethics, the naturalist insistence on bottom-up justification would presumably include justifying moral principles by appeal to their ability to subsume and explain our observation and experience, where this might include our particular moral judgments and emotions. And the naturalist insistence on fallibilism leads to skepticism about treating any moral beliefs as self-evident or beyond the need for justification. If so, then the naturalist about ethics should be skeptical of the apparent methodological contrast Mill mentions at the outset.

This helps explain the contrast Mill draws between his own ethical naturalism and the intuitionist school of ethics. He treats Whewell as the chief representative of intuitionism and criticizes his a priori methods in ethics of deriving particular moral truths from more general moral beliefs that are treated as self-evident ("Whewell on Moral Philosophy"). He dismisses any version of intuitionism that would lay claim to a faculty of moral perception that could discern what is right or wrong in particular cases.

It will be helpful to distinguish three different levels of generality in our moral claims. At the most particular level, our judgments can concern particular actions or action tokens. For instance, we might judge this particular act of lying, in these specific circumstances, to be wrong. We often try to subsume and explain such particular truths under more general claims about morally relevant factors that operate at the level of types or classes of actions. For instance, we might judge lying to be *pro tanto* wrong. Such claims could be thought of as mid-level moral principles or rules. Finally, we might try to subsume and explain disparate morally relevant factors or mid-level principles under some single or small number of very general principles. If these principles cannot be subsumed and explained in terms of other, more basic principles, then these principles are ultimate or first principles. Utilitarianism is one such putative first principle, because it attempts to ground all mid-level principles in utility.

We might characterize Mill's discussion of intuitionism in terms of distinctions that Sidgwick would later draw within intuitionism. Sidgwick distinguishes perceptual, dogmatic, and philosophical intuitionism. Perceptual intuitionism locates intuitions at the level of action tokens, dogmatic intuitionism locates intuitions at the intermediate level of action types or mid-level principles, and philosophical intuitionism locates intuitions at the level of first principles (*Method* 97–102). Sidgwick himself rejects both perceptual and dogmatic intuitionism but ultimately defends philosophical intuitionism. Mill dismisses perceptual intuitionism and focuses on, but ultimately rejects, dogmatic intuitionism.[1]

According to Mill, intuitionists and naturalists need not, and typically do not, disagree about the content of mid-level principles or moral factors. First and foremost, they disagree about the nature of moral knowledge. It is characteristic of intuitionism to claim that moral principles are knowable a priori, or independently of experience, and can be seen to be self-evident. By contrast, the naturalist claims that moral knowledge, like other knowledge, must be based on observation and experience (*U* I 3). As we will see, this sort of observation and experience can include moral observation and moral lessons from history. So Mill is making two distinguishable claims here. One is that moral beliefs are not self-evident but must be justified discursively or dialectically in terms of other beliefs we hold, including other moral beliefs. The other is the idea that at least some of this evidence will be a posteriori evidence derived from experience and observation.

With these contrasts between intuitionism and naturalism in mind, we might identify three distinct claims that seem to be part of Mill's ethical naturalism.

1. *Fallibilism*: Moral beliefs are fallible and so revisable in principle.
2. *Dialectical Method*: Moral beliefs are not self-evident; they are to be justified by their fit with other beliefs we hold, including our beliefs about particulars.
3. *Empiricism*: Moral knowledge is a posteriori insofar as the justification of moral beliefs depends on experience and observation.

Though one might embrace fallibilism and dialectical methods without a commitment to a posteriori justification, Mill's naturalism embraces all three.

---

1. Mill does not discuss philosophical intuitionism explicitly. However, I will argue that his naturalism gives him good reason to reject philosophical intuitionism as well (§34).

Moreover, there is another difference between intuitionists and naturalists inasmuch as intuitionists tend not to ascend higher than mid-level principles or, if they do, tend to recognize a plurality of ultimate principles. By contrast, Mill thinks that the application of naturalist methods to ethics should lead us to the adoption of a single first principle or, if we must recognize a plurality of first principles, then to a master-rule for adjudicating conflicts among these first principles (I 3). Exactly why we should expect to find a single first principle or a master-rule among first principles, in advance of the evidence, is a question Mill does not address directly.

This second set of methodological remarks already raises a question about the first set. It is essential to the inductive or naturalistic scientific method that theory be tested against observation and experience. That means that the structure of justification should include bottom-up support of theory on the basis of our beliefs about particulars. But Mill wants to apply this same naturalistic method to ethics. This suggests that we should be able to provide support to moral principles based on whether their implications for particular cases fit what we observe and believe about those cases. But this is just the sort of bottom-up strategy in ethics that Mill seemed to question earlier. Perhaps it is significant that Mill explicitly treats the methodological asymmetry between science and ethics as apparent only, and then goes on to embrace a form of naturalism that would cast doubt on this supposed asymmetry. Whether this is a reasonable conclusion to draw depends on the nature of the claims Mill makes in support of utilitarianism and so should be re-evaluated after we have examined those claims (§34).

Echoing Bentham, Mill insists that first principles "are not amenable of direct proof" (I 5). Proof is a form of justification familiar from axiomatic systems. Mill may think of first principles, as Bentham and James Mill do, as axioms. With an axiomatic system, other things admit of proof by derivation from axioms, but the axioms themselves do not admit of proof within the axiomatic system. If utilitarianism is a first principle, then it cannot be proved in this sense. Does that mean that first principles, such as utilitarianism, cannot be justified? That is not the conclusion Mill draws.

> If, then, it is asserted that there is a comprehensive formula, including all things which are in themselves good, and that whatever else is good, is not so as an end, but as a means, the formula may be accepted or rejected, but is not a subject of what is commonly understood by proof. We are not, however, to infer that its acceptance or rejection must depend on blind impulse, or arbitrary choice. There is a larger meaning of the word proof, in which

this question is as amenable to it as any other of the disputed questions of philosophy. The subject is within the cognisance of the rational faculty; and neither does that faculty deal with it solely in the way of intuition. Considerations may be presented capable of determining the intellect either to give or withhold its assent to the doctrine; and this is equivalent to proof [I 5].

In this discussion of methodological preliminaries, Mill does not say what form this alternative method of justification should take. An obvious place to look to fill this gap is Chapter IV's discussion "of what sort of proof the principle of utility is susceptible" (the title of that chapter).

31. A traditional reading of the proof

Mill claims that the utilitarian must claim that happiness is the one and only thing desirable in itself (IV 2). He claims that the only proof of desirability is desire and proceeds to argue that happiness is the one and only thing desired. He argues that a person does desire his own happiness for its own sake and that, therefore, happiness as such is desired by and desirable for its own sake for humanity as a whole ("the aggregate of all persons") (IV 3). He then turns to defending the claim that happiness is the only thing desirable in itself, by arguing that apparent counterexamples, such as desires for virtue for its own sake, are not inconsistent with his claim (IV 5–8).

Mill's proof is widely regarded as flawed in multiple ways. To appreciate the objections, we need to reconstruct the steps in this argument more carefully. One traditional reconstruction might look something like this.

1. Utilitarianism is true if and only if happiness is the one and only thing desirable for its own sake (and not for the sake of something else).
2. The only proof of desirability is desire.
3. Each person desires his own happiness for its own sake (and not for the sake of something else).
4. Hence, happiness, as such, is desired for its own sake (and not for the sake of something else) from the point of view of humanity (= the aggregate of persons).
5. Hence, happiness, as such, is desirable for its own sake (and not for the sake of something else).

6. Happiness is the only thing desired for its own sake (and not for the sake of something else). Other things—such as virtue, health, music, money, and power—can come to be desired for their own sakes, but then they are desired as parts of happiness.
7. Hence, happiness is the only thing desirable for its own sake (and not for the sake of something else).
8. Hence, utilitarianism is true.

Something like this reconstruction is a very natural and common way of understanding the structure of Mill's proof.

32. Spot the howler

The proof has, at least in some quarters, threatened Mill's reputation as a careful philosopher. It is commonly thought to be riddled with major mistakes—mistakes of inference and implausible assumptions. Here is a partial list of concerns about Mill's argument, as traditionally conceived.

(A) (1) is plausible only if "desirable" means *worthy* of being desired, not if it means *capable* of being desired. But (2) is most plausible if "desirable" means capable of being desired (see (C) below). But then there is a real worry that the argument trades on a tacit equivocation between these two different senses of "desirable" and that the argument is, as a result, invalid.

(B) Even so, (1) is false. Even if happiness were the one and only thing desirable for its own sake, this would establish only a claim about the good or ends. It is not a claim about duty or right action. Utilitarianism not only claims that the good is happiness but goes on to define the right in terms of promoting the good. The second claim does not follow from the first. Mill appears to recognize this insofar as he at least tacitly distinguishes the two claims (IV 9; cf. IV 2). However, he goes on to infer the second claim from the first without any independent argument.

> [I]f human nature is so constituted as to desire nothing that is not either a part of happiness or a means of happiness, we can have no other proof, and we require no other, that these are the only things desirable. If so, happiness is the sole end of human action, and the promotion of it the test by which to judge

all human conduct; from whence it necessarily follows that it must be the criterion of morality, since a part is included in the whole [IV 9].

(C) For the argument to be valid, "desirability" in premise (2) must mean worthy of being desired (as it does in premise (1)). But then (2) is false. Desire may not be the only proof of desirability, especially if there are other theoretical constraints on desirability, such as the assumption that the human good should be appropriate for the sort of beings that humans are. Such considerations could give us theoretical evidence of what is desirable. Moreover, desire is not proof of desirability. People can and do have mistaken desires for what is good. Indeed, if Mill is either a hedonist or a perfectionist he must think that people can and do have desires that fail to track their own good or happiness. Even if he is a desire-satisfaction theorist, he must recognize that people's actual desires can fail to track the preferences of competent judges.

(D) It is not clear that (3) is true. It seems as if masochists might fail to desire their own happiness for its own sake. Of course, it is hard to know what to say about masochists: Do they seek their own detriment, are they indifferent to their own happiness, or do they have a very unusual conception of their own happiness? But the fact that this seems an open question means that (3) is not obviously true. Moreover, genuinely selfless altruists would also seem to pose a problem for (3).

(E) (4) may be incoherent and certainly does not follow from (3). It's not clear that aggregates of persons have desires. Perhaps under special circumstances groups of people might form a corporate agent or person. But aggregates of persons, as such, are not persons and do not have desires. Even if they did, it is doubtful that one could infer what the aggregate desires from facts about what its members desire. That would involve a compositional fallacy.

(F) (5) is presumably equivalent to the claim that happiness is good. But is it good simpliciter or good for the aggregate? The analogy between individuals and groups would suggest that happiness should be a good for the aggregate. But presumably the intended conclusion requires that happiness be good simpliciter.

(G) It is not clear how to understand (6). One would think that the aim is to make claims that parallel (4) and (5). But then (6) needs to be understood as making another claim about aggregate psychology. And this raises some of the previous questions about aggregate psychology (see (E) above). However, much of the discussion in IV 5–8 seems to be about individual psychology. Mill seems to be saying that insofar as individuals do have intrinsic desires for things other than their own happiness, the objects of their intrinsic desires are desired as parts of their own happiness. Perhaps Mill thinks that he can infer a claim about aggregate psychology—that the general happiness is the only thing desired by the aggregate for its own sake—from this claim about individual psychology—that each desires only his own happiness for its own sake. This inference would, of course, give rise to the same sort of worries we raised about the inference from (3)–(4). In particular, we might doubt that aggregates of persons have any aims, much less ultimate aims. And even if we conceded that they did, it is not clear that we could infer facts about the desires of aggregates from facts about the desires of their members. That, we said, would seem to involve a compositional fallacy.

(H) Even if we accepted this defense of (5) and (7), this would only establish that happiness as such was the only thing desirable or good for the aggregate. It looks like we could have parallel claims about the agent's own happiness being the only thing desirable or good for the individual. But this might seem to imply that while the aggregate should pursue or promote the general happiness, individuals should pursue or promote their own happiness. While this would be a defense of something like utilitarianism for state actors, it would be a defense of ethical egoism, not utilitarianism, for individual agents. That would not be a defense of utilitarianism, as Mill explains that doctrine elsewhere.

33. An alternative reading of the proof

These are all serious worries about Mill's proof, as traditionally conceived. These objections seem so serious and so obvious that they should make us reluctant to interpret Mill as advancing this conception of the proof. Can we construct a more plausible interpretation of his proof?[2]

---

2. My alternative reading of the proof is not without precedent. There are some broad similarities between my preferred reading of the proof and interesting observations by Everett Hall, "The 'Proof' of Utility in Bentham and Mill," *Ethics* 60 (1949): 1–18, and by Crisp, *Mill on Utilitarianism*, pp. 67–88.

Indeed, a serious problem with this sort of traditional reading of the proof is that it represents Mill as apparently trying to derive utilitarianism from a prior commitment to psychological egoism. One problem with this reading is that the attempted derivation is blatantly fallacious. But in addition to these problems with the merits of the derivation there is the further problem that such a derivation would be a proof of the utilitarian first principle from a prior principle, which is precisely what Mill eschews in his methodological preliminaries (I 5). So our interpretation should not aim at proof in this strict sense.

For one thing, Mill need not confuse two different senses of desirability. His focus is what is desirable in the sense of being worthy of being desired or valuable. He does claim that desire is our only evidence of desirability (IV 3), but this is not confused. It is perhaps a mistake to say that desire is our only evidence of desirability if there are other forms of evidence, and I think Mill does recognize evidence in the form of theoretical constraints on the good, such as the constraint that the good should reflect what makes us progressive beings. But the more important issue is whether desire is evidence of desirability. In saying this, Mill need not presuppose that desire infallibly tracks desirability, which he could apparently maintain only by supposing that desiring something confers value on (obtaining) it. He can be a perfectionist, as we interpreted him, in the higher pleasures doctrine. As he recognizes there (especially the dignity passage), our desires often reflect value judgments we make, explicitly or implicitly. If so, our desires will be evidence of what we regard as valuable, and our reflectively acceptable desires may provide our best defeasible test of what things are objectively valuable, just as our actual perceptual deliverances may be our best evidence about what is visible. Evidence need not be infallible and, according to the naturalist, is not.

Mill first applies this test to what each of us desires for her own sake. His answer is that what each of us desires for his or her own sake is happiness (IV 3). We needn't interpret Mill as endorsing psychological egoism at this point. Mill is not saying that each of us can only care about her own happiness. Rather, he can be read as saying when each of us does focus on her own ends or sake, we find that each cares about her own happiness. Another way to put Mill's point is that prudential concern focuses on the agent's happiness or that happiness matters (§17).

Mill goes on to say that just as each person's own happiness is a good to that person, so too happiness, as such, is a good to the aggregate of persons. This is an evaluative claim, not a psychological claim about either individuals or groups. Consider, in this context, Mill's reply to Henry Jones in a letter of 1868, addressing his concern that Mill was concluding that each individual aims only at the general happiness.

> [W]hen I said that the general happiness is a good to the aggregate of all persons I did not mean that every human being's happiness is a good to every other human being, though I think in a good state of society and education it would be so. I merely meant in this particular sentence to argue that since A's happiness is a good, B's a good, C's a good, etc., the sum of all these goods must be a good [*CW* XVI 1414].

Moreover, Mill is making a particular kind of evaluative claim here. He is claiming that just as the agent's own happiness is the object of prudential concern, so too happiness as such is the proper object of disinterested or impartial concern.

On this reading, Mill is not trying to derive utilitarianism from egoism. Rather, he is assuming that the moral point of view is impartial in a way that prudence is not. Just as prudence aims at the agent's own happiness, so too, Mill thinks, morality, which is impartial, aims at happiness as such. On this reading, the structure of Mill's proof looks something like this.

1. Prudence involves partial concern for the agent's own sake.
2. When an agent is concerned for her own sake, she cares about her own happiness.
3. Morality, by contrast, involves an impartial concern for all.
4. When one is concerned with others for their own sakes, one is concerned with the happiness of all.
5. If the moral point of view aims at happiness as such, then it is the moral duty of each to promote happiness.
6. Hence, utilitarianism is true.

This understanding of the proof fits the general structure of Mill's argument in Chapter IV. Insofar as each of us has prudential concern for himself, each is concerned with his own happiness. But if morality is impartial, then moral concern would involve an impartial concern for happiness as such (for the happiness of the aggregate). Moreover, happiness is the only thing we care about from both the prudential and impartial points of view. Apparent counterexamples—things that we do care about intrinsically—are best interpreted as claims about the constituents of happiness. If happiness as such is the one and only thing we care about from the moral point of view, it is our moral duty to promote happiness.[3]

If this is the right way to understand Mill's proof, then his justification or defense of utilitarianism consists in assuming that the moral point of view is impartial and claiming that utilitarianism is the right way to understand impartiality. Morality is impartial, and impartiality requires taking everyone's interests into account—and not just those of some select few—and weighing them equally—and not with a thumb in the scales for some select few. Indeed, later, in Chapter V, Mill identifies impartiality and its progressive demands with both justice and morality.

> It [impartiality] is involved in the very meaning of Utility, or the Greatest-Happiness Principle. That principle is a mere form of words without rational signification, unless one person's happiness, supposed equal in degree (with the proper allowance made for kind), is counted for exactly as much as another's. Those conditions being supplied, Bentham's dictum 'everybody to count for one, nobody for more than one,' might be written under the principle of utility as an explanatory commentary. The equal claim of everybody to happiness in the estimation of the moralist and the legislator involves an equal claim to all the means of happiness.... And hence all social inequalities which have ceased to be considered expedient, assume the character not of simple inexpediency, but of injustice. The entire history of social improvement has been a series of transitions, by which one custom or institution after another, from being supposed a primary necessity of social existence, has passed into the rank of universally stigmatized injustice and tyranny. So it has been with the distinctions of slaves and freemen, nobles and serfs, patricians and plebeians; and so it will be, and in part already is, with the aristocracies of colour, race, and sex [V 36].

Here we see Mill identifying utilitarian impartiality with the demands of justice and morality itself.[4] In doing so, he sees himself as echoing Bentham's conception of utilitarianism.[5]

---

3. So I am inclined to agree with Skorupski who distinguishes between what he calls "philosophical utilitarianism," which is the combination of impartiality and welfarism, and classical utilitarianism, which tells us to maximize happiness or welfare, and who claims that the proof supports philosophical utilitarianism and that the inference from philosophical utilitarianism to classical utilitarianism is a substantive and controversial inference. See Skorupski, *John Stuart Mill*, pp. 310–13. I would add that Mill seems not to distinguish between philosophical and classical utilitarianism and so does not see the need to defend his inference from the first to the second.
4. As Crisp also notes in *Mill on Utilitarianism*, pp. 79–80.
5. Bentham's "dictum" may have been a saying of his, rather than anything he ever wrote, inasmuch as no one has ever found the exact quotation in Bentham's writings. However, the source of the dictum may be Bentham's claim "Every individual in the country tells for one; no individual for more than one" in *Rationale of Judicial Evidence*, which Mill edited and is contained in Bentham's

This interpretation of the proof also fits with Mill's remarks about the Art of Life (*A System of Logic* VI.xii.6), which we discussed earlier (§28). In the Art of Life Mill endorses a teleological conception of practical reason that applies to the different domains of prudence, morality, and aesthetics. Each domain is identified by its distinctive focus of concern, that is, its end. Of particular interest here is the division of labor between prudence and morality. Whereas prudence is concerned with the agent's own happiness and seeks to promote that end, morality is concerned with the happiness of all and seeks to promote that end. So the proof echoes his views about the Art of Life by claiming that, just as prudence aims at the agent's own happiness, so too morality, which is impartial, aims at the happiness of all.

One might wonder if utilitarianism is the only or the best way to understand impartiality. Indeed, this is one way of understanding now familiar worries about the implications of utilitarianism for issues of distributive justice and individual rights, some of which we will discuss later (Chapter 9). But this reading of the proof has the virtue of identifying Mill's defense of utilitarianism with the feature of it that made it a progressive influence historically.

34. Bottom-up justification

On this reading of the proof, Mill derives utilitarianism from two assumptions—that the moral point of view is impartial and that happiness is what matters when we care about someone for her own sake. There are two things to note about this derivation. First, it derives utilitarianism from other moral or evaluative commitments, in particular, impartiality and the assumption that happiness matters. This contrasts with the traditional reading that sees Mill as trying to derive utilitarianism from the non-evaluative premise of psychological egoism. Second, this raises the question why we should embrace these two moral assumptions. Mill argues within the proof itself that happiness matters, claiming that individuals do view their own happiness as desirable and that anything else they desire for their own sake can be viewed as part of their happiness. As we saw (§17), it's also an assumption

---

Collected Works (*Works* VII 334). See Phillip Schofield, *Utility and Democracy: The Political Thought of Jeremy Bentham* (Oxford: Clarendon Press, 2006), p. 84. As Stephen notes, Bentham himself attributes the dictum to Beccaria or Priestley (*The English Utilitarians*, vol. I, p. 178).

Mill defends in Chapter II of *Utilitarianism* when he claims that we should care about happiness, rather than contentment (II 6), and in *On Liberty* when he insists on understanding happiness in ways that make it worth caring about (III 4). Mill defends impartiality, as we have just seen, by appealing in Chapter V to its progressive credentials in breaking down forms of discrimination that we can see, at least with the benefit of hindsight, as unjust.

It is important to notice that these aspects of Mill's justification of utilitarianism involve bottom-up justification—showing that utilitarianism and its constitutive commitments are plausible because they support moral and evaluative judgments that we are prepared on reflection to endorse. This sort of bottom-up justification fits Mill's conception of his own methodology as inductive or naturalistic. As we saw (§30), he conceives of naturalism as a method that relies on experience and observation (I 3). His use of bottom-up justification of utilitarian commitments is naturalistic provided experience and judgment include moral judgment and experience. His defense of impartiality by noting its progressive historical accomplishments is a perfect example of this sort of naturalism in ethics.

But once we notice these ways in which Mill makes use of bottom-up justification in the proof of the principle of utility, we are in a position to appreciate that this is just the tip of a methodological iceberg. Bottom-up justification is really quite pervasive in *Utilitarianism*. We noted that he ends Chapter I by claiming that a proper understanding of utilitarianism is a precondition of evaluating it (I 6). But he also warns there that the doctrine is often misunderstood and that these misunderstandings result in unwarranted objections to utilitarianism. This sets the stage for the discussion in Chapter II of what utilitarianism is and is not. As we have seen, in Chapter II he considers a number of objections to utilitarianism. Typically, he responds by defending the implications of utilitarianism and arguing that the objection rests on a confusion of some kind. But in other cases he concedes the point and tries to show that utilitarians have the conceptual resources to accommodate it. A central claim in Chapter II is the doctrine of higher pleasures. In it, Mill appeals to the reflective judgments of competent and experienced judges. In all cases, Mill tries to show that utilitarianism can accommodate moral and evaluative commitments that experience has shown are worth preserving. In doing so, he is clearly defending and justifying utilitarianism using dialectical methods that also appeal to experience and observation.

Or consider again his polemic with intuitionism. Whereas the intuitionist treats the precepts of commonsense morality as ultimate moral factors whose justification is supposed to be self-evident, Mill treats these precepts as mid-level generalizations that function as secondary principles in relation to the utilitarian first principle. Mill insists that these secondary principles are important in moral reasoning but that they are neither innate nor infallible; they are precepts that have been adopted and internalized because of their acceptance value, and their continued use should be suitably regulated by their ongoing comparative acceptance value. Far from undermining utilitarian first principles, Mill thinks, appeal to the importance of such moral principles actually provides support for utilitarianism. He makes this argument in considerable detail in the case of precepts of justice in Chapter V of *Utilitarianism*, where he argues that justice is not, as intuitionists allege, a principle independent of utility, but rather a principle and associated set of emotions protecting security and other essentials of happiness, and, hence, justified by their good consequences (V 1–3, 32–38).

In these ways, Mill displays all three aspects of his commitment to naturalism (§30). Like the intuitionist, Mill assigns probative value to our particular moral judgments; but, unlike the intuitionist, he does not regard them as infallible. Indeed, many intuitions are the product of parochial or discriminatory practices and stand in the way of progressive moral reform. We should exhibit epistemic modesty in the way we hold our moral beliefs and be prepared to revise or abandon them if they cannot be justified. To justify our moral beliefs, we must employ dialectical methods and show how the belief in question fits with other reasonable commitments. In particular, in defending a moral theory, we should look for bottom-up justification, that is, the ability of the theory to subsume and explain particular moral convictions we find plausible. Though one could perhaps employ dialectical or bottom-up justification in a way that was not a posteriori, Mill's conception of dialectical method has important empirical dimensions. For example, when he appeals to the lessons of history about which policies have been parochial and exclusionary, when he appeals to the preferences of informed and experienced judges, when he appeals to secondary precepts that experience shows have greater acceptance value, and when he appeals to psychological claims about sympathy and Conscience to defend the authority of utilitarian demands, he is making empirical arguments.

So Mill thinks that dialectical methods provide evidence of utilitarian accommodation—cases in which utilitarianism, properly understood, can accommodate common moral distinctions and claims. Claims of accommodation provide naturalistic support for the utilitarian first principle. But, like most utilitarians, Mill mixes accommodation and reform. Indeed, utilitarianism could not have been a progressive influence unless it had contained elements of reform, and it could not remain a progressive influence unless some of its demands were revisionary. Reformist demands assume that our existing outlook is in some way incomplete, inconsistent, or incorrect. But they would have little appeal if they couldn't be anchored in accommodation. Revisionary claims are acceptable on naturalistic grounds provided they are forced on us by principles that subsume and explain our experience and observations well. In such cases, local revision or reform is required by considerations of global or systematic accommodation.

So Mill employs a naturalistic defense of utilitarianism insofar as he engages in accommodation. Because accommodation is background for principled reform, Mill also employs a naturalistic defense of utilitarian calls for reform. In his polemic with intuitionism, he argues that we should accept the utilitarian first principle because of the way it subsumes, explains, and regulates common moral precepts. We can now see that Mill is making a claim very much like the claim that Sidgwick will later make when he (Sidgwick) says that commonsense morality is "unconsciously" and "inchoately and imperfectly" utilitarian (*Methods* 424–27).

> It may be shown, I think, that the Utilitarian estimate of the consequences not only supports broadly the current moral rules, but also sustains their generally received limitations and qualification: that, again, it explains the anomalies in the Morality of Common Sense, which from any other point of view must seem unsatisfactory to the reflective intellect; and moreover, where the current formula is not sufficiently precise for the guidance of conduct, while at the same time difficulties and perplexities arise in the attempt to give it additional precision, the Utilitarian method solves these difficulties and perplexities in general accordance with the vague instincts of Common Sense, and is naturally appealed to for such solution in ordinary moral discussions. It may be shown further, that it not only supports the generally received view of the relative importance of different duties, but is also naturally called in as arbiter, where rules commonly regarded as co-ordinate come into conflict...[*Methods* 425–26].

Mill's mix of global accommodation and local reform commits him to Sidgwick's claim about the imperfect coincidence between utilitarianism and commonsense morality.

Mill's naturalism commits him to thinking that this imperfect coincidence provides a justification of the utilitarian first principle. Though Sidgwick recognizes that commonsense morality is inchoately and imperfectly utilitarian, he seems more ambivalent about the probative significance of this fact.[6] On the one hand, Sidgwick does sometimes assign probative significance to the imperfect coincidence of utilitarianism and commonsense morality.

> If systematic reflection upon the Morality of Common Sense thus exhibits the Utilitarian principle as that to which Common Sense naturally appeals for the further development of its system which this same reflection shows to be necessary, the proof of Utilitarianism seems as complete as it can be made [*Methods* 422].

However, this naturalistic justification of utilitarianism is inconsistent with Sidgwick's official epistemological position, because Sidgwick is a kind of intuitionist. Like Mill, Sidgwick considers and rejects forms of intuitionism that would recognize self-evident judgments about action tokens (perceptual intuitionism) or action types (dogmatic intuitionism). Nonetheless, he embraces philosophical intuitionism, which insists that true first principles can only be justified if they are self-evident by intuition. It is worth looking at Sidgwick's reasons for defending philosophical intuitionism, if only briefly, to help us better understand the disagreement between Mill and Sidgwick about the justification of first principles.

Like Mill, Sidgwick recognizes metaphysical structure among moral truths. Truths about action tokens can be subsumed and explained by morally relevant factors or mid-level principles. Provided these factors are not ultimate, they can in turn be subsumed and explained by some smaller number of abstract principles. Eventually, we must reach ultimate moral principles that subsume and explain other moral claims but which cannot be subsumed and explained under any more general or abstract principle. There could be a small number of ultimate moral principles, though in the limiting case there might be just one. Within this structure of moral truths there is *asymmetrical metaphysical dependence*—the more particular moral truths depend on the more general ones, but not vice versa.

---

6. I explore Sidgwick's ambivalence more thoroughly in "Common Sense and First Principles in Sidgwick's *Methods*," *Social Philosophy & Policy* 11 (1994): 179–201.

Sidgwick believes that this asymmetrical metaphysical dependence implies an asymmetric epistemic dependence as well (*Methods* 98–110, 200–01, 338–42, 379–87). *Epistemic ascent* is the natural way to respond to moral uncertainty or challenges to our moral convictions. We can justify more particular moral claims by tracing them to secondary principles and ultimately to the first principle(s) on which they depend, but we cannot justify first principles in terms of anything else—otherwise, they wouldn't be ultimate moral principles.[7] If epistemic dependence must be asymmetric as well, then we should accept philosophical intuitionism. Philosophical intuitionism must deny that utilitarian accommodation of commonsense morality confers justification on the utilitarian first principle. A principled investigation of commonsense morality may serve the heuristic function of helping identify possible first principles, but it cannot be part of the justification of first principles. First principles must be objects of a self-evident intuition.[8]

Mill's naturalistic methods and associated bottom-up strategies of justification assume that epistemic dependence need not be asymmetric. How could first principles depend for their justification on more particular moral convictions? We can't ask in virtue of what other morally relevant factor a first principle obtains. For if one moral factor did depend on another in this way, that would show that the first was not ultimate. But we can ask whether a putative first principle is true, or why we should accept one putative first principle, rather than another. A plausible answer is that we should accept those putative first principles as true that subsume and explain the more particular judgments that, on reflection, we think are true. No principle may subsume and explain all and only the things we take to be true antecedently, in part because our antecedent beliefs are likely to be incomplete in some respects and inconsistent in others. But we can reasonably prefer to accept a principle or set of principles that subsumes and explains more that we are prepared on suitable reflection to accept over principles that subsume and

---

7. Also see Henry Sidgwick, "The Establishment of Ethical First Principles," *Mind* 4 (1879): 106–11.
8. In principle, one could try to reconcile appeals to self-evidence with dialectical methods by insisting that while some beliefs must be self-evident in a way that confers *pro tanto* justification, dialectical justification of those beliefs provides *additional* or *more complete* justification. This is a possible view about justification. But I think it is neither Mill's nor Sidgwick's view. It cannot be Mill's because of his attack on the intuitionist appeal to self-evidence. It cannot be Sidgwick's because he believes that discursive justification of principles necessarily undermines their status as first principles.

explain less of what we believe to be true. Metaphysical dependence may be top-down, but epistemic dependence can be bi-directional.

This account of the justification of first principles explains why Sidgwick would be right to attach probative significance to the fact (if it were a fact) that commonsense morality is inchoately and imperfectly utilitarian, despite the fact that this would be in tension with his own philosophical intuitionism. It also allows us to explain and defend many of Mill's epistemological claims.

First, it allows us to explain why Mill claims that first principles are not amenable to proof in one straightforward sense. Proof is familiar within axiomatic systems. To prove something within an axiomatic system is to derive it from some more fundamental claim. But first principles cannot be derived from more fundamental claims, because they are the most fundamental claims of all. So first principles cannot be proven in that sense.

But that doesn't mean that first principles cannot be justified or that we must resort to intuitionistic claims of self-evidence. We cannot prove axioms, but we can justify their adoption or the adoption of one axiomatic system, rather than another, by showing that it allows us to prove things that we believe are true or are prepared on further reflection to believe to be true. Similarly, even if we cannot prove first principles of ethics in an axiomatic sense, we can justify adopting one, rather than another, by showing that it subsumes and explains more of our independent moral convictions, if not those antecedently held, then those we are prepared on reflection to accept as true.

And this is exactly how Mill proceeds. The "proof" in Chapter IV defends utilitarianism by appeal to moral convictions about the importance of impartiality and happiness. More generally, Mill tries to show that various important moral distinctions and claims can be accommodated by utilitarianism, at least when that doctrine is properly understood. Even where utilitarianism does call for reform, these revisions are required by considerations of global accommodation. These bottom-up strategies reflect Mill's naturalistic commitment to testing theories against experience and observation, which include our moral experiences and observations.

Finally, Mill's consistent application of naturalistic methods in ethics explains why he is careful to frame the methodological asymmetry at the beginning of Chapter I as an apparent asymmetry. We might think that the way to resolve moral disagreement requires a purely top-down strategy, different from the bottom-up strategies that are admissible in the sciences

(I 1–2). But this would not be a naturalistic strategy in ethics, as his subsequent contrast between naturalism and intuitionism shows. His actual strategies for justifying utilitarianism include just the sort of bottom-up strategies a naturalist would employ. This shows that he rejects the apparent methodological asymmetry mooted at the outset.

35. Utilitarianism's prospects

Of course, to accept Mill's naturalistic standards of justification is not to say that utilitarianism meets those standards. That, plainly, is a separate matter. It is a matter of controversy whether the mix of accommodation and reform that Mill's utilitarianism involves is credible, and that is a matter of how well utilitarianism subsumes and explains moral claims that we are prepared on reflection to accept.

Naturalistic methods favor moral theories that accommodate or fit our considered convictions. But we have already seen that the best fit overall may have revisionary implications. Our antecedent moral convictions may be incomplete or inconsistent and are defeasible. So when we try to systematize our moral convictions with principles, we may find conflicts between principles and convictions. Ideally, we make tradeoffs between our principles and our convictions, sometimes modifying a principle, sometimes revising a conviction, until our ethical views are in a kind of *dialectical equilibrium*.[9] Seeking this sort of dialectical equilibrium or fit involves both accommodation and reform. But there is a sense in which accommodation is the more fundamental demand, because we accept reform as part of the demands of systematic or global accommodation or fit. Though utilitarianism can be tested in isolation for its degree of fit, the ultimate test here should be *wide* and *comparative* in nature.

The test must be wide in the sense that justified moral theories must fit with other things we know. If naturalism requires theories to be tested against experience and observation, then acceptable moral theories must fit with other well-supported claims about the world, especially claims about how individuals and societies work. So a justified moral principle must fit

---

9. My conception of dialectical equilibrium or fit is indebted in important ways to the method of "reflective equilibrium" that Rawls advocates in *A Theory of Justice*, §§9, 87. Because equilibrium is the regulative ideal of dialectical methods, I think it makes sense to describe it as a dialectical equilibrium or fit.

with, or at least not flout, the findings of the other moral sciences, including psychology, politics, economics, and social theory. Psychological realism (§10) reflects a demand that dialectical fit in ethics be broad, and Mill's attempt to satisfy this sort of demand by appeals to sympathy and Conscience in Chapter III is one manifestation of his interest in embedding his moral and political principles in a plausible moral science.

The test must also ultimately be one of systematic comparative plausibility. We want to know how well utilitarianism subsumes and explains our reflective convictions and whether its revisionary implications are really necessitated by considerations of global or systematic accommodation. As we have just indicated, this should be a wide or broad kind of fit. Degree of fit is directly relevant to justification, understood in naturalistic terms. But if, at the end of the day, we want to know whether to accept utilitarianism, we need to know not only how good its fit is, but how its fit compares with that of other, rival theories. Does its particular mix of accommodation and reform provide a better dialectical fit with our other moral convictions and background knowledge than rival theories provide?

Of course, it's an extraordinarily complex and difficult matter to determine when the standard of systematic comparative plausibility is or would be met. Dialectical fit is a regulative ideal that we can only hope to approximate. For the most part, we apply the standard in a manner that is *fragmentary* and *piecemeal*, focusing on particular apparent strengths and weaknesses of particular theories and seeing how well the particular strengths and weaknesses survive closer scrutiny. These piecemeal inquiries bear directly on the justificatory prospects of the theories under examination, but they do not themselves, individually, answer questions of systematic comparative plausibility.

I have defended an interpretation of Mill as a perfectionist act utilitarian. It is beyond the scope of this study to reach definitive conclusions about the systematic comparative plausibility of his utilitarianism. That would be too ambitious in any case, but especially given the prior interpretive aims of this study. We can't assess Mill's form of utilitarianism until we know what it is, and that interpretive question has been my primary focus here. As a result, what we can say about the adequacy of Mill's naturalistic defense of utilitarianism must remain especially fragmentary and piecemeal. I have explained and defended Mill's perfectionist assumptions about happiness against rival interpretations and objections. We have seen that his act utilitarian commitments are more plausible than his sanction utilitarian commitments. We have also looked at concerns that utilitarianism is too demanding and explored resources within act utilitarianism and within Mill's theory of human motivation to meet this concern. We also explored, without settling, the issue of how far Mill's version of act utilitarianism can legitimately defend partiality to the near and dear. It would be foolish to suggest that we have fully addressed and satisfactorily answered those concerns about utilitarianism. However, I hope our discussion has sketched lines of inquiry worth pursuing further. We have not yet explored concerns about Mill's utilitarian conception of rights and justice. Some of those concerns will be addressed in the course of our discussion of Mill's liberal principles.

I think Mill's naturalism provides the right conception of how to test the adequacy of candidate first principles, insisting that utilitarianism subsumes and explains, better than rival theories, what is reflectively acceptable in commonsense morality and consistent with what we know about human psychology and social theory. So far, utilitarianism shows some promise in meeting this test—enough promise, I think, to merit further study.

6

Liberal preliminaries

On Liberty is the most considered statement of Mill's liberal principles, published comparatively late (1859) and after undergoing many revisions. It is also Mill's most influential statement of his liberal principles. He begins by distinguishing old and new threats to liberty. The old threat to liberty is found in traditional societies in which there is rule by one (a monarchy) or a few (an oligarchy). Though one could be worried about restrictions on liberty by benevolent monarchs or oligarchs, the traditional worry is that when rulers are politically unaccountable to the governed they will rule in their own interests, rather than the interests of the governed. In particular, they will restrict the liberties and opportunities of their subjects in ways that benefit the rulers, rather than the ruled. It was these traditional threats to liberty that the democratic reforms of the Philosophical Radicals were meant to address. Mill shares these concerns. But he thinks that these traditional threats to liberty are not the only ones to worry about. He makes clear that democracies contain their own threats to liberty—this is the tyranny, not of the one or the few, but of the majority (I 5). Mill sets out to articulate the principles that should regulate when and how governments and societies, whether democratic or not, are allowed to restrict individual liberties (I 6).

36. One very simple principle and the categorical approach

In an early and famous passage, Mill offers one formulation of his liberal commitments in terms of "one very simple principle," which is worth quoting at length.

> The object of this essay is to assert one very simple principle, as entitled to govern absolutely the dealings of society with the individual in the way of compulsion and control, whether the means used be physical force in the form of legal penalties or the moral coercion of public opinion. That principle is that the sole end for which mankind are warranted, individually or collectively, in interfering with the liberty of action of any of their number is self-protection. That the only purpose for which power can be rightfully exercised over any member of a civilized community, against his will, is to prevent harm to others. His own good, either physical or moral, is not a sufficient warrant. He cannot rightfully be compelled to do or forbear because it will be better for him to do so, because it will make him happier, because, in the opinions of others, to do so would be wise or even right. These are good reasons for remonstrating with him, or reasoning with him, or persuading him, or entreating him, but not for compelling him or visiting him with any evil in case he do otherwise. To justify that, the conduct from which it is desired to deter him must be calculated to produce evil to someone else. The only part of the conduct of anyone for which he is amenable to society is that which concerns others. In the part which merely concerns himself, his independence, is, of right, absolute. Over himself, over his own body and mind, the individual is sovereign [I 9].

There are several things worth noting about this passage.

First, notice that Mill is concerned with articulating principles to apply to restrictions on liberty in various contexts, involving different potential actors and different forms of restriction. He is perhaps most interested in cases where the state uses civil or criminal law to forbid conduct and applies sanctions for noncompliance. But he is also interested in other sorts of cases, including those in which social groups use the threat of condemnation and ostracism to limit liberty and ensure conformity and those in which one individual restricts the liberty of another.

> Protection, therefore, against tyranny of the magistrate is not enough; there needs protection also against the tyranny of prevailing opinion and feeling, against the tendency of society to impose, by other means than civil penalties, its own ideas and practices as rules of conduct on those who dissent from them. ... There is a limit to the legitimate interference of collective opinion with individual independence; and to find that limit, and maintain it against encroachment, is as indispensable to a good condition of human affairs as protection against political despotism [I 5].

At various points, it may be worth remembering the variety of restrictors and restrictions that concern Mill. But the central case that concerns him, it is still fair to say, is that of legal prohibition by the state.

Second, in this passage, Mill distinguishes paternalistic and moralistic restrictions of liberty from restrictions of liberty based upon the harm principle.

- A's restriction of B's liberty is *paternalistic* if it is done for B's own benefit.
- A's restriction of B's liberty is *moralistic* if it is done to ensure that B acts morally or not immorally.
- A's restriction of B's liberty is an application of the *harm principle* if it is done to prevent harm to someone other than B.[1]

Mill clearly says that harm prevention is a necessary condition for restrictions of liberty to be permissible. It is not clear whether he thinks that harm prevention is sufficient to justify restrictions on liberty. At other points in the text, he suggests that causing harm to another is sufficient to make the conduct eligible for regulation (IV 1–4, 6; V 2). For instance, Mill writes

> As soon as any part of a person's conduct affects prejudicially the interests of others, society has jurisdiction over it... [IV 3].

Of course, conduct being eligible for regulation or even regulation of that conduct being permissible does not mean that its regulation is required or obligatory. We will return to some of these issues later (§52). But if Mill wants to defend one very simple principle about restrictions on liberty, then harm prevention had better be a sufficient, as well as a necessary, condition for restriction. Because if harm prevention were only necessary, then it looks like we would need additional principles to determine if regulations were appropriate. So there is at least *prima facie* reason to treat Mill, at this point, as claiming that harm prevention is both necessary and sufficient for restricting liberty.

Later in the text, Mill distinguishes between genuine harm and *mere offense*. In order to satisfy the harm principle, an action must actually violate or threaten imminent violation of those important interests of others in which they have a right (I 12; III 1; IV 3, 10, 12; V 5). So he seems to be saying that the harm principle is always a good reason for restricting liberty, but that mere appeals to morality, paternalism, or offense are never good reasons for restricting liberty.

As this recounting of Mill's principles suggests, his defense of individual liberties appears to be part of what might be called a *categorical approach*. To decide whether an individual's liberty ought to be protected, we must

---

1. As we will see, the quoted passage formulates the harm principle in two non-equivalent ways—one broader and one narrower. To simplify, for present purposes, I adopt the first, broader reading here. However, I will revisit the ambiguity later (§53).

ascertain to which category the potential restriction of liberty belongs. The main categories for potential restrictions are as follows.

- Offense
- Moralism
- Paternalism
- Harm Principle

It is not just that Mill sorts restrictions on liberty by category. He also seems to permit or forbid restrictions on liberty by category, for his very simple principle appears to say that a potential restriction is permissible if and only if it is an application of the harm principle: if so, it may be regulated; if not, the restriction is impermissible and the liberty must be protected.

Of course, a given regulation might fall under more than one category. Many provisions of the criminal law, such as prohibitions on murder and assault, might be designed both to enforce fundamental moral provisions and to prevent harm to others. Prohibitions on driving while intoxicated might be defended on paternalistic grounds and by appeal to the harm principle. Presumably, Mill does not object to moralistic or paternalistic legislation that can also be defended by appeal to the harm principle. Rather, the objection is to mere offense, mere moralism, and mere paternalism—that is, to restrictions that can only be justified in these ways and cannot be justified by appeal to harm prevention. We can think of different categories of restrictions on liberty in terms of a Venn diagram in which the categories form partially overlapping ovals.

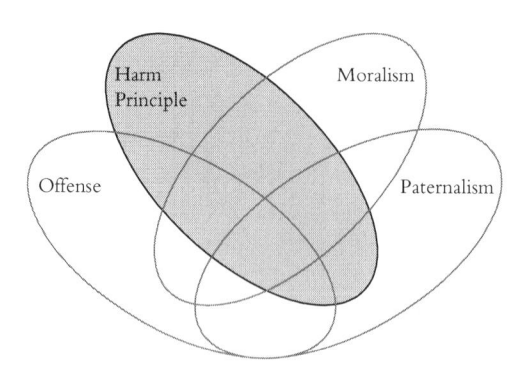

Figure 1.

According to the simple principle, any restriction within the harm prevention oval is permissible, even if it is also within other ovals, and any restriction not within the harm prevention oval is impermissible.

37. The self/other asymmetry

Sometimes, Mill suggests that the harm principle is equivalent to letting society restrict all and only other-regarding conduct. So for instance, the "one very simple principle" passage ends with this distinction.

> The only part of the conduct of anyone for which he is amenable to society is that which concerns others. In the part which merely concerns himself, his independence, is, of right, absolute [I 9].

Mill invokes this self/other asymmetry in other places as well (I 11; IV 2–10). On this view, conduct can be divided into self-regarding and other-regarding conduct. Regulation of the former is paternalistic, and regulation of the latter is an application of the harm principle. So on this view it is never permissible to regulate purely self-regarding conduct and perhaps always permissible to regulate other-regarding conflict.[2]

But the self/other asymmetry gives a misleading picture of Mill's view. As Mill eventually concedes, a great deal of conduct affects others in some way or other (IV 8). For instance, some conduct affects others adversely by causing offense. But if it causes only offense, and not genuine harm, then liberty should not be restricted (IV 3, 10). The natural way to describe Mill's position here is to say that not all other-regarding conduct can be regulated, only behavior that is both other-regarding and harmful.

Offenses tend to be comparatively trivial and ephemeral. Mere offenses do not harm. For instance, I am offended, but not harmed, by tasteless jokes. For an action to harm someone, it must set back an important interest of that person or deprive her of something to which she has a right.

> The acts of an individual may be hurtful to others or wanting in due consideration for their welfare, without going to the length of violating any of their constituted rights. The offender may then be justly punished by opinion,

---

2. See, for example, Brown, "Mill on Liberty and Morality," and Daniel Jacobson, "Mill on Liberty, Speech, and the Free Society," *Philosophy & Public Affairs* 29 (2000): 276–309, and "Utilitarianism without Consequentialism: The Case of John Stuart Mill."

though not by law. As soon as any part of a person's conduct affects prejudicially the interests of others, society has jurisdiction over it... [IV 3].

Mill sometimes ties the self/other distinction to the idea of harm.

> I fully admit that the mischief which a person does to himself may seriously affect, both through their sympathies and their interests, those nearly connected with him and, in a minor degree, society at large. When, by conduct of this sort, a person is led to violate a distinct and assignable obligation to any other person or persons, the case is taken out of the self-regarding class and becomes amenable to moral disapprobation in the proper sense of the term [IV 10].

Here Mill suggests that no matter how much conduct might affect others adversely, it only ceases to be self-regarding when it becomes genuinely harmful to others. This is clearly a technical sense of self-regarding and other-regarding categories, because self-regarding conduct, in this sense, includes much that clearly affects others negatively, for instance, by causing offense.

While Mill is sometimes drawn to this technical interpretation of the self/other asymmetry, it is, I think, an unfortunate way to express his commitments. First, it is unfortunate, because it is misleading, and it is misleading because it violates ordinary ways of thinking and talking. Much conduct is other-regarding, because it is offensive to others, but it does not involve genuine harm. Such conduct, Mill seems to think, should not be regulated. To say that such other-regarding conduct is nonetheless purely self-regarding in a technical sense only confuses an otherwise clear position. The clear position is that self-regarding conduct and other-regarding conduct are mutually exclusive and jointly exhaustive categories and that harmful conduct and offensive conduct are mutually exclusive and jointly exhaustive parts of other-regarding conduct.

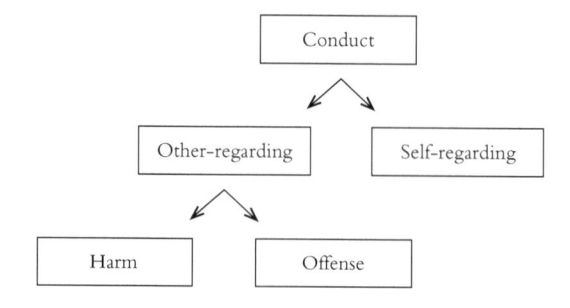

Figure 2.

According to the simple principle, only other-regarding conduct that is harmful can be regulated.

Indeed, we can see that an action is self-regarding in the technical sense just in case it is not harmful and, hence, is not a suitable object of regulation, according to the simple principle. But then calling conduct self-regarding is the conclusion of an argument about whether or not it should be regulated, not a premise. It is another way of saying it is not harmful and should not be regulated. But, if that is true, then one cannot invoke an action's self-regarding character as an explanation or justification of why it may not be regulated. This means that the self/other asymmetry is either false, if interpreted in ordinary ways, or unhelpful, if interpreted in Mill's technical sense. We make better sense of his simple liberal principle, I think, in terms of the harm principle, rather than in terms of an alleged self/other asymmetry.

38. The scope of liberty

Mill makes clear in his introductory remarks that his one simple principle does not apply everywhere. As we noted briefly before (§15), he places limits on the scope of his liberal principles, telling us that they do not apply to individuals who do not possess a suitably developed normative competence (cf. *PPE* V.xi.9).

> It is, perhaps, hardly necessary to say that this doctrine is meant to apply only to human beings in the maturity of their faculties. We are not speaking of children or of young persons below the age which the law may fix as that of manhood or womanhood. Those who are still in a state to require being taken care of by others must be protected against their own actions as well as against external injury. For the same reason we may leave out of consideration those backward states of society in which the race itself may be considered as in its nonage.... Despotism is a legitimate mode of government in dealing with barbarians, provided the end be their improvement and the means justified by actually effecting that end. Liberty, as a principle, has no application to any state of things anterior to the time when mankind have become capable of being improved by free and equal discussion. Until then, there is nothing for them but implicit obedience to an Akbar or a Charlemagne if they are so fortunate as to find one. But as soon as mankind have attained the capacity of being guided to their own improvement by conviction or persuasion (a period long since reached in all nations with whom we need here concern ourselves), compulsion, either in the direct form or in that of pains and penalties

for noncompliance, is no longer admissible as a means to their own good, and justifiable only for the security of others [*OL* I 10].

Mill recognizes that children have immature deliberative faculties and that some adults have very limited normative competence, whether due to congenital defects or social circumstance. So he implies that some threshold level of normative competence is a necessary condition for the application of the harm principle. Where this condition is not met—below the threshold of normative competence—regulations that would not otherwise be permissible may be acceptable. In particular, below the threshold of normative competence, paternalistic action by the state or other parties may be permissible. Paternalistic interference in such cases must be successful to be permissible—it must actually promote the interests of those whose liberty is being restricted. Moreover, in the case of the potentially normatively competent, that is, those adolescents and backward societies that have the potential for normative competence, paternalistic interference must be exercised in ways that help develop, rather than retard, this potential (for more on this issue, see §77).

An obvious question concerns where exactly Mill sets the threshold of normative competence below which a society is sufficiently backward that anti-paternalistic principles do not apply. Here, one might suspect Mill has in mind a defense of British colonialism. However, he does say that the threshold has been long since reached in the nations with whom we need concern ourselves. This could be evidence of Mill's parochial concerns. But Mill's thirty-five year career in the India House made him obviously very concerned about India and other colonies, so a good case could be made that he thinks the normative competence threshold is very widely met. At least, we should not assume otherwise without very good evidence.

39. The harm principle and liberal rights

It is generally thought that by applying this categorical approach to liberty and its permissible restrictions Mill is led to offer a fairly extensive defense of individual liberties against interference by the state and society. In particular, it is sometimes thought that Mill recognizes a large sphere of conduct that it is impermissible for the state to regulate. We might characterize this sphere of protected liberties as Mill's conception of *liberal rights*. We have not yet examined the extent, scope, or contours of these liberal rights. In subsequent chapters, we will see that these matters are often quite complex. But what seems clear, at this point, is that Mill sees himself deriving his conception of liberal rights from a prior commitment to the categorical approach and, in particular, to the harm principle. On this reading, Mill starts with the idea of a harm and uses the harm principle, and the associated categorical approach, to determine just which rights individuals have against the state and society. At least, this is how Mill is traditionally interpreted.[3]

This traditional reading assumes that we have a reasonably good grasp of harm, as something like the setback of an important interest in which the individual has a right, as contrasted with mere offense, which then explains and justifies limits on the rights other individuals have. Of course, more needs to be said about what is and is not harmful, and this may require refining our antecedent conception of a harm, perhaps by appealing to more definite claims about which interests are fundamental and which are not. It would be natural to refine our conception of a harm by appeal to Mill's conception of happiness or well-being, which we have argued is perfectionist in nature.

As we will see, it is hard to square every claim that Mill wants to make, or that contemporary liberals might want to make, about the contours of liberal rights with this traditional reading of Mill's justification of liberal rights. It seems unlikely that we can reconcile all and only the liberties that Mill actually recognizes with the harm principle interpreted in light of some independent conception of harm. If so, to avoid inconsistency, Mill must either abandon or supplement the harm principle, on the one hand, or reconceive harm, on the other hand.

In a provocative recent paper, "Mill on Liberty, Speech, and a Free Society," Daniel Jacobson rejects the traditional reading of Mill's strategy, arguing for what we might call a *moralized* reading of harm.[4] Jacobson sees various problems reconciling Mill's claims about liberal rights with the harm principle, as traditionally conceived. On his reading, Mill thinks that individuals do have speech rights that are harmful on most pretheoretic conceptions of

---

3. Two good traditional readings of Mill's defense of liberal rights are C.L. Ten, *Mill On Liberty* (Oxford: Clarendon Press, 1980), and Jonathan Riley, *Mill On Liberty* (London: Routledge, 1998). Riley, *Mill On Liberty*, pp. 98–9, is especially clear about not wanting to moralize harm too much.
4. Jacobson, "Mill on Liberty, Speech, and the Free Society."

harm, and they can have their liberties restricted in other ways that do not prevent harm, as that would be pretheoretically understood. We will examine such apparent conflicts between Mill's claims about liberal rights and the traditional reading of the harm principle later. What's interesting, for present purposes, is Jacobson's response to this perceived tension. His response is to claim, in effect, that Mill moralizes harm. On this view, it's not so much that harm constrains what rights we have as that what rights we have constrain what counts as a harm. On this view, I don't harm you even if I set back your interests provided that I act within my rights. If we moralize harm in this way, then there will be no difficulty squaring Mill's claims about the contours of liberal rights with the harm principle, because the harm principle claims that liberty can be restricted if and only if someone is acting in ways that exceed her rights. On this view, liberal rights are not derived from the harm principle; rather, liberal rights are prior to harm.

Of course, any such reading owes us an account of what rights Mill thinks we have. The explanation of harm had better not terminate in claims about liberal rights, because this would make Mill's position indistinguishable from intuitionist and natural rights claims that Mill rejects.

> It is proper to state that I forego any advantage which could be derived to my argument from the idea of abstract right as a thing independent of utility. I regard utility as the ultimate appeal on all ethical questions; but it must be utility in the largest sense, grounded on the permanent interests of man as a progressive being [I 11].

To vindicate Mill's consistency, the priority of liberal rights over harm would have to understand liberal rights as having a utilitarian foundation.[5]

Until we have actually looked at some of the complexities of Mill's assignments of liberal rights and strategies for justifying them, it would be premature to try to make a final decision on the comparative merits of the traditional and moralized readings of the harm principle. At this stage, I think it best to note some potential costs and benefits of these readings. On the one hand, there is a real intellectual cost to moralizing harm. On the traditional reading, Mill tries to justify his assignment of rights by appeal to the harm principle: the limit of people's rights is where they start to harm others. Here we explain rights in terms of something else, viz. harm. By contrast, on the moralized reading, we cannot appeal to harm to justify an

---

5. Unfortunately, Jacobson does not discuss the foundation of liberal rights or Mill's need for a utilitarian foundation, but his reading is compatible with recognizing this need.

assignment of rights, because whether conduct is harmful depends on the prior issue of whether it is within the agent's rights. Whether a person's liberty should be protected depends not on whether she would be harming someone by her action, but by whether she has a right to act that way. But that's precisely our question. Whereas the traditional interpretation sees Mill as trying to answer that question by invoking harm, the moralized reading leaves that question unanswered, pending an independent account of liberal rights.

Another way to make this point is to see that the harm principle, on the moralized interpretation of harm, is really just a consequence of whatever liberal rights we have and has no independent content. Conduct, on this view, only counts as harmful when it exceeds liberal rights. But then there is really nothing that could count as a counterexample to the harm principle—a liberal right that could not be derived from the harm principle—because whatever our rights are determines what's harmful in this technical, moralized sense. And if Mill were to justify his conception of liberal rights by appeal to this moralized interpretation of the harm principle, that justification would be circular, inasmuch as the moralized harm principle presupposes the liberal conception of rights.

I find the moralized reading of harm to be difficult to square with Mill's evident intention to explain the limits on liberty by appeal to a prior notion of harm. I also think it would be a hollow victory for the harm principle if it so moralizes the idea of harm that any assignment of rights could be squared with the harm principle. I sympathize with proponents of the traditional reading who see the harm principle as a substantive principle, invoking an independent notion of harm, to try to vindicate a particular assignment of liberal rights. I not only think that the harm principle is subject to counterexample and could fail to deliver the goods, I think that on any reasonable interpretation it does fail to deliver the goods, that is, it fails to show that we have some of the liberal rights that Mill thinks we have. My own suspicion is that these problems are best seen, not as reasons to moralize harm, at least not in this way, but rather as reasons to reject the one very simple principle as consisting in the harm principle. In fact, Mill's actual liberal principles are more complex than the one simple principle passage would suggest.

Having spoken against the complete moralization of the harm principle and in favor of something like the traditional interpretation, I should concede that some moralization of the harm principle may be called for. For in several places, especially where Mill is distinguishing harm from mere offense, he does insist that genuine harm must "violate a distinct and assignable obligation to [another] person or persons" (IV 10) or must violate the "constituted rights" of others (IV 3). On this view, the rights of others help determine what conduct of mine is harmful, which determines which rights I have. There is no threat of circularity here. Whether this kind of moralization of harm can be squared with the traditional reading may depend on whether the rights of others can be understood in terms of their fundamental interests. If so, something like the traditional reading of the harm principle can be vindicated, whether or not it yields the particular assignment of liberal rights Mill or we might want. These issues about the foundations of rights are ones that Mill must face in any case, if he is to square his utilitarian and liberal commitments.[6]

40. Categories, rights, and utility

There is an apparent tension between Mill's commitment to a categorical approach to basic liberties and his defense of utilitarianism. Utilitarianism treats the good as prior to and independent of the right or duty—defining duty as the promotion of good consequences. Perhaps respecting certain liberties tends to be good, but, according to direct utilitarianism, the moral quality of a particular action depends on its own consequences, and there's no reason to believe that respecting individual liberties is always optimal. By contrast, the *deontological* and *natural rights* traditions treat duty or the right as prior to and independent of the good. In particular, deontologists believe that it is not always one's duty to promote good consequences. Sometimes one has a duty to do the suboptimal act, and sometimes it is wrong to do the optimal act. Deontologists recognize moral *constraints* on pursuing the good. These constraints usually take the form of *categorical rules* to perform or refrain from certain sorts of actions (e.g. to keep promises or to refrain from lying), regardless of the consequences. A special case of this perceived

---

6. Joel Feinberg partially moralizes harm, treating it as the conjunction of the setback of an important interest and wrongful conduct. See Joel Feinberg, *Harm to Others* (New York: Oxford University Press, 1984), pp. 31–36. This is different from the sort of partial moralization I have in mind. Assume that the person doing the potential harming is A and that the person potentially harmed is B. Feinberg moralizes harm by requiring that A act wrongly to harm, whereas I am inclined to moralize partly by requiring that the interests of B which suffer the setback are ones to which he has a right. Feinberg's moralization seems closer to Jacobson's than mine, and I worry that both preclude the appeal to harm to explain why A acts wrongly and can have his liberty restricted. See §54.

conflict between categorical rules and utility is the perceived tension between utility and *rights*. For, on a common view, individual rights just are a special case of categorical rules. Individual rights, such as rights to liberties or to freedom from harm, are interpreted as "side constraints" or "trumps" on the pursuit of good consequences.[7] We might understand this apparent tension between utility and rights as follows.

1. Rights to liberties require categorical moral rules that protect those liberties from interference by other parties.
2. Utilitarianism can recognize imperfect generalizations protecting individual liberties, but not categorical moral rules.
3. Hence, utilitarianism cannot recognize rights to liberties.

This apparent tension between utility and rights is especially problematic for Mill, because he not only endorses utilitarianism but also wants to defend liberal rights. As we have seen, Mill forswears appeal to abstract right and claims that his liberal rights have utilitarian foundations (I 11). Is Mill able to reconcile his defense of utility and liberty without compromising either his utilitarianism or his defense of a right to liberties?

Many commentators have been dubious. One of Mill's earliest and most vigorous critics was James Fitzjames Stephen in *Liberty, Equality, and Fraternity* (1874).[8] Stephen considers himself a "disciple" of Mill's utilitarianism but vigorously objects to what he sees as libertarian elements in *On Liberty* that would prevent the state from engaging in paternalistic and moralistic legislation of various kinds. It is easy for liberals to dismiss Stephen's uncritical defense of paternalism and moralism. But we should be careful about what we dismiss. Stephen approaches restrictions on liberty as we might expect a utilitarian to do so.

> Compulsion is bad: (1) When the object aimed at is bad. (2) When the object aimed at is good, but the compulsion employed is not calculated to obtain it. (3) When the object aimed at is good, and the compulsion employed is calculated to obtain it, but at too great an expense.[9]

So Stephen agrees that liberty should be preserved when compulsion is on-balance bad, but he is notoriously optimistic that many forms of paternalism

---

7. See Nozick, *Anarchy, State, and Utopia*, pp. 28–35, and Ronald Dworkin, *Taking Rights Seriously* (London: Duckworth, 1977), pp. xi, 184–205.
8. James Fitzjames Stephen, *Liberty, Equality, and Fraternity* (originally published 1874), ed. R. Posner (Chicago: University of Chicago Press, 1991), p. 53.
9. Ibid., p. 85.

and moralism are not bad in these ways. We can distinguish stronger and weaker claims here.

1. A utilitarian assessment of restrictions on liberty should be case-by-case and not categorical.
2. This case-by-case utilitarian assessment will show paternalism and moralism to be optimal in many cases.

We can accept the weaker (1) without the stronger (2). Even if liberals reject (2), utilitarians seem committed to (1).[10]

Commentators who accept the tension between utility and rights disagree over how to interpret and assess Mill. There seem to be four possible resolutions of this tension:

1. The tension between utility and rights is inescapable, and Mill is simply inconsistent, endorsing both utilitarianism and individual rights to liberties.
2. The tension between utility and rights is inescapable, and Mill's utilitarianism prevents him from defending genuine individual rights.
3. The tension between utility and rights is inescapable, and Mill defends genuine individual rights, but only by abandoning his utilitarianism.
4. The tension between utility and rights is not inescapable; Mill succeeds in reconciling a form of utilitarianism with a defense of individual rights to liberties.

Mill's preliminary statement of his liberalism emphasizes both its utilitarian foundations and its categorical approach in a way that naturally raises this apparent tension between utility and rights. However, it would be premature to commit to one resolution of this tension at this point, prior to examining the substance and details of Mill's defense of basic liberties in the balance of *On Liberty*.

We should continue our study of Mill's defense of individual liberties, as he does, by turning to his defense of freedom of expression. This defense of expressive liberties is important in its own right but also because Mill thinks that there is general agreement about the importance of expressive liberties, which can be leveraged to mount a defense of a wider set of liberties of thought and action (I 16).

---

10. Interestingly, Sidgwick offers a similar evaluation of Stephen's criticism of Mill. See Henry Sidgwick, "Fitzjames Stephen on Mill on Liberty" (1873), reprinted in Henry Sidgwick, *Essays on Ethics and Method*, ed. M. Singer (New York: Oxford University Press, 2000), p. 182.

7
Freedom of expression in a liberal context

Chapter II of *On Liberty* contains Mill's now classic defense of freedom of expression. This defense of expressive liberties has proved extremely influential and finds important echoes in First Amendment jurisprudence within United States constitutional law. We need to reconstruct and assess this defense of freedom of expression. But we are left with an incomplete and perhaps misleading view of Mill's defense of expressive liberties if we read that defense outside its dialectical context in his larger defense of liberal principles. Though important in its own right, Mill's defense of freedom of expression also plays an important, though sometimes overlooked, role in his more general defense of individual liberties. Mill turns to freedom of expression immediately after his introductory chapter in the belief that there is general agreement on the importance of freedom of expression and that, once the grounds for expressive liberties are understood, this agreement can be exploited to support a more general defense of individual liberties.

> It will be convenient for the argument if, instead of at once entering upon the general thesis [the defense of various individual liberties], we confine ourselves in the first instance to a single branch of it on which the principle here stated is, if not fully, yet to a certain point, recognized by the current opinions. This one branch is the Liberty of Thought, from which it is impossible to separate the cognate liberty of speaking and writing. Although these liberties...form part of the political morality of all countries which profess religious toleration and free institutions, the grounds, both philosophical and practical, on which they rest are perhaps not so familiar to the general mind.... Those grounds, when rightly understood, are of much wider application than to only one division of the subject, and a thorough consideration of this part of the question will be found the best introduction to the remainder [I 16].

This means that a proper understanding of the significance of Mill's defense of freedom of expression requires not only reconstructing and assessing his arguments on behalf of expressive liberties but also seeing how these arguments generalize to other kinds of liberties. In this regard, it will be especially instructive to consider how his claims about freedom of expression inform his liberal principles, especially what his discussion of the best grounds for expressive liberties can tell us about the best grounds for opposing paternalism. But it is also worth exploring whether philosophical pressure runs in the other direction as well—whether Mill's discussions of liberalism, in general, and paternalism, in particular, have implications for the proper articulation of principles governing expressive liberties. This perspective requires that we view Mill's defense of freedom of expression in the context of his liberalism.

41. The blanket prohibition on paternalism

To see some of the larger significance of Mill's defense of expressive liberties, it will help to understand some aspects of his liberal principles, especially his opposition to paternalism. We have already examined Mill's initial statement of liberalism, including his concerns about tyranny of the majority and his introductory remarks about the harm principle. Recall that the one very simple principle implies that paternalism is never an appropriate reason to restrict liberty. We need to look at his explicit rationale for this anti-paternalistic position.

Mill's concern with paternalism is general and includes paternalism practiced by individuals or groups, as well as by states. But, as we have already noticed, his central focus is on paternalism practiced by the state. Mill's introductory remarks about the harm principle imply that paternalism is never an acceptable rationale for restricting liberty. Why the blanket prohibition on paternalism? In later chapters, Mill offers two explicit reasons.

First, state power is liable to abuse. Politicians are self-interested and corruptible and will use a paternalistic license to limit the freedom of citizens in ways that promote their own interests and not those of the citizens whose liberty they restrict (V 20–23). This is a concern he shares with earlier Philosophical Radicals.

But even in a democracy, where rulers are politically accountable to the governed and in which, as a result, the rulers aim at the welfare of the governed, there are reasons to be concerned about giving paternalistic license to the state. Even well-intentioned rulers will often misidentify the good of citizens.

> [T]he strongest of all the arguments against the interference of the public with purely personal conduct is that, when it does interfere, the odds are that it interferes wrongly and in the wrong place [IV 12].

Mill needn't assume that individuals cannot be mistaken about their own good, only that an agent is a more reliable judge of his own good than others. If so, even well-intentioned rulers will promote the good of the citizens less well than would the citizens themselves.

These are the sorts of consequentialist arguments against giving the state a broad discretionary power to engage in paternalistic legislation that one might expect a utilitarian to make. Moreover, they make a strong case against giving the state paternalistic license. However, they do not support a categorical ban on paternalism. In particular, these arguments provide no *principled* objection to paternalism—no objection to *successful* paternalistic restrictions A might make on B's liberty that do in fact benefit B. Perhaps some who object to paternalism are only concerned with unsuccessful paternalism. They would have no objection to successful paternalism but are simply skeptical that most paternalistic interference is successful. But for many liberals doubts about paternalism run deeper. They would be inclined to think that much, if not all, paternalism would be impermissible even if it were successful. For it is common to think that individuals have a right to make choices in their own personal affairs and that this includes a right to make choices that are imprudent.

Fortunately, Mill's view of paternalism is ultimately more complicated than these explicit consequentialist arguments suggest. In particular, he has the resources for another, stronger argument against paternalism. These resources are clearest in his defense of free speech. As noted earlier, Mill thinks that there is general agreement on the importance of free speech and that, once the grounds for free speech are understood, this agreement can be exploited to support a more general defense of individual liberties (I 16; III 1). So we might hope to find resources against paternalism in Mill's arguments against censorship.

42. Against censorship

Mill's discussion of censorship in Chapter II focuses, for the most part, on censorship whose aim is to suppress false, immoral, or unpopular opinion (II 1–2), though his principles have quite general application.[1] Here too, Mill is apparently concerned with censorship whether practiced by individuals, groups, or states. However, here, as elsewhere, he focuses on restrictions on liberty imposed by the state. He mentions four reasons for maintaining free speech and opposing censorship.

1. A censored opinion might be true (II 1–20, 41).
2. Even if literally false, a censored opinion might contain part of the truth (II 34–39, 42).
3. Even if wholly false, a censored opinion would prevent true opinions from becoming dogma (II 1–2, 6, 7, 22–23, 43).
4. As a dogma, an unchallenged opinion will lose its meaning (II 26, 43).

This is an odd foursome. First, whereas (1) and (2) are clearly related but distinct considerations, it is difficult to understand (3) and (4) independently of each other. Second, it is natural to group these four considerations into two main kinds: the first two invoke a *truth-tracking* defense of expressive liberties, while the second two appeal to a distinctive kind of *deliberative value* that free discussion is supposed to have.

43. The truth-tracking rationale

The first two claims represent freedom of expression as instrumentally valuable; it is valuable, not in itself, but as the most reliable means of producing something else that Mill assumes is valuable (either extrinsically or intrinsically), namely, true belief. Though Mill here just assumes that true belief is valuable, it is not hard to see how true beliefs would possess at least instrumental value, if only because our actions, plans, and reasoning are likely to

---

1. So, for instance, Mill does not focus on a contemporary First Amendment concern with the regulation of classified information—speech that is true but potentially dangerous. Nonetheless, the harm principle applies to speech and so provides guidance for assessing restrictions on true but potentially dangerous speech. See §47.

be more successful when based on true beliefs. Of course, the most reliable means of promoting true belief would be to believe everything. But that would bring a great deal of false belief along too, which would be disvaluable. A more plausible goal to promote would be something like the *ratio* of true belief to false belief.[2] Freedom of expression might then be defended as a more reliable policy for promoting the ratio of true belief to false belief than a policy of censorship. This rationale for freedom of expression is echoed by Justice Oliver Wendell Holmes, in his famous dissent in *Abrams v. United States*, when he claims that the best test of truth is free trade in the marketplace of ideas.[3]

Notice that this instrumental defense of freedom of expression does not require Mill's problematic claim that the censor must assume his own infallibility.

> [T]he opinion which it is attempted to suppress by authority may possibly be true. Those who desire to suppress it, of course, deny its truth; but they are not infallible. They have no authority to decide the question for all mankind and exclude every other person from the means of judging it. To refuse a hearing to an opinion because they are sure that it is false is to assume that *their* certainty is the same thing as *absolute* certainty. All silencing of discussion is an assumption of infallibility [II 3].

It may well be that censorship of opinion on the grounds of its falsity is never permissible. But Mill is wrong to say that the censor necessarily assumes that he is infallible. The censor can recognize that he, like anyone else, might be mistaken, but insist that he must nonetheless act on the best available evidence about what is true.[4] Mill's better reply is that proper recognition of one's own fallibility should generally lead one to keep discussion open and not foreclose discussion of possibilities that seem improbable.

This instrumental rationale may justify freedom of expression in preference to a policy of censorship whenever the censor finds the beliefs in question implausible. But it does not justify freedom of expression in preference to more conservative forms of censorship. If the question is what policies are likely to increase the ratio of true to false belief, we would seem to be

---

2. Even the ratio of true to false beliefs might be too crude a maximand, because we might want to weight true and false beliefs for their importance.
3. See 250 U.S. 616 (1919) (upholding the conviction of a wartime pamphleteer on behalf of the Russian revolution under the Espionage Act of 1917).
4. Other commentators have objected to Mill's making the case for censorship include an assumption of infallibility on the part of the censor. See, for instance, Stephen, *Liberty, Equality, and Fraternity*, pp. 77–78.

well justified in censoring opinions for whose falsity there is especially clear, compelling, and consistent or stable evidence. We would be on good ground in censoring flat-earthers, both literal and figurative.

Another way to see the weakness of the truth-tracking justification of freedom of expression is to notice a parallel with Mill's explicit arguments against paternalism. Mill's instrumental opposition to paternalism, we saw, could not explain principled opposition to successful paternalism—cases in which A's restriction of B's liberty does in fact benefit B. In a similar way, Mill's truth-tracking defense of freedom of expression cannot explain what is wrong with censorship that is successful in truth-tracking terms. Suppose we lived in a society of the sort Plato imagines in the *Republic* in which cognitive capacities are distributed unequally between rulers and citizens and in which maximally knowledgeable and reliable censors—call them "philosopher kings"—censor all and only false beliefs. The truth-tracking argument would provide no argument against censorship in such circumstances. This shows that the truth-tracking argument condemns only *unsuccessful* or *incompetent* censorship. For some, this may be the biggest worry about censorship; they might suspect that most censorship is incompetent or unsuccessful. But many liberals would have residual worries about *successful* or *competent* censorship. They would object to censorship, even by philosopher-kings. Answering this worry requires a more robust defense of expressive liberties.

44. The deliberative rationale

The resources for a more robust defense of freedom of expression can be found in Mill's claim that it is needed to keep true beliefs from becoming dogmatic, because this reason for valuing freedom is intended to rebut the case for censorship even on the assumption that all and only false beliefs would be censored (II 2, 21). Mill's argument here is that freedoms of thought and discussion are necessary for fulfilling our natures as progressive beings (II 20–33). We can and should read Mill as appealing to his perfectionist assumptions about happiness to defend expressive liberties.

Recall that in his introductory remarks, Mill insists that his liberal principles are "grounded on the permanent interests of man as a progressive being" (I 11). We have already had occasion to observe that Mill thinks that it is our deliberative capacities, especially our capacities for practical deliberation, that mark us as progressive beings (see §15). This is because it is our capacities to deliberate about the appropriateness of desires and plans and to regulate our emotions, desires, and actions in accordance with these deliberations—our normative competence—that makes us responsible agents, or persons. Because it is these deliberative capacities that mark us as progressive beings, the most important ingredient in our happiness or well-being consists in the exercise of these deliberative capacities.

Mill's claim that the value of freedom of expression lies in keeping true beliefs from becoming dogmatic reflects his view that freedoms of thought and discussion are necessary for developing and exercising our deliberative capacities and, hence, for fulfilling our natures as progressive beings. For instance, Mill appeals to the distinction between knowledge and mere true belief.

> [A]ssuming that the true opinion abides in the mind, but abides as a prejudice, a belief independent of, and proof against, argument—this is not the way in which truth ought to be held by a rational being. This is not knowing the truth [II 22].

If we understand knowledge, in familiar terms, as involving something like *justified* true belief, we can better understand his deliberative rationale for freedom of expression.[5] Progressive beings seek knowledge or justified true belief, and not simply true belief. Whereas the mere possession of true beliefs need not exercise one's deliberative capacities, because they might be the product of indoctrination, their justification would. One exercises deliberative capacities in the justification of one's beliefs and actions that is required for theoretical and practical knowledge. This is because justification involves comparison of, and deliberation among, alternatives (II 6, 7, 8, 22–23, 43). Freedoms of thought and discussion are essential to the justification of one's beliefs and actions, because individuals are not cognitively self-sufficient (II 38, 39; III 1). Sharing thought and discussion with others, especially about important matters, improves one's deliberations. It enlarges the menu of options, by identifying new options worth consideration, and helps one better assess the merits of these options, by forcing on one's attention new considerations and arguments about the comparative merits of the options. In these ways, open and vigorous discussion with diverse interlocutors improves the quality of one's deliberations. If so, censorship, even of false belief, can rob both those whose speech is suppressed and their audience of

---

5. Others have commented on the significance of Mill's distinction between knowledge and true belief. See, for instance, T.M. Scanlon, "A Theory of Freedom of Expression," *Philosophy & Public Affairs* 1 (1972): 204–26, and Ten, *Mill On Liberty*, pp. 126–28.

resources that they need to justify their beliefs and actions and so fulfill their natures as progressive beings (II 1).

We should be careful not to overstate the significance of this argument against censorship. Deliberative values may not always speak in favor of expanding one's option set.[6] Cognitively limited agents cannot consider all logically possible options, and careful consideration of many options—especially irrelevant options and options known to have failed—is likely to retard, rather than advance, an agent's deliberations. More options are not always better than fewer. Later, we will look at cases where promoting deliberative values may actually support limitations on liberties (§§49, 55). However, the important point, for present purposes, is that this perfectionist appeal to deliberative values can explain why it is often wrong to censor even false beliefs. In this way, Mill's defense of expressive liberties that relies on his perfectionist appeal to deliberative values is a more robust defense than the one provided by his truth-tracking arguments alone.

45. From expressive liberties to liberal principles

Though important in its own right, Mill's defense of freedom of thought and discussion also provides the resources for an argument for other basic liberties, including liberties of action of various kinds. The deliberative rationale for freedoms of thought and discussion is a special case of a more general defense of basic liberties of thought and action that Mill elaborates in the balance of *On Liberty*, but especially in Chapter III. A good human life is one that exercises one's higher capacities, and a person's higher capacities include her deliberative capacities, in particular, capacities to form, revise, assess, select, and implement her own plan of life.

> He who lets the world, or his own portion of it, choose his plan of life for him has no need of any other faculty than the ape-like one of imitation. He who chooses his plan for himself employs all his faculties. He must use observation to see, reasoning and judgment to foresee, activity to gather materials for decision, discrimination to decide, and when he has decided, firmness and self-control to hold his deliberate decision. And these qualities he requires and exercises exactly in proportion as the part of his conduct which he

---

6. Cf. Gerald Dworkin, "Is More Choice Better than Less?" in Gerald Dworkin, *The Theory and Practice of Autonomy* (New York: Cambridge University Press, 1988).

determines according to his own judgment and feelings is a large one. It is possible that he might be guided in some good path, and kept out of harm's way, without any of these things. But what will be his comparative worth as a human being [III 4]?

Here, Mill makes clear the importance of the development and exercise of deliberative capacities in a life that is fit for progressive beings. Of course, he makes similar claims about the importance of self-examination and reflective decision-making in his discussion in *Utilitarianism* of the higher pleasures doctrine, where he recognizes a categorical preference on the part of competent judges for activities that exercise their higher capacities—claiming that "it is better to be a human being dissatisfied than a pig satisfied; better to be Socrates dissatisfied than a fool satisfied" (*U* II 6).

The development and exercise of capacities for self-government requires both positive and negative conditions. Among the positive conditions it requires is an education that develops deliberative competence by providing understanding of different historical periods and social possibilities, developing cultural and aesthetic sensibilities, developing skills essential for critical reasoning and assessment, and cultivating habits of intellectual curiosity, modesty, and open-mindedness (*OL* V 12–15). Among the negative conditions that self-government requires are various liberties of thought and action. If the choice and pursuit of projects and plans are to be deliberate, then they must be informed as to the alternatives and their grounds, and this requires intellectual freedoms of speech, association, and press that expand the menu of deliberative options and allow for the vivid representation of the comparative merits of options on that menu. If there is to be choice and implementation of choices, there must be liberties of action such as freedom of association, freedom of worship, and freedom to choose one's occupation (I 12).

Indeed, liberties of thought and action are importantly related. This is apparent in the pre-eminent value Mill assigns to diversity and experimentation in lifestyle (III 1). Indeed, in his *Autobiography* Mill describes this as the central truth of *On Liberty*:

> The importance, to man and society, of a large variety in types of character, and of giving full freedom to human nature to expand itself in innumerable and conflicting directions [*CW* I 259].

Mill values diversity and experimentation in lifestyles not only insofar as they are expressions of individual self-government but also insofar as they enhance that kind of self-government. For experimentation and diversity of lifestyle expand the deliberative menu and bring out more clearly the nature and merits of options on the menu (*OL* II 23, 38; III 1). Experiments in living not only express the autonomy of the agent at the time of action, but they provide materials for the agent and others in future deliberations. But diversity and experimentation presuppose liberties of action, and in this way liberties of action, as well as thought and discussion, are essential to the full exercise of deliberative capacities (III 2, 17).

This interpretation provides Mill with a robust rationale for various liberties of thought and action; they are important as necessary conditions for exercising our deliberative capacities and so for producing the chief ingredients of human happiness. In particular, it provides a more robust defense of Mill's general anti-paternalism. For if a person's happiness depends on her exercise of the capacities that make her a responsible agent, then a principal ingredient of her own good must include opportunities for responsible choice and reflective decision-making. But then it becomes clear how self-determination is an important part of a person's good and how paternalism undercuts her good in important and predictable ways.

> If a person possesses any tolerable amount of common sense and experience, his own mode of laying out his existence is the best, not because it is the best in itself, but because it is his own mode [III 13].

Mill may still not have an argument against successful paternalism—successful paternalism that reckons in self-determination as a pre-eminent condition of an agent's good. Indeed, we will see that Mill explicitly endorses one kind of successful paternalism when he defends a prohibition on letting individuals contract into slavery (V 11; see §55). But his perfectionist defense of basic liberties does give him an argument that successful paternalism is much harder to achieve than one might have thought, because it is very hard to benefit an autonomous agent in paternalistic ways.

46. Limits on liberty

Despite this robust rationale for liberties of thought and action, it is also important to see that Mill is not treating liberty as an intrinsic good or endorsing an unqualified right to liberty.

First, we should note that Mill does not defend liberty per se, but only certain *basic liberties*. His defense focuses on three basic categories of liberty (I 12).

1. Liberties of conscience and expression
2. Liberties of tastes, pursuits, and life-plans
3. Liberties of association

Though these liberties evidently include quite a bit, there is no suggestion here that any and all liberties deserves protection. Why not? Insofar as Mill defends individual liberties by appeal to deliberative values, he can distinguish the importance of different liberties in terms of their role in practical deliberation. A central part of practical deliberation is forming ideals and regulating one's actions and plans in accordance with these ideals. But some liberties seem more central than others to the selection of personal ideals. For instance, it seems plausible that liberties of speech, association, worship, and choice of profession are more important than liberties to drive in either direction on streets designated as one-way, liberties not to wear seat belts, or liberties to dispose of one's gross income as one pleases, because restrictions on the former seem to interfere more than restrictions on the latter with deliberations and choices about what sort of person to be. If so, Millian principles defend rights to certain basic liberties, rather than a right to liberty per se. If so, Mill's liberalism should not be confused with traditional libertarianism, which does recognize a right to liberty per se.[7]

Second, even the exercise of basic liberties is limited by the harm principle, which justifies restricting liberty to engage in actions that cause harm or threaten imminent harm to others. There are interesting questions about the correct interpretation of the harm principle, which we will return to later (see §§51–54). But Mill's commitment to some version of the harm principle as a ground for restricting liberty is hard to dispute.

Third, it is important to be clear about how Mill values basic liberties. To account for the robust character of his perfectionist argument, it is tempting to suppose that Mill thinks these basic liberties are themselves important intrinsic goods.[8] After all, if liberty were intrinsically valuable, this would

---

7. For more on the distinction between Millian liberalism and libertarianism, see §§70–71.
8. See Berger, *Happiness, Justice, and Freedom*, pp. 41, 50, 199, 231–32, and James Bogen and Daniel Farrell "Freedom and Happiness in Mill's Defence of Liberty," *Philosophical Quarterly* 28 (1978), pp. 325–28.

explain why the deliberative or perfectionist rationale for basic liberties is stronger than the more limited defenses of these liberties as instrumentally valuable on truth-tracking grounds. But recall that in Mill's introductory remarks he insists that his liberal principles do not apply to individuals who do not have a suitably developed normative competence (I 10). So, for instance, the prohibition on paternalism does not extend to children with immature deliberative faculties or to adults with very limited normative competence, whether due to congenital defects or social circumstance (see §38). Such restrictions on the scope of Mill's principles make little sense if basic liberties are dominant intrinsic goods, for then it should always be valuable to accord people liberties—a claim that Mill denies. Instead, he claims that these liberties have value only when various necessary conditions for the exercise of deliberative capacities—in particular, sufficient rational development or normative competence—are in place.

We could explain this aspect of the value Mill sets on basic liberties in one of two ways. We could claim that basic liberties are not intrinsic goods per se but only *conditional intrinsic goods*. That is, basic liberties are intrinsically valuable but only when various necessary conditions, including normative competence, have been met. Alternatively, we could claim that basic liberties are *necessary conditions* on the exercise of our higher capacities. Though not valuable themselves, they are essential preconditions for exercising our deliberative capacities and thereby to the happiness of progressive beings. This would involve assigning basic liberties an important kind of extrinsic value. These two interpretations of the value Mill assigns to basic liberties agree on many points, including the importance of the scope limitations he places on his liberty principles.

If the two interpretations disagree, it would seem to be in cases in which various necessary conditions for the exercise of higher capacities are met but where the agent nonetheless does not exercise these capacities—she has the opportunity to do so but does not. Presumably, the conditional intrinsic good interpretation would require Mill to say that it is valuable to grant competent adults liberties that they will not use to exercise their higher capacities, whereas the necessary condition of happiness interpretation need not. Of course, in actual cases we will seldom know in advance whether competent agents will use their liberties to exercise their higher capacities, so both interpretations will agree on the importance of basic liberties in actual cases. In the hypothetical case where we stipulate that the competent agent will not use her liberties to exercise her higher capacities, my sense is that liberties are wasted on her. If so, this would favor the necessary condition interpretation. But this may not be the only reasonable verdict about the hypothetical case, and I don't think Mill squarely faced the choice between these two interpretations of the value of basic liberties. However, I do think his scope limitations on his liberty principles require that he not assign any unconditional intrinsic value to basic liberties. This conclusion is important, even if it is agnostic between conditional intrinsic good and necessary condition interpretations of the importance of basic liberties.

47. Limits on freedom of expression

Does Mill recognize any limitations on his defense of free speech? If one read only Chapter II of *On Liberty* one might be excused for concluding that Mill is a free speech absolutist who believes that censorship is never permissible (at least for mature competent adults). Were we to combine this free speech absolutism with the assumption that liberty can be restricted if and only if it causes harm, we would have to conclude that Mill believes that speech can never be harmful—"sticks and stone can break my bones, but words can never hurt me." However, Mill does recognize that speech can be harmful, and he applies the harm principle to speech, as well as other action, when he claims that the regulation of incendiary speech is permissible.

> [E]ven opinions lose their immunity when the circumstances in which they are expressed are such as to constitute their expression a positive instigation to some mischievous act. An opinion that corn dealers are starvers of the poor, or that private property is robbery, ought to be unmolested when simply circulated through the press, but may justifiably incur punishment when delivered orally to an excited mob assembled before the house of a corn dealer, or when handed about among the same mob in the form of a placard [III 1].

One question that the corn dealer passage raises is how much censorship would be justified by applying the harm principle.

Mill would presumably accept at least some aspects of First Amendment jurisprudence. He would agree with some version of the "clear and present danger test" recognized by Justice Holmes in his majority opinion in *Schenck v. United States*.[9]

---

9. See 249 U.S. 47 (1919) (upholding conspiracy convictions, under the Espionage Act of 1917, for the distribution of literature aiming to obstruct the military draft).

> The most stringent protection of free speech would not protect a man in falsely shouting fire in a crowded theater, and causing a panic....The question in every case is whether the words used are used in such circumstances and are of such a nature as to create a clear and present danger...

This raises the more general question of how good the match is between Mill's defense of freedom of expression and some central aspects of First Amendment jurisprudence. This is especially relevant to ascertaining which limitations Mill can and should recognize on freedom of expression, because First Amendment jurisprudence is not absolutist.

48. Deliberative values and First Amendment categories

It is a general proposition governing the adjudication of cases involving individual rights within constitutional law in the United States that when a court determines that an individual's interest or liberty is a fundamental constitutional value it accords that value special protection by subjecting legislation that interferes with that value to *strict scrutiny* or some comparable standard of judicial review. To pass strict scrutiny, legislation must pursue a *compelling state interest* in the *least restrictive manner possible*, that is, doing as little violence to the affected interests and liberties as possible, compatible with securing or promoting that compelling state interest. Strict scrutiny and its relatives contrast with a weaker standard of review, known as *rational basis review*, that is applied to legislation affecting interests and liberties that are not fundamental. To pass rational basis review, legislation need only pursue a *legitimate state interest* in a *reasonable manner*. With some notable exceptions in which courts recognize intermediate levels of scrutiny, the analysis of the importance of interests or liberties and associated standards of scrutiny is generally *bivalent*: interests or liberties are either fundamental or they are not; fundamental ones trigger strict scrutiny or some comparable standard, whereas non-fundamental ones trigger rational basis review or some comparable standard.[10]

---

10. The treatments of commercial speech, under First Amendment jurisprudence, and gender classifications, under Equal Protection jurisprudence, are among the exceptions to this rule, insofar as the Court subjects restrictions on commercial speech and regulations distributing social benefits and burdens by gender to an intermediate standard of review.

For the most part, liberties of expression are treated as fundamental liberties, because of the central role open discussion plays in both public and private deliberations. Insofar as liberties of expression are fundamental, the Supreme Court protects them by subjecting legislation that interferes with them to strict scrutiny or some comparably exacting standard, such as the clear and present danger test.

However, not all liberties of expression are treated the same. For instance, First Amendment analysis distinguishes between *content-neutral* restrictions on speech that restrict the time, manner, and place of speech but not its content and *content-specific* restrictions that restrict some forms of speech on account of the topic discussed or the viewpoint expressed in the speech. Whereas content-specific restrictions are subject to heightened scrutiny, content-neutral restrictions are subject to weaker forms of scrutiny. Deliberative values would seem to explain the Court's special concern with content-specific restrictions. Often, time, manner, and place restrictions leave open many avenues of expression and so do not significantly restrict the production, distribution, or consumption of ideas. By contrast, content-specific, especially viewpoint-specific, restrictions make it harder for certain messages to be heard and evaluated. If the representation of diverse perspectives, even mistaken ideas, can improve public and private deliberations, then there is general reason to think that content-specific restrictions constrain deliberative values in unacceptable ways.

However, not all content-specific regulations are thought to restrict fundamental liberties. First Amendment jurisprudence also distinguishes between *low-value* and *high-value* speech. The liberty to engage in low-value speech is not a fundamental liberty. As a result, content-specific regulation of low-value speech need not satisfy strict scrutiny. By contrast, other forms of speech are high-value, and the liberty to engage in them is a fundamental liberty. As a result, content-specific regulation of high-value speech must satisfy strict scrutiny or some comparable standard. The Court formulated the distinction between low-value and high-value speech in *Chaplinsky v. New Hampshire*:

> There are certain well-defined and narrowly limited classes of speech, the prevention and punishment of which have never been thought to raise any Constitutional problem. These include the lewd and the obscene, the profane, the libelous, and the insulting or "fighting" words—those which by their very utterance inflict injury or tend to incite an immediate breach of the peace. It has been well observed that such utterances are no essential part of any exposition

of ideas, and are of such slight social value as a step to truth that any benefit that may be derived from them is clearly outweighed by the social interest in order and morality.[11]

Here the Court associates central First Amendment liberties with what is an essential part of the exposition of ideas and what is of value as a step toward truth. Like Mill, the Court justifies freedom of expression as a way of promoting true belief. However, if the Court values freedom of expression only as a means of promoting true belief, then it becomes difficult to extend protection to false beliefs, as the Court has. But we need not interpret the Court as valuing freedom of expression only as a means of acquiring true beliefs. The Court appeals to what is an essential part of the exposition of ideas and what is of value as a step toward truth. We can see this rationale as invoking, as Mill also does, deliberative values about the value of free inquiry to the promotion of knowledge, and not just true belief. If we interpret the Court's rationale this way, we can provide a more wide-ranging conception of high-value speech that includes the advocacy of some false beliefs.

What would Mill think about low-value speech and the permissibility of regulating it? He might well think that some examples of low-value speech violate the harm principle. For instance, it is not hard to see how libelous speech—roughly, false and defamatory speech in which the speaker knows that her statement is false and defamatory or acts in reckless disregard of these matters—might be harmful. And some kinds of fighting words might also be harmful. Certainly, fighting words that incite pugilistic responses can be harmful, as Mill recognizes in the corn dealer case (III 1). In other situations, fighting words may cause genuine psychic harm that is serious in its consequences and goes beyond mere offense.

One might also wonder what Mill would think about the permissibility of anti-discriminatory regulations of speech of the sort embodied in employment discrimination law, hate speech regulations, and policies regulating certain kinds of pornography. Mill's commitments here would depend, in part, on whether the regulations in question targeted mere offense or genuine harm. Insofar as such regulations target genuine harm, and not mere offense, they would be defensible according to Millian principles. A very good case could be made for familiar forms of regulation of workplace harassment and discrimination on harm prevention grounds. It is perhaps less

---

11. See 315 U.S. 568 (1942) (upholding a state prohibition on the use of offensive language in face-to-face exchanges in public spaces) at 571–72.

clear whether hate speech and pornography regulations target harm, rather than mere offense. Verdicts here would presumably depend on the details of the regulations—just which kinds of speech they target—and on complicated empirical issues about the effects of hate speech and pornography.

Insofar as these forms of speech are harmful, they would be regulable under the harm principle. But the harm principle applies to high-value speech; it says that speech can be regulated no matter how valuable it is if it is harmful. If the harm principle is Mill's only reason for regulating speech, then he would appear to be committed to regulating harmful speech *in spite* of its high value. But then Mill could not really agree with *Chaplinsky*'s distinction between high-value and low-value speech and its claim that low-value speech possesses no significant expressive interest.

49. From liberal principles to expressive liberties

But this overlooks a way in which Mill might appeal to deliberative values to determine the comparative value of speech interests. To appreciate this possibility, consider how one might understand his free speech principle in light of his considered views about paternalism. Previously, we examined how his discussion of free speech could inform his liberalism and, in particular, his anti-paternalism. Here, we might explore a way in which Mill's liberalism and, in particular, anti-paternalism can inform his position on free speech.

Despite Mill's many blanket prohibitions on paternalism, he does not (consistently) reject paternalism per se. For instance, he qualifies his blanket prohibition on paternalism to allow that no one should be free to sell himself into slavery.

> The ground for thus limiting his power of voluntarily disposing of his own lot is apparent, and is very clearly seen in this extreme case....[B]y selling himself for a slave, he abdicates his liberty; he foregoes any future use of it beyond that single act. He, therefore, defeats in his own case, the very purpose which is the justification of allowing him to dispose of himself [V 11].

Because it is the importance of exercising one's deliberative capacities that explains the importance of certain liberties, the usual reason for recognizing liberties provides an argument against extending liberties to do things that will permanently undermine one's future exercise of those same capacities.

In this case, an exception to the usual prohibition on paternalism is motivated by appeal to the very same deliberative values that explain the usual prohibition. So this seems to be a principled exception to the usual prohibition on paternalism. We might call these *autonomy-enhancing* or *deliberation-enhancing* forms of paternalism.[12]

There might be similar deliberation-enhancing forms of censorship. There might be speech that does not engage or tends to undermine the very deliberative values that explain why content-specific forms of censorship are normally impermissible. On this view, whereas speech that engages or promotes deliberative values is high-value, speech that fails to engage or frustrates deliberative values would be low-value. I should note that Mill does not explicitly endorse the distinction between high-value and low-value speech or recognize deliberation-enhancing forms of censorship, but doing so would be one way to make his liberal principles more consistent and allow him to accept some central aspects of First Amendment jurisprudence. To see how such limitations on freedom of expression might work, reconsider two categories of low-value speech: libel and fighting words.

Though libel can cause harm and so could be regulated even if it were high-value speech, in spite of the fact that it is high-value, it is also arguable that libel does not properly engage deliberative values and so should be treated as low-value speech, which requires no especially compelling justification to regulate. Libel is false and defamatory speech in which the speaker knows that her statement is false and defamatory or acts in reckless disregard of these matters. It is true, as Mill claims, that the careful consideration of claims, advanced in good conscience, that are in fact false can advance deliberation by forcing us to consider the grounds of their falsity. But libelous speech is not advanced in good conscience. It is arguably a case in which more speech is not better insofar as the introduction of false and harmful claims with no concern for their truth and consequences arguably hinders, rather than promotes, reasoned assessment of issues. But then for that reason libel could be viewed as low-value speech, and its censorship could be treated as a principled exception to the usual prohibition on censorship.

---

12. Notice that Mill claims that the reasons for allowing paternalism in "this extreme case" are "evidently of far wider application" (V 11). That raises the question of what other forms of paternalism might be justified as principled exceptions to the usual prohibition on paternalism, which we will address later (§55).

Deliberative values might also explain why fighting words are low-value speech. *Chaplinsky* characterizes fighting words as those that "by their very utterance inflict injury or tend to incite an immediate breach of the peace." As a matter of subsequent constitutional doctrine, the Court has interpreted the category of fighting words narrowly, focusing on their tendency to incite violence. Fighting words, so understood, are words that in their context tend to evoke visceral and violent—rather than articulate—responses. However, it would be a mistake to focus on pugilistic responses, and this is why *Chaplinsky* rightly construes fighting words more broadly, so as to include words whose utterance would cause injury in a reasonable person. A natural response to the use of insulting epithets in many such contexts is visceral but non-violent; the target of fighting words might be intimidated and silenced as well as provoked. Whether silence or fisticuffs, the natural response is not articulate. But then fighting words simply express, without articulating, the speaker's perspective, and they invite various inarticulate responses. If so, we can see why one might reasonably claim that they do not contribute to deliberative values, but often hinder them. If so, there is a case to be made for thinking that fighting words are low-value speech and that the censorship of fighting words would be a principled exception to the usual prohibition on censorship. This is not a proposition that American courts have accepted. In particular, they have been skeptical of hate speech regulations that target a subclass of fighting words directed at individuals as members of historically marginalized groups. But in its skepticism about hate speech regulation, American constitutional doctrine is anomalous among Western liberal democracies that have embraced regulation of discriminatory speech for some time. One might argue that when the foundation of First Amendment principles in deliberative values is properly understood, a case can be made that First Amendment hate speech jurisprudence can and should be modified in the direction of other Western liberal democracies.

In this connection, it is worth noting that Mill does consider apparently similar restrictions on "intemperate" speech that exceeds "the bounds of fair discussion" (II 44). He observes that there is more to be said on behalf of such restrictions when they are applied to the expression of prevailing views than when they are applied to the expression of minority views.

> In general, opinions contrary to those commonly received can only obtain a hearing by studied moderation of language and the most cautious avoidance

of unnecessary offense, from which they hardly ever deviate even in a slightest degree without losing ground, while unmeasured vituperation employed on the side of the prevailing opinion really does deter people from professing contrary opinions and from listening to those who profess them. For the interest, therefore, of truth and justice it is far more important to restrain this employment of vituperative language than the other...[II 44].

This passage is interesting, because Mill recognizes the disparate impact of intemperate speech when employed by a majority and by a minority. If intemperate speech by the majority excludes and marginalizes minority opinions on issues that affect their interests, this looks like a harm that might justify intervention. Even if it did not qualify as a harm, it might show that the speech in question tends to retard deliberative values and so could be regarded as low-value speech. However, Mill ultimately rejects all such restrictions, claiming that it is "obvious that law and authority have no business...restraining either" (II 44). It is unfortunate that Mill does not explain why he thinks it obvious that the law should not prohibit intemperate speech by the majority, since it looks like he should recognize a case for restricting it. Perhaps he thinks that the category of intemperate speech is too broad and includes too much passionate and potentially provocative language that cannot be easily separated from the vigorous give-and-take of ideas. That would leave open the question whether there could be some more narrowly crafted restriction on speech that targets only hateful expression that threatens deliberative values and is not an essential part of the exchange of ideas.[13]

Another potential form of deliberation-enhancing censorship concerns campaign finance reform. Campaign finance reform is obviously a large and complex debate that cannot be satisfactorily addressed here. Nonetheless, we can put parts of this debate in a new perspective by viewing some such reforms as deliberation-enhancing censorship. Campaign finance reform can take many forms, from limitations on private expenditures by candidates, political parties, and individual donors to the public financing of elections. There are different rationales for different kinds of reforms. Some reforms, such as expenditure limits on private donors, have as their main

---

13. I discuss Mill's concern and caution about regulating intemperate speech and argue that Millian principles may actually support narrowly crafted hate speech regulations in David O. Brink, "Millian Principles, Freedom of Expression, and Hate Speech," *Legal Theory* 7 (2001): 119–57.

aim the regulation of influence peddling. While such reforms and rationales are important in their own right, their connections with deliberative values are unclear or, at best, indirect. Of more direct relevance to our present concerns are those campaign finance reforms that limit spending by candidates and donors or that ban private expenditures and provide for equal public funding for candidates as a way of addressing concerns about the impact of unequal resources on the character of political campaigns and political debate. At least since the landmark case of *Buckley v. Valeo*, U.S. courts have been generally skeptical about the permissibility of the limitations on political expression inherent in such reforms.[14] Skeptics of such reforms have generally viewed this as a conflict between equality and freedom of expression, concluding that the interest "in equalizing the relative financial resources of candidates competing for elective office is clearly not sufficient to justify the provision's infringement of fundamental First Amendment rights...."[15] But our Millian distinction between speech that enhances and retards deliberative values suggests a different perspective. In circumstances of significant inequalities in resources, laissez-faire political campaigning, in which campaigns are privately funded and in which candidates and donors operate under no serious restrictions on the amounts they spend, gives a significant advantage in political debate and electioneering to candidates and causes backed by the most resources. But then a laissez-faire regime makes the representation of candidates, issues, and policies hostage to economic interests in a way that is likely to prevent political dialogue from representing diverse views and tracking the merits of viewpoints as required by the sort of free and open inquiry essential to the exercise of deliberative values. Insofar as this is true, laissez-faire harms the deliberative interests of Haves, as well as Have-Nots. If we appeal to the deliberative values that justify freedom of expression to help distinguish between fundamental and non-fundamental expressive liberties, then there is an interesting case to be made for the idea that campaign finance reforms designed to redress the effects of economic inequalities on political dialogue do not infringe central

---

14. See 424 U.S. 1 (1976) (invalidating on First Amendment grounds legislation imposing limits on campaign expenditures by candidates and private donors and creating a system of public funding for Presidential campaigns). *Buckley*'s hostility to regulations on private political expenditures has only been amplified by *Citizens United v. Federal Election Commission*, 588 U.S. 50 (2010) (invalidating on First Amendment grounds restrictions on political expenditures by corporations and unions), which has freed corporations and unions to make enormous contributions to political action committees.

15. *Buckley* at 54.

expressive liberties and that such reforms would be a principled exception to the usual prohibition on the censorship of political expression.

In *Considerations on Representative Government* (Ch. 10) and "Thoughts on Parliamentary Reform" (1859) Mill expresses serious reservations about the effects of economic inequalities among candidates in elections that allow for unrestricted private expenditure by candidates and mentions publicly financed elections as a possible antidote (*CW* XIX 320). He does not object to the effects of inequalities among private donors, and he does not make explicit this deliberation-enhancing rationale for restrictions on private campaign finance.[16] But Mill does accept the premises from which this deliberation-enhancing rationale is constructed, and the conclusion would fit with his other ideas about electoral reform.

Yet another way in which Mill's conception of freedom of expression might be articulated in light of his liberal principles concerns the obligation of public institutions to represent diverse points of view. Mill insists that in order to exercise our deliberative capacities properly it is essential not only to represent diverse perspectives on important moral, political, and spiritual matters but also to represent their merits faithfully and vigorously. This discipline of fair representation of alternatives is

> so essential...to a real understanding of moral and human subjects that, if opponents of all important truths do not exist, it is indispensable to imagine them and supply them with the strongest arguments which the most skilful devil's advocate can conjure up [*OL* II 23].

What is true of the need to represent false opinion applies *a fortiori* to true opinion and opinion whose truth-value is not yet known. Mill's defense of proportional, rather than winner-take-all, representation in *Considerations on Representative Government* (Ch.VII) and state support for the arts in the *Principles of Political Economy* (V.xi.15) are examples of institutional mechanisms designed to increase the diversity and salience of political, intellectual, and artistic activities and voices so as to enhance the character of public and private deliberations. One application of this

---

16. Mill does express support for limitations on private donors to campaigns. In *Considerations on Representative Government* he endorses aspects of Thomas Hare's proposal for electoral reform, including its requirement that candidates put up £50 to stand for election, designed to distinguish serious from frivolous candidacies. Mill suggests that candidates be allowed to treat this £50 as a deposit on which they can draw for legitimate campaign expenses. He allows donors to contribute toward this deposit but no more (*CW* XIX 496).

concern with the fair representation of alternatives in the domain of expression would be support for a fairness in broadcasting doctrine, of the sort at stake in *Red Lion Broadcasting Co. v. FCC*, that would, at least in some contexts, condition access to broadcast time by some candidates and viewpoints on the provision of access to broadcast time by opposing candidates or points of view.[17] Insofar as making public speech by some conditional on the provision of public speech by others can be understood as a restriction of expressive liberties, it too can be represented as a form of deliberation-enhancing censorship.

Mill's position on the limits of freedom of expression requires reconstruction. He is clearly not a free speech absolutist, as his application of the harm principle to the corn dealer case illustrates. The more interesting question is whether he can accept some other limitations on freedom of expression of the sort embodied in some central First Amendment principles and doctrines. Millian principles provide a good rationale for First Amendment doctrines about the importance of high-value speech. While Mill does not himself explicitly distinguish between high-value and low-value speech, one way to reconcile his free speech principles with his other liberal principles would be to treat speech that fails to engage or retards deliberative values as low-value speech whose suppression could be justified as a form of deliberation-enhancing censorship, akin to the autonomy-enhancing paternalism that he explicitly recognizes.

50. Free speech and other liberal principles

Mill's defense of expressive liberties has been deservedly influential, and it is important in its own right to understand these arguments. But Mill intended his free speech principles to play a larger role in articulating and grounding more general liberal principles governing thought and action. Once we appreciate the way in which his defense of expressive liberties appeals to the distinctive value of our nature as progressive beings—specifically, our capacities as moral agents—we can see how he thinks that free speech principles, properly understood, support a broader array of individual liberties. In particular, we can see how the importance of deliberative values provides Mill

---

17. See 395 U.S. 367 (1969) (upholding the FCC's fairness doctrine and, in particular, the personal attack rule against First Amendment challenge).

with a reasonably robust defense of his general anti-paternalistic doctrine. But just as Mill's free speech principles can shed light on his liberal principles, so too his liberal principles can shed light on his free speech principles. Reconciling his expressive and liberal commitments suggests some ways of extending and qualifying his explicit commitments about freedom of expression. Though Mill initially says that he will defend one "very simple" liberal principle—the harm principle—as governing the limits of the authority that the state or anyone else may have over another, this turns out to be an over-simple statement of his liberal principles. Several potential qualifications are in order (see §§51–54). One qualification is that the harm principle need not be invoked to justify restricting liberty, for Mill endorses deliberation-enhancing forms of paternalism, as in his discussion of the permissibility of restrictions on selling oneself into slavery. This feature of his considered liberal principles has a direct bearing on freedom of expression. Mill can and does recognize permissible forms of censorship whose aim is to prevent harm, as in the corn dealer example. But if we try to square Mill's expressive principles with his other liberal principles, this suggests that he can and should recognize the permissibility of other forms of censorship whose aim is not to prevent harm but to advance the very deliberative values that explain why censorship is normally impermissible. When Mill's free speech principles are understood in this light, they provide an interesting and generally supportive perspective on some central First Amendment categories and doctrines. Viewing Mill's principles governing freedom of expression in the context of his more general liberal principles provides distinctive and instructive information about the proper interpretation of both sets of commitments.

8
Liberal principles refined

Mill's discussion of freedom of expression shows us that he wants to defend expressive and other liberties not just as instrumentally reliable goods but also as necessary conditions for the exercise of those capacities for self-examination, reflective decision-making, and deliberative control that mark us as progressive beings. Mill's explicit remarks about the limits of freedom of expression show that he allows restrictions on speech that satisfy the harm principle. But his remarks about some forms of paternalism indicate that he accepts autonomy-enhancing or deliberation-enhancing restrictions on liberty as principled exceptions to the usual prohibition on paternalism. Similar reasoning applied to speech would allow Mill to distinguish high-value and low-value speech and treat restrictions on low-value speech as principled exceptions to the usual prohibition on censorship.

If this is Mill's position, or at least a position supported by Millian principles, then this raises questions about Mill's adherence to the one very simple principle, because the rationale for these forms of censorship focuses on speech that does not engage deliberative values, rather than harm prevention. If Mill were otherwise deeply invested in the one very simple principle, this might be reason to resist the extension of deliberation-enhancing restrictions on liberty into the sphere of expressive liberties. But closer inspection of the categorical approach associated with Mill's one simple principle will show that his principles are anything but simple.

51. The harm principle

It is time to look more closely at the centerpiece of the categorical approach—the harm principle. Let's begin our scrutiny of the harm principle by rehearsing some facts about it.

First, recall that Mill distinguishes between *harm* and *mere offense*. Not every unwelcome consequence for others counts as a harm. Offenses tend to be comparatively minor and ephemeral. To constitute a harm, an action must be injurious or set back important interests of particular people, interests in which they have rights (*OL* I 12; III 1; IV 3, 10, 12; V 5). Whereas Mill appears to reject the regulation of mere offense, the harm principle appears to be the one justification he recognizes for restricting liberty.

Second, Mill envisions that the harm principle is something that we can apply prospectively to prevent someone from acting in certain ways and causing harm. He could hold that we are justified in restricting liberty only in cases in which the agent would have acted to in fact cause harm. But that sets a very high informational threshold for applying the harm principle, since in many cases all we could reasonably know is that a given action *risks* harm. Fortunately, this seems to be all that Mill requires.

> Whenever, in short, there is definite damage, or a definite risk of damage, either to an individual or to the public, the case is taken out of the province of liberty and placed in that of morality or law [IV 10].

Here Mill claims that it is enough, for purposes of the harm principle, if the action in question poses a substantial risk of imminent harm. There are interesting and important questions about what threshold of risk must be met for purposes of the harm principle, which Mill does not address in any detail. Presumably, the threshold should vary inversely with the magnitude of the harm risked, so that the probability of harm required to justify regulation is lower the greater the harm risked.

Third, it should be noted that Mill wants the harm principle to have *wide scope*. He insists that the harm principle regulates more than relations between government and individuals. Its application should include the family, in particular, relationships between husbands and wives and parents and children (V 12). Here, he prefigures some claims he will develop in *The Subjection of Women* (discussed in Chapter 11).

Fourth, though Mill often focuses simply on harm, it appears that his real focus is on *non-consensual* harm.

> But there is a sphere of action in which society, as distinguished from the individual, has, if any, only an indirect interest: comprehending all that portion of a person's life and conduct which affects only himself, or if it also

affects others, only with their free, voluntary, and undeceived consent and participation [OL I 12].

Here, Mill appears to endorse the maxim *volenti non fit injuria*, which he glosses in *Utilitarianism* as the doctrine "that is not unjust which is done with the consent of the person who is supposed to be hurt by it" (*UV* 28). As this gloss makes clear, it is not that one cannot be hurt by something one has consented to or freely risked. Rather, when one has knowingly and willingly risked something harmful, one cannot legitimately complain when that harm comes home to roost.[1] Having my nose broken surely counts as a harm, but if you broke my nose in a boxing match, I cannot fairly complain about the harm, because I consented to the risk. In such cases, there is a sense perhaps in which one has harmed oneself. However, it is important to make sure that the risk is freely assumed. Suppose that I walk on streets known to be unsafe, because alternative routes are all much more inconvenient, and that I get mugged. I don't lose my basis for complaint just because my conduct was predictably risky. To assume otherwise would be to blame the victim. Here, I think one wants to say that the existence of unsafe streets does not mean that one has consented to the risks of using them. Undoubtedly, there is work to be done in explicating the *volenti* principle. However exactly we explicate that principle, Mill makes clear that we should understand the harm principle to focus on non-consensual harms, whether that restriction is explicit or not.

We can now better approach the question of whether Mill really does treat the harm principle as the sole legitimate basis for restricting liberty. Mill clearly states that harm is the only legitimate basis for restricting liberty, which means that he thinks that it states a necessary condition on restricting liberty. We said that it was less clear if he thinks it is also a sufficient condition for restricting liberty (§35). However, it seems that Mill must think that causing harm to others is both necessary and sufficient for justifying restrictions of liberty if the harm principle is to serve as his one very simple principle for regulating conduct. Is that right?

---

1. Contrast Thomas Hobbes, *Leviathan* [1688], ed. E. Curley (Indianapolis: Hackett, 1994): "Whatsoever is done to a man conformable to his own will, signified to the doer, is no injury to him" (XV 13).

52. Is harm sufficient?

Let's look more closely at the issue about sufficiency. In various places, Mill suggests that causing harm to another is sufficient to make the conduct eligible for regulation (*OL* IV 1–4, 6; V 2). For instance, as we saw earlier, he writes

> As soon as any part of a person's conduct affects prejudicially the interests of others, society has jurisdiction over it... [IV 3].

Presumably, for society to have jurisdiction over harmful conduct means that the conduct is in principle eligible for regulation or perhaps even that regulation of that conduct is in fact permissible. But neither of these claims implies that regulation is required or obligatory. The full passage suggests that causing harm is sufficient to trigger a utilitarian calculation about the balance of evils.

> As soon as any part of a person's conduct affects prejudicially the interests of others, society has jurisdiction over it, and the question whether the general welfare will or will not be promoted by interfering with it, becomes open to discussion [IV 3].

Later, Mill makes clear that harm prevention is necessary but not sufficient to justify restrictions on liberty.

> [I]t must by no means be supposed, because damage, or probability of damage, to the interests of others, can alone justify the interference of society, that therefore it always does justify such interference [V 3].

These claims demonstrate that Mill is not committed to a simple version of the sufficiency of harm for restrictions on liberty.[2] However, these claims are compatible with Mill endorsing a weaker version of sufficiency.

> If anyone does an act hurtful to others, there is a *prima facie* case for punishing him by law or, where legal penalties are not safely applicable, by general disapprobation [I 11].

Mill might mean that harm triggers an apparent case for sanctions. This would involve an epistemic interpretation of the *prima facie* case. But an apparent case might prove to be only apparent. Another possibility is to give a metaphysical reading of the *prima facie* case. On this interpretation, causing

---

2. See Jonathan Riley, "One Very Simple Principle," *Utilitas* 3 (1991): 1–35; Riley, *Mill on Liberty*, p. 113; Crisp, *Mill on Utilitarianism*, pp. 180–1; and Miller, *J.S. Mill*, p. 117.

harm is always *pro tanto* reason—a non-negligible reason—to regulate the action, but nonetheless a reason that might be outweighed by countervailing reasons not to regulate. Perhaps effective restriction of the harmful behavior is very costly or has other harmful side-effects. If the regulation is more harmful than the behavior in question, it may be best not to regulate, despite the *pro tanto* case for regulation.

For instance, this is a common historical verdict on the American experience with Prohibition (the prohibition on the distribution and sale of alcoholic beverages enacted into law in the Eighteenth Amendment in 1919 and subsequently repealed in the Twenty-First Amendment in 1933). Of course, some supported Prohibition for moralistic reasons. Moreover, even when the consumption of alcohol did cause harm, some of that harm was arguably self-inflicted and consensual. But it's equally true that the consumption of alcohol can and does lead to non-consensual harm to others, especially spouses and children. While these harms might have established a *pro tanto* case for regulation, it is generally agreed that the costs of regulation outweighed the benefits. In particular, Prohibition provided a weak deterrent for alcohol consumption, encouraged binge drinking, and gave rise to black markets, which not only increased the costs of alcohol but also led to organized crime, corruption, and violence. On this reading of the history of Prohibition, the costs of regulation outweighed the benefits.[3]

The lessons of Prohibition support this reading of Mill's claim. If conduct is genuinely harmful, this presumably does provide a genuine reason for regulation, even in cases in which those reasons are outweighed by greater evils of regulation. This suggests that we should distinguish stronger and weaker versions of the idea that harm is sufficient to justify regulation.

- *Weak Sufficiency*: Harm to others is a *pro tanto* justification of regulation.
- *Strong Sufficiency*: Harm to others is a *conclusive* justification of regulation.

Once we distinguish these options, there is a pretty compelling case for thinking that Mill rejects strong sufficiency but embraces weak sufficiency.

---

3. Miller, in *J.S. Mill*, p. 147, makes a similar argument for thinking that the current American "war on drugs" may be a case in which the benefits of regulation are outweighed by its costs. The two issues are obviously very similar in nature; many of the same problems with Prohibition plague the war on drugs and argue for legalization. However, I think that the historical consensus on the failures of Prohibition is greater, at least at this point in time, than is the consensus in favor of legalization of various drugs. History may eventually conclude that all forms of prohibition are equally misguided (some think that now), but for now Prohibition may be the safer illustration of how a *pro tanto* case for regulation can be defeated by the costs of regulation.

But notice that if Mill rejects strong sufficiency then this compromises his one very simple principle. For only strong sufficiency shows that the harm principle is a complete guide to the regulation of liberty, telling us both when regulation is impermissible and when it is required. Even weak sufficiency implies that the harm principle must be supplemented with some other principle, such as the utilitarian principle, in order to determine if regulation is permissible, much less required. So Mill's doubts about strong sufficiency imply that his own conception of liberal rights requires more than the harm principle.

In rejecting strong sufficiency, Mill claims that actions that cause losses in a fair competition should not be regulated (V 3–4). This case would fall within Mill's "free-trade" exception, which limits the scope of the liberty principle (V 4). Unfortunately, Mill is not entirely clear about the basis for the free-trade exception. After all, losses, even in a fair competition, can be harmful. If I have a successful business selling widgets and then you move into the area selling widgets at a big discount and drive me out of business, forcing me into bankruptcy, I suffer a significant loss, making me worse off than I would otherwise have been. This is harmful in any ordinary sense.

If Mill accepts weak, rather than strong, sufficiency, then he might claim that though there is a reason to regulate harmful economic competition the costs of interfering with free markets are too great. However, this seems not be Mill's preferred response. His official position seems to be that the harm principle should not be applied to such economic harms.

> This is the so-called doctrine of Free Trade, which rests on grounds different from, though equally solid with, the principle of individual liberty asserted in this Essay. Restrictions on trade, or on production for purposes of trade, are indeed restraints; and all restraint, *quâ* restraint, is an evil: but the restraints in question affect only that part of conduct which society is competent to restrain, and are wrong solely because they do not really produce the results which it is desired to produce by them. As the principle of individual liberty is not involved in the doctrine of Free Trade, so neither is it in most of the questions which arise respecting the limits of that doctrine [V 4].

It is hard to see why exactly Mill embraces this sort of free-trade exception. A different and, I think, better reply would not suspend the operation of the harm principle in such cases but rather claim that such losses should not be understood as harms, in the relevant sense. Mill might make either of two related arguments for not treating such losses as harms. First, he might invoke the *volenti* principle and insist that the harm principle targets only non-consensual harms. He could then argue that in a market economy that ensures fair terms of cooperation, economic losses of the sort described are freely risked and so consensual, in the relevant sense. Second, Mill can and does claim that competitive losses are not harms, because they do not deprive economic actors of something to which they have a right.

> In other words, society admits no right, either legal or moral, in the disappointed competitors to immunity from this kind of suffering, and feels called on to interfere only when means of success have been employed which it is contrary to the general interest to permit—namely, fraud or treachery, and force [V 3].

Recall that Mill says that a harm involves damage to an interest to which a person has a right (I 12; III 1; IV 3, 10, 12; V 5). You may beat me out in a fair competition for a job. But I don't seem to have a right to the job. Instead, what I have is a right of fair opportunity to compete for the job. Notice that this defense of the sufficiency thesis involves some moralization of harm, by interpreting harm in terms of the violation of rights. But we are not explaining whether someone engages in harmful behavior by asking whether he is acting within his rights. Rather, we are explaining whether someone harms another by asking whether he has violated the rights of others.

What about non-economic losses and harms? Suppose you promised to marry me but literally leave me standing at the altar without notice. We can imagine circumstances in which your conduct causes me real psychological harm, which requires years of therapy to resolve. But presumably we do not think, and Mill would not claim, that you can be legally prevented from doing so. Are these counterexamples to the sufficiency claim?

Mill might claim that such cases challenge only strong sufficiency, not weak sufficiency. To preserve weak sufficiency, we would have to claim that in such cases there is a *pro tanto* case for regulation, but one that is overridden in the balance of reasons by the untoward effects of allowing state interference in matters of intimate association. How plausible this response is depends on how plausible it is to recognize even a *pro tanto* case for regulation here. One might well doubt the existence of even a *pro tanto* case for regulation. Alternatively, Mill might appeal to the strategies we discussed for economic losses. He might argue that injuries to the heart are freely risked, and so consensual, or that no one has a right not to be stood up at the altar. These strategies applied to losses of the heart have some plausibility, though perhaps not as much as when applied to economic losses.

Further counterexamples to weak sufficiency come from the criminal law doctrines of justification. A common conception of criminal punishment identifies the basis for deserved punishment as consisting in culpable or responsible wrongdoing. There are two main sorts of defense to a charge of culpable wrongdoing that, if successful, justify acquittal. *Justifications* are defenses that deny wrongdoing, whereas *excuses* are defenses that deny culpability or responsibility. In this respect, criminal law doctrine reflects the moral landscape well. Morality, as well as criminal law doctrine, distinguishes two ways of avoiding blame—justifying and excusing conduct. Traditional forms of justification admit harm but deny wrongdoing. Killing or injuring another in self-defense is harmful conduct, but if the threat was credible and the response proportionate, it is not wrong and, hence, is justified. Similarly, there are a range of cases in which an agent causes harm that would otherwise be impermissible but is permissible in the circumstances because it reflects a choice of the lesser evil in a situation of difficult choice that was not the agent's making. For instance, I can plead necessity in response to a charge of trespass if my breaking into your unoccupied cabin and using your phone without your consent was the only way to secure emergency medical treatment for my critically injured hunting companion. This sort of necessity defense undermines a finding of wrongdoing. Such justifications involve harmful conduct that is nonetheless justified.

At least, justified conduct may be harmful in these ways if we understand harm in a non-moralized way as the setback of an important interest. But if we moralize harm in the way that I have suggested Mill sometimes does, by construing it as the setback of an interest in which the individual has a right, then it is perhaps less clear that self-defense harms the target, because the target presumably does not have a right to threaten others. This would allow us to say that the agent injuring or killing another in self-defense does not harm the person he injures or kills, at least not in a technical sense. This moralization of harm is a consistent view, but it certainly strains ordinary language. It follows that if Mill is to recognize justifications, such as self-defense and the necessity defense, then he must either give up weak sufficiency or moralize harm.

53. Is harm necessary?

Is harm necessary to justify regulation? When Mill announces his one simple principle or invokes the harm principle explicitly he treats causing harm as a necessary condition of restricting liberty. However, this claim is difficult to square with various claims he makes both within *On Liberty* and elsewhere in which he is willing to countenance restrictions on individual liberty that do not appear designed to prevent harm to others. Here is a partial list of such commitments.

1. Some actions for the benefit of others may be compelled on the ground that their omission causes harm. These include: (a) giving evidence in court; (b) contributing one's fair share to the common defense and other public goods; and (c) certain kinds of mutual aid, including Good Samaritanism (I 11).
2. Each may be required to bear his fair share of the costs of securing public goods (IV 3).
3. Government may regulate trade (e.g. fixing prices or regulating manufacture), because such conduct is not purely private (IV 4).
4. The state should make education compulsory (V 12–14). (a) This is a form of paternalism toward children that is consistent with Mill's scope worry (I 10), but (b) it is also a restriction on the liberty of parents that seems not to conform to the harm principle.
5. Mill accepts many forms of social welfare legislation. He thinks that local and central governments are empowered to enact various kinds of legislation pursuant to the community's interest (*PPE* V.i.2; *CRG* 538, 541). He explicitly includes the following items on the governmental agenda: (a) the redistribution of wealth (through taxes on earned and unearned income and inheritance) so as to ensure a decent minimum standard of living and equal opportunity; (b) Poor Laws that provide work for the able-bodied indigent (*PPE* II.xii.2, V.xi.13); (c) labor regulation (e.g. regulation of the hours of factory-laborers) (*PPE* V.xi.12); (d) provision for a common defense (*OL* I 11; *PPE* V.viii.1); (e) development of a system of public education (*OL* V 12–13; *PPE* II.xiii.3, V.xi.8; *CRG* 467–70; *Autobiography* 128); (f) maintenance of community infrastructure (e.g. roads, sanitation, police, and correctional facilities) (*PPE* V.viii.1; *CRG* 538, 541); and (g) state support for the arts (*PPE* V.xi.15). Some of these regulations restrict liberty directly; others do so indirectly inasmuch as the implementation of the legislation can only be supported by compulsory taxation.

In all of these cases, liberty is restricted not, in the first instance, to prevent harm to others but rather to provide *benefits* to others.

Of these commitments, (1) alone explicitly tries to link benefits and harms by alleging that the failure to supply the benefits results in harm. But we might try to generalize this strategy to the other cases as well. How well does it work? Is the failure to provide a benefit always harmful? Can we justify restricting liberty to benefit some or promote a common good by appeal to the harm principle?

There is some plausibility in this strategy. Consider Mill's example of compelling testimony in court. If I am on trial and you can provide testimony that would give me an alibi and lead to my acquittal, I would benefit from your testimony, and it seems your failure to give testimony harms me. If so, the harm principle might be invoked to compel your testimony. Failure to provide needed aid or rescue (benefits) might lead to injury or even death (harms), and so Good Samaritan laws might be justified on grounds of harm prevention. Also, many of the public goods Mill talks about—education, national defense, sanitation, and social infrastructure—provide very important benefits, without which we would be much worse off. So perhaps they too can be brought under the harm prevention umbrella.

But this strategy is more problematic than first appears. For one thing, it is not clear that the failure to provide benefits always counts as a harm. In many cases it seems not to. Let us assume that you would benefit me by transferring all your savings to my bank account. It doesn't follow that your failure to do so harms me. Why not? Presumably, because we assess harms counterfactually: if x harms me, it makes me significantly worse off than I would have been otherwise. This makes clear that harms are assessed relative to some baseline. It's an interesting question how to set the baseline. What seems clear is that the baseline cannot be set by the restriction on liberty itself. Relative to that baseline in which you do transfer your savings to me, your failure to make the transfer does make me worse off. But that's clearly not the appropriate baseline. The baseline must have some independent rationale.

Take Mill's example of Good Samaritan laws. Suppose that I come across a small child drowning in a shallow pond or fountain, that I am uniquely positioned to rescue her, and that I can do so at little or no risk to myself. This is just the sort of aid or rescue that Good Samaritan laws compel. Do I harm the child if I fail to rescue her? Have I made the child worse off than she would otherwise have been? It's true that she will die without my intervention, but it's also true that she would have drowned had I not been there at all. For this reason, it is arguable that my failure to rescue her does not worsen her situation, which was bad before I came on the scene. Of course, I have made the child worse-off relative to the baseline situation in which Good Samaritanism is compulsory. But we were seeking an independent rationale for selecting a baseline. A potential restriction cannot set its own baseline. Relative to the situation in which the potential rescuer is not there, failure to rescue does not worsen the victim's situation and so does not harm her. This is not to deny that my failure to rescue is wrong and perhaps that the law ought to compel aid in such cases. But it does raise questions about whether we can justify Good Samaritan laws by appeal to the harm principle.

Similar questions arise in the case of compulsory testimony. We can agree that conviction of the innocent is bad for the innocent and that my provision of testimony on his behalf confers a benefit on him. Does my failure to testify harm him? Well, relative to what baseline? It can be tempting to say relative to the baseline in which I do testify. Indeed, relative to that baseline, my failure to provide testimony does make him worse off. But why should the restriction in question be allowed to set its own baseline? We need an independent rationale for the baseline.

If we resist the suggestion that failure to confer benefits *ipso facto* harms, must we reject Mill's attempt to justify these restrictions by appeal to the harm principle? Not necessarily. Consider the rescue case again. I may not harm the child by failing to rescue her, but she is clearly harmed by drowning, inasmuch as her death deprives her of many goods she would have experienced had she not died prematurely. Something similar is true in the testimony case. It is questionable whether my failure to provide testimony harms the defendant, but it is not similarly questionable whether it is harmful to him to be wrongly convicted. The point is that even if these restrictions on A's freedom, requiring him to benefit B, cannot be justified on grounds of preventing A from harming B, they may nonetheless be justified on the grounds of preventing harm to B.

This draws our attention to a significant ambiguity in the harm principle.[4] Mill talks both about preventing one from harming others and about harm prevention. Indeed, his statement of the one very simple principle mentions both.

---

4. David Lyons notes this ambiguity and its significance in "Liberty and Harm to Others," reprinted in *Rights, Welfare, and Mill's Moral Theory*. Also see Brown, "Mill on Liberty and Morality."

> That the only purpose for which power can be rightfully exercised over any member of a civilized community, against his will, is to prevent harm to others [*OL* I 9].

And

> To justify that [compulsion and sanctions], the conduct from which it is desired to deter him, must be calculated to produce evil to someone else [I 9].

But, as these examples make clear, these two claims are not equivalent. Every time I prevent one person from harming another, I also engage in harm prevention. But, as the rescue case illustrates, some cases of preventing harm may not be cases of preventing one person from harming another. So we really should distinguish two different versions of the harm principle.

- HP1 is an *anti-harming* principle: A can restrict B's liberty only in order to prevent *B from harming others.*
- HP2 is a *harm prevention* principle: A can restrict B's liberty only in order to prevent *harm to others.*

Because every case of preventing one person from harming another is a case of harm prevention, but not vice versa, HP1 is narrower than HP2. Indeed, HP1 is a proper part of HP2. Whereas HP1 justifies intervention only when the target herself would be the cause of harm to others, HP2 would justify intervention to prevent harm to others, whether that harm would be caused by the target or in some other way. Clearly, HP2 will justify more intervention than HP1. As we have seen, it is hard to justify Good Samaritan laws if HP is the sole basis for restricting liberty as long as we understand HP as HP1. If we understand HP as HP1, then we must either reject Good Samaritan laws or reject the claim that HP is the sole basis for restricting liberty. However, it looks like we could square Good Samaritan laws with HP if we interpret HP as HP2. That's some reason to interpret HP that way. But notice that if we interpret HP as HP2, then it is likely to allow a good many more restrictions on liberty than we might have thought when we focused on its anti-harming applications. The sphere of liberal rights that follow from the harm principle should be smaller according to HP2 than according to HP1.

The cases involving Good Samaritan laws and compulsory testimony involve definite benefits to particular individuals. A different worry about the necessity of harm concerns those cases involving restrictions on liberty in the compulsory provision of public goods. The problem arises primarily for laws that compel contribution of one's fair share of public goods, as in (1b), (2), (5d), and (5f). For it is part of the structure of public goods that the effect of individual contributions on provision of the public good is quite small. The negative impact of an individual's failure to contribute is both small and is spread widely over the population. But that means that even if failure to provide public goods would otherwise count as a serious loss for all and a harm, the cost of individual failures to provide for such goods does not seem to meet Mill's criteria for harmful conduct—the impact of individual failures to contribute to public goods is too small and spread too widely to constitute the breach of "a distinct and assignable obligation to any other person or persons" (IV 10). Insofar as this is a worry for the harm principle, it seems to be equally a worry for HP1 and for HP2.

Perhaps Mill can try to square the restrictions on liberty involved in the provision of public goods with the harm principle by insisting on moralizing harm at least to the extent that anything counts as harmful if it deprives individuals of that to which they have rights. Mill might argue that there is or ought to be a right to public goods, because it is very useful for society to provide such goods and enforce an individual's claim to such goods. The details of this strategy will depend on Mill's theory of rights, which we will examine later (Chapter 9). But even if individuals do have a right to public goods, there's a question of whether individual restrictions on liberty involved in the state provision of those goods can be justified as preventing harm, inasmuch as individual contributions typically have a negligible effect on the provision of the good.

A different and, I think, better response is to deny that the harm principle is intended to serve as a necessary condition on any and all restrictions on liberty. As we saw in the last chapter (§46), Mill is interested in defending *fundamental* or *basic liberties*, rather than liberty per se. In particular, he is interested in liberties of conscience and expressive liberties, liberties of tastes and pursuits, and liberties of association (I 12). He can defend these liberties as playing a more central role in our practical deliberations and our formation and pursuit of personal ideals than other liberties. But then Mill might try to justify the modest restrictions on liberty necessary to provide the benefits of significant public goods by claiming that, even if these restrictions on liberty don't prevent harms, they do not restrict fundamental liberties and they do help secure other goods, such as education, security, and sanitation, that serve as necessary conditions of our happiness.

This issue requires us to distinguish two more readings of the harm principle: one in terms of liberty per se and one in terms of basic liberties. This distinction cuts across the distinction between anti-harming and harm prevention, giving us four possible interpretations of the necessity claim.

- HP1A: A can restrict B's *liberty* only in order to prevent *B from harming others.*
- HP1B: A can restrict B's *basic liberties* only in order to prevent *B from harming others.*
- HP2A: A can restrict B's *liberty* only in order to prevent *harm to others.*
- HP2B: A can restrict B's *basic liberties* only in order to prevent *harm to others.*

Earlier, we suggested that the harm principle would be more robust and better fit with Mill's views about justified restrictions of liberty if we understood it as a harm prevention principle, essentially, as HP2A, rather than HP1A. Now we have seen how the harm principle would be more robust and better fit Mill's views about justified restrictions of liberty if we understood it to regulate restrictions on basic liberties, rather than liberty per se. This requires us to interpret the harm principle as HP2B. We might call this the *basic liberties harm prevention principle.* But if we interpret the harm principle this way, then Mill is even further from a libertarian view, at least if libertarianism is understood as the idea that the only legitimate limit on individual liberty is to prevent that individual from acting in ways that harm others.

The necessity claim that the harm principle makes is more robust if we interpret it as the basic liberties harm prevention principle. But, even so interpreted, the necessity claim is still false. For all versions of the harm principle, including this one, insist that paternalism is an impermissible rationale for restriction. But, as we have seen, Mill does not in fact accept a blanket prohibition on paternalism. He allows paternalistic restrictions on selling oneself into slavery (V 11). In a moment (§55), we will discuss the justification and scope of this exception to the normal prohibition on paternalism. But the exception itself shows that Mill does not think that the only acceptable restrictions on liberty are those that prevent harm to others. For this is a case in which it is permissible to restrict liberty, not to prevent harm to others, but to prevent a special kind of harm to self. This exception to the necessity thesis applies equally to HP1 and HP2.[5]

One might try to rationalize the prohibition on voluntary slavery contracts under the harm principle rather than paternalism. One could prohibit such contracts as a restriction not on the slave's liberty but on the liberty of the master. On this strategy, we restrict the liberty of the master to prevent him from harming the slave. But there are two problems with this way of trying to save the necessity claim within the harm principle. First, since Mill is discussing voluntary slavery contracts, any harm that the slave suffers would be consensual. But then the *volenti* principle implies that the harm in question cannot be the basis for legitimate restriction of liberty. Second, Mill clearly justifies the prohibition on voluntary slave contracts as a restriction on the slave's liberties, not those of the master. There is more to say about the significance of this prohibition on slavery contracts, which we will address shortly (§55). But it should be clear already that this prohibition appears to violate the necessity claim that is part of the harm principle.

54. Moralizing harm?

These count as important qualifications in and exceptions to the harm principle provided that we understand harm as something like the setback of an important interest. This way of conceiving harms appeals to evaluative notions about a person's interests and their importance, but not, apparently, to any specifically moral notions. Many of Mill's claims about the harm principle apparently rely on something like this unmoralized conception. Moreover, conceiving of harm as the setback of an important interest provides a reasonably good fit with common ways of thinking and speaking about harm. However, conceiving of harm in this way makes it hard to sustain the harm principle as Mill's one very simple principle.

An alternative approach to the harm principle would be to moralize our understanding of what counts as a harm. One form of moralization has a reasonably good interpretive pedigree. On this interpretation, we moralize

---

5. David Archard, "Freedom Not to Be Free: The Case of the Slavery Contract in J.S. Mill's *On Liberty*," *The Philosophical Quarterly* 40 (1990): 453–65, contains a nice discussion of Mill's prohibition of slavery contracts, with which I am generally sympathetic. But I don't see how he thinks that this sort of paternalism can be squared with Mill's harm principle, specifically the claim that harm to others is a necessary condition for restricting individual liberty.

harm to the extent of insisting that the interest that the harm sets back must be not only an important one but also one to which the agent has a right. The details of this conception of harm will not be clear until we get clearer about Mill's conception of rights, which is the topic of Chapter 9.[6] But it seems plausible that this conception of harm may help address worries about justifications, economic losses, and perhaps even emotional injuries. For though justified self-defense harms the target in the sense of setting back her interests, it's not clear that the person who engages in justified self-defense infringes the rights of the target. For it's not clear that we have a right not to be injured by those whom we threaten. Similarly, though imposing economic losses on another in fair competition or leaving someone at the altar without fair notice might set back significantly the financial or emotional interests of the injured party, it is not clear that people have a right to protection against those kinds of injuries. Moralizing harm in this way yields somewhat revisionary conclusions, inasmuch as it requires us to say that being killed or injured by another acting in self-defense is not harmful and that bankruptcy and emotional loss may not be harmful. But this kind of moralization, as we have seen, is something Mill insists on in several places (I 12; III 1; IV 3, 10, 12; V 5). It also helps make a stronger case for the necessity of harm prevention than if we leave the harm principle unmoralized. For instance, we may be able to reconcile restrictions contained in Good Samaritan laws with the harm principle if people have a right to aid. Notice that even if we moralize harm in this way, the harm principle is still explanatory. When A would harm B in this moralized sense, we can appeal to the harm A would cause as the reason why A would be acting wrongly and why A's liberty can be restricted.

Though this way of moralizing harm makes the harm principle more robust than it would otherwise be, it doesn't completely vindicate the harm principle. This is because it doesn't explain why it is permissible to restrict liberties to promote the common good or why it is permissible to engage in autonomy-enhancing paternalism. Neither kind of restriction aims at preventing harm, even in this moralized sense.

We might try to solve these residual problems with the harm principle by further moralizing harm. One might understand harm as the *wrongful* setback of an important interest. On this conception, something counts as a

---

6. As we will see, on one reading of Mill's theory of rights, rights are just protections for especially important interests. If we accept this conception of Mill's rights, there may be no substantive difference between the unmoralized conception of harm and this moralized conception.

harm just in case it involves an *unjustified interference* with the interests of others.[7] It seems to follow, on this conception, that no harm is caused provided agents act within their rights. Notice that this conception of harm can also be formulated in terms of rights, but in a different way. Whereas the previous kind of moralization defined harm in terms of the rights of affected parties, the present version appeals to the rights of agents whose liberty is in question. Also, whereas the earlier moralization claimed that an action is harmful if it violates the rights of affected parties, the present moralization claims that an action is not harmful if the agent acts within his rights.

It might help to contrast these three conceptions of harm clearly. We can contrast an unmoralized conception of harm with two different ways of moralizing it. It is easiest to state the differences in an anti-harming form, though they could presumably restated in harm prevention form.

1. A harms B insofar as A sets back an important interest of B.
2. A harms B insofar as A sets back an interest of B to which B has a right.
3. A harms B insofar as A wrongly or unjustifiably sets back B's interest or A fails to act within his rights.

Whereas (2) and (3) moralize harm, (1) does not. Though (2) moralizes harm by appeal to the rights of affected parties, (3) moralizes harm by appealing to the rights of agents whose liberty might be restricted.

Whether Mill should moralize harm and, if so, how is a difficult question. First, neither moralization of harm seems to explain away the exception to the harm principle created by Mill's paternalistic prohibition on slavery. For the prohibition on selling oneself into slavery, though it might count as a justified interference with someone's interests, is interference with the agent's own interests, not those of another. The harm prohibited is harm to self, not harm to others. Second, both ways of moralizing harm introduce a technical sense of harm that is at odds with ordinary usage. For, on both conceptions of harm, it turns out that neither killing someone in self-defense nor bankrupting him is harmful. It might be clearer to acknowledge that these are cases of justified harm. But Mill does sometimes moralize harm as in (2), and doing so allows the harm principle to be more robust than it would be without moralizing harm. I see little evidence that Mill

---

7. See Feinberg, *Harm to Others*, pp. 31–36, and Jacobson, "Mill on Liberty, Speech, and a Free Society."

intends to moralize harm as in (3). Indeed, moralizing harm in this way prevents the harm principle from doing explanatory work, as Mill evidently intends (cf. §38). In particular, it prevents us from citing the harm that an action would cause as the reason for thinking that it is an unjustified interference with another, because something only counts as harmful in the first place, on this conception, if it is unjustified. Harm, on this reading, is the conclusion of an argument about whether it is permissible to interfere with an agent's liberty, not an independent premise in that argument. Precisely because Mill appeals to harm as a reason for interference, it seems he cannot moralize harm as in (3).

If libertarianism is the claim that we have a right to any and all liberties and that liberty may only be restricted for the sake of preventing force or fraud, then I think that it is clear that Mill is no libertarian. Perhaps that should not be surprising. But it is hard to see how he can reconcile these claims about the way in which the state can and should interfere with individual liberty with his claim that liberty may be restricted only in accordance with the harm principle. Mill's simple statement of his basic principle is vastly over-simple.

55. Paternalism

Despite Mill's many blanket prohibitions on paternalism, he does not (consistently) reject paternalism per se. As we have seen, he is forced to qualify his blanket prohibition on paternalism in order to maintain his claim that no one should be free to sell himself into slavery.

> The ground for thus limiting his power of voluntarily disposing of his own lot is apparent, and is very clearly seen in this extreme case.... [B]y selling himself for a slave, he abdicates his liberty; he foregoes any future use of it beyond that single act. He, therefore, defeats in his own case, the very purpose which is the justification of allowing him to dispose of himself [V 11].

Because it is the importance of exercising one's deliberative capacities that explains the importance of certain liberties, the usual reason for recognizing liberties provides an argument against extending liberties to do things that will permanently undermine one's future exercise of those same capacities. In this case, an exception to the usual prohibition on paternalism is motivated by appeal to the very same deliberative values that explain the usual prohibition. So this seems to be a principled exception to the usual prohibition on paternalism. As we noticed before (§49), this is a *deliberation-enhancing* or *autonomy-enhancing* form of paternalism.

Notice that Mill claims that the reasons for allowing paternalism in "this extreme case" are "evidently of far wider application" (V 11). That raises the question of what other forms of paternalism might be justified as principled exceptions to the usual prohibition on paternalism. Mill does not address this question directly, at least not right away.

One might worry that all sorts of commitments, including most labor contracts, involve voluntary alienation of significant forms of deliberative control over one's decisions and actions. Surely, Mill doesn't mean to justify interference in most labor contracts simply because such commitments constrain freedom and directive control. But can he provide a principled basis for distinguishing between slavery contracts and other contracts?[8] Presumably, Mill thinks that the slavery contract limits future agency in a way and to a degree that most contracts do not. Selling oneself into slavery involves a contract in perpetuity that mandates wholesale renunciation of deliberative control. There are thus two concerns about it—it is a revocation of control in perpetuity and that revocation is systematic in character. Mill might also object to other contracts in perpetuity, even ones that involve a less wholesale renunciation of control. Indeed, he does in the *Principles of Political Economy* (V.xi.10). But he can object to some contracts in perpetuity without objecting to any and all contracts.

One kind of contract in perpetuity is the marriage contract, at least under Victorian family law. In a nearby passage, which Mill does not explicitly connect with selling oneself into slavery, he does refer to the "almost despotic power of husbands over wives" (*OL* V 12). So we might see Mill likening a wife's consent to marriage, in which she must surrender various rights of control over herself and her children, to someone contracting herself into slavery. This, of course, is a theme that Mill develops at length in *The Subjection of Women*, which we will be discussing later.

A different parallel with selling oneself into slavery, which Mill does not mention, might be a paternalistic prohibition on unjustified suicide. We can imagine cases of justifiable suicide in which someone with a terminal and

---

8. This issue is raised nicely in Frank Lovett, "Mill on Consensual Domination," in *Mill's On Liberty: A Critical Guide*, ed. C.L. Ten (Cambridge: Cambridge University Press, 2008). Lovett seems to assume that there must be a difference in kind, rather than degree, between the slavery contract, which can be prohibited, and other contracts, which cannot. This is the assumption I dispute.

degenerative illness who is racked with pain and legitimately worried about losing her normative competence seeks to end her life with dignity. This is a possibility Mill at least contemplates in *Utilitarianism* (II 12). But many, perhaps most, suicides are committed in temporary periods of depression or emotional pique. Such suicides appear to be irrational or unjustified. They involve an exercise of deliberative control that renounces all further exercise of those very capacities. One can imagine applying Mill's justification of the prohibition on selling oneself into slavery to a prohibition on unjustified suicide. Perhaps suicide would be permitted but only upon successful petition to a medical-psychological advisory board, as in the Netherlands.[9]

One can also imagine a principled paternalistic prohibition on the use of drugs likely to lead to significant permanent cognitive or volitional impairment or perhaps to certain kinds of drug addiction. Mill does discuss drunkenness in Chapter V, para. 6. There he suggests that drunkenness as such is not restrictable but becomes so when the drunk is unable to fulfill obligations toward others. This may suggest that he has no problem with the purely self-regarding drunk. But Mill seems to focus only on episodes of being drunk, for instance, being inebriated for a period of hours. He does not seem to address the condition of genuine alcoholics whose use of drink impairs their decision-making abilities (cognitive impairment) and whose addiction arguably prevents them from properly regulating their actions in accordance with their deliberations (volitional impairment). We might wonder whether some aspects of Mill's justification of the prohibition on selling oneself into slavery wouldn't apply to drug addiction. It wouldn't justify prohibition on sale or consumption, as such, but it might justify the prohibition of drug abuse and addiction. Whether it does might depend on just how complete the degree of cognitive and volitional impairment is for the drug addict, and this might vary significantly among drugs and among addicts. If the possibilities for recovery are always real, then this might limit the value of the analogy with the slavery contract.[10]

---

9. Mill endorses the permissibility of restricting the liberty of someone who would otherwise be injured on an unsafe bridge, but he says that this restriction is permissible because we can assume that the person would not attempt to cross the bridge if he knew that it was unsafe (*OL* V 5). But that doesn't address the case of the suicide.
10. For skepticism about using this autonomy-enhancing justification as the basis for a wide and undiscriminating case for prohibiting recreational drugs, see Douglas Husak, "Recreational Drugs and Paternalism," *Law and Philosophy* 8 (1989): 353–81. But even if Husak's skepticism is well-founded, that need not undermine a more discriminating regulation of a narrower class of drugs that are more addictive or that cause more significant cognitive impairment.

Laws requiring drivers and passengers to wear seatbelts or motorcyclists to wear helmets are further forms of paternalism that might be justified on the model prohibiting slavery contracts. Of course, one might claim that basic liberties are not at stake, and one might try to justify the restrictions as a fair way to mitigate the medical and insurance costs that others would be forced to pay for an agent's decision not to wear seatbelts or helmets. But one might also justify such restrictions paternalistically as avoiding catastrophic outcomes that would defeat the very value of autonomy that we normally appeal to when opposing other forms of paternalism.

In this context, one might consider other forms of epistemic protectionism that are paternalistic, at least in an extended sense. Collectively, we limit or regulate information in ways that are arguably designed to enhance deliberative values. Here, we might consider evidentiary rules at trial that limit the use of hearsay and information about the past crimes of the accused on the ground that such information often biases jury verdicts, limitations on commercial speech that are designed to protect consumers from potentially misleading information and improve their decision-making, or limitations on educational curriculum designed to focus education on viable and promising scientific and social scientific theories (no astrology or Ptolemaic astronomy).[11] The rationale for these forms of epistemic protectionism is to improve our deliberations about judgments of guilt and innocence, consumer choice, and scientific truth. In this way, they are deliberation-enhancing limitations on liberty. Strictly speaking, they need not be viewed as forms of paternalism, because they can be represented as restrictions on the liberty of one party (e.g. witnesses or attorneys, advertisers, and educators) for the sake of others (e.g. the accused, consumers, and students). Nonetheless, it makes sense to conceptualize them as forms of paternalism in a more extended sense insofar as they are limitations on speech or action that we impose on ourselves in the interest of improving our deliberations in ways that are not possible if deliberation is completely unfiltered. These too could be viewed as deliberation-enhancing forms of paternalism that we accept and that Mill presumably would too.

These applications suggest that the prohibition on selling oneself into slavery is an extreme example of a more common phenomenon. These exceptions are all cases of *successful paternalism*—that is, paternalism that

---

11. See Alvin Goldman, "Epistemic Paternalism: Communication and Control in Law and Society," *Journal of Philosophy* 88 (1991): 113–31.

does benefit the agent on balance despite the significant cost of paternalistic interference (§45). The reason that they can be cases of successful paternalism, despite the injury paternalism does to the agent's higher-order interests, is that they promote the very deliberative values that paternalism compromises. The prohibition on selling oneself into slavery is the tip of an iceberg of exceptions to the usual prohibition on paternalism. We won't know the full extent of Mill's anti-paternalism until we know the full contours of the iceberg.

Not only does Mill's anti-paternalism not rule out deliberation-enhancing paternalism, but also it does not rule out interference with an agent's choice that shapes that choice without dictating it. As we have seen, we are often imperfect deliberators with limited time and information and subject to temporal and interpersonal biases (§24). If our deliberations are unfiltered, we are likely to make very imprudent decisions. For example, if our decisions are unfiltered, we are likely to prefer an unhealthy diet to a healthy one and unlikely to save enough for our retirements. We could interfere with such choices paternalistically by banning unhealthy foods and requiring retirement savings. Alternatively, we could interfere in such a way as to yield better prudential choices by shaping choice in ways that don't deprive agents of choice. We could *nudge*, rather than coerce.[12] We could tax unhealthy foods (so as to reflect their true cost), or we could arrange for the healthy foods in the cafeteria to be more easily accessible, reserving the less accessible locations for less healthy foods. In the case of defined contribution retirement plans, we could make the maximum annual contribution the default option, which the agent could change but only through deliberate choice. As this last example shows, shaping choice is often inescapable, precisely because something has to be the default option. Why not make the prudentially better option be the default? In this way we can shape choice so as to produce better prudential outcomes without engaging in paternalistic coercion. There are obviously more and less responsible ways to shape choice, and we would want to insist that choice only be shaped in ways that do lead to better prudential outcomes. It's not clear that Mill's anti-paternalism should object to shaping choice in this way.

12. See Cass Sunstein and Richard Thaler, *Nudge: Improving Decisions about Health, Wealth, and Happiness* (New Haven: Yale, 2008). Sunstein and Thaler call their position "libertarian paternalism" to indicate that it is paternalistic insofar as it shapes choice so as to yield better prudential outcomes, but libertarian insofar as it does not dictate decisions and leaves choice to the agent.

We might conclude our discussion of Mill's anti-paternalism by considering an interesting objection to Mill's position raised by Richard Arneson. In his article "Paternalism, Utility, and Fairness"[13] Arneson raises reasonable worries about the unequal impact of Millian principles, especially his anti-paternalism. To see his point, recall the scope limitation on Mill's liberty principle (I 10; §§15, 38), which sets a threshold of normative competence below which the liberty principle does not apply and above which it applies to all equally. Arneson worries about the disparate impact of Mill's anti-paternalism on people above the threshold who nonetheless possess different degrees of normative competence. Suppose that we set the threshold at a C-level competence. Ds are saved from themselves by paternalistic intervention. But, according to Mill, paternalism is equally impermissible for C+s and A+s. But the welfare prospects of C+s and A+s are quite different under non-scalar anti-paternalist principles. A+s will fare much better than C+s under an anti-paternalism regime. This disparate impact of liberal principles, Arneson claims, gives rise to fairness and equality worries. It would be unfortunate if Mill just turned a deaf ear to these concerns. How, if at all, might he respond?

One response would be for Mill to switch from a threshold conception of normative competence and its significance to a scalar conception. Normative thresholds are always arbitrary where what they are responding to is scalar in nature. Moreover, it seems clear that normative competence is scalar in nature. But why do differences in normative competence below the threshold make no difference whatsoever, and why should small differences just below and above the threshold make all the difference. The alternative would be to embrace a sliding scale of basic liberties that tracks degree of normative competence. Good parents already work with this sort of sliding scale. Not only do children have partially developed normative competence, their level of competence is developing over time. Different responsibilities and opportunities are appropriate for them at different stages of normative development. Adolescents need to be given various sorts of deliberative opportunities and responsibilities, including the freedom to make and learn from their own mistakes in certain circumscribed ways, which prevent or minimize the chance of catastrophic outcomes. As they get older and their competence grows, they need to be given more freedom, opportunities, and responsibilities. Only in this way will the potentially competent develop normal adult competence.

13. Reprinted in *Mill's On Liberty: Critical Essays*, ed. G. Dworkin.

The difficult question is whether this sort of sliding scale could be applied to relations between state actors and children and other people at various levels of normative competence. Could we assign differential liberties to citizens in ways that track their differential levels of normative competence? Skepticism here is not unreasonable. If not, we might end up accepting Mill's threshold conception, not as a matter of ideal theory, but as a concession to pragmatic difficulties with the scalar approach.

A different response to the worry about the disparate impact of Mill's anti-paternalism would be to retain Mill's non-scalar principles but insist that C+s get a greater share of non-coercive help in reaching better prudential outcomes. Perhaps C+s could have their choices shaped more than the choices of A+s, or they could get more assistance in the form of special tutoring and remonstration. Mill allows the state to educate about the ill effects of certain activities and even discourage those activities in cases where prohibition would be impermissible (V 9). It would therefore be possible, at least in principle, for the state to concentrate its educational and persuasive efforts on those who are normatively competent but less so.

The contours of Mill's anti-paternalism are starting to take shape. Mill does not accept a blanket prohibition on paternalism. Instead, he allows and even requires paternalism both to forestall catastrophic outcomes but also to enhance the very deliberative values that normally explain why paternalism is problematic. In addition, he can favor interventions in prudential deliberations that shape deliberation without coercively dictating its outcome. Mill can and should respond to the disparate impact of anti-paternalistic principles by adopting a sliding scale of basic liberties that tracks differences in normative competence or by offering non-coercive deliberative assistance to those with diminished normative competence. Important issues remain to be settled, but it should be clear that Mill's anti-paternalism is anything but simple.

56. Offense

As we've seen, Mill distinguishes between merely offensive and genuinely harmful behavior. Whereas genuinely harmful behavior can be regulated, merely offensive behavior cannot (I 12; III 1; IV 3, 10, 12; V 5). Offense is one case where Mill distinguishes sharply between state regulation and informal social sanctions.

> The acts of an individual may be hurtful to others or wanting in due consideration of their welfare, without going to the length of violating any of their constituted rights. The offender may then be justly punished by opinion, though not by law [IV 3].

Mill goes on to describe various ways in which others are at liberty to express their distaste for someone's offensive behavior.

> Though doing no wrong to anyone, a person may so act as to compel us to judge him, and feel to him, as a fool or as a being of an inferior order....We have a right, also, in various ways, to act upon our unfavourable opinion of any one, not to the oppression of his individuality, but in the exercise of ours. We are not bound, for example, to seek his society; we have a right to avoid it (though not to parade the avoidance), for we have a right to choose the society most acceptable to us. We have a right, and it may be our duty, to caution others against him if we think his example or conversation likely to have a pernicious effect on those with whom he associates. We may give others a preference over him in optional good offices, except those which tend to his improvement. In these various modes a person may suffer very severe penalties at the hands of others for faults which directly concern only himself; but he suffers these penalties only in so far as they are the natural and, as it were, the spontaneous consequences of the faults themselves, not because they are purposely inflicted on him for the sake of punishment [IV 5].

Here, Mill distinguishes between legitimate disapprobation for permitted but offensive behavior and intentional sanctioning of such behavior, claiming that the former is permissible and that the latter is not. No doubt, there will be gray areas, involving forms of consequential social exclusion for boorish behavior, where it is not clear if the exclusion is merely legitimate disapprobation or prohibited social sanction. Despite this difficulty, Mill seems to have a coherent treatment of offense, which forbids the legal regulation of mere offense.

However, in his discussion of drunkenness, Mill does at one point allow that offenses against others may be prohibited, at least when they involve acts of public indecency.

> Again, there are many acts which, being directly injurious only to the agents themselves, ought not to be legally interdicted, but which, if done publicly, are a violation of good manners and, coming thus within the category of offenses against others, may be rightly prohibited. Of this kind are offenses against decency; on which it is unnecessary to dwell, the rather as they are only connected indirectly with our subject, the objection to publicity being equally strong in the case of many actions not in themselves condemnable, nor supposed to be so [V 7].

The immediate context is otherwise paternalistic restrictions with drink. But when drinking that is otherwise purely self-regarding (e.g. does not result in the neglect of duties to dependents) is done in public, it becomes offensive and, Mill here claims, regulable.

Is it possible to square the regulation of public indecency with Mill's blanket prohibition on offense regulation?[14] One might claim that this is best viewed as a qualification, rather than a rejection, of his opposition to offense regulation. Though still opposed to offense legislation per se, he indicates here that he is not opposed to the regulation of *public* offenses. Not everything that is permissible to do in private is permissible to do in public. But even if this is a coherent position, we might wonder if it is attractive. If behavior is impermissible to regulate in private, why is it permissible to regulate in public? Mill's answer is that when done in public, the conduct comes "thus within the category of offense against others" (V 7). But if publicity is relevant because it makes the conduct offensive, then Mill's real appeal is to offense. But then this exception threatens to swallow the rule.

Mill may not have a consistent view about offense. Except for this one potentially wide-ranging endorsement of offense regulation, he is otherwise clear in his opposition to offense regulation. How attractive is this sort of libertarian position on offense regulation?

57. A balancing test

Though societies vary considerably in how much and what forms of offensive behavior they tolerate, few, if any, accept the libertarian position that Mill sometimes suggests. Most societies allow for the regulation of nuisance, prohibiting public disturbances and placing time, manner, and place restrictions on loud or otherwise disorderly conduct. Such restrictions flout a libertarian ban on offense regulation.

It is instructive in this context to consider briefly issues that Joel Feinberg has raised about offense regulation. In his important four-volume work *The Moral Limits of the Criminal Law*, Feinberg sees himself articulating a broadly

---

14. Jeremy Waldron, "Mill and the Value of Moral Distress," *Political Studies* 35 (1987): 410–23, esp. p. 421, finds this exception so at odds with the rest of Mill's skepticism about offense regulation that he proposes that sympathetic interpreters should ignore it. However, Waldron does not address legitimate demands for time, manner, and place restrictions on public nuisance, to which Mill might be responding (discussed later in the text).

Millian conception of liberalism.[15] Feinberg follows a categorical approach to the restriction of liberty. His main modification of Millian principles, as he sees it, is to permit some forms of offense regulation. In *Offense to Others*, Feinberg begins by focusing on *nuisance*.[16] Many offensive things are nuisances; they cause passing inconvenience or disagreeable mental states or sensations. But even if many nuisances are just the price one has to pay to live in a free society, it is common for the law to regulate nuisance. Feinberg thinks that some nuisances—especially public nuisances—can justify regulation. He motivates this use of the law by describing a series of hypothetical *Bus Rides* in which the reader is asked to imagine riding public transportation and being unable get off without seriously inconveniencing herself. The reader is asked to imagine that she is on her way to an important appointment, which she will miss if she gets off the bus. In each hypothetical case (there are 31 in all) people get on the bus, sit near you (the reader), and start doing things that you find it impossible to ignore and that cause reactions in you ranging from mild annoyance or anxiety to shock and revulsion. Feinberg groups the cases into six categories: (a) affronts to the senses; (b) disgust and revulsion; (c) shock to moral, religious, and patriotic sensibilities; (d) shame, embarrassment (including vicarious embarrassment), and anxiety; (e) annoyance, boredom, and frustration; and (f) fear, resentment, humiliation, and anger (from empty threats, insults, mockery, flaunting, or taunting). Within each category of nuisance, Feinberg recognizes a spectrum of cases of offensive conduct, ranging from the reasonably tame to the extreme. He does not think that all versions of the Bus Ride justify restriction, only the most extreme.

In most, if not all, cases, the occurrence of such behavior in private, while not unobjectionable, would nevertheless present no case for restriction. If so, it appears to be crucial that the indecency is *public*. This qualification is potentially important. For it was public indecency that Mill was prepared to regulate, and if it is only public indecency that can be regulated, then we could represent these as exceptions to the usual ban on offense regulation. But we will need to know what, if anything, it is about public offense that is especially problematic, and how to determine when the offense may be permissibly regulated. To determine when nuisance regulation is permissible and when it is not, Feinberg employs a *balancing test* in which we must

---

15. Joel Feinberg, *The Moral Limits of the Criminal Law*, 4 vols. (New York: Oxford University Press, 1984–88).
16. Joel Feinberg, *Offense to Others* (New York: Oxford University Press, 1985), volume 2 of *The Moral Limits of the Criminal Law*, chs. 7–8.

weigh the seriousness of the offense against the importance of the agent's interests being regulated. But what exactly should be put in the scales?

When assessing the seriousness of an offense, Feinberg says that we must consider several factors. We should pay attention to the *magnitude* of the offense, where that is a function of the *intensity*, *duration*, and *extent* of the offense. We should also pay attention to the *degree of avoidability*, attaching less significance to offenses that are easily avoidable for the audience and more significance to offenses that fall on *captive audiences*. Also, it seems we should not attach much significance to offenses that an audience has consented to or has agreed to risk. Just as Mill focuses on non-consensual harms, for purposes of the harm principle, so too Feinberg focuses on *non-consensual offense*, for purposes of nuisance regulation.

These dimensions of offense all seem quite significant. But some of Feinberg's other claims about seriousness of offense seem more problematic. For instance, he says we do not need to consider offenses that result from *abnormally sensitive* sensibilities. That would be too constraining. But it is not clear that we are entitled to ignore all abnormal sensibilities. At least if the offended is not responsible for her unusual sensibility, why should we discount her offense? It seems that I should still take reasonable steps to avoid causing you auditory offense, even if I learn that your auditory sensitivity is abnormally acute.

Also, Feinberg eschews considerations about the *reasonableness* of the offense in determinations of its seriousness. He thinks that abnormality is a reasonable proxy for unreasonableness and worries about allowing the state to make determinations of reasonableness. But abnormality is an inadequate proxy for unreasonableness. Consider the offense that racial bigots experience at seeing interracial couples in public. Presumably, a liberal should deny that the offense resulting from a bigoted sensibility creates even a *pro tanto* case for regulating public appearances by interracial couples. But we can't secure this result by appealing to the abnormality of the bigoted sensibility. Such offense was presumably not abnormal—that is, uncommon—in the Jim Crow South. It seems we do need to appeal to the unreasonableness of the bigoted sensibility.[17] Feinberg may think that when we balance interests

---

17. One needn't think that offenses have to be reasonable for the offensive behavior to be regulated; it might be enough if they are not unreasonable. Perhaps there's nothing especially reasonable about the offense we take at the coprophagic picnickers on the bus (case #8). But if there are some offenses that are unreasonable, then I'm not sure that they should contribute to a *pro tanto* case for regulation, no matter their intensity or duration.

the scales will always favor the interests in freedom of association of the interracial couple over the interests in being free of offense by racial bigots, no matter the intensity, duration, and extent of the offense. But one might wonder if that's true, and, in any case, one might wonder whether bigoted offense creates even a *pro tanto* case for restricting interracial dating.

Finally, we might notice another potential dimension affecting the significance of offense—its *fixity*. Some, but not all, of what we find offensive is the result of culturally conditioned sensibilities. One can well imagine stable democratic regimes that would tolerate offense, and it is quite possible that societies that tolerate what we find offensive would not perceive any or as much offense in the same conduct. For instance, whereas the nuisance involved in sleep deprivation by loud and disorderly conduct in the middle of the night does not seem to be especially culturally conditioned, the offense that some take to public displays of nudity does seem to be culturally conditioned to a significant extent. But then we might attach less significance to those offenses that are not fixed and depend on the very sort of conventions and taboos that the offensive regulation enforces.

The other scale in the balance involves the interests of the offender. Feinberg appeals to the *expressive value* of the offender's interests, both to the offender himself and to society at large. Here, we might supplement Feinberg's own analysis of the expressive value of offensive behavior with Mill's claims about the expressive and deliberative value of experiments in living. Feinberg also appeals in this context to the *availability of alternative avenues of expression*. The impact on my expressive interests of regulating my offensive conduct will be less severe if that regulation leaves me many other means of expressing myself. In effect, many regulations of public indecency can be understood as analogous to time, manner, and place restrictions that regulate but do not significantly restrict expressive liberties. Provided such regulations leave alternative avenues of expression and do not have a significantly differential impact, they do not present a serious threat to expressive interests. This is perhaps the single most important fact in the case for regulating public offenses imposed on a captive audience.

Feinberg adds that people have weaker expressive claims when they enter *public space* and concludes that it is easier to justify offense regulation in public places. This may be plausible either because public fora often do involve captive audiences (increasing the significance of offense) or because regulation in public fora often leaves alternative avenues for expression (reducing the impact of regulation on expressive interests). But I doubt that public fora, as such, reduce expressive interests. If the only means of expression were public, then regulation would have a significant impact on expressive interests. And when public fora do not involve a captive audience, one may wonder whether the public nature of the offense increases its seriousness. If, for instance, we allow sex orgies in a tent in the town square between 8 a.m. and 9 a.m. on Saturdays and put warning signs on the exterior of the tent, then the offense is eminently avoidable, and I'm not sure there is a very strong liberal case for regulation. In any case, I certainly don't see why expressive interests would cease to play a role just because the locale was public.

The details of Feinberg's balancing test are complex and potentially controversial. A full discussion of them is not possible here. But it does seem safe to say that most liberal societies do in fact allow for some nuisance regulation and that if one is going to consider modifying Mill's categorical approach so as to allow the regulation of some kinds of nuisance, then one must restrict potential regulation to offense that is not unreasonable and involves a captive audience, and one must allow restriction only when the expressive interests of the offenders are modest and where offenders have ample alternative avenues of expression. Since Mill's own position on offense regulation is not fully consistent, it is hard to say how big a modification this would make in his liberal principles.

One potentially puzzling feature of Feinberg's modified Millian position on offense deserves notice. Feinberg distinguishes profound offense, which he treats separately, from the nuisances of the sort displayed on his Bus Rides.[18] He mentions several examples of profound offense, including sexual harassment in the workplace, desecration of the dead, and psychologically traumatic displays of hate, as in the neo-Nazi march in Skokie. Feinberg says that, in contrast with mere nuisances, profound offenses are less ephemeral and trivial. That makes his conclusion that profound offense regulation is harder to justify than nuisance regulation *prima facie* puzzling. But the puzzle dissolves once one understands other claims he makes about profound offense. Some actions that cause profound offense are not merely offensive but actually cause harm. This is true, Feinberg thinks, of workplace harassment. Though the injuries are psychic, not physical, they are no less real for that and do set back important professional interests of the harassed. So workplace harassment can be handled by the harm principle and need

---

18. Feinberg, *Offense to Others*, ch. 9.

not appeal to offense regulation. By contrast, Feinberg thinks, desecration of the dead and hate speech, though offensive, are not, or need not be, harmful. He claims that these profound offenses do not depend upon being personally experienced, as the offenses in the Bus Rides are, but arise from the bare knowledge of the conduct in question, and have a moral character. He believes that whereas nuisance, such as public indecency, tends to be wrong (when it is wrong) because it is offensive, profound offense tends to be offensive because of its perceived wrongness. Insofar as this is true, so-called profound offense legislation is better justified, if at all, Feinberg thinks, as legal moralism. However, Feinberg takes it to be a constitutive commitment of Millian liberalism to reject legal moralism. As a result, he tends to be more skeptical of the regulation of profound offense than he is of the regulation of nuisance.

One might respond that desecration of the dead and hate speech can involve personal offense and not just the moralized offense that depends upon the bare knowledge of the activities in question. Relatives of the deceased might experience psychological trauma witnessing desecration of the bodies of their loved ones that a disinterested observer would not, and Holocaust survivors in Skokie might also experience psychological trauma if the neo-Nazis march in their streets that a disinterested observer would not. One might well try to justify restricting these activities on offense-based, rather than moralism-based, grounds. Whether such restrictions could be justified in this way should depend on the results of applying an appropriate balancing test.

58. Legal moralism

Feinberg treats the rejection of legal moralism as a constitutive commitment of Millian liberalism. Mill, we saw, appears to reject legal moralism categorically (I 9). He goes on to reject "blue laws" that forbid work on the Sabbath (IV 20), prohibition on Mormon polygamy (IV 21), temperance legislation (V 6–7), and laws forbidding gambling and prostitution (V 8–10).[19] Indeed,

---

19. Of course, Mill objects to any marriage that does not recognize equal rights of women, but he thinks that there is nothing especially objectionable about plural marriage as such. He is clear that polygamy would have to afford wives ready exit from marriages that proved unacceptable (IV 21), and presumably he would not permit underage girls to marry.

it is Mill's anti-moralism that provokes the strongest criticism from Stephen in *Liberty, Equality, and Fraternity* and his (Stephen's) defense of the use of the criminal law to promote virtue and curb vice.

But is Mill really committed to denying legal moralism? Indeed, one might think that Mill is actually committed to legal moralism by his sanction theory of duty. Recall that Chapter V of *Utilitarianism* links the idea of duty to sanctions.

> For the truth is that the idea of penal sanction, which is the essence of law, enters not only into the conception of injustice, but into that of any kind of wrong. We do not call anything wrong unless we mean to imply that a person ought to be punished in some way or other for doing it—if not by law, by the opinion of his fellow creatures; if not by opinion, by the reproaches of his own conscience. This seems to be the real turning point of the distinction between morality and simple expediency [V 14].

If something only counts as wrong if sanctions are appropriate, then it might seem to be a necessary, perhaps conceptual, truth that the law ought to sanction immoral conduct. This seems to be the conclusion that Mill himself goes on to draw.

> It is part of the notion of Duty in every one of its forms, that a person may rightfully be compelled to fulfil it. Duty is a thing which may be *exacted* from a person, as one exacts a debt. Unless we think that it might be exacted from him, we do not call it his duty [V 14].[20]

However, there are a number of reasons to be skeptical of this rationale for legal moralism and its Millian pedigree.

Some doubts are traceable to problems with this sanction theory of duty. As we saw earlier (§27), one worry is that the appeal to sanctions seems to provide the *wrong sort of reason* to hold that behavior is wrong. It makes the wrongness of an act depend upon the appropriateness of punishing or, more generally, sanctioning it. But this inverts what many would regard as the usual dependency between wrongness and sanction. Many think that punishment or sanction is appropriate for wrong acts *because* they are wrong. This requires grounding their wrongness in some independent account; it is not the suitability for sanction that makes an act wrong. But if wrongness is

---

20. Mill goes on to say that though duty implies that an agent may be compelled not to do wrong and could not complain about such compulsion, nonetheless there may be good reasons not to compel his duty. But if sanction utilitarianism identifies wrong action as action that it is optimal to sanction, it's hard to see how there might be duties that one should not enforce.

explanatorily prior to blame and sanction, then we should reject this response-dependent conception of wrongness and claim instead that blame or sanction is a *fitting response* to wrongdoing that is culpable. On this view, the reactive attitudes aim to track (culpable) wrongdoing, not vice versa.

In any case, this indirect account of duty cannot be squared with Mill's more considered commitment to direct utilitarianism. As a result, Mill could not consistently endorse legal moralism for this reason. The direct utilitarian assesses conduct, rules prohibiting that conduct, and sanctions for noncompliance with prohibitions separately and, in each case, by its consequences, in relation to its alternatives. Insofar as Mill is a direct utilitarian, he has no commitment to sanctioning all suboptimal conduct.

Finally, we might note that, despite Mill's apparent endorsement of legal moralism in the last quoted passage, the sanction theory of duty does not entail legal moralism. The sanction theory of duty does link wrongness and sanctions, but it does not link wrongness and legal sanctions by the state. Recall that Mill distinguishes different grades of sanctions—legal (e.g. criminal) sanctions by the state, social sanctions of various kinds including ostracism and mere disapprobation, and self-reproach or blame. The first two sorts of sanctions are external, whereas the third is internal. Mill does not say that all wrong actions merit legal sanction, only that they merit some kind of sanction or other, external or internal. But then the sanction theory of duty does not imply that all wrong actions deserve to be legally prohibited and sanctioned.

So, I think we can acquit Mill of the charge of inconsistency about legal moralism. He seems pretty consistent in his rejection of legal moralism, which explains Stephen's moralistic criticisms. The debate between Mill and Stephen was revived a century later by Lord Devlin's defense of the legal regulation of homosexuality, prostitution, and pornography, and liberal criticisms of Devlin by H.L.A. Hart, Joel Feinberg, and Ronald Dworkin.[21] It can be tempting to see these debates over moralism in stark terms, as a choice between Mill and Stephen. In particular, it can be tempting to think that rejecting the legal moralism of Stephen and Devlin is a vindication of Millian anti-moralism. But that temptation should be resisted, as we will see.

21. See Patrick Devlin, *The Enforcement of Morals* (Oxford: Clarendon Press, 1965); H.L.A. Hart, *Law, Liberty, and Morality* (Stanford: Stanford University Press, 1963); Ronald Dworkin, "Liberty and Moralism," reprinted in *Taking Rights Seriously*; and Joel Feinberg, *Harmless Wrongdoing* (New York: Oxford University Press, 1988), volume 4 of *The Moral Limits of the Criminal Law*.

Of course, a great deal of morality is concerned with harm prevention, and central provisions of the criminal law prohibiting killing, rape, assault, and theft are clearly concerned to prevent especially serious moral wrongs that harm others. This means that much of the criminal law both prevents harm and enforces morality. These are not simply coincidental outcomes, inasmuch as the immorality of much criminal conduct consists in its harmfulness. This could make us wonder if there are cases of legal moralism that can't be justified by appeal to the harm principle.

Even if there is considerable overlap between harmful conduct and wrongdoing, the two are distinguishable. First, there are harms that are not wrong, such as self-defense and other kinds of moral necessity in which it is permissible to harm another as a way of avoiding greater evil. Second, there are wrongs that do not harm others. Just which things fall in this category is a matter of dispute. The traditional debate over legal moralism between Devlin and Hart concerned the legislative enforcement of sexual morality, in particular, the regulation of homosexuality, prostitution, and pornography. For the most part, both sides conceded that these activities were immoral but harmless and debated whether it could be permissible to regulate them as a matter of enforcing sexual morality. But we might reject Devlin's moralistic proposals, not because we reject legal moralism per se, but rather because we do not regard homosexuality, prostitution, or pornography as per se immoral. If these were the only candidates for harmless wrongdoing, we might wonder if there was such a thing. However, there are other plausible candidates for harmless wrongdoing, including, but not limited to, such things as criminal attempts, blackmail and extortion that do not harm the victim, broken promises that do no harm, desecration of the dead, and bestiality. If there are justified harms and harmless wrongdoing, then we can distinguish harm prevention and legal moralism and ask if we should endorse legal moralism, as well as the harm principle (see §60).

59. The Devlin debate

To understand and assess the Millian position on legal moralism, it is useful to bear in mind the debate between Devlin and his Millian critics. In Britain in 1954 the Wolfenden Committee recommended that homosexuality and prostitution should no longer be criminalized. Devlin criticized the report and defended the legislative enforcement of sexual morality, invoking two main arguments.

Devlin's first argument appeals to a society's right of self-defense. It has something like this structure.

1. Society has right to protect its own existence by prohibiting behavior that threatens its existence.
2. Homosexuality, prostitution, and pornography threaten society's existence.
3. Hence, society has a right to prohibit homosexuality and pornography.

Both Hart and Dworkin have effectively criticized this argument as unsound. Its apparent plausibility rests on a tacit equivocation between two different ways of thinking of society:

(a) a culturally elastic entity that persists through various changes in social mores
(b) a culturally inelastic entity that is defined by its current social mores.

(1) is plausible only on the (a)-reading. Indeed, so understood, it might be defended by appeal to the harm principle. (2) is plausible only on the (b)-reading. But if we read the premises so as to maximize their plausibility, then the argument is unsound because it equivocates between these two readings. On either univocal reading, the argument is valid but not sound. On the univocal (a)-reading, (1) may be true but (2) is false, and on the univocal (b)-reading (2) may be true but (1) is false. On no reading is the argument sound.

Devlin also appeals to public censure as a reason to regard the behavior as immoral and subject to regulation. Here, he seems to argue as follows.

1. Society has reason to prohibit behavior that is immoral, whether or not it causes harm.
2. Hence, society has reason to prohibit behavior that it has good reason to believe is immoral.
3. Public censure of behavior provides good reason to think that the behavior is immoral.
4. There is public censure of homosexuality, prostitution, and pornography.
5. Hence, society has a right to prohibit homosexuality, prostitution, and pornography.

Some critics, such as Dworkin, have focused on (3), claiming that public censure is not very good reason to think that the object of censure is immoral. Censure might register disgust or unfamiliarity rather than a moral judgment. Even when censure reflects moral beliefs, censure itself provides no good reason to think that the censured conduct is immoral. People have all sorts of moral beliefs that are ill-informed, dogmatic, superstitious, and the product of prejudice. One has to be able to tell some secularly plausible story about why the censured conduct is wrong before one should treat censure as a reliable indicator of immorality. Perhaps we should reject (3), as such. But also we should reject the specific suggestion that public censure of homosexuality, prostitution, and pornography provides good evidence of their immorality.

Mill and anyone else who categorically rejects legal moralism will think that the plausibility of (3) is neither here nor there. The real problem with the argument, they must claim, is (1). Much immoral conduct is harmful and that is why it is immoral. This is true of central provisions of the criminal law, such as the prohibitions on murder, rape, assault, and theft. This sort of moral legislation is fine. But moral legislation as such, in particular, moral legislation that does not aim to prevent harm, is impermissible. Criminal legislation deprives people of liberty and, as such, imposes quite significant harm. The only good reason for imposing such harm is the prevention of harm.

60. Beyond the Devlin debate

Though Devlin's critics raise real problems for his defense of moralism, that debate can remain unsatisfying. One reason is that it is contentious whether the sexual interests and activities in question are in fact immoral. Homosexuality or prostitution that involves coercion or that occurs between adults and children is wrong, as is heterosexual sex that involves either coercion or children. Violent or misogynist pornography will be wrong insofar as it is harmful. But these observations don't show that there is anything wrong with homosexuality, prostitution, or pornography per se.

It is easier to keep the philosophical issues about legal moralism in focus, I think, if we focus our attention on less disputed cases of immorality. Consider a less controversial case of a harmless immorality, for instance, a case of promise-breaking or deception that actually fails to result in harm. Junior takes his parents' car out for a joyride without permission but nothing untoward happens. Here is a case of harmless wrongdoing. Consider this moralistic argument.

1. Society has reason to prohibit behavior that is immoral, whether or not it causes harm.
2. Junior's taking the car without parental permission is a case of harmless wrongdoing.
3. Hence, society has a right to prohibit Junior's behavior.

One person's *modus ponens* is another person's *modus tollens*. Many people would reject (3), claiming that the criminal law ought not to reach into family relations in this way. Millian liberals might well claim that the case against (3) is clearer than the case for (1), so that we should appeal to the falsity of (3) to reject the moralist premise in (1). This is an instance of a more general argumentative strategy for Millian liberals. If there are any cases in which we should reject the legislative enforcement of morality, that undermines legal moralism, because immorality, as such, is not sufficient to justify regulation.

But this argumentative strategy is problematic. The *modus tollens* argument against moralism assumes that the argument in (1)–(3) is valid. But it is not. The conclusion of the argument—(3)—is an all-things-considered verdict about what the state is permitted to do. But the moralist principle (1) on which it allegedly rests asserts only a *pro tanto* or *prima facie* reason to regulate. But a *pro tanto* reason to regulate does not entail an all-things-considered reason to regulate.[22] In particular, even if there is some reason to regulate conduct, there may be countervailing reasons not to regulate it. Perhaps the costs of regulation—administrative costs and the costs of improper regulation—exceed the benefits of regulation. Earlier, we suggested that this might be one lesson from the American experience with Prohibition (§52). But this shows that the legal moralist need not regulate all harmless wrongdoing and that it is not necessary to reject legal moralism as such in order to defend liberal conclusions about the limits of state regulation. This does not vindicate legal moralism, but it does caution us that we

---

22. Critics of Devlin's second argument have focused on the truth of the premises in his argument. But this analysis shows that Devlin's second argument is (also) unsound because invalid.

cannot argue against legal moralism by citing cases in which it would be wrong all-things-considered for the state to intervene to promote virtue or reduce vice.[23] Because it is possible to reject moralistic intervention in particular cases without rejecting legal moralism, it is possible to reject Devlin's case for regulating homosexuality, prostitution, and pornography without rejecting legal moralism as such.

To be clear about Mill's anti-moralism, it might be helpful to distinguish weak and strong moralistic theses.

1. *Weak Moralism*: an action's wrongness is *pro tanto* reason to regulate it.
2. *Strong Moralism*: an action's wrongness is conclusive reason to regulate it.

The distinction is important, because, as we have just seen, one can reject strong moralism without rejecting weak moralism. It is clear that Mill rejects strong moralism. It is less clear if he also rejects weak moralism.

We can also frame this as a question about the nature and strength of Mill's skepticism about legal moralism. There are at least three forms of skepticism worth distinguishing.

1. Skepticism that moralistic interference is typically on-balance justified.
2. Skepticism that moralistic interference is ever on-balance justified.
3. Skepticism that moralistic interference is *pro tanto* justified.

These are progressively stronger forms of skepticism. Mill is not very precise in his statements of anti-moralism, but he does say that one cannot be compelled on purely moralistic grounds (I 9). It is clear that he accepts the first sort of skepticism. But that is not yet a categorical prohibition on legal moralism. Insofar as Mill seems to be staking out a categorical position, he must endorse either the second or third form of skepticism. He could apparently embrace the second kind of skepticism without embracing the third sort of skepticism.

But even the second form of skepticism about legal moralism is too strong if there are cases of harmless wrongdoing where legal regulation is not only *pro tanto* justified but also on-balance justified. Consider the following list of candidates for harmless immorality that it is nonetheless appropriate to regulate.

---

23. This is one way of understanding the significance of Michael Moore's defense of legal moralism in *Placing Blame* (Oxford: Clarendon Press, 1997), ch. 16.

1. Criminal attempts, such as attempted murder, that aim to harm but do not succeed.
2. Crimes that don't harm, because their consequences don't make anyone worse off than they would otherwise be, such as the murder of someone whose life, unbeknownst to the murderer, is not worth living or who would otherwise have died a worse death a moment later.
3. Non-harmful fraud or blackmail.
4. Actions that would be harmful but for the non-identity problem. The non-identity problem is present in cases in which one's actions determine not only how benefits and harms are distributed but also who exists to be benefited or harmed. My action may make someone—for instance, my child or a member of a future generation—badly off without harming him if he wouldn't exist if I had not acted as I did.[24]
5. Desecration of the dead.
6. Bestiality.

These all seem to be cases of conduct that is not or at least need not be harmful. Most of them would strike most people as wrong.[25] One might try to bring the first two kinds of cases under the harm principle if we can understand that principle as justifying the regulation of actions that *risk* harm. But, even if we accept that reading of the harm principle, it won't help with the other cases, which neither cause nor risk harm. Yet many would think some or all of them are properly regulated by the criminal or civil law. If any of these involve harmless immorality that it is permissible to regulate, then we must reject a categorical ban on legal moralism. The most that could be justified would be a weak skepticism about legal moralism that saw the on-balance permissibility of the legislative enforcement of morality as exceptional.

---

24. See Derek Parfit, *Reasons and Persons* (Oxford: Clarendon Press, 1984), ch. 16 and Feinberg, *Harmless Wrongdoing*, pp. 325–27.
25. Not everyone regards all of these alleged harmless immoralities as wrong. Peter Singer opines that bestiality that does not involve cruelty to animals is morally permissible. See Peter Singer, "Heavy Petting," *Nerve* (2001) <http://www.utilitarian.net/singer/by/2001----.htm>. I am not persuaded. Singer's reasons for thinking harmless bestiality permissible would seem to imply that under certain circumstances sex with children who are too young to comprehend or remember would also be permissible. But I am more confident in denying the permissibility of sex with very young children than I am accepting the permissibility of harmless bestiality. In any case, the argument for weak legal moralism only requires that there be some harmless immoralities that deserve regulation, whether or not bestiality is such a case.

61. The categorical approach revisited

Mill's "one very simple principle"—that liberty may be restricted always and only to prevent harm to another—is over-simple. So too is the related categorical approach to liberty that approves all applications of the harm principle and rejects all cases of paternalism, censorship, offense regulation, and legal moralism.

The harm principle itself is complex in several ways. Harm to others is not a sufficient ground for restricting liberty. Rather, it creates a *pro tanto* reason for restricting liberty. Determination of whether restrictions on harmful conduct are fully justified depends on balancing the evils of regulation against the harm to be prevented. This weaker form of sufficiency is the more plausible liberal claim, though various cases, including justifications involving self-defense and necessity, economic losses in fair competition, and emotional injury, raise questions about whether even weak sufficiency is too strong. Moreover, it is not clear if the harm principle justifies restricting liberty to prevent others from being harmed or only justifies restricting liberty to prevent those whose liberty is being restricted from causing harm to another. The anti-harming rationale for restricting liberty is narrower than the harm-prevention rationale. Only the broader harm-prevention rationale would explain how Mill could hope to square Good Samaritan laws and laws compelling testimony in court with the harm principle. Because the harm-prevention principle is broader, it will justify greater restrictions on liberty than the anti-harming principle. It is also unclear whether the harm principle protects all liberty or just basic liberties. A harm prevention basic liberties interpretation makes Mill's harm principle more robust but is a far cry from the common libertarian reading of Mill as limiting liberty only to prevent force or fraud.

Interacting with some of these issues about the role and adequacy of the harm principle is the question about how exactly to understand harm and, in particular, whether and, if so, how to moralize it. Often, Mill relies on an unmoralized conception of harm as something like the setback of an important interest. Such a conception underlies many of his claims and provides a reasonably good fit with common ways of thinking and speaking about harm. But Mill's considered view seems to moralize harm by conceiving of it as the setback of an important interest to which the individual has a right. Moralizing harm in this way makes the harm principle more robust than it would otherwise be but still seems to give harm prevention an explanatory role in Mill's liberal arguments. This moralization might be contrasted with a different moralization that conceives of harm as the wrongful or unjustified setback of another's interests. This conception of harm appears to deprive the appeal to harm of its intended explanatory value. In particular, it prevents Mill from citing the harm that an agent would cause as the reason for thinking that his liberty may be restricted, because, on this moralized conception, an action only counts as harmful if the agent is acting impermissibly or outside of his rights.

However these questions are resolved, it is doubtful that the harm principle is necessary to justify restrictions on liberty. Liberty may be restricted to pursue the public good in certain ways. Moreover, Mill softens his antipaternalistic position by recognizing the permissibility of restrictions on selling oneself into slavery and other autonomy-enhancing forms of paternalism. He recognizes legitimate forms of censorship designed to prevent harm to others. But he also has room to recognize restrictions on speech that advance the very deliberative values that explain why censorship is normally bad. Despite his general hostility to offense regulation, at one point Mill recognizes the permissibility of restrictions on public indecency on the ground that such conduct is offensive to others. The best resolution of Mill's inconsistent claims about offense regulation may be to adopt a test, similar to Feinberg's, that balances the legitimate interests of the audience against the expressive interests of the actor or speaker. Though Mill does seem more consistent in his opposition to legal moralism, it is not necessary to reject legal moralism as such in order to recognize the liberal conclusion that many forms of legal moralism do not do enough good in order to justify the harms they cause. Moreover, there are some forms of legal moralism that do seem to justify enforcing moral norms, even though the behavior in question does not cause harm. Though Mill does not address such forms of legal moralism explicitly, it is hard to imagine that he would reject them all.

9
Liberalism, utilitarianism, and rights

We have examined Mill's liberal principles in some detail now. In particular, we have a better grasp of which liberal rights he wants to recognize and how he wants to justify those rights. Various basic liberties are necessary conditions to the exercise of those deliberative capacities that mark us as progressive beings and that are central to our higher-order interests and happiness. Though harm prevention is generally much easier to justify than other sorts of restrictions on liberty, including paternalism, offense regulation, and moralism, Mill's one very simple principle is vastly over-simple. At most, harm prevention creates a *pro tanto* case for restriction, one that can be overcome if regulation is too cumbersome, costly, or ineffective. Some injuries do not seem to create even a *pro tanto* case for regulation, including injuries caused by self-defense, economic losses in fair competition, and emotional injuries. To square these justifications with the harm principle would require moralizing harm. Harm prevention is not necessary, as is demonstrated by autonomy-enhancing forms of paternalism and censorship and by restrictions on individual liberty incidental to pursuing the common good. Provided the state pursues a good that is genuinely common and does not interfere with basic liberties of conscience, expression, and lifestyle of its citizens, such incidental restrictions on liberty are permissible. With this more comprehensive understanding of his liberal principles and the liberal rights he recognizes, we are in a better position to address the apparent tension between his conception of liberal rights and his utilitarianism.

62. The apparent tension between utility and rights

As we saw earlier (§40), there is an apparent tension between moral appeals to utility and moral appeals to rights. Utilitarianism treats the good as prior to and independent of the right or duty—defining duty as the promotion of the good, conceived as well-being or happiness. Perhaps respecting certain liberties tends to be good, but, according to direct utilitarianism, the moral quality of a particular action depends on its own consequences, and there's no reason to believe that respecting individual liberties is always optimal. By contrast, the *deontological* and *natural rights* traditions treat duty or the right as prior to and independent of the good. In particular, deontologists believe that it is not always one's duty to promote good consequences and that sometimes it is wrong to do the optimal act. Deontologists recognize moral *constraints* on pursuing the good. These constraints usually take the form of *categorical rules* to perform or refrain from certain sorts of actions, regardless of the consequences. A special case of this perceived conflict between categorical rules and utility is the perceived tension between utility and *rights*. For, on a common view, individual rights just are a special case of categorical rules. Indeed, much contemporary work in moral and political philosophy assumes that rights, such as rights to liberties or to freedom from harm, function as "side constraints" or "trumps" on the pursuit of good consequences.[1]

It might be useful to try to identify different strands in this apparent tension between utility and rights.

1. Rights function typically to silence or trump direct appeals to utility in moral deliberation and debate.
2. Rights function typically to trump or defeat the moral value of pursing collective goods.
3. There can be a right to do something that would fail to maximize utility.
4. There can be a right to do something wrong.

---

1. See Nozick, *Anarchy, State, and Utopia*, pp. 28–35, and Dworkin, *Taking Rights Seriously*, pp. xi, 184–205.

5. It is *pro tanto* wrong to violate rights.
6. Rights are side constraints on pursuit of the good.
7. Rights are absolute; it is always on-balance wrong to violate a right.

Claims (1) and (2) both invoke Dworkin's idea that rights function as trumps, that is, as a kind of moral suit or currency that defeats other kinds of moral suits or currencies in moral and political debate. (1) is an epistemic claim about moral psychology and deliberation; it says that rights should supersede direct appeals to considerations of utility in an agent's deliberations and in public debate. By contrast, (2) is a metaphysical claim that rights are moral factors that override or defeat other moral factors involving collective advantage. Claim (3) asserts that there are rights to pursue a suboptimal course of conduct. Claim (4) assumes that there can be a right to do something wrong, in particular, a right to make certain kinds of unwise or bad choices. Claim (5) holds that one ought not violate rights. Claim (6) is Nozick's idea that rights are not themselves goods, perhaps especially important goods, but are instead side constraints on the pursuit of goods. But Nozick does not insist that rights are absolute. On some views, they may be permissibly violated when the consequences of honoring them would be not just suboptimal but catastrophic. Claim (7) goes further, insisting that rights are absolute, which presumably means that it would always be on-balance wrong to violate them.

These assumptions about rights and utility are not all equally uncontroversial. For instance, if there is a plurality of rights, it is not clear why they couldn't conflict. Indeed, we do seem to recognize such conflicts, as when we recognize a conflict between the right of the accused to a fair trial and the right to privacy of potential witnesses or a conflict between the rights of innocent to be free from harm and the right of others to self-defense, even against innocent aggressors. If there is a conflict of rights, both cannot win, and so rights cannot be absolute. Moreover, it presumably won't be wrong to abridge the right that is overridden, which raises the question whether it is always on-balance wrong to violate rights. Nor is it clear that rights can be side constraints on the pursuit of the good if they are not absolute. I raise these issues here, not to try to settle them, but to show that some of these alleged marks of rights are controversial. Though all have some plausibility and adherents, some are more plausible than others. I have tried to arrange them from the least to the most controversial.[2]

Mill's liberalism is an interesting test for this conventional wisdom that utility and rights are incompatible, because, as we have seen, he recognizes individual rights that are supposed to be grounded in considerations of utility.

> It is proper to state that I forego any advantage which could be derived to my argument from the idea of abstract right as a thing independent of utility. I regard utility as the ultimate appeal on all ethical questions; but it must be utility in the largest sense, grounded on the permanent interests of man as a progressive being [OL I 11].

To decide if Mill can ground rights in utility, it may help to see which, if any, of these claims about rights he can accept. Attention to Mill's explicit theory of rights in Chapter V of *Utilitarianism* and to his liberal principles and arguments in *On Liberty* suggests three somewhat different conceptions of rights with somewhat different implications for the reconciliation of utility and rights.

63. The sanction theory of rights

We might begin by considering Mill's explicit theory of rights introduced in Chapter V of *Utilitarianism*, which we encountered briefly before (§25). Recall that Mill there introduces the concept of a right in the context of his sanction theory of duty, which is an indirect form of utilitarianism that identifies wrong actions, not as suboptimal actions, but as actions that it is useful—on one interpretation, optimal—to sanction (V 14). Mill then introduces justice as a proper part of duty. Justice involves duties that are perfect duties—that is, duties that are correlated with rights (V 15).

> Justice implies something which it is not only right to do, and wrong not to do, but which some individual person can claim from us as a matter of right [V 15].

---

2. In "Rights, Constraints, and Trumps," *Analysis* 47 (1987): 8–14, Philip Pettit argues that side constraint and trump conceptions of rights are equivalent. But, as he recognizes, Dworkin's trumps insulate rights claims from an unspecified range of demands to pursue collective goals, whereas Nozick's constraints insulate rights claims from almost all demands to pursue collective goods (p. 12). Perhaps one could say that constraints are unusually strong trumps. But then trumps, as such, do not imply constraints.

Mill explains his theory of rights in terms of the two elements in a rights violation—an injury to the right holder and warranted punishment.

> These [two] elements are, a hurt to some assignable person or persons on the one hand, and a demand for punishment on the other....[T]hese two things include all that we mean when we speak of violation of a right. When we call anything a person's right, we mean that he has a valid claim on society to protect him in the possession of it, either by the force of law, or by that of education and opinion. If he has what we consider a sufficient claim, on whatever account, to have something guaranteed to him by society, we say that he has a right to it. If we desire to prove that anything does not belong to him by right, we think this is done as soon as it is admitted that society ought not to take measures for securing it to him, but should leave it to chance, or to his own exertions [V 24].

This is a sanction theory of rights, akin to Mill's sanction theory of duty. It says that one has a right to some interest or liberty insofar as society ought to protect that interest or liberty. But this conception of a right does not yet introduce any utilitarian considerations. Mill adds utilitarianism to the mix in his account of the conditions under which society ought to enforce an individual's claim.

> To have a right, then, is, I conceive, to have something which society ought to defend me in the possession of. If the objector goes on to ask why it ought, I can give him no other reason than general utility [V 25].

These claims introduce a form of indirect utilitarianism into Mill's conception of rights. For it implies that whether one possesses a right to particular interests or liberties in a particular case is not determined by the value of honoring or interfering with that interest or liberty but by the value of protecting it and punishing interference with it. We might call this a sanction or sanction-utilitarian conception of rights.

How, if at all, does this indirect utilitarian aspect of Mill's theory of rights afford a response to the apparent tension between utility and rights? For example, what does it imply about some possible marks of rights, which we have discussed?

If an individual's interest or liberty is sufficiently important to justify society's protection, even when protecting that right requires inconvenience or foregoing some collective benefits, then it seems clear that rights, on this conception, will typically trump claims about the value of pursuing other collective goods and should typically silence such appeals in moral reasoning and public debate as well.

It also seems clear that rights, so conceived, can conflict with considerations of direct utility. For whether a right is violated by interference with an individual's interest or liberty is determined not by the comparative utility of the interference but by the comparative utility of enforcing the individual's claim to that interest or liberty. It seems quite possible that it would be good or optimal to defend an individual's liberty in some matters, even if the individual exercises that liberty to choose suboptimal outcomes. So, for instance, it seems likely that it would be good or optimal for society to defend an individual's autonomy even in cases in which the individual chooses imprudently, for instance, by choosing a poor mate.

It is a little more complicated matter whether Mill can maintain the right to do wrong if he combines his indirect sanction theory of rights with his indirect sanction theory of duty. Here the question is whether there is a liberty to perform acts that it is optimal (or useful) to protect, even though it is optimal (or useful) to sanction the act. The answer to this question appears to be Yes. Especially if we have in mind informal sanctions in the form of self-reproach or social censure, it is not hard to imagine that there might be forms of imprudence or socially obtuse behavior that would be wrong—because it would be optimal or especially useful to sanction by self-reproach or mild social censure—which the individual would nonetheless have a right to perform—because it would be optimal or especially useful for society to protect the individual's claim to do so. If so, there can be rights to do things that are wrong (according to the sanction utilitarian conception of duty).

It is one thing for there to be a right to do something suboptimal or wrong. It is another thing to say that such a right should be respected or enforced. Mill thinks that a right is something that society ought to protect me in the possession and exercise of, and he thinks that to protect me in this way is to punish (by force of law or opinion) those who do or would interfere with my possession or exercise of that to which I have a right. But then rights violators ought to be punished by society. And so—according to the sanction theory of duty—it seems to follow that they act wrongly.

1. One has a right to x if and only if society ought to protect one's possession or exercise of x.

2. In order for society to protect a claim to x, it must punish (by law or opinion) those who interfere with the possession or exercise of x.

3. Hence, if one has a right, society ought to punish those who violate that right.
4. An act is wrong if and only if some sort of sanction ought to be applied to its performance.
5. Hence, it is wrong to violate rights.

It is a further question whether sanction utilitarian rights function as side constraints. On the one hand, their indirect utilitarian character means that rights do not depend on considerations of direct utility. Whether I have a right to freedom of speech does not depend on the utility of my speech but rather on the utility of protecting and enforcing my ability to speak. So sanction rights do seem to constrain direct appeals to utility. On the other hand, sanction rights are claims that it would be wrong to interfere with because of the utility of enforcing those claims. For this reason, it's hard to see sanction rights as vindicating Nozick's idea that rights are side constraints, not justified by the good they promote. As we've seen, it's not clear that failure to deliver side constraints flouts an adequacy condition on rights (more on this in §65).

We treated it as a separate question whether rights are absolute. It's a complicated matter whether sanction rights are absolute. On the one hand, we just saw an argument showing that it is always wrong to violate rights. If I have a right to x, then society ought to protect me in the possession, enjoyment, or use of x and ought to punish those who would interfere with x. But if those who would interfere with x ought to be punished, then, according to the sanction theory of duty, they act wrongly. Hence, it is always wrong to violate rights. But wouldn't this conclusion imply that there could be no conflicts of rights? Can't we imagine a situation in which different individuals have interests or liberties that are in conflict and cannot both be honored? Consider, for example, a conflict between the rights of innocent persons not to be harmed and the right of self-defense, even against innocent aggressors? In such cases, mightn't both parties have claims that it was useful to protect?

The answer turns, I think, on an issue that I said Mill does not address squarely, namely, the precise standard of expediency for applying sanctions. Recall that we distinguished two conceptions of that standard—usefulness, as involving something like net benefit, and optimality. One can imagine that it might be useful to protect each of two mutually incompatible claims. What's harder to understand is how it could be optimal to protect each of two mutually incompatible claims. This suggests that there could be conflicting rights according to the usefulness or net benefit criterion for applying sanctions, but not according to the optimality criterion. If there can be a conflict of rights, rights cannot be absolute.

So we need to revisit the claim that it is always wrong to violate rights. It is common to treat judgments that an action is wrong as final or conclusive moral verdicts based on a proper weighting of all the morally relevant factors. If it were always wrong—in this sense—to violate moral rights, then that would be strong evidence that moral rights are absolute. Such a commitment would seem to require the optimality criterion for applying sanctions. For anything less than the optimality criterion would not be able to ensure that it was best to apply sanctions, and if it wasn't best to apply sanctions, it's unclear why it should be all-things-considered wrong to violate the right. We can make this point another way. Assume that the relevant criterion of expediency for applying sanctions is mere usefulness, not optimality. It might be useful to protect an individual's claim to x. If so, sanction theories of rights and duty would imply that it was wrong to violate this right. But that is compatible with it being better still not to protect the individual's claim, the usefulness of protection being overridden by the greater usefulness of not protecting. But surely then we should treat its being wrong to violate the right as merely a *prima facie* or *pro tanto* moral claim, not a final or all-things-considered verdict.

This allows us to say that sanction rights are absolute just in case it is always all-things-considered, and not merely *pro tanto*, wrong to violate rights and that it is always all-things-considered wrong to violate rights just in case the criterion for applying sanctions is optimality. Use of any weaker criterion of expediency for applying sanctions will still allow us to say that it is always *pro tanto* wrong to violate rights but cannot guarantee that it will be all-things-considered wrong to violate rights, that rights will not conflict, or that rights will be absolute.

Though it is not incoherent to insist that rights are absolute and cannot conflict, this is a controversial view. If there is a plurality of rights, it's not clear why they couldn't conflict. Indeed, we do seem to recognize such conflicts, as when we recognize a conflict between the right of the accused to a fair trial and the right to privacy of potential witnesses or a conflict between the rights of innocent to be free from harm and the right of others to self-defense, even against innocent aggressors. If there is a conflict of rights, both cannot win, and so rights cannot be absolute. Moreover, it presumably won't be wrong to abridge the right that is overridden, which raises the question whether it is always wrong to violate rights. So while there is a reading of Mill's sanction theory of rights that would deliver these further claims about rights, it is not clear this is the reading we should prefer.

Whether or not we accept all these potential marks of rights, Mill's sanction theory of rights promises to accommodate many of them. Does that mean that Mill can give rights a utilitarian foundation and that the sanction theory is a promising conception of rights? Though the sanction theory accounts for many of the marks of rights, it is nonetheless problematic. Not surprisingly, the sanction theory of rights inherits the problems of the sanction theory of duty.

Recall that we found sanction utilitarianism to be internally inconsistent insofar as it combines indirect and direct utilitarian claims.

1. An act is right if and only if it is optimal to apply sanctions to its omission (the indirect claim).
2. Applying sanctions is right if and only if doing so is optimal (the direct claim).

Because the sanction theory of rights is committed to sanction utilitarianism, it inherits this inconsistency.

1. X has a right to Y if and only if society ought to protect X's claim to Y from interference (the first part of the sanction theory of rights).
2. Society ought to protect X's claim to Y from interference if and only if doing so is optimal (the second part of the sanction theory of rights).
3. Society ought to protect X's claim to Y from interference if and only if it would be optimal to blame society for failing to do so (the indirect sanction theory of duty).

As far as I can see, (2) and (3) are inconsistent. One could respond by decoupling the sanction theory of rights from the sanction theory of duty. (2) is only problematic when conjoined with the sanction theory of duty. Since we have already raised questions about the sanction theory of duty (§27), perhaps we should reject it, which would still seem to leave Mill free to accept the sanction theory of rights.

But the sanction theory of rights has problems of its own. Recall that the sanction theory of duty seemed to provide the *wrong kind of reason* for thinking an action wrong. Sanction utilitarianism says that acts are wrong because it is appropriate to sanction or punish them. But this inverts what most people believe is the relationship between punishment and wrongness. We punish wrong acts because they are wrong, which requires grounding their wrongness in something other than their suitability for punishment. Similarly, the sanction theory of rights treats the desirability of social enforcement as constitutive of the idea of a right. But this seems to get things backward. It is because we have rights that society ought to enforce them; it is not that we have rights to whatever society ought to enforce. The desirability of social enforcement seems *consequential* on the existence of the right.

This is even clearer, because there are some claims that society ought to enforce that are not rights. Among the things that society ought to recognize and protect are both rights and *privileges*. The exact line between rights and privileges is not always clear. But we recognize the distinction in claiming that some interests and opportunities that the state ought to protect are not ones that can be claimed as a matter of right. Perhaps a driver's license, access to public transportation, or certain income tax credits are best understood as privileges, rather than rights. The intuitive idea with privileges is that though there are good reasons for the state to recognize and protect them, they are not things that can be claimed as a matter of individual right or entitlement. This shows that the usefulness of social enforcement cannot be constitutive of a right, because otherwise privileges would be rights. But it also underscores the idea that even with rights, the desirability of social enforcement is consequential on, and so not constitutive of, the existence of the right.

64. Rights as secondary principles

Though the sanction theory of rights is the conception Mill introduces when he is explicitly defining rights in Chapter V of *Utilitarianism*, he has the resources for other conceptions of rights that do not presuppose indirect utilitarianism. As we have seen, in *On Liberty* Mill recognizes rights but only such rights as can be given a utilitarian grounding (I 11). That means that rights must be subordinate to the utilitarian first principle, and that suggests that Mill regards rights as especially important *secondary principles*. We have already examined Mill's conception of secondary principles in some detail (§24). On this conception, rights are rules that insulate or protect an individual's interest or liberty from certain kinds of interference and that make no direct reference to the good consequences of insulation. We should observe such rules more or less uncritically and set them aside only when adherence to them is clearly suboptimal or in cases of conflicts among such rules (rights). In such exceptional cases, we should make direct appeal to the principle of utility.

Why should we regulate our conduct by such rules? Because doing so is generally but imperfectly optimal, and because we are unable to discriminate for cases in which deviation from the rules is suboptimal without deviating from them in other cases in which it is not.[3] Why should we believe that there are interests or liberties that are generally but imperfectly optimal to protect? Mill's answer is that some interests and liberties play a more fundamental role in human happiness than others. Recall that in Chapter V of *Utilitarianism* Mill links the idea of justice and rights insofar as all injustices are not only wrong but violate rights.

> While I dispute the pretensions of any theory which sets up an imaginary standard of justice not grounded on utility, I account the justice which is grounded on utility to be the chief part, and incomparably the most sacred and binding part, of all morality. Justice is a name for certain classes of moral rules which concern the essentials of human well-being more nearly, and are therefore of more absolute obligation, than any other rules for the guidance of life; and the notion which we have found to be of the essence of the idea of justice—that of a right residing in an individual—implies and testifies to this more binding obligation [V 32; cf. V 33, 37–38].

Like other goods that are, as a class, especially valuable, Mill thinks that we should make them the object of secondary principles that regulate our deliberations and reasoning.

The special importance of the interests protected by rights suggests that Mill might claim not simply that rights are secondary principles but further that rights are *especially stringent* secondary principles. For we can assess the stringency of any moral claim by the number of other claims it defeats when they conflict. The reasons generated by secondary principles tend to defeat ordinary *pro tanto* reasons for action, which explains the stringency of secondary rules in relation to ordinary *pro tanto* reasons. But we might also recognize that some secondary principles tend to defeat others in cases of conflict, which makes the first sort of secondary principles more stringent

---

3. This is very much like the "strategy" conception of rights defended in Berger, *Happiness, Justice, and Freedom*, chs 3–4.

than the second. Mill presumably thinks that these more stringent secondary rules concern security and other necessary conditions for exercising our higher capacities. One version of the secondary principle conception of rights would identify rights with especially stringent secondary principles. However, there will be conflicts among rights of comparable stringency, and these must be resolved by direct appeal to utility.

This conception of rights as secondary principles accounts for many common assumptions about rights and their relation to considerations of utility. First, rights, on this conception, do typically silence or trump direct appeals to utility in moral deliberation and reasoning. This is precisely how secondary principles function. However, they do not silence or trump appeals to utility in all circumstances. Direct appeal to utility can and should be made when following secondary precepts is obviously or saliently suboptimal or when rights conflict with one another or other stringent secondary principles. But in normal cases, the appeal to rights ought to be treated as dispositive and not just as a heuristic in an expected utility calculation.

This conception also implies that it is typically best and, hence, right to honor rights to individual interests or liberties over moral claims about the value of pursuing collective goods by interfering with those interests or liberties. There will be cases where following the rule and, hence, respecting the right is suboptimal, but such cases will be, by design, exceptional.

If we treat rights as secondary principles, then we are committed to the claim that there are or at least could be cases in which honoring rights is suboptimal. This means that there can be a right to do something suboptimal. Moreover, as long as we cannot identify and discriminate these cases reliably and efficiently, then we will be justified in respecting rights, even when doing so is suboptimal. Exactly how we describe such cases depends on whether we combine the secondary principle conception of rights with a rule or act utilitarian account of duty. If we combine the secondary principle conception of rights with rule utilitarianism, then we should conclude that it is our duty to respect rights even in cases in which this is suboptimal. But then it seems we cannot recognize a right to do wrong over and above a right to do something suboptimal. Alternatively, if we combine the secondary principle conception of rights with act utilitarianism, we can recognize a right to do something suboptimal and wrong. In such cases, we cannot say that it is our duty to respect the right, because that would be suboptimal. But we can say that respecting the right might be part of an optimal pattern of behavior. So the act utilitarian can treat respecting rights to do that which is suboptimal in such cases as blameless or even praiseworthy wrongdoing.

Though rights can and will constrain direct pursuit of the good, they are not, on this conception, side constraints on the good. Rather they are forms of entrenching expectations that are justified by the way that such entrenchment promotes utility. Nor are rights absolute. When honoring rights is not just suboptimal but dramatically so and the agent is able to discriminate reliably for this sort of exception, she should depart from the secondary principle and not honor the associated right. Even more clearly, secondary principles can and will conflict, even the especially important secondary principles associated with rights. In such cases, we have a conflict of rights, and Mill thinks that the conflict should be resolved by direct recourse to the utilitarian first principle. It follows that rights, conceived of as especially important secondary principles, cannot be absolute. But these assumptions about rights are more controversial. It is not clear that they represent adequacy conditions on an account of rights or that the failure of the secondary principle conception of rights to vindicate them is a decisive objection to that conception (see §65).

65. Rights as pre-eminent goods

In explaining the secondary principle conception of rights, we saw that Mill explains why it is generally but imperfectly optimal to protect some interests and liberties by claiming that some interests and liberties play an especially fundamental role in human happiness (V 32–33, 37–38). But this claim suggests a distinct conception of rights, as protections of pre-eminent goods. This conception of rights rests on Mill's assumptions about happiness and the role of individual rights to basic interests and liberties in securing happiness.

Recall Mill's claim that he appeals to rights based on a conception of utility "in the largest sense, grounded on the permanent interests of man as a progressive being" (I 11). We have seen that he thinks that it is our deliberative capacities, especially our capacities for practical deliberation, that mark us as responsible and progressive creatures and that, as a result, the principal ingredients of our happiness or well-being must be activities that exercise these deliberative capacities. Indeed, in the Higher Pleasures doctrine in Chapter II of *Utilitarianism* Mill treats the Socratic life of self-examination and reflective decision-making as a pre-eminent good, which competent judges would categorically prefer to a life of lower pleasures.

This allows us to see how expressive liberties are essential for fulfilling our nature as progressive beings. Freedoms of thought and discussion are essential to the justification of one's beliefs and actions, because individuals are not cognitively self-sufficient. Sharing thought and discussion with others, especially about important matters, improves one's deliberations. It enlarges the menu of options, by identifying new options worth consideration, and helps one better assess the merits of these options, by forcing on one's attention new considerations and arguments about the comparative merits of the options. In these ways, open and vigorous discussion with diverse interlocutors improves the quality of one's deliberations. Mill introduces his discussion of expressive liberties by saying that there is general agreement about their importance and that once the grounds for these liberties are understood this agreement can be exploited to support a more general defense of individual liberties (*OL* I 16). After articulating this deliberative rationale for expressive liberties, which appeals to our capacities as progressive beings, Mill extends this rationale to a more general defense of rights to a number of basic interests and liberties, including education, freedom of worship, freedom of occupational choice, and freedom of association.

It can be tempting to suppose that Mill actually treats these as intrinsic goods, perhaps especially important intrinsic goods. But, as we saw (§46), limitations in the scope of Mill's argument show that this cannot be right; the liberty principle does not apply to children or others below the threshold of normative competence. Such restrictions on the scope of Mill's principles make little sense if basic liberties are dominant intrinsic goods, for then it should always be valuable to accord people liberties—a claim that Mill denies. Instead, he claims that these liberties have value only when various necessary conditions for the exercise of deliberative capacities—in particular, sufficient rational development or normative competence—are in place.

We saw that we could explain this aspect of the value Mill sets on basic liberties in one of two ways. We could claim that basic liberties are not intrinsic goods per se but only *conditional intrinsic goods*. Alternatively, we could claim that basic liberties are *necessary conditions* on the exercise of our higher capacities. I offered some reason to prefer the second interpretation, but the differences between them do not matter much for present purposes.

On this conception, rights to basic interests and liberties are conditional intrinsic goods or necessary conditions to the exercise of deliberative capacities, which is the pre-eminent or incomparable ingredient in human happiness. On either interpretation, rights are especially important, and the only things as important are other rights—other rights of that individual or the rights of other individuals.

On this reading, it is crucial that Mill's conception of utility is a pluralistic one in which some elements of happiness dominate others. This makes possible an act utilitarian conception of rights that treats them as protections for dominant goods and for necessary conditions of dominant goods. For then it should always be optimal to honor rights, except in cases of conflicts of rights. We should apparently resolve conflicts of rights by determining which resolution would maximize altitude-adjusted utility.

The pre-eminent goods conception of rights would explain why rights act as trumps. Consider the metaphysical dimension of trumps first. In card games, one suit or kind of card trumps other suits, so that the trumping suit defeats even a higher value card in the trumped suit. Indeed, the lowest value card in a trump suit defeats the highest value card in any other suit. Dworkin thinks of rights as a certain kind of moral factor or currency that trumps or defeats the moral factor or currency of collective advantage. In contexts where rights are not in play, considerations of majority preference, efficiency, and so forth are normally good reasons for action, whether individual or collective. But where these benefits come at the expense of rights, rights trump. The pre-eminent goods conception explains why this is so. Rights protect interests and liberties that are higher in the scale of value than other considerations. Protecting rights will then be the way to maximize value. Indeed, if Mill treats such interests and liberties as he treats higher pleasures—as being discontinuously better than other goods—then it could never be better overall to sacrifice a right in the smallest way to achieve any amount of lesser goods.

On this conception of rights, there can also be a right to something even though honoring that right would be suboptimal, and there can be a right to do wrong. But both possibilities depend on the idea that rights can conflict. Even if the goods that rights protect are incomparably better than other kinds of goods, they won't be incomparably better than each other. So we can imagine that honoring a right might be purchased at the price of honoring other rights. There should be no presumption in such conflicts that it is always optimal to honor an individual's rights. When a hand of cards includes more than one card from the trump suit, the higher value trump card wins. So if rights are trumps, we should expect that in cases of conflict of rights, the individually or collectively stronger right wins. This is like Mill's claim that conflicts among secondary principles should be resolved by direct appeal to the principle of utility.

Presumably, this commits Mill to maximizing the observance of rights or minimizing their violation, once the rights have been weighted according to their comparative importance. This is the view Nozick calls a "utilitarianism of rights."

> But a theory may include in a primary way the nonviolation of rights, yet include it in the wrong place and in the wrong manner. For suppose some condition about minimizing the total (weighted) amount of violations of rights is built into the desirable end state to be achieved. We would then have something like a "utilitarianism of rights".... This still would require us to violate someone's rights when doing so minimizes the total (weighted) amount of the violation of rights in society.[4]

This utilitarianism or consequentialism of rights must allow that it can be not only permissible but also obligatory to violate a right in order to maximize utility—but only in cases of conflicts of rights. In cases of conflicts of rights, the pre-eminent goods conception of rights could recognize a right to do something wrong, but one which can and should be overridden.

Can the conception of rights as pre-eminent goods recognize rights as side constraints? Nozick contrasts this conception of rights as goals with his own conception of rights as side constraints.

> In contrast to incorporating rights into the end state to be achieved, one might place them as side constraints upon the actions to be done: don't violate constraints C.... This view differs from the one that tries to build the side constraints C into the goal G. The side-constraint view forbids you to violate these moral constraints in the pursuit of your goals; whereas the view whose objective is to minimize the violation of these rights allows you to violate the rights (the constraints) in order to lessen their total violation in the society.[5]

So the direct utilitarian reading of Mill's conception of rights does not deliver Nozick's conception of rights as side constraints. But it is far from

---

4. Nozick, *Anarchy, State, and Utopia*, p. 28.
5. Ibid., p. 29.

clear that it is a decisive objection to it. Nozick himself notes that conceiving of rights as side constraints is potentially paradoxical.

> Isn't it irrational to accept a side constraint C, rather than a view that directs minimizing the violations of C?....If nonviolation of C is so important, shouldn't that be the goal? How can a concern for the nonviolation of C lead to the refusal to violate C even when this would prevent other more extensive violations of C? What is the rationale for placing the nonviolation of rights as a side constraint upon action instead of including it solely as the goal of one's actions?[6]

If the non-violation of a constraint is so important, shouldn't we take as our goal the minimization of violations of that constraint? Though Nozick thinks that this question is hard to answer, he does not treat it as rhetorical. His own answer is to appeal to the separateness of persons and the Kantian demand, contained in the Humanity Formula of the Categorical Imperative, that *we treat agents as ends and never merely as means*.[7] Nozick thinks that the utilitarian must treat agents as mere means and that the only way to treat them as ends is to recognize side constraints.

But this goes too fast. The Kantian requirement does not obviously require side constraints. Suppose that only by causing harm to B can A prevent individually comparable harms to C, D, and E. If A harms B only in order to protect C, D, and E, perhaps A treats B as a means, but he need not treat her as a *mere means*. To do that would require viewing her as a mere instrument or tool, not as someone whose own agency is valuable. But A need not view her that way. He can take her agency into account but nonetheless proceed with a reluctance that derives from a concern with her agency. If A could have protected C, D, and E without harming B, he certainly would have, and, if the situation changes so that he can protect them without harming B, he will gladly do so. It is not clear that A acts impermissibly in acting so as to minimize harm. But what's more important, for present purposes, is that even if A does act impermissibly in minimizing harm to rational agents, it is not at all clear that in so acting he must be treating those whom he harms as mere means. If so, we don't yet have a compelling rationale for side constraints.

---

6. Ibid., p. 30.
7. Immanuel Kant, *Groundwork for the Metaphysics of Morals* (1785), trs. J. Ellington (Indianapolis: Hackett, 1981) (Prussian Academy pagination), p. 429.

Nozick also defends side constraints by appeal to a sort of *inviolability* that individuals possess if and only if their fundamental interests are protected by side constraints. In *A Theory of Justice* Rawls also links individual rights with inviolability.[8] Perhaps there are other ways of understanding inviolability that do not involve side constraints. But to make B inviolable in this way requires turning a deaf ear to the comparable interests of C, D, and E that are in competition with B's. We might say that B's inviolability denies them moral *considerability*. Though we want to take seriously the fundamental interests of each, it is not obvious that we should endorse inviolability, because ensuring the inviolability of each denies the moral considerability of others. So while inviolability may require side constraints, it is not clear that our moral theory should embrace the inviolability of individuals.

These are large issues that cannot be properly adjudicated here. But conceiving of rights as side constraints is not unproblematic. If conceiving of rights as side constraints is paradoxical in a way that makes utilitarianism of rights less paradoxical, it may be a virtue, rather than a defect, if Mill embraces the latter, rather than the former. In sum, the jury is still out on whether an adequate theory of rights must conceive of them as side constraints.

Nozick remains agnostic about whether side constraints are absolute or whether there is some threshold level of good consequences to be secured or bad consequences to be avoided above which it would be permissible to violate rights. But both threshold and absolute conceptions of side constraints are puzzling. Side constraints with thresholds are puzzling in the ways that thresholds are always puzzling. If rights can be violated but only when the cost of honoring the rights is n (or greater), the obvious question is why does the cost of respecting rights matter not at all below n and then become decisive at n? We might adopt bright line thresholds for pragmatic reasons, but their introduction into the theory of rights seems arbitrary.[9] Alternatively, one might try to avoid the problem of thresholds by conceiving of rights as absolute. But then we must recognize far fewer rights than we ordinarily do. For rights, as ordinarily conceived, can conflict. But in a genuine conflict of rights, not all rights can be honored. So, if rights are absolute, they cannot conflict. But then we cannot have the rights we think

---

8. Rawls, *A Theory of Justice* §1.
9. See, e.g., Larry Alexander, "Deontology at the Threshold," *San Diego Law Review* 37 (2000): 893–912. One might try to avoid an absolute conception of rights without endorsing a threshold conception by treating the stringency of rights as *scalar*. I don't see why the pre-eminent goods conception of rights could not take this form.

we do. Instead, we must have a much narrower set of rights to much more highly circumscribed interests and liberties that could never conflict.

Neither the threshold nor the absolute conception of rights is incoherent. But each brings intellectual costs, such that it may not be a defect if the pre-eminent goods conception of rights cannot deliver either claim. Pending further investigation, we should not assume that it is an adequacy condition on rights that they be absolute.

66. Reconciling utility and rights

We have seen that Mill has the resources for three distinct conceptions of rights. Though the sanction theory of rights can accommodate many of the marks of rights, it is incompatible with the sanction theory of duty and, more importantly, provides the wrong sort of reason for recognizing rights. The desirability of enforcement is consequential on the prior recognition of rights; it is not constitutive of the existence of the right.

By contrast, the secondary principle and pre-eminent goods conceptions of rights do not suffer from these problems. They agree in most of their implications, and both are compatible with direct utilitarianism, specifically act utilitarianism. They agree that rights are considerations that trump ordinary appeals to collective advantage, both as a matter of moral fact and within our moral reasoning and deliberation. Though both imply that rights should in general be respected, neither implies that it always wrong to violate rights. This is in part because both imply that there can be conflicts of rights, which ought to be resolved by minimizing the (weighted) violation of rights. Neither recognizes rights as genuine side constraints on pursuit of the good, and neither recognizes rights as absolute. Because each recognizes rights that can conflict and can be overridden, each recognizes the possibility of a right to do wrong.

Each recognizes a right to do something suboptimal. The one possible difference between them concerns what more to say about such cases. Whether they say something different depends on whether the secondary principle conception is conjoined with rule or act utilitarianism. If it is conjoined with rule utilitarianism, the secondary principle conception can claim that it is right to respect rights even when doing so is suboptimal, and wrong to violate rights even when doing so is optimal. By contrast, if conjoined with act utilitarianism, the secondary principle conception should claim that it is wrong to respect rights to do something suboptimal but that if this is part of an optimal pattern of respecting rights this might count as blameless or even praiseworthy wrongdoing. The act utilitarian version of the secondary principle conception agrees with the pre-eminent goods conception of rights, inasmuch as the latter is a species of direct utilitarianism.

Though slightly different in their claims and implications, the secondary principle and pre-eminent goods conceptions are each compatible with direct utilitarianism and agree on many points. In assessing the comparative adequacy of these conceptions of rights, there is the issue of whether any of them is as plausible as non-utilitarian conceptions of rights. That will largely depend, I think, on the plausibility of the idea that rights are side constraints, a claim which these utilitarian conceptions deny. And that will depend at least in part on how paradoxical it is to construe rights as side constraints. While I have raised some of these issues, I have not tried to resolve them here. Despite the limitations of these conclusions, our discussion of the architecture and resources of Mill's different utilitarian conceptions of rights suggests the promise of Mill's claim to provide a utilitarian foundation for individual rights.

10
Liberal democracy

We get a somewhat different perspective on Mill's utilitarian and liberal principles by seeing how he applies them to social and political issues. We might start by examining Mill's defense of a democratic form of liberalism in *Considerations on Representative Government* and *Principles of Political Economy*. It is interesting to see to what extent Mill's substantive positions and arguments on these topics conform to and are informed by his utilitarian and liberal principles.

67. The case for representative democracy

In *Considerations on Representative Democracy* Mill argues that a form of representative democracy is the ideal form of government. It is not an invariant ideal, which holds regardless of historical or social circumstances. But he does think that it is the best form of government for societies with sufficient resources, security, and culture of self-reliance. In particular, Mill thinks that representative democracy is best, when it is best, because it best satisfies two criteria of all good government (Chapter II/*CW* XIX 390, 392).[1]

1. Government is good insofar as it promotes the common good, where this is conceived of as promoting the moral, intellectual, and active traits of its citizens.

---

[1]. In discussing *CRG* it will often be useful to give a general reference to a chapter number, which would be common to any edition, and a pinpoint reference to pages in *CW*. Here, "Chapter II/*CW* XIX 390, 392" provides a general reference to Chapter II of *CRG* and then a pinpoint reference to pages 390 and 392 in *CW* XIX. Where context is clear, "II/390, 392" would provide exactly the same reference.

2. Government is good insofar as it makes effective use of institutions and the resources of its citizens to promote the common good.

Presumably, (2) is really a component of (1). If so, Mill's ultimate criterion is that good government should promote the common good of its citizens.

It is interesting that Mill appeals to the common good and does not explicitly invoke his version of utilitarianism. Perhaps he wants his defense of representative democracy to rest on more ecumenical premises. But he clearly understands this political criterion of the common good in broadly consequentialist or result-oriented terms. Moreover, though he may not mention the Higher Pleasures doctrine explicitly, it is also clear that Mill understands the good of each in broadly perfectionist terms that emphasize the importance of an active and autonomous form of life that exercises intellectual, deliberative, and creative capacities.

Mill thinks that there are two ways in which democracy is, under the right circumstances, best suited to promote the common good. First, he thinks that democracy plays an important *epistemic* role in identifying the common good. Proper deliberation about issues affecting the common good requires identifying how different policies would bear on the interests of affected parties and so requires the proper representation and articulation of the interests of citizens. This part of the epistemic justification of democracy is already recognized by the demands of the Radicals for the extension of the franchise. If legislation is to advance the common good, legislators must be accountable to all, and this requires the extension of the franchise. Universal suffrage and political participation provide the best assurance that the interests of the governed will be properly appreciated by political decision-makers (III/404). But Mill's arguments about the importance of free speech and the role of diverse perspectives in improving deliberations about matters of common concern lead him to see additional epistemic benefits in democratic institutions and practices. Our cognitive and, especially, perspectival limitations present obstacles to the effective representation and assessment both of the interests of others and of the common good. We need to deliberate with others, who have different experiences and perspectives from our own, if we are to expand the deliberative menu and better assess options on the menu. In making this epistemic argument for democracy, Mill draws on some of his claims in *On Liberty* about the epistemic value of free inquiry and experimentation in lifestyle for developing our nature as progressive beings.

But Mill thinks that democracy is also the best form of government because of the *constitutive* effects of political participation on the improvement of the moral capacities of citizens (*CRG* II/404). To the extent that the governed can and do participate in public debate and elections they exercise those very deliberative capacities that it is the aim of government to develop. They learn to gather information about their options, deliberate about their merits, and choose a representative that will give expression to their ideals and preferences. But they deliberate and choose with others about a public agenda, and in so doing they cultivate abilities to form a conception of a common good, to take principled stands, to exchange reasons with others, and to learn from others.

So far, these would seem to be arguments for widespread—indeed, universal—direct democracy. In fact, unlike many of his contemporaries interested in expanding the franchise, Mill defends the extension of the franchise to women too, rejecting any restriction on their franchise as baseless (VIII/479). But Mill qualifies this defense of direct democracy in various significant ways.

Democracy presumably involves rule by the will of the people. We might say that a political system is democratic insofar as the content of its political decisions reflect the will of the people. A direct democracy, in which every citizen votes on legislation, is one way for political decisions to reflect the will of the people. But direct democracy is impractical in anything but a small community (IV/412). Mill defends *representative*, rather than direct, democracy. But representative democracy is not just more feasible. It has the further advantage of allowing the community to rely in its decision-making on the contributions of individuals with special qualifications of intelligence or character (V/424). In this way, representative democracy represents a more effective use of resources within the citizenry to advance the common good.

Moreover, Mill believes that representatives are charged with the task of voting, after free and open discussion, in support of their own considered views about what would promote the common good (X/490). Here Mill expresses doubts about an interest group model of democracy, according to which representatives are advocates of the sectarian interests of their constituents and democracy is seen as an impartial aggregation and set of compromises among sectarian interests. Instead, Mill regards representatives as fiduciaries in a public trust, in which each representative aims at a genuinely common good, and in which individual and collective deliberations are shaped by a diversity of experiences and perspectives. This picture of the proper task of representation is connected, Mill thinks, with how representatives should be elected and how elections should be viewed by voters. This is part of what Mill has in mind when he insists that the franchise be seen as a public trust, rather than a private right (X/488) and when he concludes that the ballot be fair and open, rather than secretive (X/490). Only in this way, can political participation become a school for developing the moral capacities of its representatives and citizens.

Mill does not think that representatives will craft legislation themselves, especially not on technical topics of economics, taxation, health, or law. Rather, they will delegate the work of drafting policy on such topics to civil servants with the appropriate expertise. Representatives assume responsibility for such legislation by articulating the objectives of these policies and reviewing proposed policies prior to enacting them. Only in this way will representative democracy take advantage of special expertise and competence to promote the common good (V).

Moreover, many needs are local in nature, and, even when the needs are general, their satisfaction may depend heavily on local conditions. For this reason, Mill advocates a federal system in which a central representative body has more limited functions and local or municipal representative bodies govern in matters involving local affairs or local detail, such as the creation and maintenance of local infrastructure, including roads, courts, jails, and schools (XV).

However, one important function of a central government, Mill believes, is the need to protect local political minorities from being systematically disadvantaged by local political majorities (XV/544). Here he shows his concern with individual rights against the tyranny of the majority, which was a focus of *On Liberty*, and suggests that constitutional guarantees may be better preserved by central, rather than local, authorities. Unfortunately, he does not devote much attention to exactly which individual rights should be recognized constitutionally.

Mill also insists that a representative democracy, either local or federal, should employ *proportional*, rather than winner-take-all, representation (VII/449–62; "Thoughts on Parliamentary Reform" *CW* XIX 328–29). When winner-take-all representation occurs within a series of single-member districts, there is no guarantee that political minorities will be represented, much less represented proportional to their numbers, in the larger group. But then we can see how proportional representation fits with the epistemic argument for democracy. Winner-take-all representation may eliminate or reduce effective expression of minority points of view so essential for free and informed inquiry about the common good and for respecting the interests of political minorities (VII/458).

68. The scope of the franchise, weighted voting, and expertocracy

Mill also introduces various limitations on the scope and weight of the franchise. As we will see, he argues that even in advanced societies the scope of the franchise should be less than universal. Moreover, he advocates a scheme of weighted voting that gives plural votes to citizens with special intellectual qualifications. Before discussing Mill's rationale for these limitations in the scope and weight of the franchise, they need to be viewed in context.

In his philosophical writings and in his service as a Liberal member of Parliament for Westminster from 1865 to 1868, Mill was a vigorous advocate for democratic reform. Though he may have recognized some limits in the scope of the franchise, he was a consistent, though not always successful, advocate for its *extension* beyond its then current scope. He supported extending the franchise to previously disenfranchised members of the working class, and he was a staunch advocate for female suffrage (VIII/479–81). To many, such views about the appropriate scope of the franchise seemed quite radical. Though Mill did support weighted voting, he may have seen this, at least in part, as a necessary concession to succeed in securing his primary objective of (near) universal suffrage, for he suggests that the time will soon come when weighted voting is the only viable alternative to equal universal suffrage (VIII/476). It is worth bearing this context in mind when evaluating Mill's proposals for the scope and weight of the franchise.

As we noted earlier, Mill does not defend representative democracy as ideal under all historical and social circumstances. There are some social circumstances, he thinks, in which democracy will not promote the common good. These are backward states of society in which most citizens are unfit to rule, because they lack necessary ingredients of the culture of autonomy to exercise decision-making authority responsibly. They lack discipline, or education, or an active and independent character. Different forms of government are appropriate for such backward states of advancement. In particular, Mill thinks that benevolent rule by an enlightened one or few, which aimed at the common good, would be better suited for such societies (*CRG* IV/415–18). Here, Mill is introducing a scope limitation on the defense of political rights that he recognized explicitly in his defense of basic liberties in *On Liberty*, which we discussed earlier (§§15, 38).

> It is, perhaps, hardly necessary to say that this doctrine is meant to apply only to human beings in the maturity of their faculties. We are not speaking of children or of young persons below the age which the law may fix as that of manhood or womanhood. Those who are still in a state to require being taken care of by others must be protected against their own actions as well as against external injury. For the same reason we may leave out of consideration those backward states of society in which the race itself may be considered as in its nonage.... Despotism is a legitimate mode of government in dealing with barbarians, provided that the end be their improvement and the means justified by actually effecting that end. Liberty, as a principle, has no application to any state of things anterior to the time when mankind have become capable of being improved by free and equal discussion [*OL* I 10].

There are important practical questions, which Mill does not address very clearly, about which societies cross this threshold of capacity for improvement by free inquiry and political rights.[2] But he does make clear that political participation, like free inquiry, is important as a necessary condition for the exercise of our higher capacities and has value only when a threshold level of normative competence is met.

But what is true of some societies in relation to others is also true of some individuals in relation to others within societies that cross this threshold of normative competence. This explains limitations on the scope of the franchise that Mill recognizes within such advanced civilizations. He confines the scope of the franchise to mature adults, excluding minors who would not have crossed the threshold of normative competence. He is also prepared to exclude those adults who are not literate (*CRG* VIII/470–71). This is a failure of normative competence for which society is to blame and

---

2. In speaking of backward societies here, Mill actually suggests that a "race" may lack normative competence. He may have in mind comparisons between backward and non-backward societies that are also composed of different races. I am not sure. But it seems clear that the notion of normative competence used to distinguish between backward and non-backward societies is not itself racial and that the reasons some societies are more backward than others are social ones that cut across racial categories. In other words, I think the content of Mill's claim would be fully captured if we substituted "people" for "race" in this passage.

which it is society's duty to correct (VIII/470). Mill also excludes from the franchise those adults who do not pay taxes and are on public assistance (VIII/472). Here he expresses the concern that voting gives one a say not only over one's own life but also over the lives of others and that without contributing to the production of an economic surplus one has no right to help determine how this surplus is distributed. But Mill is also committed to doubts about the normative competence of those on public assistance. Elsewhere, he insists that charities make beneficiaries dependent on benefactors in ways that compromise their autonomy and independence (*PPE* V.xi.13; *SW* 330). Insofar as this is true, it provides an additional rationale for excluding dependents from the franchise.

These are the main limitations on the scope of the franchise that Mill recognizes within advanced civilizations.[3] This may be surprising inasmuch as there are many other differences in comparative normative competence within such communities. Nor is Mill unaware of these additional differences. But he thinks that the reasons for favoring democracy apply to all those above this normative threshold. Literate manual laborers have the same claim to the franchise, Mill thinks, as anyone else. They need to stand up for their own interests and make sure they are properly reckoned in political decision-making. Moreover, they stand to benefit from political participation, because of the way it develops their deliberative capacities.

However, Mill's account of representative democracy tracks these further differences in terms of the *weight*, rather than the *scope*, of the franchise (*CRG* VIII/473). He seems to think that there is a fairly minimal threshold level of normative competence, above which all should enjoy voting rights. Nonetheless, differences of normative competence above this threshold should affect the comparative weight of one's vote. This scheme of weighted voting takes the form of a system of plural votes (*CRG* VIII; cf. "Parliamentary Reform" 322–28). Mill emphatically rejects property qualifications as suitable proxies for normative competence (*CRG* VIII/474; "Parliamentary Reform" 325) and insists on educational qualifications.

> The most direct mode of effecting this, would be to establish the plurality of votes, in favour of those who could afford a reasonable presumption of superior knowledge and cultivation.... The perfection, then, of an electoral system would be, that every person should have one vote, but that every well-educated

---

3. Mill raises, but does not settle, the question whether certain kinds of criminal offense might render one ineligible for the franchise ("Parliamentary Reform" 322n).

person in the community should have more than one, on a scale corresponding as far as practicable to their amount of education ["Parliamentary Reform" 324–25].

There is an upper limit on the system of plural votes such that the weighted votes of the educational elite will not give them a majority coalition that could advance its class interests at the expense of the uneducated (*CRG* VIII/476).

Mill recognizes that his commitment to plural voting will be controversial and may prove impractical (VIII/476). Moreover, he seems to attach more importance to his commitments to (near) universal suffrage and to proportional representation than to his proposal for weighted voting (VIII/477–78). But as long as there remain significant differences in normative competence, Mill seems to think that weighted voting should be part of ideal theory, even if it should prove impracticable. The differences depend, in significant part, on the backward state of the working classes.

> The opinions and wishes of the poorest and rudest class of labourers may be very useful as one influence among others on the minds of the voters, as well as on those of the Legislature; and yet it may be highly mischievous to give them the preponderant influence, but admitting them, in their present state of morals and intelligence, to the full exercise of the suffrage ["Parliamentary Reform" 334].

Despite these doubts about the working classes, Mill regarded himself as a friend of the working classes (cf. *Autobiography CW* I 274). This may seem surprising, but there is considerable truth to it.[4] Mill did not blame the working classes for their comparative inferiority, and he did not regard their inferiority as a natural or permanent condition. He thought that improved access to quality primary and secondary education and greater scope for civic participation would gradually improve normative competence in the working classes (*PPE* IV.vii.2). Insofar as this is true, the qualification to Mill's commitment to political equality, represented by his scheme of weighted voting, is temporary and transitional. In this sense, weighted voting is not part of ideal political theory in the way that (near) universal suffrage and proportional representation are.[5]

---

4. See also C.L. Ten, "Democracy, Socialism, and the Working Classes," in *The Cambridge Companion to Mill*, ed. Skorupski.
5. Though I find myself in general agreement with Miller's excellent discussion of Mill's democratic commitments in *J.S. Mill*, ch. 9, I think he underestimates Mill's reasons for thinking that weighted voting is ideally a temporary and transitional measure.

It is sometimes claimed that Mill's doctrine of weighted voting is a paternalistic doctrine, especially in its application to the working classes, and that it is, therefore, inconsistent with his anti-paternalistic position in *On Liberty*.[6] Though understandable, this criticism deserves scrutiny. It is not obvious that weighted voting is paternalistic, and, even if it is, it is not obvious that it is inconsistent with Mill's anti-paternalism.

First, it's not clear in what sense Mill's scheme of weighted voting is paternalistic. Weighted voting does not deny the working class a voice in forming policies that concern them. Mill is emphatic that the franchise be extended to include the working classes, because this is necessary to articulate properly their interests to political decision-makers, and because this introduces them to the public culture of reason-giving and develops their moral powers. It is true that weighted voting gives additional influence to those with fuller capacities and expertise. But it is not clear in what sense this scheme represents a restriction on the liberty of the working classes for their own benefit. It is of course true that the scheme of weighted voting does not allow the working classes to control all the decisions that affect their lives. But neither does democracy with equal votes. Democracy only ensures input on decisions affecting one's life. Weighted voting ensures that too, even if the comparative level of control it affords the working classes is somewhat less under weighted voting than under equal voting. There may be other concerns about whether weighted voting accords with equal concern and respect (see §69). But that sort of concern should not be confused with paternalism.

Even if weighted voting were paternalistic, it wouldn't follow that it was inconsistent with Mill's anti-paternalism. As we have seen, Mill's anti-paternalism contains a scope limitation, which limits its application to those who are normatively competent. But normative competence is a scalar phenomenon. There are significant differences in normative competence both below and above Mill's threshold. So just as there are some people below the threshold for whom paternalism is permissible, so too there might be differences above the threshold that justify further principled discriminations. In effect, Mill can be seen as claiming that liberties and associated rights should track significant differences in normative competence. Mill's threshold marks one significant cut-off, but the qualifications for weighted voting mark another difference-maker among those above the threshold. So, even

---

6. See Richard Arneson, "Democracy and Liberty in Mill's Theory of Government," *Journal of the History of Philosophy* 20 (1982): 43–64.

if weighted voting is paternalistic, it is arguably consistent with the principles underlying Mill's anti-paternalism.

Finally, it should be remembered that even if weighted voting can be understood as a paternalistic limitation on the liberties of the working class, it is also a temporary policy justified, Mill believes, by the real but corrigible condition of the working classes.

Even if Mill's scheme of weighted voting is not paternalistic, it does involve a commitment to *expertocracy* or rule by experts. But notice that Mill's version of expertocracy is very different from the version of expertocracy within ideal theory that we find, for example, in Plato's *Republic* and Aristotle's *Politics*.[7] Platonic and Aristotelian expertocracy is anti-democratic, involving significant scope limitations on the franchise, whereas Millian expertocracy is part of a democratic commitment to a near universal franchise. Also, whereas Plato and Aristotle treat expertocracy as part of ideal theory, Mill regards it at most as part of a transitional form of democracy, necessary only as long as the working class remain in their backward state, a condition that Mill thinks should be a priority of expertocracy to eliminate.

One question might be why Mill mixes expertocracy with democracy. If there is an aim of political decision-making that can be identified independently of the decision procedure—in Mill's case the common good—and some people are better judges of the common good than others, then why shouldn't decision-making be entrusted to them exclusively? Why shouldn't we endorse an anti-democratic expertocracy, as Plato and Aristotle do, at least as part of ideal theory? We've already seen the elements of Mill's answer. He thinks that participation by all, and not just experts, is necessary to help identify the interests of each and, hence, the common good and to help develop the moral capacities of each. Unlike Plato and Aristotle, Mill thinks that participation in public deliberations on public matters can help develop the moral powers of all, even those in a comparatively backward state. It is neglect of this constitutive benefit of political participation that compromises Platonic and Aristotelian criticisms of democracy.[8]

---

7. Whereas Plato and Aristotle both defend rule by a moral elite (of one or a few) as part of ideal theory, when an ultra-virtuous elite can be identified and made to rule, both regard some form of democracy as the best non-ideal form of government. See Plato's *Statesman* 294b–295e, 300c, 302e, 303a–b, and Aristotle's *Politics* 1254b31–1255a2, 1288a16–19, 1289b4–10, 1325b10–13, 1332b16–21.
8. For discussion of this worry about Platonic and Aristotelian anti-democratic commitments, see David O. Brink, "Eudaimonism, Love and Friendship, and Political Community," *Social Philosophy & Policy* 16 (1999): 252–89.

69. The trouble with weighted voting

Even if we admit the potential benefits of Mill's moderate expertocracy, we may think that it carries costs. Mill's version of weighted voting, we said, appeals to an educational, rather than a property or wealth, qualification. But an educational qualification may be correlated with other factors that would make an educational qualification problematic from the epistemic point of view of identifying the common good. If educational qualifications are correlated with race, ethnicity, gender, socioeconomic class, or other significant social dimensions, then educational qualifications may select for a more homogeneous and less diverse population that will not be well-positioned, in Millian terms, to reason about the common good.[9] Consider the effect of literacy tests for voting employed in Jim Crow southern states in the first half of the twentieth century in the United States. Of course, there were other means of discouraging educated blacks from voting, and the literacy tests were not applied consistently, so as to rule out illiterate whites. But if the literacy tests were applied consistently, it is arguable (or anyway imaginable) that they would have had a disparate impact, ruling out many more blacks than whites, precisely because blacks had been denied equal educational opportunity. The point is that this disparate impact would produce an epistemic disadvantage of weighting voting that would offset its epistemic advantages.

Mill did endorse literacy as a condition of the right to vote. But he understood further educational qualifications not as a condition of the franchise but rather as a condition of plural votes. Moreover, Mill is committed to eradicating these inequalities of educational opportunity that would give an educational qualification for weighted voting a disparate impact. But it is possible, in the short run at least, that an educational qualification for weighted voting would have this epistemic defect with respect to identifying the common good. It is hard to know how Mill should respond to this potential epistemic cost. We have already seen that his commitment to weighted voting was partly pragmatic, as a way of making universal suffrage more palatable to its opponents. Perhaps he would be willing to give up on weighted voting for this reason. Alternatively, he might claim that we should accept this epistemic cost to weighted voting in the transitional phase during which we raise the educational qualifications of the working class. A third alternative would be to accept weighted voting but insist that weighted votes be given only to a representative

---

9. See Estlund, *Democratic Authority*, pp. 215–19.

cross-section of those who meet the educational qualification. The idea would be to select from among those who meet the educational threshold a group of individuals that represent a diverse cross-section of the population and then give them, and only them, plural votes.[10] The last two responses preserve the commitment to weighted voting, at least as a temporary measure.

There are, however, two more serious concerns about weighted voting worth considering. One is a principled concern about whether weighted voting conflicts with requirements of equal concern and respect. It raises a question about whether weighted voting should be part of ideal theory. The other is a pragmatic concern about whether educational qualifications are sufficiently reliable proxies for differences in normative competence to justify weighted voting.

Weighted voting deviates from the norm of political equality and so might seem to offend against an ideal of equal concern and respect. Mill seems not to recognize the potentially corrosive effects of weighted voting in terms of the message it sends of second-class citizenship to the working classes. This message can be debilitating to the working classes themselves, and it can encourage those with plural votes to give the claims of the working class less consideration in their own deliberations about the common good. These concerns may seem especially acute when we are considering inequalities in basic political rights. Here, inequality arguably sends a message of inferiority.

This objection raises complicated issues. Why does political inequality imply second-class citizenship in a way that economic and other social inequalities don't? Though not all Western democracies tolerate the degree of social and economic inequality that the United States does, nonetheless most of them tolerate economic inequalities in a way that they don't tolerate political inequalities. They tend to view economic inequalities, within limits, as consistent with equal concern and respect in a way that they don't think political inequalities, as such, are consistent with equal concern and respect. In effect, there is a kind of orthodoxy in contemporary thinking about liberalism and democracy about the existence of an asymmetry between political equality and other forms of equality in which political equality is more important than other forms of equality.[11]

---

10. Estlund recognizes this possible response, but suggests that any attempt to identify a representative sub-group among the educationally qualified would be reasonably rejectable by some (*Democratic Authority*, p. 216). But the grounds for this rejection are unclear, and I suspect that Estlund appeals to an implausibly restrictive contractualist constraint here.
11. For instance, the asymmetry between political and other forms of equality is a part of the more general priority that Rawls assigns to basic liberties in relation to other social and economic goods in his special conception of justice. See *A Theory of Justice*, §§39, 46–47, 82.

One might challenge this orthodoxy in one of two ways. One might resist the asymmetry between political and other inequalities by insisting that political inequality is not special. Just as some social and economic inequalities are compatible with the right kind of equal concern and respect, so too some political inequalities may be compatible with equal concern and respect. For instance, if the basis of political liberties is normative competence, and normative competence is scalar and distributed unevenly, then one might think that an equal concern for each is compatible not just with distributing the franchise widely, but not universally, but also with having the weight of the franchise track differences in normative competence. One might also resist the asymmetry between political and other inequalities by urging that social and economic inequalities can be just as bad as political ones. Why should citizens care so much about political liberties and equality of political liberties if there are huge discrepancies in the material quality of their lives? Though different, these two reactions to the alleged asymmetry between political and social and economic equality are not incompatible. One might think that social and economic inequalities can be just as objectionable as political inequalities and also think limited and principled inequalities of both kinds are acceptable in principle.

Mill's defense of weighted voting seems to emphasize the first response. In distinguishing between the weight and scope of the franchise, he thinks that self-respect requires only that one has the vote, not that one has an equal vote, regardless of normative competence.

> There is not, in this arrangement [weighted voting], anything necessarily invidious to those to whom it assigns the lower degrees of influence. Entire exclusion from a voice in the common concerns, is one thing; the concession to others of a more potential voice, on the ground of greater capacity for the management of the joint interests, is another. The two things are not merely different, they are incommensurable. Everyone has a right to feel insulted by being made a nobody, and stamped as of no account at all. No one but a fool…feels offended by the acknowledgement that there are others whose opinion…is entitled to a greater amount of consideration than his [*CRG* VIII/474].

In effect, Mill claims that we should object to the denial of political voice but not to inequalities in political voice that track differences in normative competence. This is a defense of proportionate, rather than equal, political liberties. If Mill thinks that equal concern is owed to individuals as normatively competent agents, capable of exercising their progressive capacities, then he may think that equal concern can and should be expressed in unequal treatment in the form of weighted voting.

Mill emphasizes the first reason for denying the asymmetry of political and other forms of equality by insisting that political inequalities are not objectionable per se. But this does not prevent him from recognizing the second reason for denying the asymmetry by insisting that inequalities of either sort must be limited. As we will see shortly (§70), he defends definite limits on economic inequalities. Though he is not an egalitarian, he thinks that equality of opportunity places significant limits on the extent of permissible social and economic inequality. In his scheme of weighted voting, Mill recognizes political inequalities that are supposed to track differences in underlying normative competence. Here, proportionate justice justifies some political inequality. But these inequalities are limited—the working classes have the franchise, there is an upper limit on the political power of plural votes, and the entire scheme is only transitional in nature, to be dispensed with as soon as the backward state of the education of the working classes can be remedied. So there is a case for saying that Mill takes social and economic inequality seriously, that he denies that political equality is special, and that he accepts limited inequalities in both political and other social and economic goods.

Though Mill's defense of political inequalities is principled, it is less clear that it is compelling. On the one hand, Mill seems right to think that some political liberties and rights should track at least some differences in normative competence. Children should not have the vote. Moreover, one might agree with Mill that the insane and the illiterate should not have the right to vote. If so, we agree with Mill that voting rights should track differences in normative competence above and below the threshold of basic competence. But Mill's doctrine of weighted voting just extends this reasoning by insisting that there be further differences in the weight of the franchise that track significant differences in normative competence above the threshold of basic competence. From this perspective, according the educated plural votes is no more invidious than recognizing that children and the insane should have no vote. One must be qualified to vote, and one must have further qualifications to have one's vote matter most.

On the other hand, whether or not we embrace the asymmetry between political and other forms of equality, we may think that political inequalities can be more corrosive than Mill seems to recognize. Mill assumes that the only sort of equality worth caring about is one that insists that all count, notwithstanding that some count for more than others. But why should I care so much about being branded a nobody and not at all about being branded a lesser somebody? One might well want to harness the resources and expertise of an educated elite, perhaps, as Mill already imagines, by giving them special roles in the drafting of legislation or in setting the agenda for public deliberations. But this does not require giving the educated elite plural votes. Doing that seems to have significant symbolic value, saying that working classes should have less political standing and say. As the American experience with segregated education suggests, this official stamp of inferiority might have enervating effects on the working classes and encourage those with plural votes to ignore or underestimate the political contributions of the working classes. From this perspective, Mill displays something of a tin ear for such concerns about weighted voting. Interestingly, while he does not seem especially sensitive to concerns about the bad effects of second-class citizenship in *Considerations on Representative Government*, he seems much more sensitive to such concerns in *The Subjection of Women*. As we will see in the next chapter, Mill is acutely aware of the variety of ways in which women's contributions can be discouraged and undervalued and of the individual and social costs of women's second-class status. Had Mill been as mindful of the costs of according workers second-class citizenship as he would later be of the costs of according women second-class status, he might have been more skeptical of weighted voting than he in fact was.

So I am ambivalent. Though I understand Mill's principled arguments for weighted voting and can see why he might think they make no invidious discriminations, I am inclined to think he underestimates the divisive nature of giving some competent adults more political say than others. If these are legitimate worries, we might suppose that it is better to err on the side of equal treatment than on the side of proportionate justice. If so, we might suppose that the common good would be better promoted by equal voting than by weighted voting, even if that means foregoing some potential advantages of proportionate justice.

Furthermore, even if we accepted weighted voting and proportionate justice in principle, we might doubt that educational qualifications are a sufficiently reliable proxy for differences in normative competence to justify weighted voting. Presumably, Mill thinks that what really justifies plural votes is differential normative competence. He thinks that wealth and property qualifications are poor proxies for superior normative competence. While educational qualifications are presumably more reliable proxies than wealth or property qualifications, they too are imperfect. Some who meet the educational qualifications will nonetheless not be especially normatively competent, and the educational qualifications will leave out some with significant normative competence who nonetheless do not have the right educational pedigree. If so, the use of educational qualifications as a proxy for normative competence will be both over-inclusive, including some who are insufficiently competent despite having suitable degrees, and under-inclusive, leaving out some who are sufficiently competent but lack the necessary degrees. Mill certainly has reason to recognize that many men and women without the benefit of formal higher education have developed capacities for responsible self-government.[12] He may believe that despite these imperfections, educational qualifications are superior proxies to wealth or property qualifications and that they are sufficiently reliable to support the system of weighted voting. But even if educational qualifications are more reliable proxies for normative competence than wealth or property qualifications, one might doubt that they are reliable enough to justify weighted voting. This second worry is more acute in light of the first worry. Given the potential costs of weighted voting in terms of the corrosive effects of second-class citizenship, we should be very reluctant to accept imperfect proxies for differences in normative competence. Even if weighted voting made sense in an ideal world in which we could reliably measure superior normative competence, it does not make sense in the actual world if we lack sufficiently reliable ways of doing so. This gives us both principled and pragmatic objections to weighted voting.

70. Liberal democracy and the common good

What of the substance of democratic government? We have seen that Mill thinks that government is good insofar as it promotes the common good, where this is conceived of as promoting the moral, intellectual, and active traits of its citizens. But what kinds of principles and policies does he think would satisfy this test?

---

12. Mill himself would be a case in point. It is significant, therefore, that he does allow that literate citizens who have not gone to university should be allowed to take a test to demonstrate their normative competence and qualify for plural votes, despite their lack of a suitable degree (*CRG* VIII/476).

Though Mill is an advocate of limited government in ways that one might expect given his defense of basic liberties in *On Liberty*, he is no libertarian. He emphatically rejects the idea that legitimate government is limited to the functions of affording protection against force and fraud (*PPE* V.i.2). Instead, he thinks that there are a variety of ways in which government can and should intervene in the lives of citizens—sometimes as *coercer* but, more often, as *enabler* or *facilitator*—in order to promote the common good. Mill's claims about happiness imply that the good of each consists in the exercise of her higher capacities. This, we have seen, requires an active life in which one's activities are regulated by one's deliberations and choices. As we have seen in Mill's critical discussions of paternalism, this places limits on how others can promote one's own good. I can't promote your good, understood in this way, in ways that bypass your agency anymore than I can win a race for you. But just as I can do things to help you win the race yourself (training with you, sharing nutritional tips, and helping you plan strategy), so too I can do things that help you lead an autonomous life employing your higher faculties. I can provide various sorts of necessary conditions for your leading such a life, and I can facilitate your realizing your potential. If an individual's good consists in this sort of *self*-realization, then a government that aims at the common good should concern itself in significant part with the fair provision of *opportunities* and *resources* for welfare.

Mill thinks that it is the duty of parents to provide their children with "such education, and such appliances and means, as will enable them to start with a fair chance of achieving by their own exertions a successful life" (*PPE* II.ii.3). But this duty is not confined to parents. Early in *The Subjection of Women* Mill contrasts systems of hereditary caste, such as feudalism and social systems based on slavery, with the distinctively modern and progressive commitment to equal opportunity for welfare.

> For, what is the peculiar character of the modern world—the difference which chiefly distinguishes modern institutions, modern social ideas, modern life itself, from those of times long past? It is that human beings are no longer born into their place in life, and chained down by an inexorable bond to the place they are born to, but are free to employ their faculties, and such favorable chances as offer, to achieve the lot which may appear to them most desirable [*CW* XXI 272–73].

As with basic liberties, opportunities for welfare have value, not in themselves, but as necessary conditions for the sort of self-realization to which

Mill assigns pre-eminent intrinsic value. But they are no less important for that reason. Indeed, many of the functions of government that he recognizes can be traced to providing opportunities for self-realization.

Though Mill generally opposes paternalism, censorship, offense regulation, and moralism, he does recognize various functions that government should perform in pursuing the common good. In part because the opportunities for each depend in part upon the position and resources of others, Mill thinks that provision of fair equality of opportunity constrains permissible socio-economic inequalities (*PPE* II.ii.1).

> A just and wise legislation would abstain from holding out motives for dissipating rather than saving the earnings of honest exertion. Its impartiality between competitors would consist in endeavoring that they should all start fair. ... Many, indeed, fail with greater efforts than those with which others succeed, not from difference of merits, but difference of opportunities; but if all were done which it would be in the power of a good government to do, by instruction and by legislation, to diminish this inequality of opportunities, the differences of fortune arising from people's own earnings could not justly give umbrage [*PPE* V.ii.3].

As Mill makes clear in this passage, his concern is not with inequality as such. Though he envisions a society in which inequalities are reduced and in which a decent minimum standard of living is available to all (IV.vi.2), he does defend the profits of capitalists as a just recompense for their savings, risk, and economic supervision (II.xv.1; "Chapters on Socialism" *CW* V 734–35). Rather, Mill's concern in this passage is with inequalities derived from inequality of opportunity and those inequalities that perpetuate inequality of opportunity. To achieve equality of opportunity, Mill endorses various redistributive tax measures.[13] He defends a flat tax rate on earned income above a threshold necessary to secure a decent minimum standard of living, leaving earned income below this threshold untaxed (*PPE* II.i.3, II.xii.2, II.xii.3, V.ii.1–3, V.iii.3–5). In addition, he endorses the use of higher tax rates on unearned income and on inheritance (II.ii.1, II.ii.3–4, II.xii.3, V.ii.3, V.ii.5, V.vi.2, V.ix.1). Such taxes limit intergenerational inequalities that would otherwise constrain equality of opportunity.

Within this framework established for equal opportunity, Mill defends additional governmental functions designed to promote the common good. A prime condition of normative competence is a decent education,

---

13. Berger helps make this case in *Happiness, Justice, and Freedom*, pp. 159–86.

and Mill thinks that it is one of the central roles of the state to require and, if necessary, provide a quality education (*OL* V 12–13; *PPE* V.xi.8, V.xi.8). Mill thinks that the state can and should require parents to provide schooling for their children, ensuring that this kind of education is available to all, regardless of financial circumstances, by subsidizing the costs of education for the poor so that it is available free or at a nominal cost. While Mill is adamant that the state should make elementary education compulsory, his worries about conformity and his defense of individuality lead him to be suspicious of the state having a monopoly on the provision of education. If the state is to be a provider of education, Mill thinks that it should only be "one among many competing experiments, carried on for the purpose of example and stimulus to keep the others [private providers] up to a certain standard of excellence" (*OL* V 13). The state can and should play a greater role in the provision of education if, but only if, the market does not supply a sufficient number of quality private providers (*OL* V 13; *PPE* V.xi.8).

We have also seen that Mill thinks that charity breeds dependence, rather than autonomy. This is one reason that he defends the adoption of Poor Laws that provide, among other things, work for the able-bodied indigent (*PPE* II.xii.2). Mill also thinks that government should step in where market forces are unlikely to provide what people need or want (*PPE* V.xi.8). In this way, he thinks that it is an important function for the state, whether central or local, to create and maintain various aspects of community infrastructure, including such things as a common defense, roads, sanitation, police, and correctional facilities (*PPE* V.vii.1; *CRG* XV 541). He also thinks regulation of working conditions (hours, wages, and benefits) is permissible, because the provision of improved working conditions typically has the structure of a public or collective good for workers, each of whom stands to gain a competitive advantage by conceding a little more to capital than his peers (*PPE* V.xi.12). If left unregulated, each has an incentive to concede more to capital than his rivals, with the result that all workers are made worse-off. State intervention and regulation, Mill thinks, is the best solution to this collective action problem. He also thinks that there are other goods for which market provision will lead to underproduction, presumably because of positive externalities, which is why he thinks that the state should subsidize scientific research and the arts (*PPE* V.xi.15).

Mill's liberalism is committed to a largely secular state, democratic political institutions in which the franchise is widespread, private property rights, market economies, equal social and economic opportunity, and a variety of personal and civic liberties. To appreciate the significance of his brand of liberalism, it is helpful to focus on the substance of his conception of liberal essentials—the package of individual liberties and state responsibilities that he endorses—and the way he justifies his conception of liberal essentials. Millian liberalism is not laissez-faire liberalism, and it justifies liberal essentials as a way of promoting the common good. The distinctiveness of this brand of liberalism is perhaps best seen in contrast with two other conceptions of liberalism—a more libertarian conception of liberal essentials and their justification that dominated the British Liberal Party at mid-century and the sort of contemporary political liberalism that justifies liberal essentials as required if the state is to be neutral among rival conceptions of the good life that its citizens might hold.

71. Old and new liberalisms

It may be useful to try to locate Millian liberalism within the debate between so-called Old and New Liberalism taking place in the British Liberal Party in the second half of the nineteenth century. A good part of the agenda of the Liberal Party during much of the nineteenth century consisted in reforms that sought to undo limitations that the state placed on the liberties and opportunities of citizens, especially when these forms of state intervention tended to reinforce class privileges. This political culture was exemplified in the repeal of the Corn Laws, opposition to religious persecution, and several electoral reforms. The 1832 Reform Bill extended the franchise to the upper middle class; the 1867 Reform Act extended it to approximately one million urban workers; and the Reform Act of 1884 extended it still further to include another two million agricultural workers. But in the later part of the nineteenth century there emerged a new view about the role of such reforms within the Liberal agenda. Earlier Liberals, such as Herbert Spencer, thought that reform should be limited to the removal of state interference with individual liberty. Liberalism, on this conception, stood for individualism and laissez-faire. For instance, in *The Principles of Sociology* (1896) Spencer describes liberalism in laissez-faire terms.

> [I]n essence Liberalism stands for the freedom of the individual *versus* the power of the state. [Whereas] in essence Toryism stands for the power of the state *versus* the freedom of the individual.[14]

By contrast, the New Liberals thought that these reforms that extended economic, social, and political liberties had to be supplemented by social and economic reforms in areas of labor, education, and health designed to redress the effects of inequality. These new reforms gave the state positive, and not just negative, responsibilities that sometimes required interference with individual liberties. It was these constructive reforms that drove a wedge between the Old and the New Liberals.[15]

The New Liberalism is often associated with the work of British idealists and those influenced by them, such as T.H. Green, Bernard Bosanquet, D.G. Ritchie, and L.T. Hobhouse. It was not uncommon for British idealists, such as Bosanquet, to represent Mill as adhering to the laissez-faire doctrines of the Old Liberalism.[16] But this interpretation represents a very poor understanding of Millian liberalism and greatly exaggerates the differences between Mill and idealists, such as Green.[17] As we have seen, Mill rejects laissez-faire liberalism. Like Green, Mill is generally opposed to paternalistic and moralistic attempts to infringe basic liberties and insists on the importance of freedom of expression. But he thinks that the state has an important role to play in securing equal opportunity, ensuring a good education that will nurture normative competence, and redressing various market failures and providing various public goods. Like Green, he justifies this mix of negative and positive responsibilities for state action by appeal to a perfectionist conception of the common good that stresses the role of autonomy

---

14. Herbert Spencer, *The Principles of Sociology*, vols. I–III (New York: Appleton, 1896), vol. I, p. 606.
15. See Peter Clarke, *Liberals and Social Democrats* (Cambridge: Cambridge University Press, 1978); Stefan Collini, *Liberalism and Sociology: L.T. Hobhouse and Political Argument in England 1880–1914* (Cambridge: Cambridge University Press, 1979); and Peter Nicholson, *The Political Philosophy of the British Idealists* (Cambridge: Cambridge University Press, 1990), ch. 5. The emergence of a New Liberalism in reaction to the Old Liberalism within the British Labour Party bears some comparison with the rise and fall of the laissez-faire interpretation of substantive due process within American constitutional history, in which New Deal liberalism emerged in part as a reaction to the perceived economic and moral failings of the *Lochner*-era doctrine of economic substantive due process that treated liberty of contract as a fundamental constitutional right that constrained state action.
16. Bernard Bosanquet, *The Philosophical Theory of the State* (originally published 1899), 4th ed. (London: Macmillan, 1923), chs. III–IV.
17. See Nicholson, "The Reception and Early Reputation of Mill's Political Thought," pp. 483–88.

in self-realization. There are differences between Mill and Green in their official attitudes toward hedonism—with Mill apparently defending hedonism and Green criticizing it—and over the permissibility of temperance legislation—with Mill being more skeptical of temperance legislation than Green. But their similarities far overshadow their differences.[18] It makes sense to view Mill as laying much of the intellectual groundwork for the New Liberalism—both in its conception of liberal essentials as involving a mix of constraints on state action and positive duties the state has to help enable its citizens to lead informed and self-directed lives and in its conception of the proper justification of liberal essentials by appeal to a broadly consequentialist interest in promoting self-realization.

72. Perfectionist liberalism

Mill's perfectionist justification of liberal essentials also provides a contrast with an influential strand in recent Anglo-American philosophical defenses of liberalism that insist on *neutrality* among rival conceptions of the good life. This conception of liberal neutrality receives its most influential expression in the later work of John Rawls, notably *Political Liberalism*.[19] But this conception of liberal neutrality also finds expression in other contemporary liberal writers.[20] Despite important differences among the friends of liberal neutrality, there is significant common ground. On this conception, neutrality about the good is a constitutive commitment of liberalism, and liberal neutrality places limits on the justification of state action. Liberal governments, on this view, can and must enforce individual rights and any further demands of social justice, including those necessary to maintain peace and order. But they are not to undertake any action as a way of promoting a particular conception of the good life or a comprehensive philosophical doctrine. Each individual citizen in a liberal regime should be free to form and pursue his own conception of the good, but the state should not be in

---

18. See David O. Brink, *Perfectionism and the Common Good: Themes in the Philosophy of T.H. Green* (Oxford: Clarendon Press, 2003), §§XIII, XXIII, and XXIV.
19. John Rawls, *Political Liberalism* (New York: Columbia University Press, 1993).
20. See, for example, Bruce Ackerman, *Social Justice and the Liberal State* (New Haven: Yale University Press, 1980); Ronald Dworkin, "Liberalism" reprinted in *A Matter of Principle* (Cambridge, MA: Harvard University Press, 1985); and Will Kymlicka, *Liberalism, Community, and Culture* (New York: Oxford University Press, 1989).

the business of regulating what should be a matter of personal conscience. On matters of the good, a liberal state must be strictly neutral. It can promote the good of its citizenry only in ways that are consistent with every reasonable conception of the good.

Liberal neutrality can be motivated in reaction to natural concerns about how a perfectionist politics appears liable to restrict political and personal liberties of thought and action in its attempt to promote a particular conception of the good. It is easy to suppose that an authoritarian political regime committed to extensive paternalistic and moralistic interference with the civic and personal liberties of citizens is the inevitable outcome of perfectionist politics. For those who see anti-democratic expertocracy of the sort found in Plato's *Republic* as the logical expression of perfectionist politics, liberal essentials may seem to require neutrality about the good.

In these ways, liberal neutrality rejects perfectionist politics and raises questions about the viability of a perfectionist form of liberalism. Liberal neutrality, therefore, stands in stark contrast with Mill's perfectionist liberalism. But Millian liberalism is in fact a worthy rival of liberal neutrality. Neutrality is itself a potentially problematic commitment, and liberal essentials can be given a perfectionist foundation.[21]

Liberal neutrality should raise several concerns. For one thing, whereas liberal neutrality is neutral about the good, it is not neutral about matters of rights and social justice. This presupposes a sharp line between issues about the good and issues about the right. But this distinction may be hard to draw sharply. Presumably, central among the individual rights that liberal neutrality insists on upholding are rights against harm. But harm involves the setback of important interests, making individuals worse off than they would otherwise be. But then one can't identify harms without making some assumptions about what makes an individual's life go better or worse. Nor should we assume that one could recognize only those harms that set back interests that are part of any reasonable conception of the good. For instance, you've harmed me if you've injured me in a way that prevents me from pursuing sports as a vocation or avocation, even though there are reasonable conceptions of the good that assign no significance to sports. You've harmed me if you

---

21. In my discussion of the limits of neutrality, I have been influenced by Richard Kraut, "Politics, Neutrality, and the Good," *Social Philosophy & Policy* 16 (1999): 315–32. Also see, Joseph Raz, *The Morality of Freedom* (Oxford: Clarendon Press, 1986), and George Sher, *Beyond Neutrality* (New York: Cambridge University Press, 1997).

rendered me impotent, even though sexual intimacy is not a part of every reasonable conception of the good. In short, it is hard to see how the state can do its job of enforcing the right without making some assumptions about the good.

Consider the priority given to certain liberties. Liberals think that the state should be vigilant in protecting religious liberty, freedom of conscience, freedom of association, and occupational choice. But liberals do not think that all liberties are that important. Most liberals do not think that traffic laws, or seat belt laws, or nuisance regulations offend fundamental liberties. A natural explanation of the different value we place on different liberties is that the fundamental ones are much more important to leading meaningful lives, whereas the unimportant liberties are not similarly essential. How exactly are we supposed to justify the greater importance of some liberties in ways that are agnostic about the good life?

Moreover, there are legitimate functions of a liberal state that go beyond harm prevention that are difficult to square with liberal neutrality. The provision of basic infrastructure, including roads, sanitation, and utilities, is something that Mill and most liberals expect from the state. While such public goods may be pretty ecumenical goods, it is unlikely that they are part of all reasonable conceptions of the good or comprehensive doctrines, if only because they might not be goods to the Amish or certain brands of asceticism.

Or consider education.[22] Most liberals, including Mill, would expect the state to provide or at least ensure elementary and secondary education to all citizens and would include in that education exposure to the arts and sciences, history, politics, and culture. This would normally be defended as part of cultural literacy and the development of critical and independent judgment and so as being in the interest of those receiving the education, as well as other members of the community. But this is not strictly vocational education, and it cannot plausibly be defended as part of all reasonable conceptions of the good. Many adults who presumably have conceptions of the good that the neutralist would count as reasonable have no interest in or need for knowledge of some of these subjects. If we can only justify the state providing an education on terms that are entirely neutral among rival conceptions of the good, it seems unlikely that we will be able to justify a public education in the liberal arts.

---

22. Kraut, "Politics, Neutrality, and the Good," pp. 322–23.

Or consider Mill's defense of sexual equality, which we will examine in more detail in Chapter 11. In *The Subjection of Women* part of Mill's defense of equal educational and economic opportunities for women and reforms in Victorian marriage law that would give married women equal domestic standing with their husbands is the beneficial effect this would have on women's well-being. But it is hard to see how this claim could be defended in a way that was neutral among rival conceptions of a good life. It looks like it assumes that educational literacy, autonomy, and independence are good in themselves, not things likely to be recognized by all conceptions of the good. Mill goes on to claim that there is special value to intimate friendships predicated on equal standing, because each partner completes and complements the other (*CW* XXI 326, 334, 336). As we will see, Mill has a plausible perfectionist defense of this claim. But the special value of friendships among equals looks like a sectarian good, which a strictly neutral state could not permissibly promote.

Not only is liberal neutrality potentially problematic, but also liberalism does not presuppose neutrality. One can reject neutrality and still defend liberalism, as the perfectionist liberal does. Mill, of course, is just such a liberal. On this conception of liberalism, basic liberties are important because of their central role in a good or flourishing life. According to Millian perfectionism, the good life is not defined in sectarian terms as consisting in a particular set of activities. Rather, the good life is understood in terms of the exercise of capacities for practical deliberation that can be realized in very diverse, though limited, ways. As we saw in Chapter 3, Millian perfectionism is pluralist without being relativist (§18). Basic liberties are important because they are necessary conditions for this sort of reflective self-direction and self-realization. On this version of liberalism, the state recognizes various civil liberties and resists regular paternalism and moralism, not because it won't take a stand on questions of the good, but because it recognizes autonomy and self-realization as higher-order goods. As Richard Kraut points out, the liberal state's relation to its citizens in this respect might be analogized to a liberal parent's relationship to her adolescent child.[23] A liberal parent might well think that her teenage son should be free, within certain limits, to make his own decisions about how to dress, with whom to

---

23. Kraut, "Politics, Neutrality, and the Good," p. 325. This is an analogy, not a commitment to state paternalism. Moreover, the analogy suggests that even when a liberal parent is paternalistically motivated, her paternalistic interventions will be limited.

associate, and what activities to pursue, not because she should suspend judgment about the value of her son's choices, but precisely because she thinks that making these choices himself is better for her son and will contribute to his growth and maturation. So too, the liberal state prescinds from regulating matters of conscience and interfering with freedom of association and occupational choice, not because it does not take a stand on the value of these choices, but because it recognizes the good of autonomy as a higher-order good.

So we can explain the liberal's recognition of negative rights in perfectionist terms, without embracing neutrality about the good. Moreover, the recognition of constructive responsibilities of the state to advance the common good, common to Mill and the New Liberals, sits more easily with perfectionist liberalism than liberal neutrality. As we have seen, the commitments to provide community infrastructure, to educate in the liberal arts, and to provide government subsidies for scientific research and development and the arts make most sense if we eschew neutrality about the good and pursue a common good understood in broadly perfectionist terms.

In these ways, Millian liberalism articulates a tradition of classical liberalism that contrasts sharply with liberal neutrality. It is not possible to conduct a comprehensive examination of the comparative merits of these two forms of liberalism here. But I hope I have raised questions about the viability of liberal neutrality and shown the resources and promise of Mill's attempt to give liberalism a perfectionist foundation. In this respect, Millian liberalism has enduring significance for how best to understand and justify liberal essentials.[24]

---

24. A broadly similar verdict is reached in Alan Ryan's essay, "Mill in a Liberal Landscape," in *The Cambridge Companion to Mill*, ed. Skorupski.

11
Sexual equality

Mill applies his liberal principles to issues of sexual equality primarily and most systematically in *The Subjection of Women*, though there are anticipations of some of these concerns in *Principles of Political Economy* and *On Liberty*, among other writings. His discussion in *The Subjection of Women* is interesting for at least two reasons. For one thing, it was at the time, and still is, the only extended defense, much less discussion, of sexual equality by a major male figure in the Western tradition of moral and political philosophy. Secondly, it is one of Mill's latest and most mature works. Not only is it written after and with the benefit of *The Principles of Political Economy*, *On Liberty*, *Utilitarianism*, and *Considerations on Representative Government*, but also Mill tells us that this is a subject that has concerned him since he first started thinking about social and political issues (*CW* XXI 261). Like some of Mill's other popular works, it was a pamphlet or manifesto intended at least as much as a cultural and political tract as a scholarly work.

73. The case for sexual equality

Mill does not waste time or mince words. He denounces existing forms of sexual inequality in clear and unequivocal terms in his opening paragraph.

> [T]he principle which regulates the existing social relations between the two sexes—the legal subordination of one sex to the other—is wrong in itself, and now one of the chief hindrances to human improvement; and... it ought to be replaced by a principle of perfect equality, admitting no power or privilege on the one side, nor disability on the other [*CW* XXI 261].

To modern ears, Mill's defense of sexual equality may seem obvious, and, to some contemporary feminists, Mill's criticism of sexual inequality may not be deep or consistent enough. But, especially when viewed in historical context, Mill's defense of sexual equality was radical, courageous, and even eloquent.[1] While Mill clearly expected many aspects of his liberal principles to be controversial (*OL* I 6–8), there is considerable truth in the claim the revolutionary import of Mill's liberal principles only became clear when he later applied them to issues of sexual equality in *The Subjection of Women*.[2]

Mill's condemnation of sexual inequality is quite general. His focus tends to be on matters of general principle, with modest attention to particular reforms or policies. He rejects sexual inequality in both domestic and social contexts. Mill discusses domestic equality primarily in Chapter II. There, he focuses on the rights of wives and mothers, recognizing women's equal rights over their bodies or persons (283–86), to own and control property (284–85, 297) to control various aspects of domestic decision-making and household management (290–92), to custody and care of children (285), and to separation and divorce (285–86). But Mill is not only concerned with wives and mothers in domestic contexts. He also defends equal rights to education (315–16), to professional opportunities (299; cf. *PPE* IV.vii.3), to vote in political elections (301), and to run for political office (301). In addition to these rights, Mill presumably also endorses equal rights to freedom of expression, worship, and association. One assumes that he sees the main threats to these rights as occurring in the domestic realm and coming from husbands, fathers, and brothers.

Mill spends considerable time discussing particular inequalities that concern him and replying to potential objections to sexual equality or defenses of sexual inequality. His discussion of the principles requiring equality is fairly brief. There seem to be three main principles.

As we have seen (§70), he contrasts systems of hereditary caste, such as feudalism and social systems based on slavery, with the distinctively modern and progressive commitment to *equal opportunity for welfare* (272–73). At several points, he likens the status of women inside and outside of marriage to slavery (284–86, 323). Mill is not much impressed by those who would dispute the analogy on the ground that women are treated much better than slaves. Gilded cages are still cages that restrict freedom and opportunity. And often the cages are not gilded; Mill insists that husbands can be and often are

---

1. Here, I agree with Mary Lyndon Shanley, "The Subjection of Women," in *The Cambridge Companion to Mill*, ed. Skorupski.
2. See Nicholson, "The Reception and Early Reputation of Mill's Political Thought," p. 471.

just as violent and abusive as masters (285–86, 288–89). Indeed, with the demise of slavery in America, he views sexual inequality as the last vestige of slavery in the West.

> The law of servitude in marriage is a monstrous contradiction to all the principles of the modern world, and to all the experience through which those principles have been slowly and painfully worked out. It is the sole case, now that negro slavery has been abolished, in which a human being in the plenitude of every faculty is delivered up to the tender mercies of another human being, in the hope forsooth that this other will use the power solely for the good of the person subjected to it. Marriage is the only actual bondage known to our law. There remain no legal slaves, except the mistress of every house [323].

Mill is especially interested in opportunities for self-realization, which would include opportunities for developing normative competence and for exercising this competence in self-governed lives that realize our natures as progressive beings. These opportunities, we have seen, are not good in themselves, but they are necessary conditions for achieving these higher-order goods. This explains why Mill refers to the demand for equal opportunity for welfare as a demand of justice (325) and why it grounds a claim of right.

Mill also condemns sexual inequalities of opportunity by appeal to the social benefits lost.

> The...benefit to be expected from giving to women the free use of their faculties, by leaving them the free choice of their employments, and opening to them the same field of occupation and the same prizes and encouragements as to other human beings, would be that of doubling the mass of mental faculties available for the higher service of humanity [326; cf. 326–28].

Mill's discussion of the opportunity costs of inequality is often very abstract. At times, his concerns sound almost economic, as if he is defending sexual equality for its tendency to increase gross national product or lead to the design of better widgets or, perhaps, better poetry.

But Mill also focuses on the loss of intrinsic value associated with inequality and the intrinsic benefits that would come with sexual equality. For instance, he defends the value of marriage conceived as a form of friendship among equals, which is possible only when marriage is reformed so as to be a voluntary association among partners with equal legal rights to self-ownership, self-determination, property, and custody of children (293–95, 334–36).

Interestingly, he focuses as much on the expected benefits of marriage reforms for men as for women. He clearly thinks that men stand to benefit from these and other egalitarian reforms, such as equal educational and professional opportunities, inasmuch as the fuller development of the higher faculties of one's spouse contributes to the fuller realization of one's own higher faculties (326, 334–36). Mill's defense of the value of friendships among equals can be strengthened by consideration of his perfectionist defense of liberties of thought and action in *On Liberty*. That argument appeals to the way in which intellectual exchange and discussion with another contributes to the exercise of capacities for practical deliberation by expanding the menu of options available to interlocutors and better assessing the merits of options on the deliberative menu. Husbands whose wives are allowed and encouraged to develop their higher faculties have partners with whom they can share and discuss their ideals, plans, work, and avocations. Friendships among equals provide both emotional support and critical perspective. In this way, such friendships enable both partners to realize more fully their own deliberative capacities.

Because existing sexual inequalities, especially those within the family, are exceptions to the modern norm of equal opportunity at the heart of social justice, Mill thinks that these inequalities are bad insofar as they weaken the culture of social justice (288, 293–95).

> The example afforded, and the education given to the sentiments, by laying the foundation of domestic existence upon a relation contradictory to the first principles of social justice, must, from the very nature of man, have a perverting influence of such magnitude, that it is hardly possible [to conceive] so great a change for the better as would be made by its removal [325].

Mill also invokes the pernicious effects on boys of being socialized to expectations in which power and entitlements are not conditional on and proportional to effort or merit (324).

This focus on the way in which others—men, especially—are harmed by sexual inequalities and stand to gain by egalitarian reforms, though plausible, is a little odd and uncomfortable. It would be like defending the abolition of slavery by appealing to the real interests of the masters in abolition. Here, we might remember that *The Subjection of Women* is at least in part a political tract aimed at voters and men in positions of power and influence. One can see how such arguments might appeal to those who need argument most, namely, those not antecedently disposed to care about the status of slaves or women. But one does want to say that the most objectionable harms perpetrated by discrimination are those harms borne by the objects of discrimination themselves.

Fortunately, Mill does turn his attention to this concern about sexual inequality. Here, he focuses, as one might expect, on the harms and unhappiness that discrimination causes to women by appeal to the pre-eminent importance of individual liberties.

> Thus far, the benefits which it has appeared that the world would gain by ceasing to make sex a disqualification for privileges and a badge of subjection, are social rather than individual; consisting in an increase of the general fund of thinking and acting power, and an improvement in the general conditions of the association of men and women. But it would be a grievous understatement of the case to omit the most direct benefit of all, the unspeakable gain in private happiness to the liberated half of the species; the difference to them between a life of subjection to the will of others, and a life of rational freedom. After the primary necessities of food and raiment, freedom is the first and strongest want to human nature [336].

A hedonist might appeal to the dissatisfaction that sexual discrimination produces. While this is no doubt part of what Mill has in mind, his perfectionist conception of happiness allows him to focus directly on the harms to women's autonomy. Mill goes on to claim that personal independence is an "element of happiness" (336–37). An equal regard for the happiness of each explains why sexual discrimination is impermissible.

Here, one might expect Mill to invoke his liberal principles more explicitly. Sexual discrimination restricts the liberties and opportunities of women, yet it apparently cannot be justified by appeal to the harm principle. Indeed, sexual discrimination clearly harms women, so the restriction on men's liberty embodied in its elimination would be a clear, indeed, paradigmatic application of the harm principle.

The restrictions contained in Victorian marriage law that give husbands complete control over the person and property of their wives and that do not allow for unilateral divorce or separation make marriage a form of sexual slavery. Slavery is an impermissible restriction of the liberty of another. Slavery would be impermissible even if the wife consented to marriage (cf. 270). Mill might question whether the consent is meaningful given the social pressures to marry and to defer to their husbands, the limited options for those who do not marry, and the adverse consequences to women of expressing dissent within marriage (270). But the quality of consent should be in any case irrelevant, because we know that Mill thinks that it is impermissible to contract into slavery and that paternalistic laws that prevent such contracts are not only permissible but obligatory (OL V 11). Presumably, this is just the sort of case that Mill has in mind when he suggests that the prohibition of selling oneself into slavery is a principled exception to the usual prohibition on paternalism that has "wider application." Indeed, because Mill thinks that unreformed marriage is literally slavery (SW 271, 323), he must think, not just that consenting to marriage is relevantly like contracting into slavery, but that it *is* contracting into slavery.

74. Rebutting the case for inequality

Mill considers and replies to various actual and possible defenses of sexual inequality, whether domestic or social. In almost all cases, the apologist for inequality alleges that women are naturally inferior in relation to men along some dimension that is alleged to be relevant to the proper management of personal and public affairs. For the most part, the apologist claims that men possess some trait essential for normative competence that women lack—these might be represented as alleged female *deficits*—or that women possess some trait that men lack that threatens normative competence—these might be represented as alleged female *disqualifiers*. In either case, the apologist argues, it turns out that women are naturally inferior and so do not deserve equal treatment.

Mill actually considers a large list of potential natural differences, not restricted to deficits and disqualifiers, including claims that women are: (1) more intuitive and practical, less principled and theoretical, than men (305); (2) more focused on particulars, less capable of abstraction or generalization, than men (306); (3) more nervous and excitable than men (308); (4) less single-minded than men (310); (5) less accomplished in philosophy, science, and art than men (313–14); (6) less original than men (314–15); (7) morally superior to men (320–21); (8) more susceptible to personal bias than men (321); (9) more pacific and less aggressive than men (329–30); (10) more philanthropic than men (330); and (11) more self-sacrificing and self-abnegating than men (293).

Mill's response to these alleged differences is mixed. Sometimes, he questions whether the traits in question are unevenly distributed. But, for the most part, he seems to concede that the traits are unevenly distributed. He doesn't always agree that the female trait is a deficit or disqualifier. For instance, he thinks that being more intuitive, more practical, more focused on particulars, and less rigid allows women to compensate for deficits in the way that men typically approach decision-making. Women are less likely to follow principle for its own sake and are more likely to test principles by their real-world consequences. They are better able to multi-task and intellectually more open-minded.[3] Being morally superior and less aggressive are unqualified goods. However, he seems to concede that women are more excitable, less accomplished, and less original than men. He tries to explain these deficits in ways that do not presuppose women's natural inferiority.

Parts of this discussion are puzzling, especially the parts in which Mill defends the value of the alleged feminine trait. If these are valuable traits, but they are the product of sexual discrimination, does that provide support for the discrimination?

Fortunately, Mill has a more fundamental response to the apologists. Even if the trait is unevenly distributed and functions as a deficit or disqualifier, Mill wants to insist that there is no evidence of natural inferiority. There is no evidence of natural inferiority, because we cannot be sure that the incapacity is the product of nature, rather than nurture. In particular, because the history of sexual relations has been discriminatory, we cannot rule out the possibility that female incapacity is the product of past discriminatory treatment (275–77, 304–305, 313).

> I consider it a presumption in any one to pretend to decide what women are or are not, can or cannot be, by natural constitution. They have always hitherto been kept, as far as regards spontaneous development, in so unnatural a state, that their nature cannot but have been greatly distorted and disguised; and no one can safely pronounce that if women's nature were left to choose its direction as freely as men's, and if no artificial bent were attempted to be given to it except that required by the conditions of human society, and given to both sexes alike there would be any material difference, or perhaps any difference at all, in the character and capacities that would unfold themselves [304–305].

Mill rightly insists that incapacity that is the product of discriminatory treatment cannot be appealed to justify that discrimination. That would be circular reasoning.

---

3. Mill's claims about the differences between male and female approaches to decision-making anticipates, in some ways, later claims about differences in moral reasoning between men and women. See, for example, Carol Gilligan, *In a Different Voice* (Cambridge, MA: Harvard University Press, 1982). Mill's considered view is that we cannot assume that these differences are natural or innate, rather than the product of differential treatment and education.

Mill can explain differential accomplishments in philosophy, science, and the arts by appeal to social barriers to women's participation in these fields (313–18) and to competing domestic demands that are placed on them (318–19). In this connection, it is worth noting that Mill can concede not only differential accomplishments of the sexes but differential capacity, in at least one sense. For Mill can and should distinguish between *actual* capacity and *potential* capacity. Actual capacities determine what an agent is now able to do, whereas potential capacities determine what actual capacities she can develop. For instance, I have no actual capacity to speak Russian, but presumably I do have a potential capacity to speak Russian. By contrast, I don't have even a potential capacity to fly or run a three-minute mile. Actual capacities are a function of potential capacities and suitable training, opportunities, and responsibilities. If I have not been given a proper education and training with suitable deliberative opportunities and responsibilities at various points in my development, my potential competence may not be actualized. Even if everyone had equal potential capacities, we should expect unequal actual capacities in systems where education and deliberative opportunities and responsibilities have been distributed unequally. This is how Mill's case for sexual equality can concede not only that men are more accomplished than women but also that they have greater capacity in one sense, that is, greater actual capacity. However, their greater actual capacity is no evidence that they possess greater potential capacity.

But this *Appeal to Nurture*, as we might call it, applies to all the differences between the sexes. In particular, it applies to feminine traits that seem like assets as well as to those that seem like deficits or disqualifiers. But then Mill cannot argue for women's rights on the ground that they bring distinctive natural talents to domestic or social contexts. Mill should claim that we just have very little evidence about what natural assets and liabilities women or men possess. The moral that Mill draws from the Appeal to Nurture is that equal rights should prevail in the absence of any good evidence about the way in which natural assets and liabilities (potential capacities) are distributed sexually. Equality is the presumption, even if it is a rebuttable presumption, and the presumption can only be rebutted on the basis of adequate empirical evidence (262).

Indeed, Mill thinks that we do have some evidence that women possess equal (potential) capacity for managing their own affairs and those of the community well. The evidence comes from the good job women have done in those exceptional circumstances in which they have been given political rule and suitable training for that role (274–75, 302–04). Though this is a small sample, the percentage of women who have ruled well when given the opportunity is actually higher, Mill claims, than the percentage of men who have ruled well when given the opportunity.

75. The vices of charity and self-abnegation

It is worth discussing two traits associated with women, often thought to be virtues, which Mill treats as vices or at least insists on criticizing. These are *philanthropy* (330–31) and *self-sacrifice* or *self-abnegation* (292–93). Mill does not deny that women have these traits more than men, but he clearly thinks that this is the result of traditional divisions of social labor in which women are schooled to defer to their husbands and care for the family and in which women of means (whose husbands are wealthy) are encouraged to take up philanthropic causes. Moreover, he thinks that these artificial traits are morally problematic. Why?

In the case of philanthropy, we should distinguish between benevolence and charity. Mill has no problem with benevolent impulses to improve the lot of the poor. What he objects to are charitable schemes that provide food or money to the poor without making them self-reliant.

> The great and continually increasing mass of unenlightened and shortsighted benevolence, which, taking the care of people's lives out of their own hands, and relieving them from the disagreeable consequences of their own acts, saps the very foundations of the self-respect, self-help, and self-control which are the essential conditions both of individual prosperity and of social virtue—this waste of resources and benevolent feelings in doing harm instead of good, is immensely swelled by women's contributions, and stimulated by their influence [330].

Forms of beneficence that make the beneficiary dependent on the benefactor do the beneficiary no lasting good and actually harm him or her. This follows directly from Mill's perfectionist conception of happiness in which a chief ingredient of happiness is autonomous control of the shape and content of one's life. Real beneficence, though it might include temporary relief and support, must take the form of providing educational and vocational opportunities that will make the poor more self-reliant.

Why does Mill associate this pernicious form of charity especially with women? He thinks that it is no accident and should be no surprise that female philanthropists should make this mistake, inasmuch as they treat the poor just as men treat them (330). In both cases, the beneficiary is made to rely on the benefactor's largess for his or her own well-being, rather than becoming properly equipped to care for himself or herself.

Self-sacrifice is not bad in itself. Indeed, Mill thinks that it would be much better if men tended to be more self-effacing and self-abnegating. The problem is that women have an exaggerated sense of self-sacrifice. They have too little concern for their own selves and too great a concern and sense of responsibility for the welfare of others.

> If women are better than men in anything, it surely is in individual self-sacrifice for those of their own family. But I lay little stress on this, so long as they are universally taught that they are born and created for self-sacrifice. I believe that equality of rights would abate the exaggerated self-abnegation which is the present artificial ideal of feminine character, and that a good woman would not be more self-sacrificing than the best man: but on the other hand, men would be much more unselfish and self-sacrificing than at present, because they would no longer be taught to worship their own will as such a grand thing that it is actually the law for another rational being [293].

Indeed, men's exaggerated sense of entitlement and inflated self-concern are just the corollaries of women's exaggerated sense of self-sacrifice and diminished self-concern. It is the one set of attitudes that make the other possible. Both extremes are wrong and require correction, which, of course, requires changes in cultural norms and the way men and women are educated. Mill anticipates later feminist claims in insisting that, so far from praising women's selflessness, we should be encouraging them to have a greater regard for themselves.[4]

76. Is the sexual division of labor natural?

We have seen that in rebutting potential defenses of sexual inequality by appeal to various alleged dimensions of natural inferiority, Mill insists that we cannot determine whether traits commonly found in women are the product of nature or nurture without suitable social experimentation,

---

4. For a good contemporary statement of this view, see Jean Hampton, "The Wisdom of the Egoist: The Moral and Political Implications of Valuing the Self," *Social Philosophy & Policy* 14 (1997): 21–51.

including, most importantly, the social experiment of sexual equality. In particular, there is the very real possibility that the traits alleged to justify sexual discrimination are the product of past discriminatory practice.

However, it is arguable that Mill does not carry his Appeal to Nurture far enough.[5] At several points, he expresses the conviction that most women raised in a culture of equal opportunity and with a full menu of options from which to select will prefer a traditional sexual division of labor in which they perform domestic functions while their husbands pursue professions in civil society, and he approves of this traditional division of labor.

> When the support of the family depends, not on property, but on earning, the common arrangement, by which the man earns the income and the wife superintends the domestic expenditure, seems to me in general the most suitable division of labour between the two persons.... In an otherwise just state of things, it is not, therefore, I think, a desirable custom, that the wife should contribute by her labour to the income of the family [297].

Of course, Mill is right that a wife should not *also* have to earn a living outside the home if she is working full time within the home. But Mill gives no reason for thinking that women should have families or that, if they do, they, rather than their husbands, should be responsible for matters domestic. Indeed, Mill's view seems to be that for women extra-domestic vocations should be reserved primarily for those without children or whose children are already grown (338). He seems here to assume that the traditional sexual division of labor is natural. Of course, it is possible that the traditional sexual division of labor would emerge in a system of equal opportunity. But this is conjecture. Indeed, one might have thought that his own claims about how the system of unequal opportunity has repressed women's creative and managerial capacities would have suggested that the traditional sexual division of labor was probably not robust. In defending or at least speculating about the robustness of the traditional sexual division of labor, Mill appears to be ignoring his own Appeal to Nurture.

---

5. Julia Annas vigorously defends a variant of this conclusion in "Mill and the Subjection of Women," *Philosophy* 52 (1977): 179–94. She distinguishes between Mill's reformist claims (that accept a traditional sexual division of labor but try to make marriage more humane and give women the right to vote) and radical claims (that treat virtually all aspects of the sexual division of labor as the product of sexual discrimination and that demand wholesale egalitarian changes in women's personal, domestic, economic, political, and social roles). She sees Mill's ambivalent response to the normative significance of these alleged feminine traits as a reflection of his ambivalence between his reformist and radical agenda. Cf. Susan Okin, *Women in Western Political Thought* (Princeton: Princeton University Press, 1979), ch. 9, esp. pp. 226–30.

77. Transitional justice?

For Mill, women are, through no fault of their own, a backward class. This backwardness is correctable and temporary. In this respect, the situation of women is relevantly similar to the situation of the working classes. This raises the question of whether the right policy is to afford women full personal and political rights immediately or whether to treat them, as he does the working classes, in accordance with principles of transitional justice until such time as their backwardness has been corrected.

Recall that in *On Liberty* Mill limits the scope of his defense of basic liberties to those in the maturity of their faculties and leaves out of consideration "backward states of society" (I 10). He makes clear here that the argument for basic liberties applies only to those who meet some threshold level of normative competence. This, we saw, is because basic liberties are important as necessary conditions for exercising one's deliberative capacities but have no value when other necessary conditions—such as basic normative competence—are not in place. Exactly where Mill sets this threshold is unclear. On the one hand, he clearly contemplates that some societies might be too backward. On the other hand, he suggests that "all nations with whom we need concern ourselves" have met this threshold. Presumably, colonial societies, such as India, were societies that concerned Mill. So perhaps he thinks that the threshold for application is comparatively low and that the scope of basic liberties is correspondingly wide.

We might notice two aspects of the issue that Mill is discussing to which he does not draw much attention. First, we might note that even though Mill seems to have in mind some threshold level of normative competence below which basic liberties are not important and above which they are important, the underlying phenomenon of normative competence is presumably *scalar* and admits of degree (cf. §§38, 55). In principle, it seems, the argument for basic liberties in any particular case (with any particular agent) should track the degree of normative competence the agent possesses, whether above or below any particular threshold. If so, then selecting any one point on the scale of normative competence as setting a normative threshold above which basic liberties have full normative significance and below which they have none must be arbitrary and justified, if at all, on pragmatic or administrative grounds.

Second, Mill does not directly address here whether the backwardness in question is *correctable*. We can distinguish between those whose backwardness is correctable and those whose backwardness is not. Presumably, the backwardness of some is uncorrectable. This is currently true of those whose who are born with significant cognitive impairments. It is also true of those who were once competent but whose competence has now deteriorated as part of some irreversible degenerative process. But, for many, backwardness is a potentially temporary and correctable condition. This is true of most children. They are incompetent only because they are immature. Under normal circumstances, they will mature as they age and acquire more competence, eventually crossing the threshold of basic competence. Mill implies that the same is true of backward societies. With suitable changes in their economic, social, and political institutions, members of such societies can become competent. Drawing on our distinction between potential and actual capacities, we might say that basic competence is a kind of actual capacity, but many people who lack this actual capacity have the potential capacity to acquire this actual capacity.

But in cases where backwardness is correctable, we are under special obligations to make the corrections. This raises questions about *transitional justice*. Even if we do not have the same obligations of justice toward the competent and the backward, we have obligations of justice toward those whose backwardness is correctable to help them acquire competence. Mill doesn't really deal with these questions of transitional justice in *On Liberty*. But he needs to.

Consider the case of children. Presumably, transitional justice requires that we provide them with an education—in the broadest sense—that develops their normative competence. To do so, we really need to recognize both their potential competence and the scalar character of actual competence. We should not treat children or other potentially competent individuals the way we would treat the permanently childlike. We need to try to teach them skills and allow them to acquire varied experiences safely. Children need to play an active part in their own development and education. In particular, they need to be given various sorts of deliberative opportunities and responsibilities, including the freedom to make and learn from their own mistakes in certain circumscribed ways, which prevent or minimize the chance of catastrophic outcomes. As they get older and their competence grows, they need to be given more freedom, opportunities, and responsibilities. Only in this way will the potentially competent develop actual competence.

These ideas about transitional justice raise the question whether the history of sexual discrimination has put women in a comparatively backward state that should be addressed by an account of transitional justice. One way to pursue this issue is by thinking about how Mill responds to what he regards as the backward condition of the working classes.

We noted earlier that, as an advocate of greater equality of income, equality of educational opportunity, the extension of the franchise, healthcare reform, and labor regulations that tended to improve the safety and quality of factory work, Mill saw himself, with good reason, as a friend of the working classes (§68). Nonetheless this friendship was mixed with doubts about their present intellectual and moral abilities. This comparative incompetence was not a natural condition, and Mill hoped to improve their competence by better education, better working conditions, and greater scope for civic participation. This commitment to improving their lot, however, was tempered by concerns about letting them dominate civic life in their current backward state. As we saw (§§67–68), this ambivalence is clearly expressed in Mill's conception of democracy in *Considerations on Representative Government*. He thought that the proper representation of workers' interests in political decision-making required that they be allowed to vote. He also thought that their political participation required them to be better educated and that their active participation in civic affairs would improve their competence. But he worried about Parliament being dominated by "a low grade of intelligence" (*CRG* VII/448), and he endorsed a scheme for weighted voting in which everyone voted but plural votes were given, not on the basis of wealth, but on the basis of education (VIII). In matters of political economy, Mill was generally supportive of workers' cooperative associations, which introduced democratic principles into the governance of the workplace. Such associations, like their political counterparts, were to be welcomed insofar as they better protected workers' interests and extended the scope of the autonomy of workers. But, also like their political counterparts, they introduced the threat of bad and, in particular, inefficient economic management until such time as workers were better educated (*PPE* IV.vii.6).

So, in the case of the working classes, Mill recognized their comparative backward condition as a temporary condition, but as one that affected the political and economic liberties they should be permitted, if not in the long run, at least in the transitional phase during which their competence would be raised. Whatever one thinks of these qualifications to the political and economic liberties of the working classes, it is a striking fact that Mill does not mention similar qualifications to the domestic, social, and political liberties of women. This is striking, inasmuch as one might think that the same sort of social conditions that explain the comparative backwardness of the working classes and call for the application of a scheme of transitional justice for them would also explain the comparative backwardness of women and call for a scheme of transitional justice for them.

Indeed, one might wonder whether Mill wasn't committed to accepting an account of transitional justice that treated women more like the recipients of public charities than like the working class. For both law and custom treat women, as Mill repeatedly criticizes, as dependent on the wills of their fathers, husbands, and brothers. But in this respect, at least, they are likely to develop the same culture of dependency and deference that Mill criticizes public and private charities for fostering (*SW* 330). Indeed, we know that Mill disqualifies those on parish relief from the franchise (*CRG* VIII/472–73). It is not that, like the (literate) working class, their votes count for less than those of the better educated. Rather, they are excluded from the franchise altogether, until such time as they are productively employed. But if he accepted this analogy, Mill would seem forced to exclude women from the franchise altogether, at least as a temporary measure, required by transitional justice.

Mill does not address these issues of dependency as clearly as he should. However, he may want to reply by distinguishing productive employment and wage labor. In rejecting the idea that women should be expected to work outside the home for wages as well as assume domestic responsibilities, with this constituting overtime or moonlighting (*SW* 297), Mill treats domestic labor as productive work, even though it is not compensated as such. Indeed, domestic tasks of household management and raising children obviously call for considerable practical skills. Managing a family's domestic affairs is in many ways like managing a small firm. So Mill can distinguish the backward condition of women in systems of sexual inequality from the more backward condition of those subsisting on charity. Though he must recognize regrettable forms of dependency that existing sexual inequality breeds, these are offset to a considerable degree by women's domestic responsibilities. As a result, women are not so dependent that Mill should treat them, even transitionally, as he would treat those on parish relief.

What about the comparison with the backward condition of the working classes? Mill may well apply the same principles of transitional justice to women as to the working class. For in defending female suffrage in *Considerations on Representative Government* he denies that gender justifies differential treatment.

> In the preceding argument for universal, but graduated suffrage, I have taken no account of difference of sex. I consider it to be entirely irrelevant to political rights, as difference in height, or in the colour of the hair. All human beings have the same interest in good government; the welfare of all is alike affected by it, and they have an equal need of a voice in it to secure their share of its benefits [VIII/479].

Mill seems to be advocating the same educational and professional qualifications for plural voting for women as for men. So his principles of transitional justice appear, after all, to be gender-neutral. They will justify fractional suffrage for women only to the extent that women receive less education than their male counterparts. Because Mill thinks that the progressive application of principles of sexual equality will equalize access of men and women to educational opportunities, any fractional suffrage women must endure should be temporary in nature.

So Mill is committed by gender-neutral principles to fractional suffrage for women during the period of transitional justice in which equal opportunity is established and becomes part of the domestic, social, and legal culture. Whether fractional suffrage is justified even in these limited circumstances depends on Mill's defense of weighted voting. The defense of plural votes for those of superior normative competence (or at least a representative cross-section thereof) is surprisingly robust. However, we did raise two worries about weighted voting (§69). The first worry concerned the potentially corrosive effects of political inequalities that introduce a form of second-class citizenship. Though Mill does not seem especially sensitive to concerns about the bad effects of second-class citizenship in *Considerations on Representative Government*, he recognizes and is quite sensitive to such concerns in *The Subjection of Women*. Here is a case where Mill's actual concern with sexual inequalities might lead him to be more concerned about political inequalities in weighted voting. The second worry concerned the use of educational qualifications as a proxy for normative competence. While educational qualifications provide a better proxy for normative competence than wealth or property qualifications, even educational qualifications are imperfectly correlated with normative competence, proving both over-inclusive, giving plural votes to some with educational degrees who are not especially competent, and under-inclusive, denying plural votes to those who are especially normatively competent but lack the right educational pedigree. Even if weighted voting made sense in an ideal world in which we could reliably measure superior normative competence—

something that the first concern with second-class citizenship might lead us to doubt—it does not make sense in the actual world if we lack sufficiently dependable ways of doing so.

78. Millian feminism

There is one significant blemish on Mill's feminist credentials. He sometimes assumed that a traditional sexual division of labor was natural in the sense that it was likely to emerge in a culture of equal opportunity for all. His mistake was not in supposing that this could be true but in supposing that it was likely to be true. Given Mill's recognition that the existing division of labor was produced and sustained in conditions of sexual discrimination and unequal opportunity, there is no basis for supposing that this division of labor would survive a culture of equality. Here, Mill neglects his own Appeal to Nurture. Even here, it is Mill himself that supplies the resources for criticizing his assumption. That ought to provide partial mitigation of his mistake.

Otherwise, Mill's feminist credentials are sterling. He is a keen critic of domestic and social forms of inequality, recognizing the harm such practices cause women and the ways in which they deform the lives of boys and men too. Victorian marriage law, the denial of the franchise, and lack of social and economic opportunities violate the higher-order interests of women. These rights violations are a matter of serious social injustice. The corollary of these criticisms is that Mill is a staunch defender of equal opportunity for women and an eloquent spokesman for the way in which a culture of equality would transform the lives of girls and women, liberating their creative potential and emotional sensibilities, and make possible more productive social cooperation and friendships among equals.

Mill's discussion of sexual equality is one place where the perfectionist underpinnings of his liberal principles play an important role and add to the depth of his criticisms of sexual discrimination and his case for sexual equality. His defense of sexual equality highlights the genuinely progressive aspects of his utilitarian and liberal commitments.

Epilogue

[T]he Greatest Happiness Principle...is a mere form of words without rational signification, unless one person's happiness, supposed equal in degree (with the proper allowance made for kind), is counted for exactly as much as another's.... The equal claim of everybody to happiness in the estimation of the moralist and legislator, involves an equal claim to all the means of happiness, except in so far as the inevitable conditions of human life, and the general interest, in which that of every individual is included, set limits to the maxim; and those limits ought to be strictly construed.... All persons are deemed to have a *right* to equality of treatment, except when some recognised social expediency requires the reverse. And hence all social inequalities which have ceased to be considered expedient, assume the character not of simple inexpediency, but of injustice, and appear so tyrannical, that people are apt to wonder how they ever could have been tolerated; forgetful that they themselves perhaps tolerate other inequalities under an equally mistaken notion of expediency, the correction of which would make that which they approve seem quite as monstrous as what they have at last learnt to condemn. The entire history of social improvement has been a series of transitions, by which one custom or institution after another, from being supposed a primary necessity of social existence, has passed into the rank of an universally stigmatized injustice and tyranny. So it has been with the distinctions of slaves and freemen, nobles and serfs, patricians and plebeians; and so it will be, and in part already is, with the aristocracies of colour, race, and sex [*U* V 36].

Having examined Mill's utilitarian and liberal principles and their applications to democratic politics and sexual equality in some detail, we are now in a position to take stock of his contributions to the utilitarian and liberal traditions and appreciate the sense in which these contributions were progressive.

79. Making utilitarianism more progressive

Mill's Philosophical Radical forebears, especially Bentham and his father James Mill, were hedonistic utilitarians who applied their utilitarian principles self-consciously and directly to social, political, and legal institutions and called for democratic reforms, including the extension of the franchise. Mill continued this Radical legacy, but he extended it and transformed it significantly. Many of these transformations are reflected in changes he introduced into utilitarianism itself.

Mill recognized the tension between utilitarianism and psychological egoism, latent in the Radical tradition. He resolved it by criticizing and rejecting psychological egoism, recognizing the diversity of human motivation and stressing the possibilities for sympathetic identification with the interests of others and the cultivation of moral sentiments.

Mill also rejected the tendency of the Radicals to assume that a utilitarian should always apply utilitarian principles directly to practical problems, calculating expected utility at every choice point. There are opportunity costs to calculating expected utility, there is often limited information at the time of decision, and calculations are often subject to familiar temporal and personal biases. We can reject the idea that utility should always be our guide without leaving agents adrift. Communities have developed secondary principles that function as generally but imperfectly optimal heuristics that can and should regulate much conduct. However, these secondary principles are not sacred. They should be reassessed from time to time to ensure their continued comparative utility, and they should be set aside in favor of direct appeal to the utilitarian first principle in cases in which following the heuristic would be clearly and significantly suboptimal and in cases in which secondary principles, each of which has a utilitarian justification, conflict.

Mill's defense of the importance of secondary principles within utilitarianism implies another critique of the Radicals. They tried to remake personal and public morality from the ground up, substituting the principle of utility for more familiar discrete moral precepts about honesty, fidelity, fairness, rights, and justice. Such a program was psychologically unrealistic. It also failed to see the utilitarian justification of regulating our conduct by these discrete moral precepts. The intuitionists were wrong to treat these moral precepts as ultimate and self-evident, but they were correct to stress their importance to moral life. However, commonsense morality is not adequate as it stands. It requires theoretical unification, which will show some common moral precepts to be unprincipled and in need of reform. But, for the most part, familiar moral precepts can be accommodated by the right kind of utilitarianism. This mix of accommodation and reform commits Mill to Sidgwick's thesis that commonsense morality is unconsciously, inchoately, and imperfectly utilitarian. Mill, perhaps more clearly than Sidgwick, sees that this fact simultaneously vindicates the probative value of common moral precepts and provides the most satisfactory justification of utilitarianism. In this, he makes an important advance over the unsatisfactory justificatory claims Bentham and the other Radicals made on behalf of utilitarianism.

Important as these changes in utilitarianism are, perhaps Mill's most important break with the Radical legacy he inherited is his conception of happiness itself. The change comes in Mill's doctrine of higher pleasures in Chapter II of *Utilitarianism*. Though Mill formulates that doctrine as a modification within hedonism, in fact he conceives of higher pleasures as activities and pursuits that employ our higher, deliberative faculties. Such activities and pursuits are uniquely valuable not because they would be the objects of informed and idealized preference by competent judges. Rather, they would be the objects of idealized preference because they are valuable and appeal to our sense of dignity. This perfectionist reading of the higher pleasures doctrine dovetails nicely with Mill's claims about our happiness as progressive beings in *On Liberty* and elsewhere. In fact, he grounds this perfectionist conception of happiness in our capacities as moral agents, capable of responding to reasons for action, which promises to explain why this conception of happiness should be normative for us. Such an objective conception of happiness may seem elitist, but it is in fact compatible with an attractive form of pluralism and preserves the common assumption that happiness is what matters when we are concerned for anyone for his own sake.

Mill's early critics, such as Sidgwick and Green, were right to see that this perfectionist doctrine could not be squared with hedonism, but they were wrong to think that Mill was fundamentally inconsistent. Though his break with his hedonist legacy would have been clearer if he had eschewed talk of pleasure consistently, his higher pleasures doctrine is best interpreted in perfectionist terms, and it is this perfectionist understanding of happiness that accounts for some of the most distinctive and progressive aspects of his utilitarian outlook.

80. From progressive utilitarianism to liberalism

Mill's Radical forebears were interested in democratic reforms that extended the franchise. Though this was a progressive kind of reform, which challenged institutions of class and privilege, the Radicals were not much concerned about threats within democracy, such as the tyranny of the majority. Tyranny of the majority threatens individual rights, and the antidote to tyranny of the majority is to constrain majority decision-making by individual rights. Though Bentham did recognize legal rights in the sense of legal entitlements, he was notoriously hostile to the idea of natural rights, calling the idea "nonsense on stilts" (*Anarchical Fallacies* in *Works* II 501). It was Mill who recognized clearly worries about the potential excesses of majority rule, embraced the liberal idea that individuals have rights against each other and the state that limit what others may permissibly do to them, tried to articulate the contours of these liberal rights, and gave them a utilitarian foundation.

Initially, Mill identifies liberalism with "one very simple principle," the harm principle, apparently claiming that preventing harm is necessary and perhaps sufficient for restricting liberty—rejecting paternalism, moralism, and offense regulation along the way. But, as Mill articulates his liberal principles and applies them, it becomes apparent that this one simple principle is only a rough first approximation. Though the harm principle remains very important, it is neither sufficient nor necessary for restricting liberty. Some injuries do not create even a *pro tanto* case for regulation. If Mill is to deny that these injuries are harmful, he must moralize harm. He can and should do so, but only in ways that allow him to assign harm an explanatory role in his liberal arguments. To do this, he should understand harm as the setback of an important interest to which the affected party has a right. Moreover, Mill does not even think that harm prevention is necessary to justify regulation. He allows that the state may restrict liberty in small and predictable ways incidental to the provision of the common good, and he recognizes autonomy-enhancing forms of paternalism. One might respond to these various worries about the harm principle by completely moralizing harm, in effect, defining A's harm of B in terms of A's liberal rights. We do better, I think, to read Mill as qualifying his simple principle. The harm principle states an important presumption about liberty and its limits, but liberal rights defy such simple formulas. Both the importance of basic liberties and their limitations depend on Mill's perfectionist conception of happiness, in particular, his claim that a uniquely important ingredient in someone's well-being is a kind of self-realization that requires normative competence and autonomy. This perfectionist defense of liberalism provides a plausible alternative to more recent interpretations of liberalism that rest on a commitment to neutrality among conceptions of the good.

Defending liberal rights raises questions about Mill's utilitarian commitments. As James Fitzjames Stephen observes, Mill's liberal categories may seem inconsistent with case-by-case utilitarian assessment.[1] The tension between utility and rights may seem no less serious if our liberal categories turn out to be complex, rather than simple. But Mill explicitly seeks to reconcile the tension between utility and rights, providing a utilitarian foundation for rights. Despite its initial promise, Mill's explicit conception of rights, the sanction theory of rights, suffers from the same sort of worries that plagued his sanction theory of duty. Mill does better sticking with his predominant commitment to direct utilitarianism. Thus, he can treat liberal rights as important secondary principles that insulate individual interests and liberties from utilitarian reasoning in many, but not all, contexts. He can also appeal to the structure contained in his perfectionist conception of happiness, according to which autonomous self-government and its prerequisites, including basic liberties, are pre-eminent goods that trump other lesser goods. These resources provide Mill with a plausible claim to reconcile utility and rights. Whether this utilitarian conception of rights is fully adequate depends in part on the plausibility of the rival conception of rights as side constraints on the pursuit of the good.

Mill relies on his perfectionist defense of liberal rights to defend a form of representative democracy that aims to promote a common good. Near universal suffrage is important both for epistemic reasons, helping representatives identify the interests of their constituents and the common good, and for constitutive reasons, helping citizens establish normative competence and providing greater scope for the exercise of their normative powers. Perfectionist elements also explain Mill's controversial calls for weighted voting and a democratic form of expertocracy. Weighted voting might make sense as part of ideal theory insofar as it treats political influence as a matter of degree that should track underlying differences in normative competence. However, weighted voting may underestimate the corrosive effects of

1. Stephen, *Liberty, Equality, and Fraternity*, p. 85.

political inequalities, even within ideal theory, and it is problematic for non-ideal theory insofar as we lack sufficiently reliable measures of normative competence that would justify weighted voting and expertocracy. These difficulties may explain Mill's willingness to concede the impracticality of those doctrines. Perfectionist liberalism also explains Mill's rejection of laissez-faire and his recognition of a positive role for the state in enabling self-realization and the promotion of the common good. In these ways, we can see Mill laying the groundwork for aspects of the New Liberalism.

But the real import of Mill's perfectionist liberalism is perhaps clearest in his defense of sexual equality. Mill is fierce and often eloquent in his condemnation of sexual discrimination in matters political, economic, and domestic, and in his call for egalitarian reforms premised on equality of opportunity. He was not justified in his assumption that the traditional division of sexual labor is natural. But Mill himself supplies the resources for the critique of this assumption in his repeated insistence that we cannot make inferences about which traits are natural based on the current distribution of traits if that distribution is itself the product of discriminatory treatment. This blind spot does not prevent Mill from seeing and articulating forcefully the grave injustices of Victorian marriage law, the denial of female suffrage, and the limited social and economic opportunities available to women. In his calls for reform and his pleas for a culture of sexual equality, Mill's progressive utilitarian and liberal commitments do significant work.

81. Equality as a progressive principle

An interesting and unresolved issue in Mill's utilitarian and liberal commitments concerns the role of equality in his progressive principles. As the epigraph (quoted at the head of this Epilogue) makes clear, Mill treats equality as a principal demand of justice and morality. He recognizes that there are some reasons to depart from equal treatment, but he seems to treat these departures as exceptional and to recognize a presumption in favor of equality. He thinks that central among the demands of justice are demands for equal concern and treatment and that history has shown us that many forms of inequality that were once accepted as natural have proven to be serious injustices. Nonetheless, Mill does not provide any systematic discussion of equality. There are at least two issues worth raising here. One issue is how egalitarian Mill's moral and political commitments are and in what ways they are egalitarian. A second issue is how concerns about equality interact with other elements of Mill's utilitarian liberalism. Both issues are complicated and deserve fuller treatment than I can provide here.

The epigraph indicates that Mill regards equality of some kind as a central demand of justice, and, as such, it is something to which individuals have a right. We have seen various ways in which he treats demands for equal concern and treatment as important. Utilitarianism says that everyone's interests matter, not just those of a privileged few, and that everyone's interests matter equally, no one's interests mattering more than anyone else's. When Mill defends liberal rights, these are rights that each person has and that protect her from the tyranny of majority preference. In arguing for the extension of the franchise, Mill seeks to ensure that political officials are accountable to all. It is true that the doctrine of weighted voting involves a departure from the norm of equal political influence. But Mill thinks that this is a principled exception to the norm of political equality insofar as it makes political influence better track differences in underlying normative competence, and he sees it as a transitional measure only, to be adopted while society works to redress artificial inequalities in normative competence (differences in actual competence not due to differences in potential competence). Mill does not require strict social and economic equality. Just as he allows that paternalism, while normally impermissible for normatively competent adults, is permissible for backward states of society, so too he allows that inequalities that might be problematic in economically stable societies might be more permissible in conditions of economic development if they introduce incentives that spur economic growth that leads to economic stability and benefits all (*PPE* IV.vi.2). As we have seen, in mature economies ("stationary states") Mill accepts social and economic inequalities, but he thinks that permissible inequalities are limited by the norm of equal opportunity. Equality of opportunity also plays a central role in Mill's condemnation of particular sexual inequalities and his defense of an ethos of sexual equality.

It is common to distinguish between equal concern and equal treatment.[2] Equal concern requires equal regard or consideration for affected parties in individual or collective decision-making, whereas equal treatment

---

2. See, for example, Dworkin, *Taking Rights Seriously*, p. 227, and Thomas Nagel, "Equality" reprinted in Thomas Nagel, *Mortal Questions* (New York: Cambridge University Press, 1979), pp. 123–24.

requires equal shares or outcomes. Equal concern seems a more fundamental demand than equal treatment. Sometimes equal concern takes the form of equal treatment, but at other times equal concern arguably requires unequal treatment. One might show two people equal concern and yet treat them differently if their situations and needs are relevantly different. For example, I might have equal concern for my two children, but if one has special needs, I am likely to treat them differently and may devote more time or resources to the one with special needs. Similarly, healthcare policy seems to display equal concern for citizens if it directs greater medical resources to those with special medical needs (provided they are not responsible for having greater medical needs in the first place). Moreover, A and B can be treated with equal concern, despite their unequal income, if they are accorded equal opportunity for employment and A prefers leisure to income and B prefers income to leisure. With this distinction between equal concern and equal treatment in mind, we might say that Mill clearly embraces a conception of equal concern, in particular, one that assigns great importance to equal opportunity. Though this kind of equality often requires equal treatment, Mill thinks that it is compatible with limited inequalities in political rights, in the form of weighted voting, and modest social and economic inequalities.

If genuine egalitarianism requires strict equality of treatment or outcome, then Mill is not a genuine egalitarian. But that conception of egalitarianism would be overly restrictive and few would satisfy it. Mill does insist on equal concern for normatively competent agents, to which he thinks equality of opportunity is central. Equality of opportunity limits social and economic inequalities but does not preclude them. In accepting weighted voting, Mill rejects the idea that political inequalities are per se impermissible and in doing so rejects a common asymmetry between political and economic equality. Weighted voting, he thinks, is a case in which equal concern for people *qua* rational agents does not require equal treatment or equal rights. But even these inequalities are limited and entirely transitional in nature. Speaking somewhat loosely, we might say that Mill is committed to rough, rather than exact, equality. But this kind of rough egalitarianism is one kind of egalitarianism.

What is hard to pin down is the exact justificatory role that equality is supposed to play in Mill's utilitarian and liberal commitments. A central issue here is whether equality is an independent ultimate value or its value is exhausted by its role in promoting general happiness. Consider equality of opportunity. In his more applied writings, including *Principles of Political Economy* and *The Subjection of Women*, Mill treats equal opportunity as a basic, apparently non-derivative, right. But it is hard to see how this could be squared with Mill's utilitarianism. Equality might be treated as an important secondary principle or as in some way contributing to the general happiness, but it is difficult to see how it could be a first principle, coordinate with the utilitarian standard. Direct utilitarianism implies both that it is our duty to promote happiness and that what maximizes happiness is our duty. As such, utilitarianism is concerned with the total amount of happiness and not with its distribution except insofar as this affects total happiness.

If Mill really accepts equality of opportunity or other egalitarian norms as axioms, coordinate with the utilitarian standard, then he is not a pure utilitarian but rather holds some sort of mixed standard in which utility and equality are independent variables. The rough idea would be that we are to promote happiness in a way that is constrained by equality of opportunity and any other fundamental norms of equality. This would be a form of consequentialism with utilitarian and egalitarian elements. Though we moderns might feel forced to describe such a view as a form of consequentialism, rather than utilitarianism, Mill might not have seen the difference or thought it important.[3]

Though I am not sure that this interpretation of the role of equality in Mill's progressive principles can be ruled out completely, there is another interpretation of the justificatory status that Mill assigns to equal concern that involves no departure from utilitarianism. On this interpretation, equal opportunity and other forms of rough equality figure as theorems in relation to the utilitarian axiom, rather than as axioms themselves. For starters, we might note that the appeal to equality of opportunity appears basic and underived in Mill's more practical writings in which he presumably aims to be more ecumenical about first principles. That's fully consistent with thinking that his preferred view is to justify such fundamental precepts within a utilitarian framework. That is certainly his strategy in his treatment of the demands of justice in *Utilitarianism* and his treatment of rights

---

3. Sidgwick considers supplementing utility with equality in a way that seems to treat equality as a tie-breaker among distributions that are equi-optimal or at least reasonably perceived to be so (*Methods* pp. 416–17). Interestingly, he doesn't see this as involving any departure from utilitarianism.

to basic liberties in *On Liberty*. To pursue this strategy, Mill must show how various forms of equality contribute importantly to promoting the general happiness.

Of course, it is often true that the way we distribute goods and opportunities affects total happiness. In particular, it is often true that more equal distributions of goods and opportunities promote total happiness. This is true in part because of the principle of diminishing marginal utility, which claims that as a person increases her consumption of a given resource the marginal utility of additional units of that resource decreases. So, all else being equal, more equal distributions of resources produce more total utility. This may be part of how Mill would treat equality as a derived value, which promotes utility. Moreover, Mill seems to think that inequalities are often objectionable on grounds of utility. It is not just that inequalities adversely affect those who have less and give rise to envy, though these things are true and important. Mill frequently argues that everyone is better off when inequalities are removed, even those whose comparative advantage is removed in the process. For example, censorship deprives censors, as well as the censored, of the opportunity to test ideas and exercise their deliberative capacities. Similarly, Mill thinks, others benefit from my experiments in living, which not only express my deliberative capacities but also enlarge the deliberative menu and enhance assessment of the alternatives. And sexist domestic, social, and political practices injure husbands, brothers, and sons, as well as the women who are principally harmed, so that removing these inequalities can be justified by the social benefit that this produces for everyone. Of special interest here is Mill's defense of an ideal of friendship among equals. We saw that he thinks that only in a friendship in which friends have equal status and rights can they find the right sort of association that fosters intimacy and cooperation, makes each answerable to the other, and enables each to realize his or her higher nature. Mill has reason to recognize friendship among equals as a microcosm for ideal social organization. On this view, equality of opportunity and substantial political and economic equality are necessary for a genuine community in which individuals are answerable to each other and dedicated to the common good in ways that enable them to realize their higher natures. Significant inequalities in opportunity and status make it difficult to treat social and political associations as cooperative ventures involving mutual accountability and mutual benefit, and they interfere with commitment to and pursuit of a common good.

This style of justifying equality, like the appeal to diminishing marginal utility, makes the value of equality derivative. It represents the value of equality as an extrinsic or relational good. But that needn't prevent Mill's egalitarian commitments from being robust, and it needn't involve a departure from his perfectionist utilitarianism.

82. Mill's legacy

I have not claimed that Mill's utilitarian and liberal commitments are immune to serious criticism or that his moral and political philosophy is fully consistent. On several important issues, Mill might have been clearer about his commitments or recognized potential concerns. These issues include his break with hedonism, his choice between direct and indirect utilitarian standards, the centrality of the harm principle, whether or not he wants to moralize harm, the legitimacy of offense regulation, his preferred strategy for reconciling utility and rights, and his treatment of equality, especially his reconciliation of equal concern and weighted voting. Moreover, I have raised philosophical questions about these and other doctrines, sometimes finding satisfactory answers, sometimes not. But Mill's inconsistencies, real and apparent, are interesting because they manifest recognition of disparate commitments and ideals that he wants to accommodate and reconcile. If the reconciliations fail, then we have learned something important about the structure and limits of these doctrines and ideals. If the reconciliations succeed, then we've learned that traditional antinomies may be unnecessary and that we can incorporate the insights of rival traditions into a more attractive comprehensive view. Though Mill's utilitarian and liberal commitments are not entirely free of inconsistency, I have tried to defend an interpretation of those commitments as largely and fundamentally consistent and as informed, in crucial ways, by a perfectionist conception of happiness as consisting in the exercise of our higher capacities. This sort of perfectionist conception of happiness has much to recommend it. It supports a distinctive and attractive form of utilitarianism and explains many of Mill's most distinctive liberal claims.

Our focus has been on Mill's contributions to the utilitarian and liberal traditions and only incidentally on the contributions of others. So it would be out of place to try to justify verdicts about the comparative value of Mill's contributions. Nonetheless, Mill's stature in these traditions cannot be questioned. Historically, he was a foundational figure in both traditions, and we have explored the philosophical interest and resources of his main contributions to those traditions. Many would regard Mill as the most important and influential figure in the utilitarian tradition and among the most important and influential figures in the development of liberalism. I hope my reconstruction and assessment of Mill's principal contributions help explain the basis of such verdicts.

Utilitarianism and liberalism are traditions with enduring, and not merely historical, significance. By better understanding Mill's contributions to the utilitarian and liberal traditions, we learn something important not just about the history and origins of these traditions but also about their best formulations and prospects.

Mill's perfectionist conception of happiness has much to recommend it, or so I have argued. This is a significant contribution, whether or not we embed this conception of happiness within a utilitarian moral outlook. Happiness or well-being is the value at which the virtues of prudence and beneficence both aim. Even if all of morality cannot be explained in utilitarian terms, Mill's conception of happiness would be relevant to much of morality and prudence.

Though it is a controversial doctrine, utilitarianism retains an important influence on popular and academic moral thinking. Mill's ambivalence between direct and indirect versions of utilitarianism highlights an important choice utilitarians have to make, and a critical examination of his claims suggests reasons to prefer direct utilitarianism. He teaches us the importance of secondary principles to approximating any first principle of morality, utilitarian or otherwise, and the delicate balance between the demands of accommodation and reform of our pre-existing moral outlook. Finally, he shows the difference one's assumptions about the good can make to utilitarian and, more generally, consequentialist analysis—a difference reflected dramatically in the role his perfectionist assumptions about happiness play in his reconciliation of utility and liberal rights.

Liberalism is a much less controversial doctrine, at least in modern Western democracies. The divisive issue is not so much whether liberalism is right, but which version of liberalism is right. Mill's statement of liberal principles and, in particular, his defense of expressive liberties has been deservedly influential. Mill's one very simple principle is vastly over-simple, but it is Mill himself who points out many of the refinements necessary to that simple starting point. Central to his defense of basic liberties and their limitations is a conception of the person as a morally responsible agent and a corresponding perfectionist conception of happiness or welfare in terms of autonomous self-government. The resulting form of liberalism recognizes rights to basic liberties, but eschews libertarianism, and justifies a liberal concern with the common good, which denies neutrality among conceptions of the good. Controversial though this perfectionist conception of liberalism may be, no intelligent discussion of liberalism can ignore it.

Finally, Mill's application of his utilitarian and liberal commitments to representative democracy, political economy, and sexual equality provides compelling examples of the way first principles can support progressive reforms.

Bibliography

For publication details for Mill's work, see A Note on Mill's Texts this volume. This is a very select bibliography of other primary and secondary work that I have drawn on directly or indirectly. It is selective, because Mill scholarship is voluminous and my knowledge of it is limited.

Ackerman, Bruce. *Social Justice and the Liberal State* (New Haven: Yale University Press, 1980).

Anderson, Elizabeth. "John Stuart Mill and Experiments in Living," reprinted in *Mill's Utilitarianism: Critical Essays*, ed. Lyons (New York: Rowman and Littlefield, 1997).

Annas, Julia. "Mill and the Subjection of Women," *Philosophy* 52 (1977): 179–94.

Archard, David. "Freedom Not to Be Free: The Case of the Slavery Contract in J.S. Mill's On Liberty," *The Philosophical Quarterly* 40 (1990): 453–65.

Arneson, Richard. "Mill's Doubts about Freedom under Socialism," in *New Essays on Mill and Utilitarianism*, ed. Copp, *Canadian Journal of Philosophy*, Supp. Vol. V (1979).

Arneson, Richard. "Mill versus Paternalism," *Ethics* 90 (1980): 470–89.

Arneson, Richard. "Paternalism, Utility, and Fairness," reprinted in *Mill's On Liberty: Critical Essays*, ed. Dworkin (New York: Rowman and Littlefield, 1997).

Bain, Alexander. *James Mill: A Biography* [1882] (London: Thoemmes, 1995).

Bain, Alexander. *John Stuart Mill: A Criticism with Personal Recollections* (London: Longmans, 1882).

Bentham, Jeremy. *Of Laws in General* [1782], ed. H.L.A. Hart (London: Athlone Press, 1970).

Bentham, Jeremy. *An Introduction to the Principles of Morals and Legislation* [1789], ed. J. Burns and H.L.A. Hart (London: Athlone Press, 1970).

Bentham, Jeremy. *The Works of Jeremy Bentham*, ed. J. Bowring (London: Longmans, 1838).

Berger, Fred. *Happiness, Justice and Freedom: The Moral and Political Philosophy of John Stuart Mill* (Berkeley: University of California Press, 1984).

Bogen, James and Farrell, Daniel. "Freedom and Happiness in Mill's Defence of Liberty," *The Philosophical Quarterly* 28 (1978): 325–28.

Bosanquet, Bernard. *The Philosophical Theory of the State* [1899], 4th ed. (London: Macmillan, 1923).

Bradley, F.H. *Ethical Studies* [1876], 2d ed. (Oxford: Clarendon Press, 1927).

Brink, David. "Mill's Deliberative Utilitarianism," *Philosophy & Public Affairs* 21 (1992): 67–103.
Brink, David. "Common Sense and First Principles in Sidgwick's Methods," *Social Philosophy & Policy* 11 (1994): 179–201.
Brink, David. "Eudaimonism, Love and Friendship, and Political Community," *Social Philosophy & Policy* 16 (1999): 252–89.
Brink, David. "Millian Principles, Freedom of Expression, and Hate Speech," *Legal Theory* 7 (2001): 119–57.
Brink, David. "Mill's Moral and Political Philosophy," *Stanford Encyclopedia of Philosophy*, ed. E. Zalta <http://plato.stanford.edu/archives/fall2008/entries/mill-moral-political>.
Brink, David. "Mill's Liberal Principles and Freedom of Expression," in *Mill's On Liberty: A Critical Guide*, ed. Ten (Cambridge: Cambridge University Press, 2008).
Brink, David. "Mill's Ambivalence about Rights," *Boston University Law Review* 90 (2010): 1669–1704.
Brink, David. "Mill's Ambivalence about Duty," in *Mill on Justice*, ed. L. Kahn (London: Palgrave, 2012).
Brown, D.G. "Mill on Liberty and Morality," *Philosophical Review* 81 (1972): 133–58.
Brown, D.G. "What is Mill's Principle of Utility?" reprinted in *Mill's Utilitarianism: Critical Essays*, ed. Lyons (New York: Rowman and Littlefield, 1997).
Brown, D.G. "Mill's Act-Utilitarianism," reprinted in *Mill's Utilitarianism: Critical Essays*, ed. Lyons (New York: Rowman and Littlefield, 1997).
Butler, Joseph. *Fifteen Sermons Preached at Rolls Chapel* [1726] (London: Bell & Sons, 1953).
Capaldi, Nicholas. *John Stuart Mill: A Biography* (Cambridge: Cambridge University Press, 2004).
Clarke, Peter. *Liberals and Social Democrats* (Cambridge: Cambridge University Press, 1978).
Cohen, G.A. *Rescuing Justice & Equality* (Cambridge, MA: Harvard University Press, 2008).
Collini, Stefan. *Liberalism and Sociology: L.T. Hobhouse and Political Argument in England 1880–1914* (Cambridge: Cambridge University Press, 1979).
Copp, David, ed. *New Essays on Mill and Utilitarianism, Canadian Journal of Philosophy* Supp. Vol. V (1979).
Crisp, Roger. *Mill on Utilitarianism* (London: Routledge, 1997).
Cullity, Garrett. *The Moral Demands of Affluence* (Oxford: Clarendon Press, 2004).
Devlin, Patrick. *The Enforcement of Morals* (Oxford: Oxford University Press, 1965).
Donner, Wendy. *The Liberal Self: John Stuart Mill's Moral and Political Philosophy* (Ithaca: Cornell University Press, 1993).
Dorsey, Dale. "The Authority of Competence and Quality as Extrinsic," *British Journal of the History of Philosophy* (forthcoming).
Dryer, J.P. "Justice, Liberty, and the Principle of Utility in Mill," in *New Essays on Mill and Utilitarianism*, ed. Copp, *Canadian Journal of Philosophy*, Supp. Vol. V (1979).

Dworkin, Gerald. "Is More Choice Better than Less?" reprinted in *The Theory and Practice of Autonomy* (New York: Cambridge University Press, 1988).
Dworkin, Gerald. "Paternalism," reprinted in *The Theory and Practice of Autonomy* (New York: Cambridge University Press, 1988).
Dworkin, Gerald. *The Theory and Practice of Autonomy* (New York: Cambridge University Press, 1988).
Dworkin, Gerald, ed. *Mill's On Liberty: Critical Essays* (New York: Rowman and Littlefield, 1997).
Dworkin, Ronald. "Liberty and Moralism," reprinted in *Taking Rights Seriously* (London: Duckworth, 1977).
Dworkin, Ronald. *Taking Rights Seriously* (London: Duckworth, 1977).
Dworkin, Ronald. "Liberalism" reprinted in Dworkin, *A Matter of Principle* (Cambridge, MA: Harvard University Press, 1985).
Eggleston, Ben. "Rules and their Reasons: Mill on Morality and Instrumental Rationality," in *John Stuart Mill and the Art of Life*, ed. B. Eggleston et al. (Oxford: Clarendon Press, 2011).
Eggleston, Ben, Miller, Dale, and Weinstein, David, eds. *John Stuart Mill and the Art of Life* (Oxford: Clarendon Press, 2011).
Estlund, David. *Democratic Authority* (Princeton: Princeton University Press, 2008).
Feinberg, Joel. *The Moral Limits of the Criminal Law*, 4 vols (New York: Oxford University Press, 1984–88).
Feldman, Fred. *Pleasure and the Good Life* (Oxford: Clarendon Press, 2004).
Feldman, Fred. *What is this Thing Called Happiness?* (Oxford: Clarendon Press, 2010).
Gilligan, Carol. *In a Different Voice* (Cambridge, MA: Harvard University Press, 1982).
Goldman, Alvin. "Epistemic Paternalism: Communication and Control in Law and Society," *Journal of Philosophy* 88 (1991): 113–31.
Gorovitz, Samuel, ed. *Mill's Utilitarianism: Text and Critical Essays* (Indianapolis: Bobbs-Merrill, 1971).
Gray, John. *Mill on Liberty: A Defence* (London: Routledge, 1983).
Green, T.H. *Prolegomena to Ethics* [1883], ed. D. Brink (Oxford: Clarendon Press, 2003).
Hall, Everett. "The 'Proof' of Utility in Bentham and Mill," *Ethics* 60 (1949): 1–18.
Hampton, Jean. "The Wisdom of the Egoist: The Moral and Political Implications of Valuing the Self," *Social Philosophy & Policy* 14 (1997): 21–51.
Hare, R.M. *Moral Thinking: Its Levels, Methods, and Point* (Oxford: Clarendon Press, 1981).
Harrison, Ross. *Bentham* (London: Routledge, 1983).
Hart, H.L.A. *The Concept of Law* [first edition 1961], 2d ed. (Oxford: Clarendon Press, 1994).
Hart, H.L.A. *Law, Liberty, and Morality* (Stanford: Stanford University Press, 1963).
Hart, H.L.A. *Essays on Bentham* (Oxford: Clarendon Press, 1982).
Hart, H.L.A. "Between Utility and Rights" reprinted in *Essays on Bentham* (Oxford: Clarendon Press, 1982).
Himmelfarb, Gertrude. *On Liberty and Liberalism: The Case of John Stuart Mill* (New York: Knopf, 1974).

Hume, David. *A Treatise of Human Nature* [1739], ed. P.H. Nidditch (Oxford: Clarendon Press, 1978).
Hume, David. *Enquiry Concerning the Principles of Morals* [1777], ed. P.H. Nidditch (Oxford: Clarendon Press, 1975).
Hurka, Thomas. *Perfectionism* (Oxford: Clarendon Press, 1993).
Hutcheson, Francis. *A System of Moral Philosophy* [1755], in *British Moralists*, vol. I, ed. Selby-Bigge (Oxford: Clarendon Press, 1897).
Huxley, Aldous. *Brave New World*, 2d ed. (New York: Harper and Row, 1946).
Irwin, Terence. "Mill and the Classical World," in *The Cambridge Companion to Mill*, ed. Skorupski (Cambridge: Cambridge University Press, 1998).
Irwin, Terence. *The Development of Ethics*, 3 vols (Oxford: Clarendon Press, 2007–09).
Jacobson, Daniel. "Mill on Liberty, Speech, and the Free Society," *Philosophy & Public Affairs* 29 (2000): 276–309.
Jacobson, Daniel. "J.S. Mill and the Diversity of Utilitarianism," *Philosophers' Imprint* 3 (2003): 1–35.
Jacobson, Daniel. "Utilitarianism without Consequentialism: The Case of John Stuart Mill," *Philosophical Review* 117 (2008): 159–91.
Kavka, Gregory. *Hobbesian Moral and Political Theory* (Princeton: Princeton University Press, 1986).
Korsgaard, Christine. "Two Distinctions in Goodness," *Philosophical Review* 92 (1983): 169–95.
Kraut, Richard. "Two Conceptions of Happiness," *Philosophical Review* 88 (1979): 167–97.
Kraut, Richard. "Politics, Neutrality, and the Good," *Social Philosophy & Policy* 16 (1999): 315–32.
Kymlicka, William. *Liberalism, Community, and Culture* (New York: Oxford University Press, 1989).
Lewis, David. "Mill and Milquetoast," reprinted in *Mill's On Liberty: Critical Essays*, ed. Dworkin (New York: Rowman and Littlefield, 1997).
Lively, J. and Rees, J., eds. *Utilitarian Logic and Politics* (Oxford: Clarendon Press, 1978).
Lovett, Frank. "Mill on Consensual Domination," in *Mill's On Liberty: A Critical Guide*, ed. Ten (Cambridge: Cambridge University Press, 2008).
Lyons, David. *The Forms and Limits of Utilitarianism* (Oxford: Clarendon Press 1965).
Lyons, David. *In the Interest of the Governed* (Oxford: Clarendon Press, 1970).
Lyons, David. "Utility as a Possible Ground of Rights," *Nous* 14 (1980): 17–28.
Lyons, David. "Liberty and Harm to Others," reprinted in *Rights, Welfare, and Mill's Moral Theory* (Oxford: Clarendon Press, 1994).
Lyons, David. "Mill's Theory of Justice," reprinted in *Rights, Welfare, and Mill's Moral Theory* (Oxford: Clarendon Press, 1994).
Lyons, David. "Mill's Theory of Morality," reprinted in *Rights, Welfare, and Mill's Moral Theory* (Oxford: Clarendon Press, 1994).
Lyons, David. *Rights, Welfare, and Mill's Moral Theory* (Oxford: Clarendon Press, 1994).
Lyons, David. "Human Rights and the General Welfare," reprinted in *Mill's Utilitarianism: Critical Essays*, ed. Lyons (New York: Rowman and Littlefield, 1997).

Lyons, David, ed. *Mill's Utilitarianism: Critical Essays* (New York: Rowman and Littlefield, 1997).
Macaulay, T.B. "Mill's Essay on Government: Utilitarian Logic and Politics" [1852], reprinted in *Utilitarian Logic and Politics*, ed. Lively and Rees (Oxford: Clarendon Press, 1978).
Martin, Rex. "Mill's Rule Utilitarianism in Context," in *John Stuart Mill and the Art of Life*, ed. B. Eggleston et al. (Oxford: Clarendon Press, 2011).
Mill, James. *An Essay on Government* [1824] reprinted in *Utilitarian Logic and Politics*, ed. Lively and Rees (Oxford: Clarendon Press, 1978).
Mill, James. *An Analysis of the Phenomena of the Human Mind*, vols I–II [1829], 2d. ed. A. Bain, A. Findlander, G. Grote, and J.S. Mill (London: Longmans, 1878).
Miller, Dale. *J.S. Mill: Moral, Social, and Political Thought* (Cambridge: Polity Press, 2010).
Miller, Dale. "Mill, Rule Utilitarianism, and the Incoherence Objection," in *John Stuart Mill and the Art of Life*, ed. B. Eggleston et al. (Oxford: Clarendon Press, 2011).
Millgram, Elijah. "Mill's Proof of the Principle of Utility," *Ethics* 110 (2000): 282–310.
Moore, G.E. *Principia Ethica* (Cambridge: Cambridge University Press, 1903).
Moore, Michael. *Placing Blame* (Oxford: Clarendon Press, 1997).
Mulgan, Tim. *The Demands of Consequentialism* (Oxford: Clarendon Press, 2001).
Murphy, Liam. *Moral Demands in Nonideal Theory* (Oxford: Clarendon Press, 2000).
Nagel, Thomas. "Equality," reprinted in Thomas Nagel, *Mortal Questions* (New York: Cambridge University Press, 1979).
Nicholson, Peter. *The Political Philosophy of the British Idealists* (Cambridge: Cambridge University Press, 1990).
Nicholson, Peter. "The Reception and Early Reputation of Mill's Political Thought," in *The Cambridge Companion to Mill*, ed. Skorupski (Cambridge: Cambridge University Press, 1998).
Norcross, Alistair. "A Scalar Approach to Utilitarianism," in *The Blackwell Guide to Mill's Utilitarianism*, ed. H. West (Oxford: Blackwell, 2008).
Nozick, Robert. *Anarchy, State, and Utopia* (New York: Basic Books, 1974).
Okin, Susan. *Women in Western Political Thought* (Princeton: Princeton University Press, 1977).
Packe, Michael. *The Life of John Stuart Mill* (New York: Macmillan, 1954).
Parfit, Derek. *Reasons and Persons* (Oxford: Clarendon Press, 1984).
Plamenatz, J.P. *The English Utilitarians*, 2d ed. (Oxford: Blackwell, 1958).
Rawls, John. *A Theory of Justice* (Cambridge, MA: Harvard University Press, 1971).
Rawls, John. *Political Liberalism* (New York: Columbia University Press, 1993).
Rawls, John. *Collected Papers*, ed. S. Freeman (Cambridge, MA: Harvard University Press, 1999).
Rawls, John. "Two Concepts of Rules" reprinted in *Collected Papers*, ed. S. Freeman (Cambridge, MA: Harvard University Press, 1999).

Raz, Joseph. *The Morality of Freedom* (Oxford: Clarendon Press, 1986).
Regan, Donald. "The Value of Rational Nature," *Ethics* 112 (2002): 267–91.
Riley, Jonathan. "One Very Simple Principle," *Utilitas* 3 (1991): 1–35.
Riley, Jonathan. "On Quantities and Qualities of Pleasure," *Utilitas* 5 (1993): 291–300.
Riley, Jonathan. *Mill On Liberty* (London: Routledge, 1998).
Riley, Jonathan. "Is Qualitative Hedonism Incoherent?" *Utilitas* 11 (1999): 347–58.
Riley, Jonathan. "Interpreting Mill's Qualitative Hedonism," *The Philosophical Quarterly* 53 (2003): 410–18.
Robson, John. "Civilization and Culture as Moral Concepts," in *The Cambridge Companion to Mill*, ed. Skorupski (Cambridge: Cambridge University Press, 1998).
Ryan, Alan. *The Philosophy of John Stuart Mill*, 2d ed. (London: Macmillan, 1988).
Ryan, Alan. "Mill in a Liberal Landscape," in *The Cambridge Companion to Mill*, ed. Skorupski (Cambridge: Cambridge University Press, 1998).
Saunders, Ben. "J.S. Mill's Conception of Utility," *Utilitas* 22 (2010): 52–69.
Sayre-McCord, Geoffrey. "Mill's 'Proof'" of the Principle of Utility: A More than Half-Hearted Defense," *Social Philosophy & Policy* 18 (2001): 330–60.
Scanlon, T.M. "A Theory of Freedom of Expression," *Philosophy & Public Affairs* 1 (1972): 204–26.
Scheffler, Samuel. *Human Morality* (Oxford: Clarendon Press, 1994).
Schmidt-Petri, Christoph. "Mill on Quality and Quantity," *The Philosophical Quarterly* 53 (2003): 102–104.
Schneewind, Jerome. *Sidgwick and Victorian Moral Philosophy* (Oxford: Clarendon Press, 1977).
Schofield, Philip. *Utility and Democracy: The Political Thought of Jeremy Bentham* (Oxford: Clarendon Press, 2006).
Selby-Bigge, L.A. *British Moralists*, 2 vols (Oxford: Clarendon Press, 1897).
Shanley, Mary. "The Subjection of Women," in *The Cambridge Companion to Mill*, ed. Skorupski (Cambridge: Cambridge University Press, 1998).
Sher, George. *Beyond Neutrality* (New York: Cambridge University Press, 1997).
Sidgwick, Henry. "Fitzjames Stephen on Mill on Liberty" [1873], reprinted in *Henry Sidgwick, Essays on Ethics and Method*, ed. M. Singer (New York: Oxford University Press, 2000).
Sidgwick, Henry. "John Stuart Mill," *Academy* 15 May 1873.
Sidgwick, Henry. "The Establishment of Ethical First Principles," *Mind* 4 (1879): 106–11.
Sidgwick, Henry. *Outlines of the History of Ethics* [1886] (London: Macmillan, 1967).
Sidgwick, Henry. *The Methods of Ethics*, 7th ed. (London: Macmillan, 1907).
Singer, Peter. "Famine, Affluence, and Morality," *Philosophy & Public Affairs* 1 (1972): 229–43.
Singer, Peter. "Heavy Petting" *Nerve* (2001) <http://www.utilitarian.net/singer/by/2001----.htm>.
Skorupski, John. *John Stuart Mill* (London: Routledge, 1989).

Skorupski, John, ed. *The Cambridge Companion to Mill* (Cambridge: Cambridge University Press, 1998).
Skorupski, John. "The Fortunes of Liberal Naturalism," in *The Cambridge Companion to Mill*, ed. Skorupski (Cambridge: Cambridge University Press, 1998).
Slote, Michael. "An Empirical Basis for Psychological Egoism," *Journal of Philosophy* 61 (1964): 530–37.
Smart, J.J.C. "An Outline of a System of Utilitarian Ethics," in Smart and Williams, *Utilitarianism: For and Against* (Cambridge: Cambridge University Press, 1973).
Smart, J.J.C. and Williams, Bernard. *Utilitarianism: For and Against* (Cambridge: Cambridge University Press, 1973).
Spencer, Herbert. *The Principles of Sociology*, vols I–III (New York: Appleton, 1896).
Stephen, James Fitzjames. *Liberty, Equality, Fraternity* [1874] (Chicago: University of Chicago Press, 1991).
Stephen, Leslie. *The English Utilitarians* [1900], vols I–III (New York: Augustus Kelley, 1968).
Sturgeon, Nicholas. "Mill's Hedonism," *Boston University Law Review* 90 (2010): 1705–29.
Sumner, Wayne. *Welfare, Happiness, & Ethics* (New York: Oxford University Press, 1996).
Ten, C.L. *Mill on Liberty* (Oxford: Clarendon Press, 1980).
Ten, C.L. "Democracy, Socialism, and the Working Classes," in *The Cambridge Companion to Mill*, ed. Skorupski (Cambridge: Cambridge University Press, 1998).
Ten, C.L., ed. *Mill's On Liberty: A Critical Guide* (Cambridge: Cambridge University Press, 2008).
Thompson, Dennis. *John Stuart Mill and Representative Government* (Princeton: Princeton University Press, 1976).
Urmson, J.O. "An Interpretation of the Philosophy of J.S. Mill," reprinted in *Mill's Utilitarianism: Critical Essays*, ed. Lyons (New York: Rowman and Littlefield, 1997).
Waldron, Jeremy. "Mill and the Value of Moral Distress," *Political Studies* 35 (1987): 410–23.
Weinstein, David. "Interpreting Mill," in *John Stuart Mill and the Art of Life*, ed. B. Eggleston et al. (Oxford: Clarendon Press, 2011).
West, Henry. "Mill's 'Proof' of the Principle of Utility" reprinted in *Mill's Utilitarianism: Critical Essays*, ed. Lyons (New York: Rowman and Littlefield, 1997).
West, Henry. *An Introduction to Mill's Utilitarianism* (New York: Cambridge University Press, 2004).
Williams, Bernard. "A Critique of Utilitarianism," in *Utilitarianism: For and Against*, ed. Smart and Williams (Cambridge: Cambridge University Press, 1973).
Wilson, Fred. "Mill on Psychology and the Moral Sciences," in *The Cambridge Companion to Mill*, ed. Skorupski (Cambridge: Cambridge University Press, 1998).
Wilson, Fred. "John Stuart Mill," *Stanford Encyclopedia of Philosophy* <http://plato.stanford.edu/archives/spr2012/entries/mill>.

Index

a posteriori 13, 116, 127
a priori 13, 106, 115–16
Abrams v. United States 153
abstinences 96–8
acceptance value 81, 90, 93, 95–8, 127
accommodation x, 38–9, 42–3, 45,
    126–8, 130–3, 279, 287–8
Ackerman, Bruce 255 n. 20
act utilitarianism 9, 81–2, 84–98, 110–12,
    225–6, 232–3
actions:
    inexpedient 99, 103
    obligatory 9, 104
    optimal x, 81, 94–5, 100, 146, 215
    permissible 104
    right 9, 81–5, 95, 102, 119
    suboptimal 94–7, 100, 103–5, 146, 217
    supererogatory 100, 104
    wrong 101–2, 107, 204–5, 217, 223
adaptive strategy 70
adults 62, 91, 142, 160–1, 208, 239
agents 61–3, 71–2, 250
aggregates 118–23
Agule, Craig xvi, xvii
Alexander, Larry 231 n. 8
altruism 6–7, 15–18, 104, 120
analytical history of philosophy xiii, xiv
Annas, Julia 270 n.
anti-paternalism xii, 62, 142, 150, 158,
    165, 172, 194–6, 213, 242–3
Appeal to Nurture 267, 270, 276
Archard, David 187 n.
Aristotle 47 n., 243
Arneson, Richard xiv-xvi, 59 n. 21, 195,
    242 n.
art of life 108–10, 125
arts 34, 48–9, 170, 181, 252, 257, 259, 267
associates 42–3, 106, 197

associationism 29, 31–2
asymmetry 117, 131–2
    of political and economic
        equality 245–7, 284–6
    self/other 139–41
audience, captive 200–2
Austin, John 1, 86, 88
authority 35–7, 62, 153, 168,
    172, 238
autonomy xii, 166, 191, 281, 289
axioms 5, 21–4, 30, 117, 131, 285

backward states of society 61, 141, 238–9,
    271, 283
balancing test 198–203, 212
Bazargan, Saba xvi
Beccaria, Cesare 21, 125
beneficence 20, 43–4, 105, 268, 288
Bentham, Jeremy ix, 1, 34
    on democratic reforms 9, 19–21,
        278–80
    on the justification of
        utilitarianism 22–5, 117
    on pleasure 11–14, 47–9, 52, 65
    on psychology 3–7, 8, 41
    see also felicific tendencies
Berg, Amy xvi
Berger, Fred xiv, 84 n., 87 n., 159 n. 8,
    224 n., 251 n.
bestiality 206, 211
blackmail 206
blame 43–4
blameless wrongdoing, *see* wrongdoing,
    blameless
Bogen, James 159 n. 8
Bosanquet, Bernard 254
Bradley, F.H. 56
Brink, David 168 n., 243 n. 8, 255 n. 18

Brown, D.G. 84 n., 97 n., 109 n. 28, 139 n., 183 n.
Buckley v. Valeo 169
bus rides 199–203
Butler, Joseph 6–7, 27

campaign finance reform 168–70
capacities 61, 63, 72–3, 141–2, 251–2, 267
  actual and potential 267, 272
  deliberative 63, 66, 71, 77, 154–61, 165, 170, 190, 214, 226–8, 236, 240, 263, 271, 286
Capaldi, Nicholas 2 n.
categorical approach to liberties 135, 137, 142–6, 148, 173, 199, 202, 212–13
categorical rules 21–2, 146–7, 215
censorship 152–6, 161–72, 208, 212–13, 286
Chaplinsky v. New Hampshire 163–7
charity 240, 252, 268–9, 274
children:
  education 250–2
  normative competence 61–2, 91, 141–2, 160, 195–6, 239, 247, 272
choice 61, 156, 194
Citizens United v. Federal Election Commission 169
civilization 37, 136, 184, 239, 240
Clarke, Peter 254 n. 15
class ix, xiii, 1, 5, 70, 238, 241–4, 245–9, 253, 271–6, 280
clear and present danger 161–3
Collini, Stephen 254 n. 15
common good 19–20, 214, 234–8, 243, 249–53, 259, 280–2, 286
commonsense morality 25, 38–40, 45, 104–6, 113, 127–31, 134, 278–9
competence, normative 61–2, 141–2, 192–6, 239–51, 262, 265, 271–5, 281–3
competent judges 49–58, 63–5, 70, 120, 126–7, 157, 227, 279
competition 178–9, 188, 212, 214, 231
conscience 33, 36–7, 44, 99, 111, 127, 133, 159, 166, 185, 204, 214, 256–9
consent 175, 180, 191, 200, 264–5
  see also volenti principle
consequentialism xv, 79–81, 109, 139, 151, 229, 235, 255, 285, 288

constraints:
  theoretical 17, 28, 39–44, 66, 73, 80, 122, 245, 281
  see also side constraints
content-neutrality:
  and the good 73, 255–9, 281, 289
  and speech 163
contextual history of philosophy xiii–xiv
contracts 187, 191, 193, 265
  in perpetuity 78, 191
  see also slavery contracts
coordination 91–2, 285
corn dealer case 161, 164, 171–2
the crib test 68
Crisp, Roger xv, 50 n. 5, 55 n., 58 n. 16, 121 n., 124 n. 4, 176 n.
Cullity, Garrett xvi, 45 n.

Darwall, Stephen xvi, 59 n. 21, 68 n. 25
decision procedure 84, 89, 98, 243
  see also guide to conduct
deficits 265–7
deliberation 61–3, 154–6, 165–72
deliberative capacities 63, 66, 71, 77, 154–60, 165, 170, 190, 214, 226–8, 236, 240, 263, 271, 286
deliberative rationale 154–6, 227
deliberative values 78, 156, 159, 162–72, 190, 193–6, 213
deluded schoolboy 69–70
demands 15–19, 35, 38–45, 105–6, 124–8, 132, 198, 217, 235, 255, 267, 282–5, 288
democracy 18–19, 151, 234–59, 273, 280–1
deontology 107, 146, 215
dependence:
  epistemic 24–5, 130–1, 252
  metaphysical 24–5, 129–31, 252
desire-satisfaction 63–73, 120
Devlin, Patrick 205–10
dialectical equilibrium 132–3
dignity 50, 56–7, 61–3
direct utilitarianism:
  and blame 43–4, 105–8
  defined 81
  reading Mill as 84–8, 96–8, 112, 205, 281, 288
  and rights 146, 205, 215, 219–20, 232–3

discrimination:
    faculty of 61, 98, 156
    improper 126, 164, 248, 260–77, 282
    see also secondary principles
disparate impact 168, 195–6, 244
dispositional value 88
disqualifiers 264–7, 274
Dorsey, Dale xvi, 58 n. 18
duty 79–80
    and act utilitarianism 81–2, 84–98, 102–6, 110–12, 225–6, 232–3
    and interest 15–20
    and rule utilitarianism 81–2, 85–98, 101–2, 225–6, 232–3
    and sanctions 33–8, 98–108, 111–12
Dworkin, Gerald 156 n.
Dworkin, Ronald 147 n., 205, 207–8, 215 n., 216–17, 228 n. 20, 255, 283 n.

education:
    as civic project 123, 181–2, 185–6, 196, 227, 241, 252–4, 257–8, 261–2, 268, 272–3
    educational qualifications 240–9, 275
    Mill's 2
Eggleston, Ben 94 n. 15
egoism:
    predominant 7–8, 17–20, 33, 35, 37, 44
    psychological 3–8, 15–20, 28–9, 30–7, 278
elections 168, 170, 236–7, 261
    see also campaign finance reform
empathy 33–4, 37, 44–5
epistemic benefits of democracy 235
epistemic protectionism 193
equality ix, 250–1, 261–2, 282–7
    democratic 245–9
    economic 169–70, 245–7, 283–6
    equal concern and equal treatment distinguished 283–4
    of opportunity 250–1, 261–2, 283–7
    political 241, 245–7, 282–4
    sexual 258, 260–76, 282–3
Estlund, David 40 n., 244 n., 245 n. 10
expediency 99–103, 111, 204, 220–1, 277
experience machine 69–70
experiments in living 72, 158, 201, 286
expertocracy 243–9, 256, 281–2

expression, see freedom of expression
expressive liberties, see freedom of expression

faculties 51–6, 61–2, 141–2, 156, 160, 239, 250, 262–3, 271, 279
fallibilism 115–16
fallibility 153
Farrell, Daniel 159 n. 8
Feinberg, Joel 146, 189 n, 198–203, 205 n., 211 n. 24
Feldman, Fred 14 n., 58–9, 68 n. 25
felicific tendencies 83–8
feminism 269, 276
fighting words 164, 167
First Amendment 152 n., 161–72
franchise 1, 19, 235–47, 253, 273–4, 276, 278–83
freedom of expression 149–72
    and campaign finance reform 168–70
    and censorship 152–6
    and clear and present danger 161–2
    and content-neutrality 163
    and contrast between high-value and low-value speech 163
    and corn dealer case 161
    and deliberative rationale 154–6, 165–72
    and fairness in broadcasting 170–1
    and fighting words 164, 167
    and First Amendment 149, 162–5
    and intemperate speech 167–8
    and knowledge 152–4, 164
    and libel 163–4, 166
    and liberalism 149–50, 156–8, 165–72
    limits on 161–71
    and time, manner, and place restrictions 163
    and truth-tracking rationale 152–4
friendship 10, 72, 78
    among equals xvii, 78, 258, 262–3, 276, 286

Gilligan, Carol 266 n.
Goldman, Alvin 193 n.
good 4, 10–14, 47
    common good 234–5, 249, 253
    and happiness 4, 67–72
Good Samaritan duties 181–8, 212

government 18–19, 234–8, 249–53
greatest happiness principle 46, 82, 277
  see also proportionality doctrine
Green, T.H. 56, 60, 254–5, 279
Grote, George 1, 41
guide to conduct 25, 84, 90, 98, 278
  see also secondary principles

Hall, Everett 121 n.
Hampton, Jean 269 n.
happiness xii, 4, 46–7, 67–72
  and contentment 53–4, 64
  and desire-satisfaction 63–7
  hedonism about 63–7
  human 8–10, 60, 63, 158, 224, 226, 228
  objectivism about 69–71
  perfectionism about xii, 60–72, 79
  pluralism about 72–3
  and prudence 288
  and satisfaction 69
  sentient 8
  subjectivism about 68–72
  and utilitarianism viii, 46, 79, 81, 279
  as what matters 68–72
  see also the crib test
Hare, R.M. 94 n.
harm 137, 139, 144–5, 174, 187–90
  consensual or not 174–5, 178–9
  distinguished from offense 137, 139, 174, 196
  explanatory role 141, 144–5, 188–90
  justified 189, 206
  moralized or not xi, 143–6, 187–90
  and rights 142–6
  and risk 174
  as setback of important interest 137, 139, 143–6, 187–9, 212, 256, 280
harm principle 136–9, 173–90
  anti-harm and harm prevention distinguished 184–6, 212
  and categorical approach 135–9, 142–6, 212–13
  and free speech 159, 161–2
  and free trade 178–9, 181
  HP1 and HP2 184–7
  and liberal rights 142–6
  liberty and basic liberties distinguished 159, 163, 185–6
  moralized 143–6

  as necessary 137, 175, 181–7
  and public goods 181, 185
  and samaritanism 182–4
  and self/other asymmetry 139–41
  as one very simple principle 136–9, 280–1
  as sufficient 137, 176–80
  see also consent; volenti principle
harmless immorality 206–11
Harrison, Ross 21 n.
Hart, H.L.A. 57 n., 205–7
hedonism 4, 10–14, 63, 64
  attitudinal 58–60, 64, 74–6
  Benthamite 47–9, 67
    see also Bentham, on pleasure
  consistency of 52–8
  and dignity 56–7
  and higher pleasures 46–60, 226–7
  hybrid 59–60, 64
  objective and subjective pleasures distinguished 51–2, 54–5
  and perfectionism 60–3, 67–78
  and pluralism 72–3
  psychological 3–7, 26–7, 66–7
  qualitative 52–3, 65–6
  quantitative 54–5, 60
  and utilitarianism 8–9, 21–5, 47–9, 278–9
  see also deluded schoolboy; experience machine
Helvetius, Claude Adrien 21
higher pleasures, and hedonism 47–9, 51–8
Holmes, O.W. 153, 161–2
homosexuality 205–10
Hume, David 18 n.
Hurka, Thomas 67 n.
Hutcheson, Francis 50 n.
Huxley, Aldous 70

ideal theory 77–8, 89, 234–8, 241–5, 281–2
  and non-ideal theory 243 n. 7, 282
ideals 159, 185, 236, 263, 287
impartiality 1, 13, 15, 19, 38, 42–4, 96, 123–6, 236, 251
inconsistency:
  in Bentham 6, 8
  alleged in Mill x, 55, 63–4, 67, 205

in sanction theory of rights 222
in sanction utilitarianism 96, 110–11,
  143, 222
indecency 197–203, 213
indirect utilitarianism 81–2, 94
  and rule utilitarianism 81–2, 85–95
  and sanction utilitarianism 98–108,
    218–20
individuality 197, 252
inequalities 245–8, 250–1, 261–2, 283–7
  alleged asymmetry between political
    and economic 245–7
  of opportunity 250–1, 261–2, 283–7
  political 245–8
  and self-respect 246
  see also equality
innate 33, 36–7, 92, 127, 266
interests 5–6, 30, 137, 143
  and happiness 143, 228
  higher-order 228, 262, 276
  other-regarding 139–41
  representation of 235, 237–8, 240
  self-regarding 139–41
interference:
  paternalistic 142, 151, 189, 194
  with a tendency 87–8
intrinsic goods 72, 77–8, 159–60, 227–8
  conditional 160, 227–8
intuitionism 21, 92–3, 115–18, 127, 129
  contrasted with naturalism 115–18,
    127, 129
  contrasted with utilitarianism 21,
    92–3, 127
  dogmatic 116, 129
  perceptual 116, 129
  philosophical 116, 129–31
  and secondary principles 92, 115–16,
    127–32
  and self-evidence 92, 115–16, 127, 129
Irwin, Terence xiv–xv, 21 n. 17, 79 n.

Jacobson, Daniel 103 n., 109–10, 139,
  143–4, 146, 189 n.
judge, *see* competent judges
justice 21, 99–100, 124–5, 262
  and intuitionism 92–3, 127
  and the proof 124
  and rights 99–100, 262
  and utility 92–3, 100

justification 21–5, 113–18, 125–34
  axiomatic 21, 23–5, 131
  bottom-up 24–5, 114–15, 117, 125–32
  contrasted with excuse 180
  and intuitionism 115–18, 127
  and naturalism 113–18, 126–32
  and the proof 118–25
  top-down 24–5, 114–15

Kavka, Gregory 7 n. 7
Kitcher, Philip xvi
Korsgaard, Christine 47 n.
Kraut, Richard 68 n. 24, 69 n. 27, 256 n.,
  257 n., 258 n.
Kymlicka, William 255 n. 20

labor 181, 191, 240, 254, 273
  sexual division of 268–70, 276, 282
laissez-faire 169, 253–4, 282
legal moralism:
  and the Hart-Devlin debate 205–8
  and liberalism 203, 209, 213
  strong and weak distinguished 210
libel 163–6
liberalism ix-x, 135–9, 249–59, 280–2,
  288–9
  and the categorical approach to
    liberty 135–9
  contrasted with libertarianism 190,
    250, 253–5, 289
  and education 251–2, 257
  and the harm principle 135–9, 142–6,
    173–90
  and neutrality 255–9
  old and new 253–5
  and one simple principle 135–9
  and perfectionism 255–9, 280–2
  and public goods 181, 184–6,
    252, 257
  and rights 142–8, 214, 232–3, 281
libertarian paternalism 194 n.
libertarianism:
  and Mill 159, 186, 190
  as one form of liberalism 289
liberties 159–61, 185–6, 227, 245–6
  basic liberties 159, 163, 185–6
  as conditional intrinsic goods
    160–1, 227
  fundamental 163, 185–6

liberties (cont.)
   as necessary condition of value 160–1, 227
   priority of 245–6
   scope limitations 61–2, 141–2, 160–1, 195, 227, 238–43
lint collector 70, 78
literacy 244, 257–8
Lovett, Frank 191 n.
Lyons, David xiv, xvi, 80 n. 3, 94, 97 n. 17, 101–2, 107 n., 108, 183 n.

markets 177–9, 252–4
   marketplace of ideas 153
marriage 203
   as a form of slavery 191, 261–5, 276, 282
   as a relationship among equals 258, 262–3
Martin, Rex 94 n.
mid-level principles 115–17, 127, 129
Mill, James ix, 1–2, 19
   on democratic reforms ix, 1, 5, 17, 19, 21, 278
   on pleasure 3, 11, 31, 33, 278
   on psychology 4–5, 8, 17, 31, 33, 117
Miller, Dale 50 n. 5, 94 n. 15, 111 n., 176 n., 177 n., 241 n. 5
Millgram, Elijah 56 n. 13, 57 n. 14
Molesworth, William 1
Moore, G.E. 56
moralism, *see* legal moralism
morality 79–82, 98–106, 108–10, 140
   commonsense morality 25, 38–9, 45, 106, 113, 127–31, 134, 278–9
   and duty 79–82, 98–106, 108–10
   distinguished from prudence 35–6, 108–10, 120, 125, 288
   and harm 139–41, 203–11
   and sanctions 35–8
      see also sanctions; sanction utilitarianism
   as a standard of conduct 82–4
motivation 2–8, 26–38, 82–4, 278
   conscience 33, 36–7, 44, 99, 111, 127, 133
   egoism 2–8, 26–33
   predominant egoism 7–8, 17–18, 33, 35, 37

psychological realism 39–40, 44
sanctions 35–7
   see also sanctions; sanction utilitarianism
sympathy 7, 33, 36–7, 44
Mulgan, Tim 45 n.
Murphy, Liam 45

natural inferiority 266, 269–70
natural rights x, 144, 146, 215, 280
naturalism:
   contrasted with intuitionism, *see* intuitionism, contrasted with naturalism
   defined 114–16
nature versus nurture 4, 266–70, 276
necessity:
   and the harm principle 137, 175, 181–7
   moral 180
   and the moralization of harm 187–90
neutrality 73, 255–9, 281, 289
Nicholson, Peter viii n. 2, xvii, 254 n. 15, 261 n. 2
non-ideal theory, *see* ideal theory, and non-ideal theory
Norcross, Alistair xvii, 81 n. 6
normative competence 61–2, 141–2, 160–1, 195, 227, 238–43, 251–2, 267
   actual 195, 267, 272
   and education 251–2
   and equality 195
   and paternalism 195
   potential 195, 267, 272
   scalar and threshold conceptions distinguished 195–6
   and scope limitations on the liberty principle 61–2, 141–2, 160–1, 195, 227, 238–43
   and voting 239–49
Nozick, Robert 69–70, 147 n. 7, 215 n., 216, 217 n. 2, 220, 229–31
nuisance 198–203, 257

obligation 9, 35, 42, 80–1, 96–100
offense 137–9, 196–203
   and abnormal sensibilities 200
   and balancing test 199–203
   and captive audience 200
   consensual or not 200, 202

distinguished from harm 137, 139, 174, 196
extent 200
intensity 200
magnitude 200
Mill's consistency about 198
profound 202–3
and public indecency 197–8
reasonableness of 200–1
Okin, Susan 270 n.
one very simple principle vi, 135–9, 145, 150, 173–5, 178, 183, 187, 212, 214, 280, 288
opportunity 250–1
  as a constraint on inequality 251
  equality of 250–1, 261–2, 283–7
optimality x, 81–2, 91–2, 94–8, 101, 104, 106, 220–2
options 14, 77, 106, 155–8, 227, 235–6, 263–4, 270
other-regarding conduct 139–41

Packe, Michael 2 n.
pain 3–4, 11, 74–5
  see also sanctions
Paley, William 21
Parfit, Derek xvii, 211 n. 24
partiality 42–4
  see also impartiality
participation 235–43, 267, 273
paternalism 136–8, 150–1, 165–6, 190–6
  autonomy-enhancing 166, 172, 191
  blanket prohibition on 137, 150, 186–7, 190–6
  and deliberative capacities 158
  and epistemic protectionism 193
  and equality 195–6
  and the necessity of the harm principle 186–7
  and nudges 194
  and slavery contracts 165–6, 172, 190–1
  successful 151, 154, 158, 193–4
  and weighted voting 242–3
perfectionism xii, 60–3, 67–72, 255–9, 279–89
  as a conception of happiness xii-xiii, 60–73, 279
  contrasted with hedonism and desire-satisfaction 63–7

and the crib test 68, n. 25
and democracy 235, 243, 247
as an element in a mixed conception 75–8
and freedom of expression 154–6, 165–72
and higher pleasures 60–73, 75–8
and liberalism 255–9
and pluralism 72–3, 258–9
predominant 75–8
and progressive nature viii, 60–3
its purity 75–8
and rights 226–8
and sexual equality 263–4, 276, 282, 289
permissibility 100, 103–5
perplexity 114, 130
Philosophical Radicals, *see* Radicals
Plato 20, 70, 154, 243, 256
pleasure 3–4, 10–14, 26–8, 46–60, 63–7
  attitudinal pleasure 58–9
  Bentham's views about 4, 10–14, 47–9
  certainty 12–13
  cognitive conception of 66, 76
  and contentment 53–4
  contrast between higher and lower 46–60
  contrast between subjective and objective 51–2, 54–5
  and the deluded schoolboy 69–70
  duration of 11–12, 47–8
  as an evaluative concept 10–14
  and the experience machine 69
  extent 14, 47–8
  fecundity 13–14, 48
  hedonism 52–60
  higher pleasure 46–60
  and hybrid view 59–60
  intensity of 11–12
  James Mill's views about 11
  lower pleasure 47
  magnitude 14, 47–8, 53
  propinquity 12–13
  as a psychological concept 3–8, 10–14, 52, 58
  purity 14, 48
  and satisfaction 5, 53–4
  sensory 14
  and swine 47
  valuational pleasure 27, 66, 76
plural votes, *see* voting, weighted

pluralism, *see* happiness, pluralism about; higher pleasures, and pluralism; perfectionism, and pluralism
poetry 2, 47–9, 55, 60, 262
pornography 164–5, 205–8, 210
power:
   individual 41–2, 165, 190, 191, 242, 262–3
   state 9, 136, 150–1, 251, 254
   see also capacities; tendencies
praise 43, 105–6
praiseworthy wrongdoing, *see* wrongdoing, praiseworthy
predominant egoism, *see* egoism, predominant
preferences:
   of competent judges 49, 53–8, 63–5, 120, 127
   and satisfaction 11, 72, 120
Price, Richard 21
Priestley, Joseph 21, 125
principles 22–5, 41, 82–4, 89–98
   as decision procedures 82–4
   first principles 22–5, 89–98
   as guides 82–4
   mid-level 115–16, 127, 129
   secondary 84, 89–98, 223–6
   as standards of conduct 41, 82–4
privileges 223, 253, 264
progress 37, 44
   and civilization 37
   and equality 124–5, 277, 282–7
   and individual rights 124–5, 144, 277
progressive beings 61–3, 154–6, 157, 160, 214
progressive nature 61–2
progressive principles ix, xiii 37, 44, 277–87
   and reform 124–5, 277–87
   and sympathetic identification 37, 44
Prohibition 177, 209
proof 27–9, 118–25, 131
   alternative reading of 121–5
   in axiomatic systems 23–5, 131
   and justification 118–25
   in a larger sense 117–18
   traditional reading of 118–21
property 161, 240, 244, 248–9, 253, 261–4, 270, 275

proportionality doctrine 46, 63–7, 82–8, 110
prostitution 203–10
proxies 245–9, 275
prudence 35–6, 89, 108–10, 123, 125, 288
psychological egoism 3–9, 26–33
   Bentham on 3–8, 15–20, 30–1
   Butler on 6–7, 27
   James Mill on 4–5, 19–20, 30–1
   Mill's attitude toward 26–33
   plausibility of 5–8, 27–8
   predominant egoism 7–8, 17–18, 33, 35, 37
   psychological hedonism 3–5, 26–8, 32
   Sidgwick on 26–7, 66
psychological hedonism, *see* hedonism, psychological
psychological realism 39–40, 44, 133
public goods 181–5, 254, 257
Pummer, Theron xvi
push-pin 47–51

quality and quantity of pleasure 48–50, 53–8

race 61, 124, 141, 239 n., 244, 250, 277
Radicals ix, xiii, 1–3, 5, 10, 15–21, 23, 31, 52, 85, 135, 235, 280
rational basis review 162
rational nature 77 n., 78; *see also* normative competence; perfectionism
Rawls, John 39, 45, 70 n. 28, 80 n. 4, 93, 132 n., 231 n. 8, 245 n. 10, 255
Raz, Joseph 256 n.
Red Lion Broadcasting Co. v. FCC 171
reflective equilibrium 132 n.
reform 1, 124–5, 253, 277–87
   and accommodation 38–9, 45, 132–4
   and Radicals ix, xiii, 253, 279
   reform bills 1, 253
Regan, Donald 77 n.
regulation 137–41, 174, 176–80, 181, 196–8, 202, 273, 280
   costs of 176–8, 209
   nuisance 198–203, 257
Reid, Thomas 21
representation 157, 163, 169–71
representative democracy 18–19, 234–8, 240, 281

representatives 236–7, 281
resources 37, 44, 49, 105, 169, 234–6, 248–51, 268, 284–6
restrictions 135–8, 158–70, 264
   content-neutral 163
   deliberation-enhancing 166–71, 191
   paternalistic 135–8, 150–1, 190–6
   permissibility of 135–8, 212–13
   time, manner, and place 163
Ricardo, David 1
Riley, Jonathan xvii, 50 n. 4, 143 n. 3, 176 n.
rights 99–100, 142–8, 214–33, 280
   as absolute 216, 220–2, 231–2
   conflicts among 216, 221, 232
   and harm 99–100, 142–6
   and inviolability 231
   liberal rights 142–6
   as pre-eminent goods 226–33
   and privileges 223
   sanction theory of 99–100, 217–23, 232
   as secondary principles 223–6, 232–3
   as side constraints 215–17, 229–32
   as trumps 215–17, 228–9
   utilitarianism of 229
   and utility x, 146–8, 214–33
   women's 262
risk 173–5
rulers 18–19, 31, 135, 154
rules:
   coarse-grained 91
   fine-grained 91, 95
   of thumb 82, 89–94
Rutherford, Donald xv
Ryan, Alan 109 n. 26, 259 n.

sacrifices 39–43, 53–4, 265–8, 269
sanction utilitarianism 98–108
   apparent advantages of 103–6
   and the art of life 108–12
   criticized 106–8
   explained 98–103
   its hybrid character 107–8
   and legal moralism 204–5
   and supererogation 103–5
sanctions 35–7, 98–103, 109–10, 204–5
   and blame 99, 109–10
   and duty 35, 98–103, 109–10, 204–5
   external 36
   internal 36–7

psychological 35–7
   and punishment 99, 204–5
   and rights 98–101, 217–23
   and utilitarianism 34–8, 98–108
Sartorius, Rolf 94 n. 16
satisfaction 53–4, 63–5, 68–71
   of desire 63–5, 68–71
   as mental state 53–4, 69
Saunders, Ben xv–xvi, 54 n.
Scanlon, T.M. 155 n.
Scheffler, Samuel 39 n. 7, 91 n.
Schenck v. United States 161
   see also clear and present danger
Schmidt-Petri, Christoph 50 n. 6
Schofield, Philip 124 n. 5
school of sentiments 37, 263
scope of liberty 141–2
secondary principles 84, 89–98, 223–6, 278
   and decision procedures 84
   and direct utilitarianism 94–8
   and intuitionism 92–3, 115–18, 127, 129
   in relation to first principles 89–98, 115–18, 127
   and rights 223–6
   stringency of 224–5
self-defense 180, 188–9, 216, 220–1
self-evidence 92, 115–16, 127–31
self-government 157–8, 249, 281, 289
self-interest 5–8, 15–20, 29, 32–3, 34–7
self-love 18 n., 21, 35, 44
self/other asymmetry 139–41
self-realization 60, 77–8, 250–1, 255–8, 262, 281–2
self-regarding conduct 5, 29, 109, 139–41, 192, 198
self-reproach 99, 110, 219
sentiments 22, 33, 37, 263, 278
sexual division of labor 269–70, 276
sexual equality 258, 260–77, 282–3, 289
Sher, George 256 n.
side constraints 147, 215–16, 220, 226–33, 281
Sidgwick:
   on the distinction between standards and motives 83–4
   Sidgwick's thesis 25, 38, 45, 128–31, 279
   and intuitionism 21, 116, 129–31

Singer, Peter 39, 41–2, 211 n. 25
Skorupski, John viii n. 1, 124 n. 3
slavery contracts 158, 165, 172, 186–9, 190–6, 213, 265
Slote, Michael 32 n.
Socrates 51, 54, 56–7, 61, 157
speech, *see* freedom of expression
Spencer, Herbert 253–4
standard of conduct 82–4
   contrasted with decision procedures 9, 83–4, 89, 98
   and secondary principles 84–5, 89
Stephen, James Fitzjames 147, 148 n., 153 n., 204–5, 281
Stephen, Leslie 5 n., 7 n. 7, 19 n., 21 n. 16, 124 n. 5
Stewart, Dugald 21
strict scrutiny 162–3
Sturgeon, Nicholas xvii, 53 n. 9
sufficiency:
   and the harm principle 137, 177–9
   of immorality for punishment 204–5
   strong and weak distinguished 177–9
suicide 191–2
Sumner, Wayne 59 n. 21
supererogation 100, 103–5
Sweeney, Bonny xvii
sympathy 7, 18, 30–4, 45
   and conscience 33, 37, 44–5, 127, 133

taxation 181, 194, 223, 237, 240, 251
Ten, C.L. xv, xvii, 143 n. 3, 155 n., 241 n. 4
tendencies 85–8, 97
testimony 182–4, 212
threshold:
   normative competence 62 n. 142, 195–6, 239–40, 242, 247, 271–2
   and the harm principle 174
   rights and side constraints 231–2
time, manner, and place restrictions 163, 198, 201
transitional justice 124, 241–3, 244–7, 271–7, 283–4
trumps 147, 215–17, 228–9
truth-tracking rationale 152–4
tyranny 135–6, 150, 237, 277, 280, 283

Urmson, J.O. 79–80, 85–93
Utilitarianism ix, 2–3, 8–9, 21–5, 79–82, 278–9, 288
   and abstinences 96–8
   act utilitarianism 9, 81–2, 84–98, 102–6, 110–12, 225–6, 232–3
   and the art of life 108–12
   Benthamite 8–9, 21–5, 47–9, 278–9
   and categorical rules 21, 82, 146–8
   and decision procedures 41, 278
   and demands 15–16, 21, 39–45
   direct xi, 81
   and felicific tendencies 85–9
   and happiness 71, 79
   and higher pleasures 279
   indirect xi, 81
   and indirection 89, 94
   and justice 21, 99–100
   and partiality 40–5
   perfectionist 79, 279
   as progressive doctrine ix, 1, 278–9
   proof of 117–25, 131
   and rights x, 99–100, 214–33
   rule 81–2, 85–98, 101–2, 225–6, 232–3
   and rules 89–98, 101–2, 146–8
   sanction 98–108, 111–12
   and Sidgwick's thesis 25, 128
   as standard 41, 82–4
utility 4, 286
   diminishing marginal 286

value 4, 10–14, 47
   actual 12–13
   expected 12–13
   extrinsic 47
   instrumental 47
   intrinsic 47
very simple principle, *see* one very simple principle
volenti principle 175, 178, 187
voluntarism 16, 18
voting 1, 236, 238–49, 253
   extent of franchise ix, 236, 238–43
   weighted 238–49

Waldron, Jeremy 198 n.
Watkins, Eric xvi
Weinstein, David xv, 94 n. 15

welfare x, 71, 139, 151, 176, 181, 195, 197, 250, 261–2, 269, 275
    see also happiness
West, Henry 51 n., 96 n.
Whewell, William 21, 92, 103 n., 115
Williams, Bernard 39, 45 n. 6
women's rights 260–5, 271–6
    domestic 261
    and equal opportunity 261–2
    and marriage 261–2
    political 261, 274–5
    and the presumption in favor of equality 267
    and transitional justice 271–6
    and the vote 236, 238, 274–5
working classes 241
    backward state of 241, 271, 273–4
    and cooperative associations 273
    Mill's friendship with 241, 273
    and reform 241, 253, 273
    and representation 241, 273
    and transitional justice 241, 273
wrongdoing 16, 180, 205–6
    blameless 95 6, 205–6, 226, 233
    harmless 206, 209–11
    praiseworthy 95–7, 226, 233

Printed and bound by CPI Group (UK) Ltd, Croydon, CR0 4YY